A Biographical Dictionary of
Major League Baseball Managers

A Biographical Dictionary of Major League Baseball Managers

JOHN C. SKIPPER

McFarland & Company, Inc., Publishers

Jefferson, North Carolina, and London

Library of Congress Cataloguing-in-Publication Data

Skipper, John C., 1945–
A biographical dictionary of major league baseball managers / John C. Skipper.
p.   cm.
Includes bibliographical references and index.

ISBN 0-7864-1021-3 (illlustrated case binding : 50# alkaline paper)

1. Baseball managers — United States — Biography — Dictionaries.
2. Baseball managers — United States — Statistics.   I. Title.
GV865.A1 S5158   2003   796.357'092'2 — dc21   2002014108

British Library cataloguing data are available

On the cover: a photograph of John
McGraw (Baseball Hall of Fame Library)

Manufactured in the United States of America

*McFarland & Company, Inc., Publishers
Box 611, Jefferson, North Carolina 28640
www.mcfarlandpub.com*

For my brother, Thomas L. Skipper

Acknowledgments

The author wishes to thank the following individuals and organizations for their help, ideas, suggestions and encouragement: The National Baseball Hall of Fame in Cooperstown, New York, and the Society for American Baseball Research, headquartered in Cleveland, for their research resources and their cooperation in helping find or verify the smallest details; Andy Alexander, director of the Mason City Public Library, Mason City, Iowa, for sharing his ideas and his knowledge; Craig Farrar of Portland, Oregon, for his colorful insights based on his own research and observations of several managers; and Thomas L. Skipper of Oak Park, Illinois, whose phenomenal memory for names, dates and places makes him a valuable resource for minimizing the search for proverbial needles in haystacks.

Special thanks go to my wife, Sandi Skipper, not only for the hundreds of hours she spent alone, without complaint, as this project was completed — but more importantly for understanding.

Table of Contents

Preface

Earl Weaver put his best defensive team on the field early, rather than make late-inning defensive replacements. And he also didn't like to bunt, figuring that if you played for one run, that's all you'd get. By contrast, Whitey Herzog, a contemporary of Weaver's, became one of baseball's great managers by utilizing players who could bunt and by playing for one run over and over and over again.

Jimmy Dykes didn't believe in basing his starting lineup on left-right percentages. Rather than loading his lineup with left-handed batters against right-handed pitchers or vice versa, Dykes put his best nine players on the field every day. By contrast, Casey Stengel played the lefty-righty percentages to the hilt and platooned his way into the Hall of Fame with the great New York Yankee teams of the 1950s.

These are men whose lives and livelihoods revolved around vastly different philosophies, but each served a term — or several of them — as a major league baseball manager, one of life's most precarious occupations in terms of day-to-day job security. If you were to add up the wins and losses of every manager, the totals should be equal because, obviously, someone wins and someone loses every game, except for those that end in a tie. But the overwhelming majority of baseball managers have losing records. The difference is made up by the few highly successful managers — John McGraw, Joe McCarthy, Sparky Anderson and a few others — whose teams won many more games than they lost.

Bum Phillips, the former Houston Oilers football coach, once said, "There's only two kinds of coaches — them that's been fired and them's that's gonna be." The same is true of major league baseball managers. Alvin Dark, who managed the San Francisco Giants, San Diego Padres, Cleveland Indians, Kansas City A's and Oakland A's, titled his autobiography *When in Doubt, Fire the Manager.* The following pages chronicle the professional lives of this group of men who rose to the top of their chosen profession, and in so doing, were destined to be losers for the most part, in terms of wins and losses, and were almost certainly destined to be fired.

In setting up criteria for inclusion in the book, certain benchmarks were established.

The first professional league, the National Association of Professional Baseball Players, was founded in 1871— so that is the starting point for the data collected in this book. The American League was organized in 1901. Between 1876 and 1901, several leagues started and folded, among them the Union League, the Players League and the American Association. Managers who participated in these leagues are in this book because they were a part of professional baseball in the same sense that the National League was a part. Similarly, when the Federal League arose in 1914 and 1915 as a competitor to the National and American leagues, it was, for its short lifespan, part of major league baseball. Therefore, Federal League managers are also included.

The philosophies, strategies, strengths and foibles of the more than 500 men who have been at the helm of baseball teams in the past 125 years are covered herein, with all manner of resources — from interviews to shared data to anecdotes from owners, coaches and players. Just as in other sports, some managers became "the man of the moment" — someone who seemed to be the missing ingredient, the person who achieved success quickly where others fell short. Dick Williams won a pennant in his first year with the Boston Red Sox in 1967, for instance. Harvey Kuenn won a pennant with the Milwaukee Brewers in 1982 as a midseason replacement when the team was floundering. Jim Leyland spent several frustrating years with the Pittsburgh Pirates, who seemed always good enough to win the division, never good enough to take the pennant. Then he won the World Series in his first year as manager of the Florida Marlins. But the record also indicates that for those few who became the man of the moment, the moment didn't last long.

Many are those who toiled a long time before achieving measurable success. Casey Stengel and Joe Torre are examples of managers who were able to hang around long enough to reverse their fortunes, each as a manager of the New York Yankees. Before coming to the Yanks, each had managed other teams whose poor play saddled each with a lifetime record of more than 100 games below .500. Then came several successful years with the Yankees that propelled Stengel into the Hall of Fame. Torre now seems a cinch to get there too.

Sparky Anderson, after having managed more than 20 years with the Cincinnati Reds and Detroit Tigers, and after having won World Series championships in both leagues, may have said all that can, in the end, be said about his profession: "The players make the manager. It's never the other way." To be sure, from the great patriarch, Harry Wright, to the latest semi-anonymous interim, a stoic bunch, resigned to laying their fortunes in the hands of younger, less experienced but sometimes miraculously talented, athletes.

Despite all assurances to the contrary, no manager will permanently replace his predecessor; every franchise trails behind it a long, knotted string of foiled and fired managers. Some are there briefly, for only a game or two. Some stay for decades. Connie Mack stayed for more than 50 years, easily setting the longevity record (though he was considerably aided by the fact that he also owned the team that he managed, the Philadelphia A's). Mack, incidentally, lost more than he won.

Sometimes the managers themselves, and not their bosses, decide that they've had enough. Eddie Sawyer, who had suffered through a 64–90 season in 1960 as manager of the Philadelphia Phillies, quit after the Phillies lost their first game in 1961. In 1977, Eddie Stanky, who managed the Cardinals in the 1950s and the White Sox in the 1960s, was brought out of retirement to take the reins of the Texas Rangers. He managed Texas for one game, which the Rangers won, and then quit.

There is a bibliography at the end of this work that is testimony to the fact that research begets research, that no book such as this could be done without the work of many others who have set out to achieve the same objective in previous generations.

Every effort has been made to include the precise dates of tenure for the managers. If the date is uncertain, the information is not included. There is not a comprehensive source for these dates. Here are the surest routes to rich, reliable information: the *Official Bulletin*, published by the office of the Commissioner of Baseball; contract cards filed in the archives of the National Baseball Hall of Fame Library; back issues of the *New York Times* and *The Sporting News*; and resources such as the *Baseball Magazine* collection of the Society for American Baseball Research (SABR). The commissioner's bulletins were not published prior to 1927. The contract cards, which officially document that a particular individual was the field manager of a major league ball club, provide conflicting information in some cases. Often, a manager signed a contract card at a time that was convenient, in some cases weeks after he had started managing the club. For instance, Jack Barry was appointed as manager of the Boston Red Sox in January of 1917 but did not sign his contract card until May. Another problem in verifying starting dates is the number of managers in the early part of the 20th century who were player-managers. Contract cards for some reflect the date they were hired as player only. Exit cards do not exist.

One other factor is worth noting. Interim managers — those men appointed to manage on a temporary basis — usually between the time one manager is fired and another is hired — are included.

Split Seasons

Two major league seasons, 1892 and 1981, were halved, producing discrete records and standings for each half. Where they appear in the managers' records, the halves are presented as full seasons, each getting a line of its own. Tony LaRussa's 1981 season with the White Sox, for instance, is rendered

| 1981 | Chi | 31–22 | .580 | Third |
| 1981 | Chi | 23–30 | .430 | Sixth |

The upper line represents the season's first half.

League Abbreviations

N	National League	U	Union Association
A	American League	F	Federal League
AA	American Association	P	Players League
NA	National Association		

Within the statistical record of any manager, league abbreviations are provided when a city was home to more than one team for the year specified.

The Managers

Marion Danne "Bill" Adair

Born February 10, 1916, Mobile, Alabama; Chicago White Sox, September 4–13, 1970

Bill Adair was a highly successful minor league manager, winning nine pennants in his first 12 years. But he never got a shot at a major league managing role except for a brief stint with the Chicago White Sox in 1970. When Don Gutteridge was fired as Chicago's manager, Adair filled in for 10 games before Chuck Tanner was hired to guide them the rest of the way.

Though Adair's tenure was brief, he was the most successful of the three managers that year. Gutteridge left with the team's record 49–87. Adair stepped in and had a 4–6 record before Tanner took over and finished the season with a 3–13 mark.

Year	Team	Record	Pct.	Standing
1970	Chi (A)	04–6	.400	Sixth

Joseph Wilbur Adcock

Born October 30, 1927, Coushatta, Louisiana; died May 3, 1999, Coushatta; Cleveland Indians, October 3, 1966–October 1, 1967

The Cleveland Indians went 41 years without winning a championship. During that period, they hired and fired many managers. One of them was Joe Adcock, a slugging first baseman during his playing days who was a mainstay on two Milwaukee Brave championship teams and who hit four home runs and a double in a game against the Dodgers in 1953. Indians general manager Gabe Paul liked Adcock and hired him to manage the club in 1967, just after Adcock had retired from playing. Adcock was known as a likable but demanding manager who could be grouchy when things didn't go well. Utility outfielder Leon Wagner, in seizing Adcock's style, said the feisty manager liked to work on players' weaknesses. Wagner, who was not known for his modesty, said he was trying to identify a weakness of his own so he could get more playing time. In Adcock's only year as manager, the Indians finished in last place.

Year	Team	Record	Pct.	Standing
1967	Cleve	75–87	.463	Eighth

5

Robert Edward Addy

Born 1838, Rochester, New York; died April 10, 1910, Pocatello, Idaho; Philadelphia White Stockings, 1875; Cincinnati Red Stockings, 1877

Bob Addy, nicknamed "The Magnet," was a rightfielder for the 1876 Cincinnati Red Stockings, a charter member of the National League. Early in the 1877 season, Josiah Keck, a meat packer and president of the Red Stockings, told his team he was tired of losing money, that "the dog was dead." He was disbanding the team. Many players scurried to get jobs on other teams. Meanwhile, Keck managed to sell the Red Stockings to a group of businessmen. They named outfielder Addy as manager. Addy's previous claim to fame: He is believed to be the first player ever to slide while stealing a base. Taking over a team that was in shambles, Addy guided the Red Stockings to a sixth place finish and was replaced before the 1878 season. During his 43-game tenure, the Red Stockings signed a pitcher named Candy Cummings, credited with inventing the curve ball.

Year	Team	Record	Pct.	Standing
1875	Phil (NA)	12–31	.279	Sixth
1877	Cin	12–31	.279	Sixth
2 years		**8–23**	**.258**	

Robert Gilman Allen

Born July 10, 1867, Marion, Ohio; died May 14, 1943, Little Rock, Arkansas; Cincinnati Reds, 1900

Bob Allen's one-year tenure with Cincinnati is remembered more for things that happened off the field. Most of the Reds' grandstand burned down in a late-season fire (in the middle of the night, so no one was hurt). But the greatest disaster was of the Reds' own doing: They traded a young, unproven pitcher named Christy Mathewson to the Giants for veteran Amos Rusie. Mathewson won 373 games in his career. Rusie was winless with the Reds. While all of this was happening, Allen's Reds finished seventh in an eight-team league.

Year	Team	Record	Pct.	Standing
1900	Cin	62–77	.446	Seventh

Felipe Rojas Alou

Born May 12, 1935, Hanier, Dominican Republic; Montreal Expos, May 22, 1992–May 31, 2001

Felipe Alou took young talent and made the most of it, and then had to do it again and again. Under his care talented youngsters Larry Walker, Randy Johnson, Pedro Martinez, and Vlad Guerrero, to name a few, developed quickly and soon blossomed into the sorts of impact players the Expos could not afford. And it was Alou's sensitivity to the talent he had, to the strengths of those on his roster, that led to an ever-changing team strategy. While his tendency was the quick hook, the defensive substitution, and the sacrifice bunt, the extent to which he indulged such preferences varied, sometimes radically, from year to year. He took over as manager of the Montreal Expos in 1992 and guided the team to a second place finish. In 1993, they finished second again, winning

94 games. In his third year at the helm, Alou, known for a quiet, steady hand and for patience, had his Expos in first place with a 74–40 record when a players' strike ended the season. From that point on, Alou battled elements he could not control. After the 1994 season, Expo management decided to downsize to lower their budget, and the veterans departed for greener pastures. Alou had to work with unproven youngsters, and he managed a fifth place finish in 1995. Then the roof fell in, almost literally. Structural damage at the ballpark caused the Expos to play about a month of road games at the end of the 1997 season, never good for a team's won-loss record. By this time, with management unloading all of the good players and the Expos struggling, fans had started to lose interest. By 1999, Alou was managing a team that nightly drew less than 10,000 patrons at home games. When the Expos ended May of 2001 with a 21–32 record, headed for the fourth straight 90-plus loss season, Alou was fired and replaced by Jeff Torborg.

Year	Team	Record	Pct.	Standing
1992	Mont	70–55	.550	Second
1993	Mont	94–68	.580	Second
1994	Mont	74–40	.649	First
1995	Mont	66–78	.458	Fifth
1996	Mont	88–74	.543	Second
1997	Mont	78–84	.481	Fourth
1998	Mont	65–97	.401	Fourth
1999	Mont	68–94	.420	Fourth
2000	Mont	67–95	.414	Fourth
2001	Mont	21–32	.396	
9 years		**691–717**	**.491**	

Walter Emmons Alston

Born December 1, 1911, Venice, Ohio; died October 1, 1984, in Oxford, Ohio; Brooklyn Dodgers/Los Angeles Dodgers, November 24, 1953–September 29, 1976

Walter Alston managed the Dodgers in Brooklyn and Los Angeles for 23 years. His teams won seven National League championships and four World Series titles — including the Dodgers' first-ever World Series championship in 1955.

Alston didn't fit the mold of a baseball manager. He was bald, polite and college-educated. He looked more like a school teacher and was qualified to be one, earning a bachelor's degree from Miami of Ohio. Alston was a mild-mannered man who rarely argued with umpires and didn't want his players to, either. He had the philosophy on called-third strikes that if the pitch was close enough to argue about, it was close enough to swing at.

But he was also strong. Randy Jackson, a utility infielder for Alston in the late 1950s, recalls seeing his manager break up a clubhouse fight by stepping between the two players, picking one up in one arm, the other in the other arm, and telling them to settle down.

His Dodger teams usually combined speed, defense and good pitching to finish at or near the top of the league. "Baseball is made up of many things, of which the long ball is but one vital facet," he wrote in his autobiography. "The steal, the hit-and-run, the fast double play, the big catch in the outfield and the big stop in the infield help make even an ordinary ball game a spectacular one." Using Alston's formula for success, the Dodgers finished in the first division in 18 of his 23 years as manager.

Pitcher Rick Sutcliffe, who broke in under Alston, said Alston believed managers played a big part in the outcome of one-run games. If a team won by two or three runs, the pitchers probably made the difference, if a team won by more than three runs, the hitters decided the game, according to Alston.

During his tenure, the Dodgers had the best one-two pitching tandem in all of baseball in Sandy Koufax and Don Drysdale, the best base stealer of the 1960s in Maury Wills, and the premier relief pitcher of the early 1970s in Mike Marshall.

Alston's teams won with finesse more than with power. And he didn't have to platoon much because his Dodger teams were always well stocked with switch hitters — Wills, Junior Gilliam, Jim Lefebvre, Wes Parker, Dick Schofield, Paul Popovich, Ted Sizemore, to name a few. Alston often had his swiftest runners batting in the lead-off spot, with good bunters and hit-and-run men in the second slot to set the table for his run producers. The Dodgers led the

Walter Alston

National League in sacrifice bunts five times between 1959 and 1965. During Alston's tenure, his teams led the league in stolen bases 10 times.

His attention to the smallest detail is demonstrated by his insistence that umpires enforce rules on balks. Alston knew his Dodger teams, with speedsters like Wills and Willie Davis, depended on getting a good lead off of first base. He said many pitchers, in their haste to throw over to first and so hold his runners on, were failing to come to a full stop in the set position — the very definition of a balk. Alston believed enforcement of that one rule could win him games.

The Dodgers had the best farm system in the major leagues, and Alston frequently brought up fast, young kids who could pinch run and play defense. He also had veteran players over the years who, though they could no longer run, could still pinch hit.

He played the percentages, juggling his lineup during a game to have the right players in for the right situations. It wasn't flashy but it often worked. There is no greater example of Alston's knack for timely lineup switches than the subtle change he made in the sixth inning of the seventh game of the 1955 World Series. The Dodgers were clinging to a 2–0 lead when Alston decided to make a defensive adjustment. He moved Junior Gilliam, who had been playing left field, to second base, his natural position, and inserted speedy outfielder Sandy Amoros into left field.

The Yankees got two men on base and Yogi Berra sliced a ball into the left field corner. Amoros, who had been playing the left-handed hitting Berra straight-away, raced over, reached out and made a spectacular catch. It saved the ball game. The Dodgers went on to win, 2–0, to capture the World Series title.

Alston had a tough act to follow. His predecessor, fiery Chuck Dressen, had managed Dodger teams that missed winning the pennant in 1951 by one game — the playoff game in which Bobby Thomson homered for the Giants — and then won National League pennants in 1952 and 1953, though they lost the World Series to the New York Yankees both years.

After the 1953 season, Dressen wanted a long-term contract. Dodger owner Walter O'Malley responded by firing his pennant-winning manager and hiring Alston, whose entire major league experience consisted of one at-bat in 1936, in which he struck out. In 1955, Alston's second season, the Dodgers won the National League pennant and then beat the Yankees (with the help of the Amoros catch) in the World Series. Brooklyn won the National League title again in 1956. In 1958, the Dodgers moved to Los Angeles, where they won National League crowns in 1959, 1963, 1965, 1966 and 1974, capturing World Series championships in 1963 and 1965. Alston retired after the 1976 season with 2,040 victories in 23 years at the helm. Only John McGraw with the New York Giants and Connie Mack with the Philadelphia A's managed one team longer than Alston managed the Dodgers.

"Look at misfortune the same way you look at success," he once said. "Don't panic. Do your best and forget the consequences."

He never lost sight of how his owner wanted it done: Alston signed one-year contracts for 23 consecutive years.

Year	Team	Record	Pct.	Standing
1954	Brklyn	92–62	.597	Second
1955	Brklyn	98–55	.649	First
1956	Brklyn	93–61	.604	First
1957	Brklyn	84–70	.545	Third
1958	LA	71–83	.461	Seventh
1959	LA	88–68	.564	First
1960	LA	82–72	.532	Fourth
1961	LA	89–65	.578	Second
1962	LA	102–63	.618	Second
1963	LA	99–63	.611	First
1964	LA	80–82	.494	Sixth
1965	LA	97–65	.599	First
1966	LA	95–67	.586	First
1967	LA	73–89	.451	Eighth
1968	LA	76–86	.469	Seventh
1969	LA	85–77	.525	Fourth
1970	LA	87–74	.540	Second
1971	LA	89–73	.549	Second
1972	LA	85–70	.548	Third
1973	LA	95–66	.590	Second
1974	LA	102–60	.630	First
1975	LA	88–74	.543	Second
1976	LA	90–68	.570	Second
23 years		**2040–1613**	**.558**	

LEAGUE CHAMPIONSHIP SERIES

Year	Team	Record	Pct
1974	Los Angeles	3–1	.750

WORLD SERIES

Year	Team	Record	Pct.
1955	Brooklyn	4–3	.571

Year	Team	Record	Pct.
1956	Brklyn	3–4	.429
1959	LA	4–2	.667
1963	LA	4–0	1.000
1965	LA	4–3	.571
1966	LA	0–4	.000
1974	LA	1–4	.200
7 years		**20–20**	**.500**

Joseph Altobelli

Born May 26, 1932, Detroit, Michigan; San Francisco Giants, October 7, 1976–September 6, 1979; Baltimore Orioles, November 11, 1982–June 13, 1985; Chicago Cubs, May 22, 1991

Joe Altobelli was an outstanding minor league manager and had a pennant winner and World Series champion with the Baltimore Orioles in 1983. Yet his legacy as a major league manager is that he seemed to be filling in, wherever he went, and no matter how long he served. The San Francisco Giants had six managers in the 1970s. Altobelli took over in 1977 and finished fourth. The team moved up to third in 1978 and was in fourth place in 1979 when he was fired after 140 games. Earl Weaver, the Orioles' Hall of Fame manager, retired after the 1982 season, but he left a pretty good team for Altobelli, his successor. The Orioles won the pennant and the World Series in Altobelli's first year but fell to fifth place in 1984 and were in fifth place when he was fired after 55 games of the 1985 season. Cal Ripken, Sr., had the club for one game, and then Weaver came out of retirement and managed three more years. Altobelli landed a job coaching with the Cubs, and when Don Zimmer was fired in 1991, served as interim manager for one game.

Year	Team	Record	Pct.	Standing
1977	SF	75–87	.463	Fourth
1978	SF	89–73	.549	Third
1979	SF	61–79	.436	Fourth
1983	Balt	98–64	.605	First
1984	Balt	85–77	.525	Fifth
1991	Chi (N)	0–1	.000	Fourth
6 years		**408–381**	**.518**	

LEAGUE CHAMPIONSHIP SERIES

Year	Team	Record	Pct.
1983	Balt	3–1	.750

WORLD SERIES

Year	Team	Record	Pct.
1983	Balt	4–1	.800

John Joseph Amalfitano

Born January 23, 1934, San Pedro, California; Chicago Cubs, September 25–30, 1979; July 25, 1980–October 22, 1981

Joey Amalfitano, a utility infielder with the New York Giants and Chicago Cubs most of his career, was something like a "utility manager" with the Cubs for three years. He was interim manager for the last seven games of the 1979 season, finishing out the year for Herman Franks, who resigned. The Cubs then hired Preston Gomez, who lasted 90 games into the 1980 season, leaving with a 38–52 record. Amalfitano, a Cub coach, was called on once again to finish the season. He compiled a 26–46 record. He got his first opportunity as full-time manager in 1981, a year in which the season was split because of a player strike. The Cubs' combined record that year was 38–65. Amalfitano, not rehired for the 1982 season, once again returned to the coaching box. Overall, he managed in 182 games over parts of three years—equal to a little more than one full season.

Year	Team	Record	Pct.	Standing
1979	Chi (N)	2–5	.286	Fifth
1980	Chi	26–46	.361	Sixth
1981	Chi	15–37	.288	Sixth
1981	Chi	23–28	.451	Fifth
3 years		**66–116**	**.363**	

George Lee "Sparky" Anderson

Born February 22, 1934, Bridgewater, South Dakota; Cincinnati Reds, October 9, 1969–November 28, 1978; Detroit Tigers, June 12, 1979–October 2, 1995

Sparky Anderson presided over a "Big Red Machine" that won five pennants in seven years for the Cincinnati Reds. Later, in the Junior Circuit, he won a championship with a Detroit Tiger team that was in first place every day of the 1984 season.

He was known for finding a role for all of his players, particularly early on in his career, and enticing them somehow to produce. He was intense and yet fiercely loyal to his players. In return, he got their respect.

Anderson hit .218 for the Phillies in 1959, his only year as a big league player. When he took over as manager of the Reds in 1970, he inherited a team that had improved steadily under Dave Bristol for the past three seasons. At 36, Anderson was the youngest manager in the major leagues, and the Reds won the National League championship in his first season, playing in a new ballpark, Riverfront Stadium.

The Reds finished in first place in 1970, 1972, 1973, 1975 and 1976. In future Hall of Famers Joe Morgan, Johnny Bench and Tony Perez, and all-time hit leader Pete Rose, Anderson had ample offense to play for the big inning, though his teams ran nearly as much as they slugged. His 1976 Reds led the National League in team batting average, doubles, triples, home runs, stolen bases and walks. That's evidence of a team that could do it all, offensively: hit, run and hit with power.

Though Anderson could count on a big-inning offense in those years, he was practical, never letting his starters get into too much trouble. He was known, in fact, as "Captain Hook" because he went to the bullpen early and often. His teams led the league in saves in 1970, 1972, 1974, 1975 and 1976. The 1975 Reds won 108 games, yet Gary Nolan and Jack Billingham were the team leaders in wins with only 15 apiece. But Rawley Eastwick, a right-hander, had 38 saves, and Will McEnany, a left-hander, had 15—so the lefty-righty combination out of the bullpen played a part in nearly half of their wins. The same pattern took shape in 1976 when the Reds won 102, led again by Nolan's 15 victories, but buttressed by Eastwick's 36 saves, Pedro Borbon's eight McEnany's seven, as the bullpen participated in exactly half of the wins.

Sparky's formula in those days was simple: let the hitters swing, pull the starting pitchers before they get too badly hurt, and double-whammy the opposition with left-handers and right-handers coming out of the bullpen.

"Baseball is a simple game," said Anderson. "If you have good players and you keep them in the right frame of mind, then the manager is a success. The players make the manager. It's never the other way."

He took over the Detroit Tigers in 1979 and guided them to league championships in 1984 and 1987. Reminiscent of his great Reds teams, the '84 Tigers had solid hitting from Kirk Gibson, Lance Parrish, Alan Trammel and Lou Whitaker, strong pitching from starters Jack Morris (19 wins), Dan Petry (18 wins) and Milt Wilcox (17 wins), but also a bullpen featuring left-hander Willie Hernandez (9 wins, 32 saves) and right-hander Aurelio Lopez (10 wins, 14 saves.) Together, Hernandez and Lopez had a hand in 65 of Detroit's 104 wins.

After the players' strike cut short the 1994 season and delayed the opening of the 1995 campaign, play resumed on condition that talks would continue at the end of the 1995 season. Spring training in 1996 opened with replacement players taking the field because the players' union had not reached agreement with owners.

Anderson did not want to field a team of inferior players and announced his retirement. He had managed 26 years, had seven league championships and made it to the World Series five times. He had an 18–9 record in league championship play and was 16–12 in World Series games. His teams finished first seven times, second seven times and third four times. He is the only manager to have won World Series championships in both the National and American leagues. He was elected to the Hall of Fame in 2000.

Year	Team	Record	Pct.	Standing
1970	Cin	102–60	.630	First
1971	Cin	79–83	.488	Fourth
1972	Cin	95–59	.617	First
1973	Cin	99–63	.611	First
1974	Cin	98–64	.605	Second
1975	Cin	108–54	.667	First
1976	Cin	102–60	.630	First
1977	Cin	88–74	.543	Second
1978	Cin	92–69	.571	Second
1979	Det	56–49	.533	Fifth
1980	Det	84–78	.519	Fourth
1981	Det	31–26	.544	Fourth
1981	Det	29–23	.558	Second
1982	Det	83–79	.512	Fourth
1983	Det	92–70	.568	Second
1984	Det	104–58	.642	First
1985	Det	84–77	.522	Third
1986	Det	87–75	.537	Third
1987	Det	98–64	.605	First
1988	Det	88–74	.543	Second
1989	Det	59–103	.364	Seventh
1990	Det	79–83	.488	Third
1991	Det	84–78	.519	Second
1992	Det	75–87	.463	Sixth
1993	Det	85–77	.525	Third
1994	Det	53–62	.461	Fifth
1995	Det	60–84	.417	Fourth
26 years		**2194–1834**	**.545**	

LEAGUE CHAMPIONSHIP SERIES

Year	Team	Record	Pct.
1970	Cin	3–0	1.000
1972	Cin	3–2	.600
1973	Cin	2–3	.400
1975	Cin	3–0	1.000
1976	Cin	3–0	1.000
1984	Det	3–0	1.000
1987	Det	1–4	.200
7 years		**18–9**	**.667**

WORLD SERIES

Year	Team	Record	Pct.
1970	Cin	1–4	.200
1972	Cin	3–4	.421
1975	Cin	4–3	.579
1976	Cin	4–0	1.000
1984	Det	4–1	.800
5 years		**16–12**	**.571**

Adrian Constantine "Cap" Anson

Born April 17, 1852, Marshalltown, Iowa; died April 14, 1922, Chicago, Illinois; Philadelphia Athletics, 1875; Chicago White Stockings, 1879–January 31, 1897; New York Giants, June 10, 1898–July 7, 1898

Adrian "Cap" Anson was baseball's first superstar and was an imposing figure both physically and figuratively. Standing more than 6 feet tall and weighing more than 200 pounds, he was an extremely large man for his era. He also had an anything-to-win attitude and a surly personality. Part of his game plan was to intimidate the opposition and the umpire in any way he could, and often that meant employing his quick, sarcastic wit. His teammates were not spared the ill treatment. When, for instance, Hugh Duffy, a much smaller man, showed up to play for Chicago, Anson looked him over and said, "Where's the rest of you?" Anson would frequently stand on the sidelines and boisterously mock the opposing players, too. A professional showman in the off-season, Anson would sometimes come to the ballpark wearing a costume of one kind or another to distract the opposing players.

He played for 27 years, serving as player-manager for 20 of those years. Anson was a great hitter who had a lifetime batting average of .329 and 2,995 hits. (In his day, there was no particular significance to accumulating 3,000 hits, and it appears he gave no thought to staying on.) He hit over .300 in 18 seasons and averaged an RBI every five at-bats for his career.

While he was doing all of this, Anson managed the Chicago White Stockings to league championships in 1880, 1881, 1882, 1884 and 1885. He is credited with being one of the first, if not the first, to use signals to communicate with hitters and to move his defense around.

In 1880, after signing two good pitchers, Larry Corcoran and Fred Goldsmith, and needing some way to use them, Anson is believed to have come up with another first. Teams until that time had often featured a single pitcher, whom they used — game in, game out — until he was so tired that he required time off. Then someone else would start in place of him until he was ready again. Anson had a different idea with Corcoran and Goldsmith, though. He decided to pitch them alternately — thereby creating the first pitching rotation.

Anson is also credited with being the first to platoon his players. And when he took his ball club to Hot Springs, Arkansas, to sweat off extra pounds and get into shape for the coming season, he established yet another baseball tradition: spring training.

Perhaps he summarized his managerial style and strategy the best when he said, "Round up the strongest men who can knock a baseball the farthest and the most often, put yourself on first base and win." (Anson was a first baseman.)

Anson's name is also associated with an incident that helped shape the shameful side of baseball. On July 19, 1888, his Chicago ball club was scheduled to play against Newark. George Stovey, a black man, was to pitch for Newark. Anson refused to take the field against Stovey, who voluntarily agreed not to pitch. Baseball historians say Anson was not alone in his thinking, but July 19, 1888, is the day the color line was established in baseball. It would keep black athletes out of the major for 59 years, until Jackie Robinson made his appearance with Brooklyn.

In 20 years as a National League manager — 19 with Chicago and a brief stint with New York — Anson's teams finished first five times, second four times and third twice. His clubs won 1,296 games while losing 947, a percentage of .578.

Year	Team	Record	Pct.	Standing
1875	Phil (NA)	4–2	.667	Second
1879	Chi (N)	41–42	.661	Second
1880	Chi	67–17	.798	First
1881	Chi	56–28	.667	First
1882	Chi	55–29	.655	First
1883	Chi	59–39	.602	Second
1884	Chi	62–50	.554	Fourth
1885	Chi	87–25	.777	First
1886	Chi	90–34	.726	First
1887	Chi	71–50	.587	Third
1888	Chi	77–58	.570	Second
1889	Chi	67–65	.508	Third
1890	Chi	84–53	.718	Second
1891	Chi	82–53	.713	Second
1892	Chi	70–76	.479	Seventh
1893	Chi	56–71	.441	Ninth
1894	Chi	57–75	.432	Eighth
1895	Chi	72–58	.554	Fourth
1896	Chi	71–57	.555	Fifth
1897	Chi	59–73	.447	Ninth
1898	NY (N)	9–13	.409	Sixth
21 years		**1296–947**	**.578**	

Lucius Benjamin Appling

Born April 2, 1907, High Point, North Carolina; died January 3, 1991, Cumming, Georgia; Kansas City Athletics, August 20, 1967–October 1, 1967

Luke Appling was a Hall of Fame ballplayer for the Chicago White Sox who had a lifetime batting average of .310 and once hit .388. His managerial career was not as successful. He had a 40-game tenure with the Kansas City A's in 1967, succeeding Alvin Dark whose troops compiled a 52–69 record. Under Appling, who had been one of Dark's coaches, the A's lost three out of every four games they played. He never managed again. The next year, the A's moved to Oakland with Bob Kennedy as their manager.

Year	Team	Record	Pct.	Standing
1967	KC	10–30	.250	Tenth

William R. Armour

Born September 3, 1869, Homestead, Pennsylvania; died December 2, 1922, Minneapolis, Minnesota; Cleveland Bronchos, December 1, 1901–1904; Detroit Tigers, October 28, 1904–1906

Bill Armour had been managing a team in Dayton, Ohio, when he was picked to take over the Cleveland Broncos in 1902, the second year of the American League. He acquired Toledo's Addie Joss, who went on to have a brief but successful Hall of Fame career in the major leagues. When several of his pitchers went down with injuries, Armour appealed to his friend, sportswriter Henry Edwards, to run a story in the *Cleveland Plain Dealer* saying Armour was looking for pitchers. One of the people who responded to the ad, Otto Hess, pitched 10 years in the major leagues and won 20 games in 1906. His major league debut came on the day he answered the ad, as Armour started him against the Washington Senators and he won, 7–6. Later that same year, Armour hired a fan out of the stands to pitch. The fan, Charlie Smith, won two games that year and won 60 in a 10-year major league career.

Cleveland also picked up Napoleon Lajoie, one of baseball's genuine stars, in mid-season. He became such a hit in Cleveland that in 1903, when a contest was held to rename the team, the fans chose "Naps" as the new name. When Armour resigned toward the end of the 1904 season, Cleveland management had no trouble picking a successor. Lajoie became player-manager.

Armour then managed Detroit for two years. In 1906, the Tigers finished sixth with a 71–78 record, Armour's only losing record. Nonetheless, he was fired. The next year, Hugh Jennings won the pennant with young talent that had developed under Armour's guidance. Among the band of youngsters was a rightfielder named Ty Cobb.

Year	Team	Record	Pct.	Standing
1902	Cleve	69–67	.507	Fifth
1903	Cleve	77–63	.550	Third
1904	Cleve	86–65	.570	Fourth
1905	Det	79–74	.516	Third
1906	Det	71–78	.477	Sixth
5 years		382–347	.524	

Kenneth Joseph Aspromonte

Born September 22, 1931, Brooklyn, New York; Cleveland Indians, November 9, 1971–October 3, 1974

Ken Aspromonte is one of the many middle infielders to become a major league manager. Aspromonte was primarily a second baseman but played every infield position in a career that saw him move from Washington to Boston to Cleveland to the Los Angeles Angels, then back to Cleveland before moving on to the Milwaukee Braves and finally to the Chicago Cubs, all in a matter of seven years.

His managerial career was not that complicated. He managed the Indians from 1972 through 1974, finishing fifth, sixth and fourth. In his short tenure, he was known for getting the most out of the talent he had, which wasn't much. Nonetheless, he was let go after his most successful season.

"The biggest thing in managing a major league team is to establish some sort of authority without making it smothering discipline," Aspromonte said in an interview while managing the Indians.

One unique piece of strategy he had in running the ball club, according to former players, was to keep Gaylord Perry happy — with good reason. In 1972, the Indians won 72 games; Perry won 24 of them. In 1973, the Indians won 71; Perry won 19. In 1974, the Tribe won 77; Perry won 21. He was therefore accorded special privileges, such as taking a cab to and from the ballpark instead of boarding the team bus. Aspromonte said his pitcher had earned the right to do things his own way.

Despite a fourth place finish in 1974 — a marked improvement over the previous two years — Aspromonte was fired and was succeeded by Frank Robinson, the first black manager in the major leagues.

Year	Team	Record	Pct.	Standing
1972	Cleve	72–84	.462	Fifth
1973	Cleve	71–91	.438	Sixth
1974	Cleve	77–85	.475	Fourth
3 years		**220–260**	**.458**	

James Phillip Austin

Born December 8, 1879, Swansea, Wales; died April 6, 1965, Laguna Beach, Florida; St. Louis Browns, September 7–17, 1913; 1918, 1923

"Utility manager" might best describe the position Jimmy Austin held in three short stints with the St. Louis Browns, each for a few weeks, each five years apart. He had been a third baseman for the New York Highlanders and was traded to the Browns in 1911. When manager George Stovall was fired in 1913, Austin was named player-manager for eight games. He lost six of them. In 1918, the Browns fired manager Fielder Jones and once again called on Austin. He managed in 14 games, winning six, losing eight. He was not rehired. In 1923, Austin began his third and longest stint as Browns manager, this time for 52 games, winning 23, losing 29. He never managed again but resurfaced to play third base for the Browns — fittingly, one game in 1925, one game in 1926 and one game in 1929. His managing style can best be described as accommodating, at least to management, when they needed someone to put a finger in the dike.

Year	Team	Record	Pct.	Standing
1913	StL (A)	2–6	.250	Seventh
1918	StL	6–8	.750	Fifth
1923	StL	23–29	.442	Fifth
3 years		**31–43**	**.419**	

Delmar David Baker

Born May 3, 1892, Sherwood, Oregon; died September 11, 1973, San Antonio, Texas; Detroit Tigers, September 28–30, 1933; August 6, 1938–November 24, 1942

Del Baker, a former major league catcher, filled in as Detroit Tiger manager at the end of the 1933 season, and then was hired again by the Tigers after player-manager Mickey Cochrane was the victim of a near fatal beaning. His 1940 Tiger team won the American League pennant, ending the New York Yankee streak of four straight World Series championships. He had a team loaded with veterans, including future Hall of Famers Charlie Gehringer, Hank Greenberg, Earl Averill and Hal Newhouser. Yet it was the heroics of an unknown rookie — someone Baker was willing to take a chance on — that clinched the pennant. Going into the last weekend of the season, Detroit led Cleveland by one game and finished the season with a three-game series against the Indians at Cleveland. In the opener, Baker took the biggest chance of his managerial career, starting rookie Floyd Giebell against Cleveland ace Bob Feller. The strategy: Try to beat the Indians' best pitcher with a rookie. If Detroit lost, Baker could use veterans like Newhouser and Schoolboy Rowe in the next two days — and neither of them would have to face Feller. And if Giebell got in trouble early against the Indians, Baker had forewarned Newhouser that he would be coming in. But Giebell beat Feller, 2–0. After the game, Baker said, "Even if I make 100 bad guesses before I retire, they can't take this away from me. I had a hunch the kid would deliver."

"The kid" had been 1–10 at Toledo in 1939 and was 15–17 with Buffalo when Detroit called him up. His major league career lasted three years. He won a total of three games.

Year	Team	Record	Pct.	Standing
1933	Det	2–0	1.000	Fifth
1938	Det	37–20	.649	Fourth
1939	Det	81–73	.526	Fifth
1940	Det	90–64	.584	First
1941	Det	75–79	.487	Fourth
1942	Det	73–81	.474	Fifth
6 years		**358–317**	**.530**	

WORLD SERIES

Year	Team	Record	Pct.
1940	Det	3–4	.473

Johnny B. "Dusty" Baker

Born June 15, 1949, Riverside, California; San Francisco Giants, December 16, 1992–present

Dusty Baker was a major league outfielder for 19 years, mostly with the Atlanta Braves and Los Angeles Dodgers. He became manager of the San Francisco Giants in 1993 and was promptly named the National League Manager of the Year as the Giants finished second in the Western Division. He was named Manager of the Year again in 1997 when the Giants won the division championship. In 1998, the Giants tied with the Cubs for the National League wild card spot and lost a one-game playoff to the Cubs at Wrigley Field. In Baker's first seven years as a manager, the Giants finished first once, second three times and fourth three times.

Baker is an aggressive, hands-on manager whose tendency is to go with a set lineup rather than to platoon. He is also an active manager who tries to make things happen both when the Giants are at bat and in the field. His teams are usually among the league leaders in use

Dusty Baker

of the hit-and-run, enhanced by having good contact hitters such as Robby Thompson hitting ahead of run producers like Barry Bonds. Defensively, a Baker trait is to try to keep opposing runners from getting too much of a lead. Giant pitchers led the National League in pitchouts in 1994, 1995 and 1996.

Year	Team	Record	Pct.	Standing
1993	SF	103–59	.630	Second
1994	SF	55–60	.470	Fourth
1995	SF	67–77	.460	Fourth
1996	SF	68–94	.410	Fourth
1997	SF	90–72	.550	First
1998	SF	89–74	.540	Second
1999	SF	86–76	.530	Second
2000	SF	97–65	.599	First
2000	SF	90–72	.556	Second
8 years		**745–649**	**.534**	

LEAGUE CHAMPIONSHIP SERIES

Year	Team	Record	Pct.
1997	SF	3–4	.473
2001	SF	3–4	.473
2 years	**6–8**	**.473**	

George Irvin Bamberger

Born August 1, 1925, Staten Island, New York; Milwaukee Brewers, January 20, 1978–March 6, 1980; June 6, 1980–September 5, 1980; New York Mets, October 20, 1981–June 3, 1983; Milwaukee Brewers, September 27, 1984–September 25, 1986

George Bamberger appeared in ten games over three seasons as a major league pitcher, with no wins to show for it. As a manager, he achieved quick success, winning more than 90 games in each of his first two seasons with the Milwaukee Brewers. His teams finished third and second, respectively, in 1978 and 1979. He decided to take some time off in 1980, but his hiatus was short-lived. His successor, Buck Rodgers, took sick leave in mid-season and Bamberger was called on to fill in. He had a 47–45 record when Rodgers returned to the helm.

Bamberger was pitching coach of the Baltimore Orioles in the late 1960s — teams featuring Jim Palmer, Dave McNally, Moe Drabowsky, Tom Phoebus and Mike Cueller. When he became manager of the Brewers several years later, his success in Milwaukee came fast and was directly related to the development of a young pitching staff. In 1977, the Brewers finished sixth with a 67–95 record. Their three top pitchers had records of 10–14 (Jim Slaton), 7–10 (Larry Sorenson) and 5–8 (Mike Caldwell). In 1978, Bamberger's first year, Slaton had signed with Detroit, Caldwell was 22–9 and Sorenson was 18–12. In 1979, Slaton was back at 15–9, Caldwell was 16–6 and Sorenson was 15–14.

In 1982, he became manager of the New York Mets but did not have the same caliber of players he had in Milwaukee. The Mets finished last in 1982 and were headed that way again when Bamberger was relieved of his duties after 46 games in 1983. Milwaukee brought him back in 1985, and under his direction the Brewers finished fifth. In 1986, with 10 games left in the season and Milwaukee in sixth place at 71–81, Bamberger was once again fired.

Year	Team	Record	Pct.	Standing
1978	Mil	93–69	.574	Third
1979	Mil	95–66	.590	Second

Year	Team	Record	Pct.	Standing
1980	Mil	47–45	.511	Second
1982	NY (N)	65–97	.401	Sixth
1983	NY (N)	16–30	.348	Sixth
1985	Mil	71–90	.441	Sixth
1986	Mil	71–81	.467	Sixth
6 years		**458–478**	**.489**	

David James Bancroft

Born April 20, 1891, Sioux City, Iowa; died October 9, 1972, Superior, Wisconsin; Boston Braves, November 12, 1923–October 13, 1927

Best remembered as a player, Dave Bancroft was a Hall of Fame infielder in the major leagues for 16 years, accumulating 2,004 hits and playing a stellar defensive shortstop for the Philadelphia Phillies, New York Giants, Brooklyn Dodgers and Boston Braves. His Braves teams finished eighth, fifth, seventh and seventh. After his major league playing, managing and coaching days were over, Bancroft managed women's baseball teams.

Year	Team	Record	Pct.	Standing
1924	Bos (N)	53–100	.346	Eighth
1925	Bos	70–83	.458	Fifth
1926	Bos	66–86	.434	Seventh
1927	Bos	60–94	.390	Seventh
4 years		**249–363**	**.407**	

Frank Carter Bancroft

Born May 9, 1846, Lancaster, Massachusetts; died March 31, 1921, Cincinnati, Ohio; Worchester Ruby Legs, 1880; Detroit Wolverines, 1881–1882; Cleveland Blues, 1883; Providence Grays, 1884–1885; Philadelphia Athletics, 1887; Indianapolis Hoosiers, 1889; Cincinnati Reds, 1902

Frank Bancroft was one of the pioneer managers in major league baseball, beginning his career in 1880 and bouncing around to seven teams in nine years. His lifetime statistics show a .531 winning percentage, though in six of his nine years he was well below that. In 1884, his Providence team won 84 and lost only 28, the last of three consecutive winning seasons for Bancroft.

Year	Team	Record	Pct.	Standing
1880	Wor (N)	40–43	.482	Fifth
1881	Det (N)	41–43	.488	Fourth
1882	Det	42–41	.506	Sixth
1883	Cleve (N)	55–42	.567	Fourth
1884	Prov (N)	84–28	.750	First

1885	Prov	53–57	.482	Fourth
1887	Phil (AA)	22–25	.468	Fifth
1889	Ind (N)	25–42	.373	Seventh
1902	Cin (N)	10–7	.588	Seventh
9 years		**372–328**	**.531**	

Samuel E. Barkley

Born May 24, 1858, Wheeling, West Virginia; died April 20, 1912, Wheeling; Kansas City Cowboys, 1888

Sam Barkley served briefly in organized baseball's early years, managing the Kansas City team in the fledgling American Association and winning 26 of 69 games. It was his only year as a big league manager.

Year	Team	Record	Pct.	Standing
1888	KC (AA)	26–43	.377	Eighth

William Harrison Barnie

Born January 26, 1853, New York City, New York; died July 15, 1900, Hartford, Connecticut; Baltimore Orioles, 1883–1889; Brooklyn-Baltimore Gladiators, 1890; Baltimore, 1891; Philadelphia Dodgers, 1891; Washington Senators, 1892; Louisville Colonels, 1893–1894; Brooklyn Athletics, 1897–1898

In 14 years as a manager, Bill Barnie could produce only three winners. But he was a colorful, witty man who kept the press amused with his anecdotes and rumors — and he also knew how to run a ball club economically. Those two traits kept him in good graces with owners and allowed him to float fairly easily from one managing job to another. It also allowed him to make baseball's top 10 list of losingest skippers: Barnie's teams lost 183 more games than they won. Only seven other managers in baseball history have a worse record of losing more games than they won.

Year	Team	Record	Pct.	Standing
1883	Bal (AA)	28–68	.292	Eighth
1884	Bal	63–43	.594	Sixth
1885	Bal	41–68	.376	Eighth
1886	Bal	48–83	.366	Eighth
1887	Bal	77–58	.570	Third
1888	Bal	57–80	.416	Fifth
1889	Bal	70–65	.519	Fifth
1890	B–B (AA)	15–19	.441	Eighth
1891	Bal	68–61	.527	Third
1891	Phil (AA)	4–3	.571	Fourth
1892	Wash (N)	13–21	.382	Ninth
1893	Louis (N)	50–75	.400	Eleventh
1894	Louis	36–94	.277	Twelfth
1897	Brklyn	61–71	.462	Sixth
1898	Brklyn	15–20	.429	Ninth
14 years		**646–829**	**.438**	

Edward Grant Barrow

Born May 18, 1868, Springfield, Illinois; died December 15, 1951, Port Chester, New York; Detroit Tigers, 1903–1904; Boston Red Sox, 1918–1920

Ed Barrow was a no-nonsense person who never played major league baseball. He won his biggest fame and achieved his greatest success as general manager of the New York Yankees in the 1920s. Prior to that, he managed two clubs: the Detroit Tigers in 1903 and 1904 and the Boston Red Sox 14 years later. He is best remembered for one piece of strategy — taking his best pitcher and making him an outfielder. The pitcher was Babe Ruth, who had hit 20 home runs while pitching six years for the Red Sox. Barrow decided to see what he could do if he hit every day. In making this change, he was relinquishing a pitcher who won 89 games and lost only 46 in six years on the mound for Boston. The strategy paid off. Ruth hit a record 29 home runs for the Red Sox in 1919. Two years later, both Barrow and Ruth were with the Yankees, where Barrow began a great career as a general manager. He never managed in the major leagues again — but the one strategic move he made as manager of the Red Sox changed baseball history.

Year	Team	Record	Pct.	Standing
1903	Det (A)	65–71	.478	Fifth
1904	Det	32–46	.410	Seventh
1918	Bos (A)	75–51	.595	First
1919	Bos	66–71	.482	Sixth
1920	Bos	72–81	.471	Fifth
5 years		**310–320**	**.492**	

WORLD SERIES

Year	Team	Record	Pct.
1918	Bos (A)	4–2	.667

John Joseph Barry

Born April 26, 1887, Meriden, Connecticut; died April 23, 1961, Shrewsbury, Massachusetts; Boston Red Sox, January 1917–June 10, 1918

Jack Barry was the shortstop in Connie Mack's famed "100,000 infield" with the old Philadelphia A's. Mack dismantled the A's after the 1914 season and Barry landed with the Red Sox where he played for several years. In 1917, he was named player-manager under a strange set of circumstances: Bill Carrigan had managed the Red Sox to two straight World Series championships in 1915 and 1916 but was fired, inexplicably, by owner Joe Lannin after the 1916 season. Barry then led the Red Sox to a second-place finish before he too was dismissed. Ed Barrow took the club in 1918 and won another pennant and World Series.

Barry was a good bunter and believed in the value of bunting. His 1917 Red Sox team still holds the major league record for sacrifice bunts: 310. That's an average of a little more than two sacrifice bunts every game.

Barry, in his one-year stay at Boston, made one managerial move that created some baseball history. On June 23, 1917, Babe Ruth was the starting pitcher for the Red Sox against the Washington Senators. Ruth walked Ray Morgan, the Senators' lead-off man, and argued so vehemently with umpire Brick Owen that Owen threw him out of the game. Barry called on Ernie Shore to relieve Ruth. Morgan was caught stealing and Shore retired the next 26 batters.

Year	Team	Record	Pct.	Standing
1917	Bos (A)	90–62	.592	Second

Joseph V. Battin

Born November 11, 1851, Philadelphia, Pennsylvania; died October 11, 1937, Akron, Ohio; Pittsburgh Alleghenys, 1883–1884; Chicago-Pittsburgh, 1884

Joe Battin had an undistinguished three-year career in the 1880s in which he had a .174 winning percentage in 23 games.

Year	Team	Record	Pct.	Standing
1883	Pitt	2–11	.154	Seventh
1884	Pitt	1–3	.250	Eleventh
1884	Chi-Pitt	1–5	.200	Sixth
2 years		**4–19**	**.174**	

Henry Albert Bauer

Born July 31, 1922, East St. Louis, Illinois; Kansas City Athletics, June 19, 1961–October 1, 1962; Baltimore Orioles, November 19, 1963–July 10, 1968; Oakland Athletics, October 1, 1968–September 19, 1969

Hank Bauer played on powerhouse New York Yankee teams from 1948 through 1959 and was in the World Series nine times. He hit safely in 14 consecutive World Series games — a record he shares with Roberto Clemente — and is in the top 10 in eight offensive categories for World Series play. He played his last two seasons in Kansas City and then signed on to manage the A's. He ran into something there that he didn't have to contend with in New York — owner Charles O. Finley. The A's had a bad ball club and an eccentric owner. Bauer lasted two years, finishing eighth and ninth. In 1964, he took the helm of the Baltimore Orioles and developed them into one of the best teams of the era. The Orioles averaged 96 wins in the next three years and finally won the pennant in 1966. Bauer and his coaches developed a great young pitching staff that included names like Wally Bunker (19–5 as a rookie in 1964), Dave McNally (11–6 in his second full season in 1965, 13–6 in 1966 and a 22-game winner in 1968) and Jim Palmer (15–10 in his second season in 1966 on his way to a Hall of Fame career).

Bauer had a good bullpen in Baltimore, too, with veteran right-handers Stu Miller, Moe Drabowsky, Eddie Fisher, Dick Hall and Eddie Watt. The Orioles set the record in 1966 for fewest complete games by a pennant winner, but Bauer pushed the right buttons at the right time to get 49 saves out of his bullpen, an extremely high number for those days. Stu Miller led the staff with 18.

The Orioles had some offensive strength in Triple Crown winner Frank Robinson, slugging first baseman Boog Powell and star third baseman Brooks Robinson. Brooks Robinson said Bauer was easy to play for because he didn't platoon much, had a set lineup and players knew exactly what was expected of them every day.

In the 1966 World Series, Baltimore swept the mighty Dodgers, shutting them out in the last three games. A key pitching move occurred in the first game when McNally got nicked for a couple of runs early. Bauer chose Drabowsky to relieve McNally in the third inning. He shut out the Dodgers the rest of the way and struck out 11, still the World Series record for relief pitchers.

In two more years, Bauer was gone, but the Baltimore pitching staff was established and helped provide pennants for his successor, Earl Weaver. Bauer managed Oakland in

1969 and had the A's at 80–69 with two weeks left in the season when Finley fired him. That team had two young starting pitchers, Catfish Hunter and Blue Moon Odom, and a closer named Rollie Fingers who would lead the club to five straight division championships and three straight World Series championships.

So Bauer, who played with Mickey Mantle and Yogi Berra and managed Frank Robinson and Reggie Jackson, helped build pennant winners with the development of young pitching staffs, and by making the right moves at the right times with those staffs.

Year	Team	Record	Pct.	Standing
1961	KC	35–57	.380	Eighth
1962	KC	72–90	.444	Ninth
1964	Bal	97–65	.599	Third
1965	Bal	94–68	.580	Third
1966	Bal	97–63	.606	First
1967	Bal	76–85	.472	Sixth
1968	Bal	43–37	.538	Third
1969	Oak	80–69	.537	Second
8 years		**594–534**	**.527**	

WORLD SERIES

Year	Team	Record	Pct.
1966	Bal	4–0	1.00

Don Edward Baylor

Born June 28, 1949, Austin, Texas; Colorado Rockies, October 27, 1992–September 28, 1998; Chicago Cubs, November 1, 1999–July 5, 2002

Don Baylor had a reputation as a winner and as one of the best clutch hitters in baseball during his 19-year career, all in the American League. He was the league's Most Valuable Player in 1979 when he hit 36 home runs and drove in 139 for the California Angels. And his reputation as a clutch hitter made him one of the most sought-after players by pennant contenders looking to pick up someone late in the season for the stretch drive. In his last three seasons, Baylor played in three World Series for three different teams: the Boston Red Sox in 1986, the Minnesota Twins in 1987 and the Oakland A's in 1988. Prior to that he played for division winners in Baltimore in 1973 and 1974 and with California in 1979 and 1982.

He became manager of the Colorado Rockies expansion team in 1993 and, two years later, had them in the National League playoffs as the wildcard entry. Baylor was able to make do with a young pitching staff that had to suffer through 81 home games in Mile High Stadium and, later, Coors Field; in each park the high altitude made conditions just right for home-run hitters. Many final scores wound up in double figures. But Baylor had a power-hitting lineup led by Larry Walker, Dante Bichette, Vinny Castilla and Andres Galarraga, all of whom hit over 30 home runs. Galarraga also won the batting title. The Rockies were eliminated in the first round of the playoffs, but they were the darlings of baseball for having reached the post-season in their third year of existence.

Because of the ballpark his team played in, Baylor might have been influenced by his first manager, Earl Weaver, who was a master at using his pitching staff but admitted that a three-run homer was part of his winning strategy. Baylor had the players to produce the three-run homers, he just had to keep the Rockies in the game until the homers came. Consequently, he led the league in use of relief pitchers in 1993, 1995 and 1996, using 453, 456 and 449, respectively. But Baylor also liked to try to make things happen on the basepaths. His 1993 Rockies team led the National League in hit-and-run attempts. His 1995 team led the league in stolen-base attempts. He is also credited with being a great hitting coach, helping players like Galarraga, whom Baylor managed in Colorado and instructed as a batting coach later with Atlanta.

In 2000, Baylor replaced Jim Riggleman as manager of the Chicago Cubs. Injuries riddled his pitching staff and Chicago finished last for the second year in a row. In 2001, the Cubs rebounded. Buoyed by a starting pitching staff of John Lieber, Kerry Wood, Kevin Tapani, Jason Bere and Julian Tavares, and a bullpen anchored by left-hander Jeff Fassaro and right-hander Tom "Flash" Gordon, the Cubs led the Central Division most of the way. General manager Andy MacPhail acquired infielder Delino DeShields, outfielder Michael Tucker, pitcher David Weathers and slugger Fred McGriff, all in late July, to help solidify an already good ball club.

But the following year, the Cubs got off to another poor start, and Baylor was replaced by Bruce Kimm just before the All-Star break.

Year	Team	Record	Pct.	Standing
1993	Colo	67–95	.410	Sixth
1994	Colo	53–64	.450	First
1995	Colo	77–67	.530	Second
1996	Colo	83–79	.510	Third
1997	Colo	83–79	.510	Third
1998	Colo	77–85	.470	Fourth
2000	Chi (N)	65–97	.401	Fifth
2001	Chi	88–74	.543	Third
2002	Chi	34–49	.410	Fifth
9 years		**627–679**	**.480**	

DIVISIONAL PLAYOFF

Year	Team	Record	Pct.
1995	Colo	1–2	.333

David Gus "Buddy" Bell

Born August 27, 1951, Pittsburgh, Pennsylvania; Detroit Tigers, November 9, 1995–September 1, 1998; Colorado Rockies, October 20, 1999–April 26, 2002

Buddy Bell, a major league infielder for 18 years and son of major league outfielder Gus Bell, began his managing career as the successor to Sparky Anderson at Detroit in 1996. The Tigers struggled to a 53–109 record, and Bell led American League managers in use of relief pitchers, going to the bullpen 426 times. The Tigers improved by 26 games in 1997, finishing just four games below .500 at 79–83. In Bell's third year, Detroit sank again, and he was gone after 137 games and the club buried in fifth place. He resurfaced a year later as manager of the Colorado Rockies. He stayed in Denver for more than two years, but was replaced by Clint Hurdle when the Rockies sank to the National League's lowest winning percentage in late April 2002.

Year	Team	Record	Pct.	Standing
1996	Det	53–109	.320	Fifth
1997	Det	79–83	.480	Third

1998	Det	52–85	.370	Fifth
2000	Colo	82–80	.506	Fourth
2001	Colo	73–89	.451	Fourth
2002	Colo	6–16	.273	Fourth
6 years		**345–426**	**.447**	

John Benjamin

No biographical data available; Elizabeth Resolutes, 1873

Little information is recorded about the life and baseball career of John Benjamin. He is listed as manager of the Elizabeth, New Jersey, team in the National Association in 1873, three years before the National League was formed. Benjamin was in and out after his team lost 21 of the 23 games he was at the helm.

Year	Team	Record	Pct.	Standing
1873	Eliz	2–21	.087	Eighth

Vernon Adair Benson

Born September 19, 1924, Granite Quarry, North Carolina; Atlanta Braves, May 12, 1977

It was 1977. The Atlanta Braves were in turmoil. As was their custom, they were losing far more than they were winning. Cable TV magnate Ted Turner, who owned the team, was building a dynasty in which he could market his baseball team nationally via cable television. But the Braves kept losing. Turner asked manager Dave Bristol to step aside. Turner took over the team himself for one game and lost. Coach Vern Benson was also called on for one game — and he won. Then Turner brought Bristol back for the rest of the season and Benson remained on the sidelines, undefeated as a major league manager.

Year	Team	Record	Pct.	Standing
1977	Atl	1–0	1.000	Sixth

Lawrence Peter "Yogi" Berra

Born May 12, 1925, St. Louis, Missouri; New York Yankees, October 24, 1963–October 17, 1964; New York Mets, April 2, 1972–August 6, 1975; New York Yankees, December 16, 1983–April 28, 1985

Yogi Berra was an All-Star catcher for the New York Yankees who was also a successful manager. Berra's experience as a catcher in handling pitchers played a big part in his success as a manager. He is one of the few managers who won pennants in both the American and National leagues and yet he is best remembered for his achievements as a player and for his off-the-cuff humorous comments about baseball and about life around him.

Berra played in 14 World Series; the Yankees won 10 of them. He still holds many World Series records: games played, 75; times at bat, 259; hits, 71; and doubles, 10. He is second all-time in World Series runs scored, 41; second in RBIs, 39; third in home runs, 12; and third in walks, 32. He was the first man to hit a pinch-hit home run in World Series history (1947) and he also hit a grand-slam home run (1956).

He played for the Yankees from 1946 through 1963. When he was named to replace the highly successful Ralph Houk as Yankee manager in 1964, there was concern the move wouldn't work because of Berra's close relationship with the players. It is said that when

Berra got the job, he was so excited he sat down and wrote out his pitching rotation for the entire 1964 season, without taking into consideration injuries, rainouts or all the other things that could change the pitching lineup.

Houk had become the Yankee general manager and watched as the Bronx Bombers, winners of four straight American League championships, had to battle Chicago and Baltimore for the top spot and found themselves four games out of first place in mid–August.

Bill Veeck, former owner of the Cleveland Indians, St. Louis Browns and Chicago White Sox, observed in a newspaper column that the Yankee front office had concluded that the Yankees would not win it in 1964, that it was Berra's fault and that he would be fired at the end of the season.

Any thoughts Berra would be too cozy with the players to impose discipline ended in August after the Yankees had lost four straight to the White Sox at Comiskey Park. In a highly publicized incident, utility infielder Phil Linz played his harmonica on the bus taking the players from the ballpark. Berra hollered at him to stop; Linz misunderstood and, encouraged by his teammates, kept playing. According to most accounts, a fight and a fine (for Linz) soon followed. The action seemed to bring the lackluster Yankees to life. They won 11 straight and went 22–6 in September to win the pennant by one game.

But the Yankees lost the World Series in seven games to the Cardinals and Berra was unceremoniously fired. The Yankees then hired Johnny Keane, the Cardinal manager, to replace him. The Yankees went into an uncharacteristic slide for the next several years. Meanwhile, Berra hooked on as a coach for the Mets. When Gil Hodges died suddenly of a heart attack on Easter Sunday 1972, the Mets named Berra to replace him. In 1973, he guided the Mets to a first-place finish in a wild National League season that saw five teams with a shot at the championship going into the final weekend. He managed the Mets until 1975. In 1984, after Yankee owner George Steinbrenner fired Billy Martin for the third time, Berra was brought back to manage the Yankees again. He guided them to a third-place finish. In 1985, the Yankees got off to a 6–10 start. Steinbrenner fired Berra and brought Martin back. An embittered Berra vowed never to set foot in Yankee Stadium again, a promise he kept for 15 years.

In assessing Berra's style as a manager, it is necessary to separate the man from the myth. On the ballfield, he was not a clown. Lou Piniella, a Yankee player who was to become a successful manager with the Yankees, Cincinnati Reds and Seattle Mariners, said Berra taught him a lot about handling pitchers.

According to Piniella, Berra knew that every pitcher has his pitch count, beyond which he is considerably less effective. So the important thing was to know what each pitcher was capable of, and to get him out of the game when he'd reached his limit, no matter the score of the game or what the inning. Berra was a master at that, said Piniella.

Berra believed if a pitcher is to be useful for eight or 10 years he can't be irresponsibly used — can't be pushed beyond his limit, even for the short-term gain that a victory represents.

In 1984, one of Berra's projects was young Dave Righetti, a 26-year-old left-hander in his fifth major league season. In the previous two seasons, Righetti was used as both a starter and a reliever and had worked a combined 400 innings. On July 4, 1983, Righetti threw a no-hitter against the Boston Red Sox, winning 4–0.

Berra converted him to relief pitching. Righetti made 64 appearances in 1984, all in relief. His 2.34 earned run average was among the league leaders, and he registered 31 saves in just 96.1 innings of work. Righetti was a fine relief pitcher for many years after Berra left the Yankees.

Years earlier, when he took over the Mets, Berra's perceived easy-going attitude was in stark contrast to Hodges' hardline, no-nonsense approach. Berra was more like Casey Stengel, his old Yankee manager: funny at times, but hard-working and sincere, with an "aw shucks" kind of modesty.

In early August of 1973, with the Mets buried toward the bottom of the National League East, Berra uttered his now famous, "It ain't over till it's over." It is a line that has gotten laughs over the years, but it was Berra's version of a rallying cry at the time. And the Mets rallied in the next six weeks to win the pennant.

Year	Team	Record	Pct.	Standing
1964	NY (A)	99–63	.611	First
1972	NY (N)	83–73	.532	Third
1973	NY	82–79	.509	First
1974	NY	71–91	.438	Fifth
1975	NY	56–53	.514	Third
1984	NY (A)	87–75	.537	Third
1985	NY (A)	6–10	.375	Third
6 years		**484–444**	**.519**	

LEAGUE CHAMPIONSHIP SERIES

Year	Team	Record	Pct.
1973	NY (N)	3–2	.600

WORLD SERIES

Year	Team	Record	Pct.
1964	NY (A)	3–4	.429
1973	NY (N)	3–4	.429
2 years		**6–8**	**.429**

Terry Paul Bevington

Born July 26, 1956, Akron, Ohio; Chicago White Sox, June 3, 1995–September 30, 1997

Terry Bevington was a catcher in the New York Yankee and Milwaukee Brewer organizations who never made it to the major leagues as a player. He became a minor league manager at the age of 24, winning division titles in five of his first nine seasons. Bevington was the third-base coach of the Chicago White Sox from 1990 to 1995 and became their manager when Gene Lamont was let go. The White Sox had an 11–20 record. Under Bevington, they went 57–56 the rest of the way. In his first full season, 1996, Chicago rose to 85–77, finishing second behind Cleveland. In 1997, the White Sox were second again, though a distant second with an 80–81 record. Bevington was fired and managed Syracuse in the International League in 1998. In 1999, he was back in the major leagues, as third base coach for the Toronto Blue Jays.

With the White Sox, Bevington had a powerful 3-4-5 punch in his lineup with Frank Thomas, Albert Belle and Robin Ventura, but there wasn't much offense beyond that. In 1997, the White Sox were in second place, 3½ games behind the Cleveland Indians at mid-season, when owner Jerry Reinsdorf shocked the baseball world by trading starting pitcher Wilson Alvarez and ace relief pitcher Roberto Hernandez to the San Francisco Giants for prospects — in effect conceding the division title to the Indians.

Bevington was a fiery manager who was ejected from games eight times but was unable to instill the same kind of fire in his team. He and his clubs had the misfortune to compete in the same division as Cleveland, which dominated the Central Division of the American League in the 1990s.

Year	Team	Record	Pct.	Standing
1995	Chi (A)	57–56	.505	Second
1996	Chi	85–77	.524	Second
1997	Chi	80–81	.495	Second
3 years		**222–214**	**.509**	

Hugo Francis Bezdek

Born April 1, 1883, Prague, Czechoslovakia; died September 19, 1952, Atlantic City, New Jersey; Pittsburgh Pirates, 1917–1919

Hugo Bezdek gained sports fame as one of Penn State University's first great football coaches, a job he took after he resigned as manager of the Pittsburgh Pirates. Prior to taking the Pirate job, he had been a successful football coach at the University of Arkansas. He took over a Pirate team in turmoil in 1917. Many of its players had enlisted to fight in World War I. Nixey Callahan had managed the Pirates in 1916 and for part of 1917. In midseason, he disappeared for several days and the Pirates' star, Honus Wagner, filled in for him. Callahan emerged several days later, reportedly in a drunken stupor. But the Pirates wanted no more of his antics. They hired Bezdek, a big, burly Czechoslovakian who had never played major league baseball, to lead them the rest of the way. Not surprisingly, the Pirates finished eighth. But Bezdek led them to a fourth-place finish in 1918. They finished fourth again in 1919 and were making steady upward progress. But Penn State beckoned, and Bezdek returned to coaching college football. He was also the athletic director at Penn State. He coached 12 years at Penn State and compiled at 65–30 record.

At Arkansas, he was 29–13 in five years. He was later elected to the College Football Hall of Fame. Bezdek also coached the Cleveland Rams in the National Football League in 1937 and 1938, making him the only man ever to have coached an NFL team and managed a major league baseball team.

With the Pirates, Bezdek's influence was in his leadership rather than his knowledge of the game or in strategy. He knew the importance of discipline, of conditioning and of asking the right questions of the right people. In certain game situations, he would seek the advice of veteran players or ask questions like: How would McGraw have handled that?

Year	Team	Record	Pct.	Standing
1917	Pitt	30–59	.337	Eighth
1918	Pitt	65–60	.520	Fourth
1919	Pitt	71–68	.510	Fourth
3 years		**166–187**	**.470**	

Bickerson

(First name unknown; year and place of birth and death unknown); Washington Statesmen, 1884

Not much is known about Mr. Bickerson except that his last name is listed in the records of the Washington Ball Club of the American Association in 1884, when he managed in one game, which Washington lost.

Year	Team	Record	Pct.	Standing
1884	Wash	0–1	.000	Twelfth

Joseph Lee "Dode" Birmingham

Born August 6, 1884, Elmira, New York; died April 24, 1946, Tampico, Mexico; Cleveland Naps, 1912–1915

Joe Birmingham managed the Cleveland Naps for two full seasons and for parts of two others — with extremely different results. He took over a struggling Nap team in 1912 and won 21 of the 28 games left in the season. The Naps finished sixth. He showed he had no trouble taking control when he benched Nap Lajoie, who was in a hitting slump. Lajoie was so popular in Cleveland that the team, originally called the Bronchos, was renamed the Naps in his honor. But he and Birmingham never hit it off. The Naps finished third under Birmingham in 1913. In 1914, they finished eighth, but that wasn't the worst of their problems. Cleveland fans were losing interest in the ball club. In an incredible move, Cleveland owner Charley Somers transferred his minor league Toledo ball club to Cleveland in an effort to give fans baseball to watch every day. He even began shuttling players back and forth between the two teams. The result was that minor league baseball became a huge draw in Cleveland. There are reports that as many as 80,000 attended a game. Meanwhile, Birmingham had to make do with a makeshift Naps team led by a star player who hated him. The Naps finished last with a record of 51–102. Birmingham was fired 28 games into the 1915 season with the Naps in sixth place at 12–16. Soon after that, Lajoie was shipped off to Philadelphia and the team changed its name to the Indians. But for Birmingham, the damage was done. He never managed in the major leagues again.

Year	Team	Record	Pct.	Standing
1912	Cleve	21–7	.750	Sixth
1913	Cleve	86–66	.566	Third
1914	Cleve	51–102	.333	Eighth
1915	Cleve	12–16	.429	Sixth
4 years		**170–191**	**.471**	

Adelphia Louis "Del" Bissonette

Born September 6, 1899, Winthrop, Maine; died June 9, 1972, Augusta, Maine; Boston Braves, July 20, 1945–November 6, 1945

Del Bissonette took over a bad Boston Braves team in mid-season 1945, inheriting a 42–49 record from his predecessor, Bob Coleman. Bissonette guided the Braves to a 25–36 record, moving them from seventh to sixth place by the end of the season. It was his only shot at managing. Billy Southworth was hired for the 1946 season.

Year	Team	Record	Pct.	Standing
1945	Bos (N)	25–36	.410	Seventh

Russell Aubrey "Lena" Blackburne

Born October 23, 1886, Clifton Heights, Pennsylvania; died February 29, 1968, Riverside, New Jersey; Chicago White Sox, July 18, 1928–October 1929

Lena Blackburne took over for Ray Schalk in the middle of the 1928 season and was able to move the Chicago White Sox up from sixth to fifth place by the end of the season, winning 40 and losing 40. In his first full season, however, Chicago plummeted to seventh place with a 59–93 record. Blackburne's managing career was over.

Year	Team	Record	Pct.	Standing
1928	Chi (A)	40–40	.500	Sixth
1929	Chi	59–93	.388	Seventh
2 years		**99–133**	**.427**	

Raymond Francis Blades

Born August 6, 1896, Mount Vernon, Illinois; died May 18, 1979, Lincoln, Illinois; St. Louis Cardinals, November 6, 1938–May 7, 1940

Ray Blades had a .301 lifetime batting average that included 11 seasons with the St. Louis Cardinals. He took over a Cardinal team that had finished sixth in 1938 under Frankie Frisch, who had directed the play — and the antics — of the Gas House Gang of the early 1930s. Blades had a successful career as a minor league manager but he brought an unusual style to the major leagues. He constantly juggled his lineup and freely substituted players during the course of a game. It was not unusual for Blades to use three or four pitchers in a game even when the outcome was not in doubt. And in 1939, every move he made seemed to work.

The Cardinals battled the Cincinnati Reds right down to the wire, finishing second behind them. The St. Louis pitching staff had two pitchers with more than 50 appearances, two with more than 40 appearances and two others with more than 30. In 1940, the magic didn't take hold. The club lost 24 of its first 39 games and Blades was fired, never to manage in the major leagues again.

Year	Team	Record	Pct.	Standing
1939	StL (N)	92–61	.601	Second
1940	StL	15–24	.384	Seventh
2 years		**107–85**	**.557**	

Walter Blair

Born October 13, 1883, Arnot, Pennsylvania; died August 20, 1948, Lewisburg, Pennsylvania; Buffalo Bisons, 1915

Walter Blair had a fleeting moment as a big-time baseball manager when the Federal League was a competitor to the American and National Leagues. The new league grabbed some active major league ballplayers, some prospects and some over-the-hill players and tried to make a go of it. The league was short-lived, but not as short as Blair's managerial career, which lasted two games as manager of the Buffalo ball club.

Year	Team	Record	Pct.	Standing
1915	Buff (F)	1–1	.500	Eighth

Oswald Louis Bluege

Born October 24, 1900, Chicago, Illinois; died October 15, 1985, Edina, Minnesota; Washington Senators, April 21, 1943–November 19, 1947

Ossie Bluege was a third baseman for the Washington Senators from 1922 to 1939 and played on all three Senator pennant winners (1924, 1925 and 1933). He was well known to Senator fans when he was named to replace Bucky Harris as the manager in 1943. He is not remembered so much for his strategy or innovative concepts as for how his teams hopped up and down the standings.

The Senators, coming off a seventh-place finish in 1942, moved up to second in Bluege's first year. Then in 1944, Washington slipped to eighth place. The Senators shot up to second place in 1945, then back to sixth in 1946. In 1947, Washington finished seventh again — and two bad seasons in a row spelled doom for Bluege, who was fired at the end of the season. One of the reasons why teams in that era flip-flopped in the standings was that they lost many players to World War II. With players coming and going and teams scrambling to find substitutes to fill in, play was inconsistent.

Year	Team	Record	Pct.	Standing
1943	Wash	84–69	.549	Second
1944	Wash	64–90	.416	Eighth
1945	Wash	87–67	.565	Second
1946	Wash	76–78	.494	Fourth
1947	Wash	64–90	.416	Seventh
5 years		**375–394**	**.488**	

Bruce Bochy

Born April 16, 1955, Landes de Bussac, France; San Diego Padres, October, 21, 1994–present

Bruce Bochy was a major league catcher for 10 years and has been a highly successful manager of the San Diego Padres. Managing in the era of free agency, when rosters change drastically from one year to the next, Bochy's teams won two Western Division championships in his first five years. His 1998 club made it to the World Series but lost four straight games to the New York Yankees.

Bochy's experience handling pitchers during his playing career is evident in his style of managing. In 1996, the Padres had 32 games in which the opponent scored two runs or fewer, and yet San Diego used three pitchers or more in all of those games. This is an indication of the 1990s style of situational pitching — lefty pitcher versus righty hitter or vice versa, set-up men and closers. But it is significant to note that the Padres won the division that year — that all the maneuvering worked.

Year	Team	Record	Pct.	Standing
1995	SD	70–74	.480	Third
1996	SD	91–71	.560	First
1997	SD	76–86	.460	Fourth
1998	SD	98–64	.600	First
1999	SD	74–88	.450	Fourth
2000	SD	76–86	.469	Fifth
2001	SD	79–83	.488	Fourth
6 years		**564–552**	**.505**	

WORLD SERIES

Year	Team	Record	Pct.
1998	SD	0–4	.000

John Boles

Born August 19, 1948, Chicago, Illinois; Florida Marlins, July 9, 1996–October 4, 1996; October 2, 1998–May 28, 2001

John Boles managed the Florida Marlins before and after they won the World Series. He replaced Rene Lachemann as manager in 1996 and brought them to the finish with a 40–35 record, good for third place. Boles left when Jim Leyland was lured to Florida and, provided with a dazzling array of free agents, Leyland's Marlins beat the Cleveland Indians in the World Series. But Marlins owner Wayne Huizenga unloaded his big payroll the next year and the Marlins tumbled in the standings. Leyland left to manage Colorado and Boles returned to the helm in Florida. He was relieved of his duties on May 28, 2001, with the Marlins struggling on the field and criticizing the manager and his coaches publicly off the field.

Year	Team	Record	Pct.	Standing
1996	Fla	40–35	.530	Third
1999	Fla	64–98	.390	Fifth
2000	Fla	79–82	.491	Third
2001	Fla	22–26	.458	Fourth
4 years		**205–241**	**.460**	

Thomas Henry Bond

Born April 2, 1856, Granaard, Ireland; died January 24, 1941, Boston, Massachusetts; Worcester Ruby Legs, 1882

Tommy Bond was among the many pioneer managers in major league baseball who got his early training from watching and playing the games of rounders and cricket across the ocean. Bond, Born in Ireland, managed the short-lived Worcester ball club in 1882 and had no other presence in the managerial ranks.

Year	Team	Record	Pct.	Standing
1882	Wor (N)	5–22	.185	Eighth

Robert Raymond Boone

Born November 19, 1947, San Diego, California; Kansas City Royals, October 7, 1994–July 9, 1997; Cincinnati Reds, October 12, 2000–present

Bob Boone was a major league catcher for 19 years who won seven Gold Glove awards and is second all-time in games played by a catcher. Carlton Fisk caught in one more. As a manager, Boone demonstrated the same aptitude that many catchers-turned-managers do: he liked to make things happen. Sometimes managers are forced to do this because they don't have the talent on the field for things to happen on their own. Boone managed Kansas City in an era when the Cleveland Indians dominated the American League Central Division and every other team was a distant also-ran. The Royals managed to finish second in the strike-shortened 1995 season and then finish fifth the next two years. Boone was fired midway into the 1997 season.

Boone was forever shuffling his lineup, trying to find the right combination. In 1996, the Royals used 152 lineups in a 162-game season, easily the most in the league. He used 172 pinch hitters. Only Tom Kelly at Minnesota used more. He used 53 pinch runners.

Only Art Howe at Oakland, Terry Bevington at Chicago, Joe Torre in New York and Kevin Kennedy in Texas used more.

Boone's Royals executed the hit-and-run 172 times and attempted stolen bases 280 times — leading the major leagues in both categories. The Royals also led the league in sacrifice bunt attempts during Boone's years.

His style was reminiscent of Gene Mauch's. It made for lively baseball but did not produce championship teams. In 2001, he became manager of the Cincinnati Reds.

Year	Team	Record	Pct.	Standing
1995	KC	70–74	.480	Second
1996	KC	75–86	.460	Fifth
1997	KC	36–46	.430	Fifth
2001	Cin	66–96	.407	Fifth
4 years		**247–302**	**.450**	

Stephen Boros

Born September 3, 1936, Flint, Michigan; Oakland A's, November 17, 1982–May 24, 1984; San Diego Padres, February 24, 1986–October 28, 1986

Steve Boros had a tough act to follow — Billy Martin — when he became manager of the Oakland A's in 1984. He moved them from fifth to fourth place in his first year and, 44 games into the next season, was four games below .500 when he was fired. Boros was hired to manage the San Diego Padres in 1986 and brought them home in fourth place before he was fired again. A remarkable statistic from Boros' managerial career: He managed parts of three seasons for two teams in two different leagues, and yet his winning percentage was almost exactly the same every year. In this respect, his teams were models of consistency.

Year	Team	Record	Pct.	Standing
1983	Oak	74–88	.457	Fourth
1984	Oak	20–24	.455	Fourth
1986	SD	74–88	.457	Fourth
3 years		**168–200**	**.456**	

James Leroy Bottomley

Born April 23, 1900, Oglesby, Illinois; died December 11, 1959, St. Louis, Missouri; St. Louis Browns, July 21, 1937–December 14, 1937

Jim Bottomley was a Hall of Fame first baseman for the St. Louis Cardinals who had a lifetime batting average of .310 and had one game in which he drove in 12 runs. Like so many other Hall of Fame players, he did not experience the same success as a manager. He was brought in to take over the St. Louis Browns in 1937, replacing another Hall of Famer, Rogers Hornsby, with the Browns buried in last place with a 25–50 record. He didn't fare any better. The Browns won only 21 of 80 games with Bottomley in charge, losing 59 and tying 1. He never managed again.

Year	Team	Record	Pct.	Standing
1937	StL (A)	21–59	.263	Eighth

Louis Boudreau

Born July 17, 1917, Harvey, Illinois; died August 10, 2001, Harvey, Illinois; Cleveland Indians, November 25, 1941–November 10, 1950; Boston Red Sox, November 27, 1951–October 10, 1954; Kansas City Athletics, November 18, 1954–August 6, 1957; Chicago Cubs, May 4, 1960–October 4, 1960

Lou Boudreau was the youngest player-manager in baseball history when he took over the Cleveland Indians in 1942 and guided them through several unproductive seasons. But in a three-year span after World War II, the Indians went from sixth place in 1946 to the World Series championship in 1948. The Indians won 89 and 92 in 1949 and 1950. But they finished third and fourth in those two years and Boudreau was gone.

John Berardino, a ballplayer-turned-actor who played for Boudreau in Cleveland, said Boudreau benefited from having veteran coaches around him. One, Bill McKechnie, had been a major league manager for 25 years and never got the credit he deserved for mentoring the young Boudreau in Cleveland, according to Berardino.

Boudreau had been a popular manager for most of his time in Cleveland. When Boston hired him in 1952 after several years close to the top, Boudreau, now 34, announced he would produce a winner there, even if it meant trading Ted Williams. It was a brash statement that put him in disfavor with both players and fans. He never did completely overcome the hostility, and his teams finished sixth, fourth and fourth.

After Williams' third stint in the armed services in the early 1950s, he said he would quit if Boudreau remained manager. Williams stayed and Boudreau was fired after the 1954 season.

Hired to manage the Kansas City A's in 1956, Boudreau faced a whole new set of challenges. The A's had left Philadelphia, but they brought the same pitching staff to Kansas City. They finished sixth at 63–91 in 1955, eighth at 52–102 in 1956 and were eighth at 36–67 when Boudreau was fired in 1957.

His fourth managerial stint came in 1960, when he was a radio broadcaster for the Chicago Cubs. When the Cubs started the season 6–11 under Charlie Grimm, Cub owner Philip K. Wrigley engineered a unique switch — Grimm to the broadcast booth and Boudreau to the dugout. Grimm never managed again, and neither did Boudreau after guiding the Cubs to a 54–83 record the rest of the way. The next year, Boudreau was broadcasting again, and the Cubs were trying a rotating coaching system instead of a manager. That didn't work, either, but Boudreau was observing it all from the radio press box.

Boudreau was an innovator throughout his managerial career and was not afraid to try new approaches to winning. Bill Veeck is given deserved credit for breaking the color line in the American League with the signing of Larry Doby with the Indians in 1947. A manager has to take what the front office gives him, and it was up to Boudreau to make sure that integration worked on the field, in the clubhouse and in the team's travels. By 1948, Doby was a star on the pennant-winning team. Another black man, Satchel Paige, was a 42-year-old rookie on that club. Boudreau found a home for him in the Indians bullpen, where he was 6–1 with a 2.48 earned run average.

He also devised the "Ted Williams Shift," a defensive strategy in which his third baseman, Kenny Keltner, played just on the right side of second base while shortstop Boudreau moved over between first and second, in the second baseman's normal position. Centerfielder Pat Seerey moved into right–center-field while left fielder George Case played a shallow leftfield. The shift left only left-fielder Case on the left side of the diamond.

Ironically, Boudreau devised the shift after Williams had beaten the Indians by hitting three home runs in a game — hits that obviously no shift could have prevented. Boudreau knew Williams was a dead-pull hitter. In the 1946 World Series, Cardinal manager Eddie Dyer used a variation of it and held Williams to five hits.

Boudreau had one other innovation worth noting in Cleveland. He converted Bob Lemon from an outfielder to a pitcher. Lemon credited Boudreau with transforming him from a mediocre outfielder to a pitcher who wound up in the Hall of Fame. Another Hall of Fame pitcher, Bob Feller, said Boudreau instilled in him the confidence he needed when he got off to a shaky start upon returning to the Indians after World War II.

In Kansas City, Boudreau had a thin pitching staff that couldn't keep the A's competitive. In 1957, Boudreau and his successor, Harry Craft, shuttled 20 pitchers to the mound — and none of them worked enough innings to qualify for listing in the league's earned run average standings.

He also platooned a lot in Kansas City, sometimes to the consternation of his players. Gus Zernial, the slugging right-handed hitting outfielder, tells the story of coming to the plate with the bases loaded in the first inning and seeing the left-handed hitting Enos Slaughter also step to the plate. Slaughter told Zernial he was pinch-hitting for him — in the first inning! Zernial was angry at Boudreau but said nothing as Slaughter doubled and three runs scored.

Boudreau is the only man to play for and manage two professional sports teams. In 1938 and 1939, he played for and coached the Hammond, Ind., professional basketball team where one of his teammates was John Wooden, who rose to greatness as coach of the UCLA basketball championship teams of the 1960s and '70s.

In his playing days, Boudreau was considered the best shortstop of his era. He played 15 years, had a lifetime batting average of .295 and was elected to the Hall of Fame in 1970.

Year	Team	Record	Pct.	Standing
1942	Cleve	75–79	.487	Fourth
1943	Cleve	82–71	.536	Third
1944	Cleve	72–82	.468	Fifth
1945	Cleve	73–72	.503	Fifth
1946	Cleve	68–86	.442	Sixth
1947	Cleve	80–74	.519	Fourth
1948	Cleve	97–58	.626	First
1949	Cleve	89–65	.578	Third
1950	Cleve	92–62	.597	Fourth
1952	Bos (A)	76–78	.494	Sixth
1953	Bos	84–69	.549	Fourth
1954	Bos	69–85	.448	Fourth
1955	KC	63–91	.409	Sixth
1956	KC	52–102	.338	Eighth
1957	KC	36–67	.350	Eighth
1960	Chi (N)	54–83	.397	Eighth
16 years		**162–1224**	**.487**	

WORLD SERIES

Year	Team	Record	Pct.
1948	Cleve	4–2	.667

Lawrence Robert Bowa

Born December 6, 1945, Sacramento, California; San Diego Padres, October, 28, 1986–May 29, 1988; Philadelphia Phillies, Oct 12, 2000–present

Larry Bowa was a fiery competitor and a good shortstop with the Philadelphia Phillies from 1970 to 1981 and played on the Phillies National League championship team in 1980. He then played for the Chicago Cubs and was the shortstop on Chicago's 1984 division winner — the Cubs first championship since 1945. After playing a year with the San Francisco Giants, the Padres hired Bowa as their manager in 1987. The Padres finished sixth in 1987 and were in fifth place with a dismal 16–30 record in 1988 when Bowa was given the ax by the Padres front office. He returned to manage the Philadelphia Phillies in 2001, leading the club to a surprising second-place finish in the NL East.

Year	Team	Record	Pct.	Standing
1987	SD	65–97	.401	Sixth
1988	SD	16–30	.348	Fifth
2001	Phil	86–76	.531	Second
3 years		**167–203**	**.451**	

Frank Eugene Bowerman

Born December 5, 1868, Romeo, Michigan; died November 30, 1948, Romeo; Boston Pilgrims, February 10, 1909–July 21, 1909

Frank Bowerman was a catcher with some of the great Baltimore teams of the 1890s. But the winning ways did not carry over to his managerial career. He was dismissed after losing 55 of 78 games in the 1909 season and never managed again.

Year	Team	Record	Pct.	Standing
1909	Bos (N)	23–55	.295	Eighth

William J. Boyd

Born December 22, 1852, New York, New York; died September 30, 1912, Jamaica, New York; Brooklyn Atlantics, 1875

Bill Boyd played every position but catcher in parts of four seasons before getting his brief chance to manage. That came in 1875 for Brooklyn in the National Association, a year before the National League began. Boyd managed in two games and Brooklyn lost them both.

Year	Team	Record	Pct.	Standing
1875	Brklyn	0–2	.000	Twelfth

Kenton Lloyd Boyer

Born May 20, 1931, Liberty, Missouri; died September 7, 1982, St. Louis; St. Louis Cardinals, April 29, 1978–June 9, 1980

Ken Boyer was a star third baseman for the St. Louis Cardinals for 11 years and was extremely popular with the St. Louis fans. He took over as manager 18 games into the

1978 season. The Cardinals finished fifth. The Cardinals improved to a third-place finish in 1979 but had lost 33 of 51 games in 1980 when Boyer was fired.

Year	Team	Record	Pct.	Standing
1978	StL	62–82	.431	Fifth
1979	StL	86–76	.531	Third
1980	StL	18–33	.353	Sixth
3 years		**166–191**	**.465**	

William Joseph Bradley

Born February 13, 1878, Cleveland, Ohio; died March 11, 1954, Cleveland; Brooklyn Dodgers, 1914

Bill Bradley's only shot at being a big league manager came in 1914 with the upstart Federal League. He brought his Brooklyn team home in fifth place, winning as many games as he lost. The Federal League lasted two years. Bradley lasted only one.

Year	Team	Record	Pct.	Standing
1914	Brklyn (F)	77–77	.500	Fifth

Robert Randall Bragan

Born October 30, 1917, Birmingham, Alabama; Pittsburgh Pirates, November 2, 1955–August 2, 1957; Cleveland Indians, September 29, 1957–June 26, 1958; Milwaukee/Atlanta Braves—October 17, 1962–August 9, 1966

Bobby Bragan, a former major league infielder, was called on to manage the Pittsburgh Pirates during their transition years. They weren't as awful as they had been in the early 1950s, but they weren't yet good. His 1956 team featured Roberto Clemente, Dick Groat, Elroy Face and Bob Friend, all of whom would play on the 1960 pennant winner, long after Bragan was gone. The Pirates finished seventh in 1956 and were eighth in 1957 when Bragan was fired. Cleveland hired him to manage the Indians in 1958, but the talent pool wasn't much better than it had been in Pittsburgh. He was fired after 67 games.

Bragan was a thinking man's manager, someone who didn't automatically play the percentages. As manager of the Braves, he explained his way of thinking. He said if a man had one foot in an oven and the other in a bucket of ice, the percentages would say the man was comfortable. So Bragan, rather than going strictly by the book, was a man of many strategies but was seldom presented the situations in which he could try them out. At Pittsburgh, he shuffled his batting order frequently, trying to find the right combination. He believed that with so many different combinations of possible batting orders, the right lineup could mean many extra runs over the course of a season.

For instance, Bragan believed, contrary to conventional baseball strategy, that a power hitter could be a good lead-off man because of the number of extra at-bats that player would get during the course of the season. He could never test his theory in Pittsburgh or Cleveland because of the lack of punch elsewhere in the lineup. But when Bragan went to Milwaukee, he experimented with Henry Aaron in the lead-off spot a few times. And in 1966, he had Felipe Alou, who had usually been a three, four or five hitter, leading off most of the season.

The results were just as Bragan had expected. Alou led the National League in at-bats with 666, 101 more than he had in any previous season. Alou also had 218 hits, 41 more than he had ever had, and his 31 home runs beat his previous high of 26. In the lead-off spot, he was getting more good pitches to hit. His 122 runs scored were 26 more than his previous high, and he had his best batting average, .327. Alou was a base runner many of the times Aaron hit his 44 home runs and catcher Joe Torre hit any of his 36. Bragan's theory seemed to be working. But the Braves finished fifth, the same as they had in 1964 and 1965 and actually won one fewer game than they had in 1965. Bragan didn't last the season.

The Braves moved to Atlanta and new owner Ted Turner dismissed him when the team had fallen to a 52–59 record. He never managed in the major leagues again.

Year	Team	Record	Pct.	Standing
1956	Pitt	66–88	.429	Seventh
1957	Pitt	36–67	.350	Eighth
1958	Cleve	31–36	.453	Fifth
1963	Mil	84–78	.519	Sixth
1964	Mil	88–74	.543	Fifth
1965	Mil	86–76	.531	Fifth
1966	Atl	52–59	.468	Fifth
7 years		**443–478**	**.481**	

Robert Earl Brenly

Born February 25, 1954, Coshocton, Ohio; Arizona Diamondbacks, October 30, 2000–present

Bob Brenly, a major league catcher for nine years, won the World Series with the Arizona Diamondbacks in his first year as manager, helped by pitching greats Curt Schilling and Randy Johnson.

Year	Team	W–L	Pct.	Standing
2001	Ariz	92–70	.568	First

DIVISIONAL PLAYOFFS

Year	Team	W–L	Pct.
2001	Ariz	3–2	.800

LEAGUE CHAMPIONSHIP SERIES

Year	Team	W–L	Pct.
2001	Ariz	4–1	.800

WORLD SERIES

Year	Team	W–L	Pct.
2001	Ariz	4–3	.571

Roger Philip Bresnahan

Born June 11, 1879, Toledo, Ohio; died December 4, 1944, Toledo; St. Louis Cardinals, October 13, 1908–October 22, 1912; Chicago Cubs, November 18, 1914–January 5, 1916

Roger Bresnahan was a Hall of Fame catcher for John McGraw's New York Giants who is credited with two innovations: shinguards, which he began wearing in 1907, and a batting helmet, which he experimented with for only a short time after he was beaned in a game.

He was innovative in his short career as a manager, too. In 1912, his St. Louis Cardinal team set the major league record for use of relief pitchers. Bresnahan's Cardinal team finished seventh with a dismal 63–90 record, and he went to the bullpen 134 times during the season.

In modern day baseball, relief pitchers are almost a daily occurrence. (In 1995, Don Baylor went to the bullpen 456 times for the Colorado Rockies.) But in Bresnahan's day, it was unusual. The previous high mark for use of relief pitchers had been 115 in 1911 by Fred Tenney with the Boston Rustlers, a team that won only 44 games and lost 107. In 1910, the Philadelphia Phillies and Boston Braves each went to the bullpen 107 times. No other teams in history had topped the 100 mark.

Bresnahan took over a Cardinal team that had finished seventh two years in a row and got them up to fifth place in 1911. But after the sixth-place finish in 1912, Bresnahan was sent packing. He emerged to manage the Chicago Cubs to a fourth-place finish in 1915, but that wasn't good enough. The Cubs let him go. Bresnahan never managed in the major leagues again.

Year	Team	Record	Pct.	Standing
1909	StL	54–98	.355	Seventh
1910	StL	63–90	.412	Seventh
1911	StL	75–74	.503	Fifth
1912	StL	63–90	.412	Sixth
1915	Chi (N)	73–80	.477	Fourth
5 years		**328–432**	**.432**	

James David Bristol

Born June 23, 1923, Macon, Georgia; Cincinnati Reds, July 13, 1966–October 8, 1969; Milwaukee Brewers, November 24, 1969–May 28, 1972; Atlanta Braves, September 1, 1975–May 10, 1977; San Francisco Giants, September 6, 1979–December 9, 1980

As a first-year manager, Dave Bristol took over a Cincinnati Reds team in 1966 from another first-year manager, Don Heffner, who was relieved of his duties with the Reds nine games below .500. Bristol guided them to a 39–38 finish, good for sixth place in the 10-team league. The Reds had a young team that was on the brink of stardom but wasn't there yet. Bristol had Tony Perez at first, Pete Rose at second, Tommy Helms at third and Tommy Harper, Vada Pinson and Deron Johnson in the outfield. What he didn't have was Frank Robinson, who had been traded to Baltimore in the off-season. He won the Triple Crown for the Orioles while Bristol got 12 wins from Milt Pappas, a pitcher who came over in the Robinson deal. The Reds gradually improved under Bristol and won 89 games in 1969 for a third place finish. Then he was off to manage the transplanted Seattle Pilots now in Milwaukee and called the Brewers.

While Cincinnati was winning the National League pennant with Perez, Rose, Helms and catcher Johnny Bench, Bristol's Brewers won 65 in 1970, 69 in 1971 and were 10–20 in 1972 when Bristol was fired. He was hired to manage the Atlanta Braves in 1976, a team for which Phil Niekro won 17 games and the rest of the staff won 53. The Braves finished last. In 1977, Atlanta suffered through a 17-game losing streak early in the season and were headed for their second straight last-place finish when flamboyant owner Ted Turner inserted himself as manager for a game. The Braves lost. Coach Vern Benson managed for one game and won it. Then Bristol managed the rest of the way to a 61–101 record. He was fired at season's end but reappeared at the end of the 1979 season as manager of the San Francisco Giants, taking over at the end of the season for Joe Alto-belli. Bristol was 10–12 and brought the Giants to a fifth-place finish in 1980, his last season as a major league manager.

Except for Cincinnati, Bristol's teams didn't have much power, and his pitching was always suspect. He developed a style of playing for one run at a time, rather than relying on the big inning. It is more than coincidence that Bristol's Reds, Brewers and Giants teams led the league in sacrifice bunts. In Atlanta, in his one full season, interrupted by Turner's and Benson's one-game stints, the Braves were second in the league in bunts.

Year	Team	Record	Pct.	Standing
1966	Cin	39–38	.506	Seventh
1967	Cin	87–75	.537	Fourth
1968	Cin	83–79	.512	Fourth
1969	Cin	89–73	.549	Third
1970	Mil (A)	65–97	.401	Fifth
1971	Mil	69–92	.429	Sixth
1972	Mil	10–20	.333	Sixth
1976	Atl	70–92	.432	Sixth
1977	Atl	8–21	.276	Sixth
1977	Atl	53–79	.402	Sixth
1979	SF	10–12	.455	Fourth
1980	SF	75–86	.466	Fifth
11 years		**658–764**	**.464**	

Edward P. Brown

No biographical data available; St. Louis Brown Stockings, 1882

Ed Brown was one of the pioneer managers in professional baseball, taking over the St. Louis ball club in the old American Association in 1882 and finishing out the season. He won 10 of 21 games and never managed again.

Year	Team	Record	Pct.	Standing
1882	StL (AA)	10–11	.476	Fifth

Freeman Brown

Born January 31, 1845, Hubbardstown, Massachusetts; died December 27, 1916, Worcester, Massachusetts; Worcester Ruby Legs, 1881–1882

In the early days of the National League, small towns fielded teams. One of them was in Worcester, Massachusetts. Freeman Brown managed in Worcester, retired in Worcester and died in Worcester. His managerial career lasted parts of two seasons in which his teams were buried in last place.

Year	Team	Record	Pct.	Standing
1881	Wor (N)	32–50	.390	Eighth
1882	Wor	4–19	.174	Eighth
2 years		**36–69**	**.343**	

Lewis J. Brown

Born February 1, 1858, Leominster, Massachusetts; died January 16, 1889, Boston, Massachusetts; Chicago White Stockings, 1879

Lew Brown was a seldom-used catcher for Boston, Providence and Chicago in the infant years of baseball. He managed the Chicago White Stockings (forerunners to the Cubs), for eight games in 1879 and bowed out after losing seven of them.

Year	Team	Record	Pct.	Standing
1879	Chi (N)	1–7	.125	Fourth

Mordecai Peter Centennial "Three Finger" Brown

Born October 19, 1876, Nyseville, Indiana; died February 14, 1948, Terre Haute, Indiana; St. Louis Terriers, 1914

Three Finger Brown, a Hall of Fame pitcher for the Chicago Cubs in the early 1900s, took a shot at managing with the St. Louis franchise in the renegade Federal League, which raided the major leagues for players and lasted two years.

Brown won 50 and lost 63 in the Federal League — his only tour of duty as a manager.

Year	Team	Record	Pct.	Standing
1914	StL (F)	50–63	.442	Eighth

Thomas T. Brown

Born September 21, 1860, Liverpool, England; died October 27, 1927, Washington, D.C.; Washington Senators, 1897–1898

Washington's first franchise was in the National League in the 19th century. The ball club struggled much like it did for so many years in the 20th century. Tom Brown was brought on to finish out the 1897 season and won six more games than he lost for a team that finished 11th. In 1898, when the team won only three of its first 16 games, Brown was fired. Brown's dismal managerial career followed a 17-year playing career in which he stole more than 657 bases.

Year	Team	Record	Pct.	Standing
1897	Wash (N)	52–46	.531	Eleventh
1898	Wash	3–13	.188	Eleventh
2 years		**55–59**	**.482**	

Earle Francis Brucker

Born May 6, 1901, Albany, New York; died May 8, 1981, San Diego, California; Cincinnati Reds, July 29, 1952–August 5, 1952

Earle Brucker caught for the Philadelphia Athletics for five years. He managed the

Cincinnati Reds for five games. Filling in between the firing of Luke Sewell and the hiring of Rogers Hornsby, Brucker won three and lost two. He never managed again in the major leagues.

Year	Team	Record	Pct.	Standing
1952	Cin (N)	3–2	.600	Seventh

Albert C. Buckenberger

Born January 31, 1861, Detroit, Michigan; died July 1, 1917, Syracuse, New York; Columbus Solons, 1889–1890; Pittsburgh Alleghenys, 1892–1894; St. Louis Browns, 1895; Boston Beaneaters, 1902–1904

Al Buckenberger never played in the major leagues but managed for nine years, finishing at .500 or above only three times. He hung around long enough to be included in a fairly exclusive club — men who managed in more than 1,000 games. Beyond that, his greatest baseball achievement might be the development of first-rate baseball talent, including Jake Beckley, Joe Kelley and Connie Mack. All are in the Hall of Fame and Mack became the winningest major league manager.

Year	Team	Record	Pct.	Standing
1889	Col (AA)	60–78	.435	Sixth
1890	Col	42–42	.500	Fifth
1892	Pitt	55–43	.561	Sixth
1893	Pitt	81–48	.628	Second
1894	Pitt	53–55	.491	Seventh
1895	StL	16–32	.333	Eleventh
1902	Bos (N)	73–64	.533	Third
1903	Bos	58–80	.420	Sixth
1904	Bos	55–98	.359	Seventh
9 years		**493–540**	**.477**	

Charles Buffinton

Born June 16, 1861, Fall River, Massachusetts; died September 23, 1907, Fall River; Philadelphia Athletics, 1890

Charlie Buffinton was another of the many pre–1900 managers who didn't last long. Buffinton had his chance with the Philadelphia franchise in the Players League. He was the last of three managers the team employed that year and was not invited back after posting a 21–25 record.

Year	Team	Record	Pct.	Standing
1890	Phil (P)	21–25	.457	Fifth

James Leanord Bullock

Born January 13, 1845, Bristol, Rhode Island; died August 12, 1914; Providence Grays, 1880–1881

Jim Bullock took over as manager of the Providence team in the National League and had spectacular success, winning 20 more games than he lost. Thirty-four games into the next season, with his team at .500, Bullock was gone, never to manage again.

Year	Team	Record	Pct.	Standing
1880	Prov (N)	52–32	.619	Second
1881	Prov	17–17	.500	Third
2 years		**69–49**	**.585**	

John Joseph Burdock

Born in 1851, Brooklyn, New York; died November 28, 1931, Brooklyn; Boston Red Caps, 1883

Jack Burdock was one of baseball's pioneer managers, but not for long. He managed the Boston ball club in 1883 and had a 31–26 record when his managerial career came to a close. John Morrill took over and the team won 32 of its next 41 games to claim the league championship.

Year	Team	Record	Pct.	Standing
1883	Bos (N)	31–26	.544	Second

James Timothy Burke

Born October 12, 1874, St. Louis, Missouri; died March 26, 1942, St. Louis; St. Louis Cardinals, 1905; St. Louis Browns, 1918–1920

The St. Louis Cardinals had three managers in 1905. The second of them was Sunset Jimmy Burke. He replaced Kid Nichols, who won only 19 of the Cardinals' first 48 contests. Burke did even worse, winning only 17 of 49 games. Thirteen years later, he resurfaced with the St. Louis Browns and accomplished something unusual — gradual improvement of the Browns. Under Burke, they finished sixth in 1918, fifth in 1919 and then fourth — ascending to the first division — in 1920. Despite the improvement, Burke was let go at the end of the season.

Year	Team	Record	Pct.	Standing
1905	StL (N)	17–32	.347	Sixth
1918	StL (A)	29–32	.475	Sixth
Year	Team	Record	Pct.	Standing
1919	StL (A)	67–72	.482	Fifth
1920	StL (A)	76–77	.497	Fourth
4 years		**189–213**	**.470**	

George Walter Burnham

Born May 20, 1860, Albion, Michigan; died November 18, 1902, Detroit, Michigan; Indianapolis Hoosiers, 1887

George "Watch" Burnham was 27 years old when he got his chance to manage a big league team. He lasted about a month as Indianapolis could only manage six wins in his 28 games at the helm.

Year	Team	Record	Pct.	Standing
1887	Ind (N)	6–22	.214	Eighth

Thomas Everett Burns

Born March 30, 1857, Honesdale, Pennsylvania; died March 19, 1902, Jersey City, New Jersey; Pittsburgh Pirates, 1892; Chicago Cubs, 1898–1899

Tom Burns managed a Pittsburgh team in 1892 that had future Hall of Famers Jake Beckley and Joe Kelley but could do no better than 25–30 before Burns was relieved of his duties. He returned to manage Chicago for two years. In 1898, his team finished 20 games above .500. The next year, his troops slipped to 75–73, ending Burns' managerial career.

Year	Team	Record	Pct.	Standing
1892	Pitt	25–30	.455	Sixth
1898	Chi	85–65	.567	Fourth
1899	Chi	75–73	.507	Eighth
3 years		**185–168**	**.524**	

William Edwin Burwell

Born March 27, 1895, Jarbalo, Kansas; died June 11, 1973, Ormond, Beach, Florida; Pittsburgh Pirates, September 29, 1947

Bill Burwell, a former major league pitcher, was a coach with the Pittsburgh Pirates and took over as manager when Billy Herman quit with one game left in the 1947 season. The Pirates won their last game, keeping them from finishing in last place. Billy Meyer was hired to manage the club the following year. Burwell never got another chance to manage in the major leagues.

Year	Team	Record	Pct.	Standing
1947	Pitt	1–0	1.000	Seventh

Owen Joseph "Donie" Bush

Born October 8, 1887, Indianapolis, Indiana; died March 28, 1972, Indianapolis; Washington Senators, 1923; Pittsburgh Pirates, November 12, 1926–September 4, 1929; Chicago White Sox, November 29, 1929–October 27, 1931; Cincinnati Reds, November 29, 1932–April 25, 1934

Donie Bush was a major league shortstop for 15 years before he was named player-manager of the Washington Senators in 1923. He guided the Senators to a fourth-place finish but was not rehired. Instead, the Senators went with Bucky Harris, their third straight player-manager, and Washington won the pennant.

Bush got his opportunity to manage a championship team when he took over the Pittsburgh Pirates. The Bucs won their second pennant in three years and then ran into a New York Yankee team regarded as one of the greatest teams of all time. The Yankees swept them in the World Series.

The Pirates had three future Hall of Famers in their starting lineup: Lloyd and Paul Waner and Kiki Cuyler. Bush was a disciplinarian and his handling of Cuyler resulted in one of the biggest controversies of 1927. There are several versions as to what started the trouble, but all suggest that Bush was unhappy with Cuyler's attitude, feeling Cuyler was selfish and not a team player. In August, Bush benched Cuyler. Some say it was because Cuyler loafed while running the bases. Others say Cuyler complained about being moved down in the batting order. Whatever the reason, Bush quit playing his star outfielder. Cuyler had hit .357 and .321 in 1925 and 1926, had led the league in runs scored both years and had driven in 102 and 92 runs, respectively. In 1927, Cuyler appeared in only 85 games, and Bush refused to play him in the World Series. After the season, Cuyler was traded to Chicago where he played on two pennant-winning teams for the Cubs.

Bush stayed to manage the Pirates through August of 1929. When the team went into a slump that left them out of pennant contention, Bush was fired but was hired in 1930 to manage the Chicago White Sox. He didn't have the Waner brothers or Cuyler in Chicago and won just 62 and 56 games in two seasons there. His next stop, and his last one, was in Cincinnati, where he won only 58 games with the Reds in 1933.

Year	Team	Record	Pct.	Standing
1923	Wash	75–78	.490	Fourth
1927	Pitt	94–60	.610	First
1928	Pitt	85–67	.559	Fourth
1929	Pitt	67–51	.568	Second
1930	Chi (A)	62–92	.403	Seventh
1931	Chi	56–97	.366	Eighth
1933	Cin	58–94	.382	Eighth
7 years		**497–539**	**.480**	

WORLD SERIES

Year	Team	Record	Pct.
1927	Pitts	0–4	.000

Ormond Hook Butler

Born November 18, 1854, West Virginia; died September 12, 1915, Baltimore, Maryland; Pittsburgh Alleghenys, 1883

Ormond Butler was one of many men in the American Association who was given a chance to manage. But not much of a chance. Butler managed the association's Pittsburgh team for 53 games in 1883, but could win only 17 of them and was dismissed, never to manage again.

Year	Team	Record	Pct.	Standing
1883	Pitt	17–36	.321	Seventh

Charles H. Byrne

Born September 18, 1843, New York, New York; died January 4, 1898, New York; Brooklyn Gladiators, 1885–1887

Charlie Byrne lasted longer than many of his contemporaries in the early days of professional baseball, and he had a pretty good run. Byrne took over the Brooklyn club in the middle of the 1885 season and won 25 of 39 games, moving the club up from seventh to fifth place. In his next season, Brooklyn came in third but dropped to sixth the next year and Byrne was gone.

Year	Team	Record	Pct.	Standing
1885	Brklyn	25–14	.641	Fifth
1886	Brklyn	76–61	.555	Third
1887	Brklyn	60–74	.448	Sixth
3 years		**161–149**	**.519**	

James Joseph "Nixey" Callahan

Born March 18, 1874, Fitchbourg, Massachusetts; died October 4, 1934, Boston, Massachusetts; Chicago White Sox, 1903–1904; 1912–1914; Pittsburgh Pirates, 1916–1917

Nixey Callahan was an outfielder who sometimes pitched in a career that started in 1894. He interrupted his playing career to manage the Chicago White Sox in 1903 and 1904, but midway through his second season, with the White Sox mired in fourth place, he and management agreed he'd be better off going back to the outfield. He returned to managing the White Sox in 1912 and was more successful this time around, guiding them to a fourth-place finish. But they tumbled to fifth in 1913 and sixth in 1914, causing Callahan's second dismissal.

In 1916, the Pittsburgh Pirates hired him to succeed their legendary skipper, Fred Clarke, who at one point had 14 consecutive winning seasons. Clarke retired when the talent had become a little thin. Callahan finished sixth in 1916. After 60 games in the 1917 season, the Pirates were dead last and Callahan disappeared — literally. He was missing for three days during a Pittsburgh homestand and was next seen drunk on the streets of Philadelphia. He never reappeared as a major league manager.

Year	Team	Record	Pct.	Standing
1903	Chi (A)	60–77	.438	Seventh
1904	Chi	22–18	.550	Fourth
1912	Chi (A)	78–76	.506	Fourth
1913	Chi	78–74	.513	Fifth
1914	Chi	70–84	.455	Sixth
1916	Pitt	65–89	.422	Sixth
1917	Pitt	20–40	.333	Eighth
7 years		**393–458**	**.462**	

William Henry Cammeyer

Born March 20, 1821, New York, New York; died September 4, 1898, New York; New York Giants, 1876

Bill Cammeyer's career as a baseball manager was short but historic. He is remembered for managing one of the original eight teams when the National League had its first season in 1876. He will not be remembered, however, for juggling his pitching staff too much. New York had a record of 21–35. His ace, Bobby Mathews, was 21–34. Cammeyer, who was 55 when he made his managerial debut, did not manage again.

Year	Team	Record	Pct.	Standing
1876	NY (N)	21–35	.375	Sixth

Charles Columbus "Count" Campeau

Born October 17, 1863, Detroit, Michigan; died April 3, 1938, New Orleans, Louisiana; St. Louis Browns, 1890

Count Campeau was the last of three managers for the St. Louis ball club in the American Association in 1890 and steered the club into third place, behind Louisville and Columbus. He never managed again.

Year	Team	Record	Pct.	Standing
1890	StL (AA)	33–26	.559	Third

Joseph D. Cantillon

Born August 19, 1861, Janesville, Wisconsin; died January 31, 1930, Hickman, Kentucky; Washington Senators, 1907–1909

Joe Cantillon had Walter Johnson and not much else to work with when he took over as manager of the Washington Senators in 1907. In the next three years, the Senators averaged 99 losses a year. Johnson, who was a rookie in Cantillon's first year, won 5, 14 and 13 from 1907 to 1909. Cantillon was not rehired for 1910, the year that Johnson, now a fully developed veteran, started a string of 10 consecutive seasons of winning 20 or more games.

Year	Team	Record	Pct.	Standing
1907	Wash	49–102	.325	Eighth
1908	Wash	67–85	.441	Seventh
1909	Wash	42–110	.276	Eighth
3 years		**158–297**	**.347**	

Max George Carey
(*Real name: Maximilian Carnarius*)

Born January 11, 1890, Terre Haute, Indiana; died May 30, 1976, Miami, Florida; Brooklyn Dodgers, October 23, 1931–February 23, 1934

Max Carey was a switch-hitting outfielder for the Pittsburgh Pirates who hit .458 in the 1925 World Series and got the winning hit off of Walter Johnson of the Washington Senators. He was an exciting baserunner who worried the defense, distracted the pitcher and made things happen: he twice stole second, third and home in the same game. He held the major league record for career putouts by an outfielder until Willie Mays broke it 50 years after Carey retired.

He was hired after the 1931 season to manage the Brooklyn Dodgers, following the 18-year tenure of Wilbert "Uncle Robbie" Robinson. Uncle Robbie had been popular but Dodger fans were hungry for a winner. The Dodgers hadn't finished in the first division in eight years.

Carey, who was strict and serious in contrast to the easygoing Robinson, won approval from the fans with two quick moves — hiring Casey Stengel as a coach and acquiring slugging outfielder Hack Wilson, whose 56 home runs for the Cubs in 1930 stood as the National League record for 68 years. Wilson, because of his almost egg-shaped build and his penchant for peculiar behavior, quickly became a fan favorite. But Carey did some house cleaning, too. When the popular Babe Herman refused to sign a contract and did not report for spring training, he was traded to Cincinnati. Dazzy Vance, once one of the game's best pitchers but now struggling to be a .500 pitcher, was traded to St. Louis after the 1932 season. Carey brought the Dodgers up to a third place finish in 1932 but could do no better than sixth in 1933. Dodger management thought they could do better and hired Stengel to replace Carey who never managed again in the major leagues. He did manage a women's professional team before he retired.

Year	Team	Record	Pct.	Standing
1932	Brklyn	81–73	.526	Third
1932	Brklyn	65–88	.425	Sixth
2 years		**146–161**	**.476**	

Thomas Francis Aloysius Carey

Born in 1849, Brooklyn, New York; died February 13, 1899, Los Angeles, California; Baltimore Lord Baltimores, 1873; New York Mutuals, 1874

Tom Carey was an infielder for nine seasons, the first five in the National Association, the last four in the newly formed National League. While playing for Baltimore and New York in 1873 and 1874, he managed both teams for a while and had winning records in each stint. He never managed again.

Year	Team	Record	Pct.	Standing
1873	Balt	14–9	.609	Third
1874	NY	13–12	.520	Second
2 years		**27–21**	**.562**	

William Francis Carrigan

Born October 22, 1883, Lewiston, Maine; died July 8, 1969, Lewiston; Boston Red Sox, 1913–1916; November 30, 1926–December 20, 1929

Bill Carrigan had been a journeyman catcher for the Boston Red Sox when he was asked to take on the added responsibilities as manager in 1913 when he was just 29 years old. Carrigan had a reputation of being stern and strong. His nickname was "Rough." In 1914, his first full season as manager, Carrigan took a headstrong young pitcher under his wing—Babe Ruth—and eventually won two pennants with Ruth becoming the ace of the staff. The Red Sox beat the Phillies in five games in the 1915 World Series and took the Brooklyn Dodgers, also in five games, in 1916. But Carrigan did not return for the 1917 season. He did return to manage the Red Sox in 1927 after the club had finished in last place two years in a row. By this time, Babe Ruth was the Sultan of Swat for the New York Yankees and Boston had been stripped of much of its talent by owner Harry Frazee, who had purchased the team from Joseph Lannin and who needed money to pay off debts. The undermanned Red Sox finished last three years in a row and Carrigan retired.

Year	Team	Record	Pct.	Standing
1913	Bos (A)	40–30	.571	Fourth
1914	Bos	91–62	.595	Second

1915	Bos	101–50	.669	First
1916	Bos	91–63	.591	First
1927	Bos	51–103	.331	Eighth
1928	Bos	57–96	.373	Eighth
1929	Bos	58–96	.377	Eighth
7 years		**489–500**	**.494**	

World Series

Year	Team	Record
1915	Bos (A)	4–1
1916	Bos	4–1
2 years		**8–2**

Robert Caruthers

Born January 5, 1864, Memphis, Tennessee; died August 5, 1911, Peoria, Illinois; St. Louis Cardinals, 1892

Bob Caruthers was one of the greatest pitchers of the 19th century, winning 218 games and losing only 99 for St. Louis and Brooklyn. In 1892, his last year as a player, he also managed for 48 games, but the Cardinals managed to win only 16 of them.

Year	Team	Record	Pct.	Standing
1892	StL (N)	16–32	.333	Twelfth

Philip Joseph Cavarretta

Born July 19, 1916, Chicago, Illinois; Chicago Cubs, July 22, 1951–March 29, 1954

Phil Cavarretta was a tough, no-nonsense ballplayer and manager who was not opposed to settling differences with his fists. Lenny Merullo, an infielder on the Chicago Cubs last pennant winning team in 1945, tells the story of a rhubarb that started when Merullo slid hard into second base in a game against Brooklyn. Cavarretta, who was Merullo's roommate, was incensed after the game because he thought PeeWee Reese helped incite the fight and nobody took him on. At Cavarretta's insistence, Merullo confronted Reese the next day and another fight broke out — the logical conclusion as far as Cavarretta was concerned.

He played first base for the Cubs from 1934 through 1953 and was named manager in 1951, replacing Frankie Frisch. The Cubs could do no better than seventh. He guided them to a .500 record and fourth place in 1952 but they slipped back to seventh in 1953.

His habit of speaking out cost him his job in 1954. He told reporters in spring training that the Cubs were a second division team. Cubs owner Phil Wrigley didn't like it. He fired Cavarretta and hired Stan Hack to replace him. Cavarretta slipped over to the south side of Chicago where he played first base for the White Sox for two years before retiring.

Year	Team	Record	Pct.	Standing
1951	Chi (N)	27–47	.365	Seventh
1952	Chi	77–77	.500	Fifth
1953	Chi	65–89	.422	Seventh
3 years		**169–213**	**.442**	

Oliver Perry Caylor

Born December 14, 1849, Dayton, Ohio; died October 19, 1897, Winona, Minnesota; Cincinnati Reds 1885–1886; New York Metropolitans, 1887

"O.P." Caylor was a writer and baseball enthusiast who was pressed into managing two teams in the American Association in the 1880s. His Cincinnati team finished second in 1885 but slipped to fifth in 1886 and Caylor was not asked to return as manager. He started a baseball publication called the *Daily Baseball Gazette* and traveled east to New York. When the Giants faltered under manager Bob Ferguson, Caylor agreed to step in. He managed the New York club for 39 games in 1887, winning only 10 of them. When New York let him go, he vowed never to manage again and went back to his first love, writing.

Oliver Perry Caylor

Year	Team	Record	Pct.	Standing
1885	Cin (AA)	63–49	.543	Second
1886	Cin	65–73	.471	Fifth
1887	NY (AA)	10–29	.256	Seventh
3 years		**138–151**	**.478**	

Frank Chance

Born September 9, 1877, Fresno, California; died September 15, 1924, Los Angeles, California; Chicago Cubs, August 5, 1905–September 28, 1912; New York Highlanders, January 8, 1913–September 12, 1914; Boston Red Sox, October 26, 1922–February 17, 1924

Taking over for Frank Selee on August 5, 1905, Frank Chance led the Chicago Cubs to 40 victories in 63 games, securing with the late-season push a 90-win season for the North Siders. In the seven seasons that followed Chance's team would win more than 100 games four times, including 116 in 1906 — still the major league record for most wins in a season (the 2001 Seattle Mariners tied the mark).

Chance was a scrappy first baseman who never turned down an opportunity to settle a dispute with his fists when he thought the situation called for it. He was a good handler of pitchers — and he had good pitchers to handle. Mordecai "Three Finger" Brown was the ace of the staff.

Chance's Cubs knew how to get on base, and they knew how to move runners around the bases. The Cubs led the league in sacrifice bunts in 1905 and 1906 and from 1908 through 1912. (In 1907, they were two bunts shy of leading the league.) Beyond that, the strategy and style were as blunt as Chance's words: "You do things my way or meet me after the game."

Chance blended the art of executing the fundamentals, a pitching staff that consistently led the league in shutouts and earned run average, and a tenacious attitude that dared the opponent to beat the Cubs. But he did it all with a team molded and developed by Selee, who became ill in 1905 and was forced to quit.

Later, when Chance managed two other teams, he didn't come close to the success he had with the Cubs. He managed the New York Highlanders and Boston Red Sox and could get no higher than sixth place in three dismal years. Those seasons took some of the glitter off of Chance's overall managerial statistics. Still, his winning percentage of .593 is one of baseball's all-time bests.

Year	Team	Record	Pct.	Standing
1905	Chi (N)	40–23	.635	Third
1906	Chi	116–36	.763	First
1907	Chi	107–45	.704	First
1908	Chi	99–55	.643	First
1909	Chi	104–49	.680	Second
1910	Chi	104–50	.675	First
1911	Chi	92–62	.597	Second
1912	Chi	91–59	.607	Third
1913	NY (A)	57–94	.377	Seventh
1914	NY (A)	61–76	.445	Sixth
1923	Bos (A)	61–91	.401	Eighth
11 years		**1597–932**	**.593**	

World Series

Year	Team	Record
1906	Chi (N)	2–4
1907	Chi	4–0
1908	Chi	4–1
1910	Chi	1–4
4 years		**11–9**

John Curtis Chapman

Born May 8, 1843, Brooklyn, New York; died June 10, 1916, Brooklyn; Louisville Colonels, 1877; Milwaukee Grays, 1878; Worcester Ruby Legs, 1882; Detroit Wolverines, 1883–1884; Buffalo Bisons, 1885; Louisville Colonels, 1889–1892

Jack Chapman was a well-traveled manager in the 19th century, managing six teams in parts of 10 seasons. He managed the Louisville team two different times in two different leagues. His career began with Louisville in the National League in 1877, the second year the league existed. He then managed four other teams before returning to Louisville to manage its American Association entry from 1889 to 1891 and then its National League team again in 1892, his last year as a manager. His 1890 Louisville team won the championship. He had only one other team that finished over .500. His overall winning percentage of .417 is the lowest of all managers with 10 or more years of experience.

Year	Team	Record	Pct.	Standing
1877	Louis (N)	35–25	.583	Second
1878	Mil (N)	15–45	.250	Sixth
1882	Wor (N)	9–25	.265	Eighth
1883	Det (N)	40–58	.408	Seventh
1884	Det	28–84	.250	Eighth
1885	Buff (N)	12–19	.387	Seventh
1889	Louis (AA)	1–9	.100	Eighth
1890	Louis	88–44	.667	First
1891	Louis	55–84	.396	Seventh
1892	Louis (N)	23–35	.397	Ninth
10 years		**306–428**	**.417**	

William Benjamin "Ben" Chapman

Born December 25, 1908, Nashville, Tennessee; died July 7, 1993, Hoover, Arkansas; Philadelphia Phillies, June 29, 1945–July 16, 1948

Ben Chapman was a speedy, hard-hitting, hard-playing outfielder who had a .302 lifetime batting average with several major league teams. In 1945, he took over a Philadelphia Phillies team that was headed for an eighth-place finish. In 1946, though sporting only a 69–85 record, the Phillies managed to move up to fifth place. They were seventh in 1947 and seventh after 79 games in the 1948 season when Chapman was fired.

Chapman is best remembered as the manager who opposed Jackie Robinson's breaking the color barrier. He supported a planned boycott by players—a scheme that never materialized—and hurled insults at Robinson every time the Phillies played the Dodgers.

His scrappy attitude and often unkind comments might have been tolerated better had the Phillies been winning. But they weren't, and when in early 1948 Chapman complained that the Phillies needed a baseball man in the front office, owner Bob Carpenter fired him.

Year	Team	Record	Pct.	Standing
1945	Phil (N)	29–58	.333	Eighth
1946	Phil	69–85	.448	Fifth
1947	Phil	62–92	.403	Seventh
1948	Phil	37–42	.468	Seventh
4 years		**197–277**	**.416**	

Harold Homer Chase

Born February 13, 1883, Los Gatos, California; died May 18, 1947, Colusa, California; New York Highlanders, September 23, 1910–November 21, 1911

Hal Chase was a first baseman for the New York Highlanders who convinced team management that manager George Stallings ought to be replaced, even though Stallings had moved them from second division to pennant contender in the space of three years. Not only did management listen to Chase, they hired him to replace Stallings. Chase took over with 11 games left and the Highlanders in second place. They won nine of the 11 to remain second. The following season, they were back in sixth place and Chase's managerial career was over. But he continued to play several more years and retired after the 1919 season with a lifetime batting average of .291. His career is tainted by the fact that he associated with gamblers and was suspected several times of playing poorly in order to cause his team to lose.

Year	Team	Record	Pct.	Standing
1910	NY (A)	9–2	.818	Second
1911	NY	76–76	.500	Sixth
2 years		**85–78**	**.521**	

John Edgar Clapp

Born July 17, 1851, Ithaca, New York; died December 17, 1904, Ithaca; Middleton Mansfields, 1872; Indianapolis Hoosiers, 1878; Buffalo Bisons, 1879; Cincinnati Reds, 1880; Cleveland Blues, 1881; New York Gothams, 1883

John Clapp was another of the many 19th-century managers who helped mold the game of baseball but didn't stay in one city long enough to mold a reputation. He managed six teams for part or all of one season. Only once did a team of his finish above .500.

Year	Team	Record	Pct.	Standing
1872	Mdltn	5–19	.208	Eighth
1878	Ind	24–36	.400	Fifth
1879	Buff	46–32	.590	Third
1880	Cin	21–59	.263	Eighth
1881	Cleve	32–41	.438	Seventh
1883	NY (N)	46–50	.479	Sixth
6 years		**174–237**	**.423**	

Fred Clifford Clarke

Born October 3, 1872, Winterset, Iowa; died August 14, 1960, Winfield, Kansas; Louisville Colonels, June 16, 1897–1899; Pittsburgh Pirates, 1900–September 8, 1915

Fred Clarke's Pittsburgh Pirate teams won four pennants in the first decade of the 20th century and finished with a better than .500 record for 14 consecutive seasons.

He was a player-manager for 12 years — and his team's production went down considerably when he retired from playing to manage full-time. Clarke was a fleet-footed outfielder who got four singles and a triple in his first major league game and in 1897 hit .407 but did not win the batting title because Wee Willie Keeler hit .422.

Throughout his managerial tenure, Clarke had one of the game's greatest players, Honus Wagner. Wagner won eight batting titles, led the league in slugging six times, doubles eight times, triples three times, runs batted in four times and stolen bases five times.

Clarke's teams won over 90 games nine times in his 16-year career, including a stretch of eight times in nine years. But as Wagner neared the end of his career, his brilliant play diminishing, the team started to tail off. At the end of the 1915 season, Clarke, who is still Pittsburgh's winningest manager, was let go.

He managed in baseball's first World Series in 1903, losing to Boston, five games to three. His teams finished first in 1901 and 1902, as well, but the World Series had not yet been created. Two contemporary managers were Frank Chance of the Cubs and John McGraw of the Giants — so pennant races were hard fought and championships hard won.

The Pirates managed to beat out both the Cubs and the Giants in 1909, and Pittsburgh won the World Series with a shrewd piece of strategy from their manager. Pittsburgh had won 110 games behind the solid pitching of starters Howie Camnitz (25–6), Vic Willis (22–11), and Lefty Leifield (19–8). Two other strong pitchers that year, both

Fred Clarke

with previous World Series experience, were Sam Leaver (8–1) and Deacon Phillipe (8–3). Their combined record was 82–29.

But Pittsburgh also had a rookie named Charles "Babe" Adams who had a hot second half and finished 12–3. Clarke bypassed his starting rotation and went with Adams in the first game of the World Series. Adams won it and Clarke went with him in games four and seven. Adams won those also, ending up with three complete games and an earned run average of 1.33.

Long after his managing days were over, Clarke was involved in a player rebellion. In his retirement, he invested some money in the Pirates and was named a vice president. He enjoyed it so much that he often sat on the bench during games, in suit and tie. The fans loved it too, for they remembered his days as manager with fondness. In August of 1926, Clarke reportedly suggested to manager Bill McKechnie that he bench Max Carey who was in a slump. Carey found out about it and was outraged that Clarke was trying to run the team. Carey and other players talked to the press about it.

Clarke, now a Pirate executive, wanted the complaining players punished. The result: The Pirates suspended Carey and put him on waivers. Two other players were released. One was Adams, Clarke's hero in the 1909 World Series. McKechnie was fired at the end of the season. Clarke went home to his farm in Kansas. He died there in 1960 at the age of 88.

Year	Team	Record	Pct.	Standing
1897	Lou	35–52	.402	Ninth
1898	Lou	70–81	.464	Ninth
1899	Lou	75–77	.493	Ninth
1900	Pitt	79–60	.568	Second
1901	Pitt	90–49	.647	First
1902	Pitt	103–36	.741	First
1903	Pitt	91–49	.650	First
1904	Pitt	87–66	.569	Fourth
1905	Pitt	96–57	.627	Second
1906	Pitt	93–60	.608	Third
1907	Pitt	91–63	.591	Second
1908	Pitt	98–56	.636	Second
1909	Pitt	110–42	.724	First
1910	Pitt	86–67	.562	Third
1911	Pitt	85–69	.552	Third
1912	Pitt	93–58	.616	Second
1913	Pitt	78–71	.523	Fourth
1914	Pitt	69–85	.448	Seventh
1915	Pitt	73–81	.474	Fifth
19 years		**1602–1179**	**.576**	

World Series

Year	Team	Record	Pct.
1903	Pitt	3–5	.375
1909	Pitt	4–3	.571
2 years		**7–8**	**.467**

John J. "Jack" Clements

Born July 24, 1864, Philadelphia, Pennsylvania; died May 23, 1941, Norristown, Pennsylvania; Philadelphia Phillies, 1890

Jack Clements was a catcher-outfielder for 17 years, most of them with the Philadelphia Phillies. For a brief time in 1890, he served as player-manager and did pretty well, as Philadelphia won 13 of 19 games under his direction.

Year	Team	Record	Pct.	Standing
1890	Phi (N)	13–6	.684	First

James Lawrence Clinton

Born August 10, 1850, New York, New York; died September 3, 1921, Brooklyn, New York; Brooklyn Eckfords, 1872

Big Jim Clinton had a less than illustrious career as a baseball manager. In 1872, his Brooklyn ball club lost all 11 games it played with Clinton as manager. He never got another opportunity.

Year	Team	Record	Pct.	Standing
1872	Brklyn	0–11	.000	Tenth

Tyrus Raymond Cobb

Born December 18, 1886, Narrows, Georgia; died July 17, 1961, Atlanta, Georgia; Detroit Tigers, December 18, 1920–November 3, 1926

Ty Cobb was one of the greatest ballplayers who ever lived. His .367 lifetime batting average remains baseball's highest. When he retired, he held 43 major league records. He led the American League in hitting 12 times, in slugging percentage eight times, in hits seven times and in stolen bases six times.

He became the playing manager of the Detroit Tigers when many other changes were taking place in baseball: the "dead ball" era was ending; George Herman "Babe" Ruth was emerging as the home run king; and federal judge Kenesaw Mountain Landis had been named the sport's first commissioner in the wake of the "Black Sox" scandal of 1919.

Cobb continued to hit well while he was managing, batting .389 in 1921 and .401 in 1922 — but the record shows that the Tigers did better when he was playing than when he was managing *and* playing

Baseball history is filled with records of good or mediocre players who became great managers — Walter Alston, Tom Lasorda, Sparky Anderson, Bobby Cox, Whitey Herzog — and also of great players who could not generate greatness in the teams they managed — Cobb, Ted Williams, Christy Mathewson, and Frankie Frisch are examples.

Cobb's style and strategy as a manager were molded in him as a player. He was serious, disciplined and stressed the importance of fundamentals. Because of this, his dislike for Babe Ruth was intense. And it got personal. Ruth was everything that Cobb wasn't — a big man with a jovial personality who made headlines by hitting home runs and who made no effort to stay in shape. Cobb's teammates recall times when Cobb would see Ruth in the batting cage before a game and would walk by the cage, take two or three sniffs and say something like, "What smells around here?" He also started calling Ruth "nigger" because of Ruth's swarthy complexion, thick lips and broad nose. Brashness was Cobb's style both as a player and as a manager.

Cobb was a fanatic about executing fundamentals. He worked endlessly with his players on bunting, stealing bases and the hit-and-run. And Cobb liked to play the percentages.

Several times in his managerial career, his starting pitcher was a right-hander who worked to one batter and then was relieved by a left-hander — or vice versa — to catch opposing managers offguard who had loaded their lineups with left-handed or right-handed hitters. Cobb also platooned players regularly.

His temper often got in the way of any strategy. In a game at Yankee Stadium in 1921, pitcher Dutch Leonard failed on two bunt attempts. Cobb was so angry, he sent up a pinch hitter to finish the at-bat. In that one, impulsive move, he had wasted a pinch hitter, crippled the pinch hitter by sending him up with two strikes, and had to bring in a new pitcher when the Tigers took the field.

Three days after that incident, Cobb became so angry with umpire Billy Evans that he challenged Evans in the umpires dressing room after the game. Both men stripped to the waist, went outside and participated in a bloody fight witnessed by many, including Cobb's 11-year-old son, Tyrus, Jr.

Tiger management and Tiger fans put up with Cobb's temper tantrums because Cobb had the Tigers on the move. After consecutive sixth-place finishes, they finished third in 1922, second in 1923 and third again in 1924. But they slipped to fourth in 1925. In 1926, after a sixth-place finish, Cobb was through as a manager. Baseball writers said he just could not relate to players who did not have the same fire and passion that he had.

But Cobb did inspire individual greatness. Harry Heilmann was a first baseman-outfielder for the Tigers. From 1914 to 1920, he hit over .300 twice. In Cobb's six years as Tiger manager, Heilmann hit .394, .356, .403, .346, .393 and .367. His average soared at the same time the "live ball" came into play, but Cobb's mentoring clearly had an impact. Before the 1921 season, Cobb convinced Heilmann to stand farther back in the batter's box, reposition his feet and adjust his hand-spread on the bat. After Heilmann made those changes, he won four batting titles.

Year	Team	Record	Pct.	Standing
1921	Det	71–82	.464	Sixth
1922	Det	79–75	.513	Third
1923	Det	83–71	.532	Second
1924	Det	86–68	.558	Third
1925	Det	81–73	.526	Fourth
1926	Det	79–75	.513	Sixth
6 years		**479–444**	**.519**	

Gordon Stanley "Mickey" Cochrane

Born April 6, 1903, Bridgewater, Massachusetts; died June 28, 1962, Lake Forest, Illinois; Detroit Tigers, December 3, 1933–August 6, 1938

Mickey Cochrane was one of baseball's greatest catchers and might have been one of the game's greatest managers had a near-fatal beaning not cut short both careers.

Cochrane, a mainstay on Connie Mack's great Philadelphia A's teams, was traded to the Detroit Tigers in 1934 and became their manager. Under Cochrane, Detroit won the pennant in 1934 and 1935 and finished second in 1936 and 1937. On May 25, 1937, Cochrane, who was still the Tigers' regular catcher, leaned into a pitch thrown by the Yankees' Bump Hadley and was severely beaned. He was unconscious when he was taken off the field and remained in the hospital 10 days. He never played again, finishing with a lifetime batting average of .320 — still the highest ever for a catcher.

He managed from the bench in 1938. The Tigers missed his hitting and his leadership on the field. They were in fourth place after 97 games and Cochrane was fired. He never managed again.

Year	Team	Record	Pct.	Standing
1934	Det	101–53	.656	First
1935	Det	93–58	.616	First
1936	Det	83–71	.539	Second
1937	Det	89–65	.578	Second
1938	Det	47–50	.485	Fourth
5 years		**413–297**	**.582**	

WORLD SERIES

Year	Team	Record	Pct.
1934	Det	3–4	.429
1935	Det	4–2	.667
2 years		**7–6**	**.538**

Andrew Howard Cohen

Born October 25, 1904, Baltimore, Maryland; died October 29, 1988, El Paso, Texas; Philadelphia Phillies, April 15, 1960

Andy Cohen was an infielder for the New York Giants for three years in the 1920s and hit .281 in 262 games. In 1960, the Philadelphia Phillies parted company with veteran manager Eddie Sawyer after one game. The Phillies were about to hire Gene Mauch, who would lead them for the next several years. In between the time Sawyer left and Mauch came on, the Phillies played one game, under the direction of interim manager Andy Cohen, and won it. Cohen never managed again in the major leagues.

Year	Team	Record	Pct.	Standing
1960	Phil	1–0	1.000	Fourth

Gerald Francis Coleman

Born September 14, 1924, San Jose, California; San Diego Padres, October 1, 1979–October 4, 1980

Jerry Coleman was one of the "Yankee 12"—that elite group of ballplayers who played on the Yankee pennant winners from 1949 to 1953. He was a broadcaster for the San Diego Padres when he was lured out of the booth to manage the team for one year. The Padres finished sixth and Coleman was finished as their manager.

It's difficult to determine a manager's pattern or strategy from just a year, but one statistic jumps out with respect to Coleman's reign. San Diego Padre pitchers issued 113 intentional walks in 1980—the second most in major league history. Only the 1974 Padres, under John McNamara, issued more (116).

Year	Team	Record	Pct.	Standing
1980	SD	73–89	.451	Sixth

Robert Hunter Coleman

Born September 26, 1890, Huntingburg, Indiana; died July 16, 1959, Boston, Massachusetts; Boston Braves, February 12, 1944–July 20, 1945

Bob Coleman had been a catcher for parts of three years whose major league playing career ended in 1916. Twenty-eight years later he was recruited to replace Casey Stengel as manager of the Boston Braves. Stengel was destined for greater success later. Coleman was not. His Braves finished sixth in 1944 and were in seventh place half way through the 1945 season when Coleman was replaced by Del Bissonette.

Year	Team	Record	Pct.	Standing
1944	Bos (N)	65–89	.422	Sixth
1945	Bos	42–49	.462	Seventh
2 years		**107–138**	**.437**	

Edward Trowbridge Collins, Sr.

Born May 2, 1887, Millerton, New York; died March 25, 1951, Boston, Massachusetts; Chicago White Sox, December 11, 1924–November 11, 1926

Eddie Collins, the Hall of Fame second baseman of the Philadelphia A's and Chicago White Sox, was later a successful general manager for the Boston Red Sox for many years. During his time with the White Sox, he was a player-manager for two years, 1925–26. The club was still reeling from the effects of the Black Sox scandal, which was exposed in 1920 and the banishments began in 1921. Collins brought the team fifth-place finishes in his two years before going back to Philadelphia, where he played a few more years before retiring. He then became the Red Sox general manager and signed Ted Williams.

Year	Team	Record	Pct.	Standing
1925	Chi (A)	79–75	.513	Fifth
1926	Chi (A)	81–72	.529	Fifth

Jimmy Collins

James Joseph Collins

Born January 16, 1870, Buffalo, New York; died March 6, 1943, Buffalo; Boston Somersets, 1901–1904; Boston Puritans, 1905–1906

Jimmy Collins, a Hall of Fame third baseman at the turn of the 20th century, had a roller coaster career as a manager. In his first four years, Collins, as player-manager of the Somersets, finished first twice, second once and third once. But in 1905, his newly named Puritans finished fourth, and in 1906, with Boston mired in last place, Collins was fired. Two unusual aspects of Collins' pennant winners: The 1903 Red Sox played in the first World Series, beating the Pittsburgh Pirates, five games to three, after falling behind three games to one. In 1904, the Red Sox once again won the American League title, but there was no World Series; Giants manager John McGraw refused to play after the embarrassment the National League had suffered the year before.

Year	Team	Record	Pct.	Standing
1901	Bos (A)	79–57	.581	Second
1902	Bos	77–60	.562	Third

Year	Team	Record	Pct.	Standing
1903	Bos	91–47	.659	First
1904	Bos	95–59	.617	First
1905	Bos	78–74	.513	Fourth
1906	Bos	44–92	.324	Eighth
6 years		464–389	.544	

WORLD SERIES

Year	Team	Record	Pct.
1903	Bos (A)	5–3	.625

John Francis "Shano" Collins

Born December 4, 1885, Charlestown, Massachusetts; died September 10, 1955, Newton, Massachusetts; Boston Red Sox, December 1, 1930–June 20, 1932

Shano Collins brought the Red Sox to a sixth-place finish in 1931, the first time in seven years that Boston had finished out of the cellar. In 1932, the Red Sox slipped back to eighth place again, but Collins witnessed only part of it. He departed after the Red Sox lost 46 of the first 57 games. He did not manage again in the major leagues.

Year	Team	Record	Pct.	Standing
1931	Bos (A)	62–90	.408	Sixth
1932	Bos	11–46	.193	Eighth
2 years		73–136	.349	

Terry Collins

Born May 27, 1949, Midland, Michigan; Houston Astros, November 17, 1993–October 4, 1996; California/Anaheim Angels, November 4, 1996–September 3, 1999

Terry Collins managed for six years and had his club near the top of the standings in all but two of those years. In his first season managing the Houston Astros, 1994, the team was floundering in fifth when the players walked out on strike. In 1995, the Astros finished second and followed that with a second-place finish in 1996. Collins moved on to manage Anaheim and, after two straight second-place finishes, the club signed free-agent slugger Mo Vaughn from Boston. The acquisition had pundits picking the Angels to win the Western Division championship in 1999. But the club faltered and in September, with the Angels reeling at 51–82, Collins called a press conference and tearfully resigned, saying the team's failure was his responsibility. He was replaced by coach Joe Maddon, who guided the Angels to a 19–10 finish. Mike Scioscia was named manager for the 2000 season.

Collins' didn't platoon much, but he did use his bench often. His Houston clubs led the National League in use of pinch hitters in 1994 and 1995 and was near the top in 1996. His 1995 Astro team also led the National League in stolen base attempts and hit-and-run attempts — in part because of his style of play but also because of the type of ball club he had and his home ballpark, the Astrodome, which was not a home run haven.

Year	Team	Record	Pct.	Standing
1994	Hous	66–49	.570	Fifth
1995	Hous	76–68	.520	Second
1996	Hous	82–80	.505	Second

Year	Team	Record	Pct.	Standing
1997	Ana	84–78	.510	Second
1998	Ana	85–77	.520	Second
1999	Ana	51–82	.383	Fifth
6 years		**444–434**	**.505**	

Charles Albert Comiskey

Born August 15, 1859, Chicago, Illinois; died October 26, 1931, Eagle River, Wisconsin; St. Louis Browns, 1883; 1885–1889; Chicago Pirates, 1890; St. Louis Browns, 1891; Cincinnati Reds, 1892–1894

Charles Comiskey's place in baseball history is darkened some by the shadow of the Black Sox scandal of 1919. The conspirators claimed they threw the Series in part because they wanted to get back at Comiskey for paying them so little.

Long before Comiskey was an owner, he was a manager — and a good one. His .607 winning percentage in 11 years remains the second best in the history of baseball, behind only Joe McCarthy's .614. He managed the St. Louis Browns of the American Association for seven years and Chicago and Cincinnati for shorter stints.

Comiskey's teams were known for their toughness and for good pitchers who did not give up much. The Browns led the league in earned run average five times but never led the league in either hits allowed or walks. Comiskey's 1891 St. Louis team used relief pitchers 39 times, a record at the time.

Part of his strategy was to give his team a home field advantage. Comiskey encouraged St. Louis fans to taunt the opposing team. They became so abusive that players on the visiting team often feared for their safety. In the 1885 championship series against Cap Anson's Chicago White Stockings, the second game was stopped because of fights on the field and a riot in the stands.

In 1901, Comiskey contributed to baseball history by helping his friend Ban Johnson form the American League. They had a falling out after the 1919 World Series because Johnson hesitated to investigate hints of wrongdoing when Comiskey suspected trouble during the Series.

Year	Team	Record	Pct.	Standing
1883	StL (AA)	12–6	.667	Second
1885	StL	79–33	.705	First
1886	StL	93–46	.669	First
1887	StL	95–40	.704	First
1888	StL	92–43	.681	First
1889	StL	90–45	.667	Second
1890	Chi (P)	75–62	.547	Fourth
1891	StL (AA)	86–52	.623	Second
1892	Cin (N)	82–68	.547	Fifth
1893	Cin	65–63	.508	Sixth
1894	Cin	55–75	.423	Tenth
11 years		**824–533**	**.607**	

Roger Connor

Born July 1, 1857, Waterbury, Connecticut; died January 4, 1931, Waterbury; St. Louis Browns, 1896

Roger Connor was the greatest home run hitter of the 19th century and is the answer to a trivia question: When Babe Ruth swatted his 137th home run in 1921, whose all-time home run record had be broken?

Connor, a member of baseball's Hall of Fame, was not nearly as successful a manager. He lasted 46 games with St. Louis in 1896, winning only nine of them.

Year	Team	Record	Pct.	Standing
1896	StL (AA)	9–37	.196	Eleventh

Allen Lindsey "Dusty" Cooke

Born June 23, 1907, Swepsonville, North Carolina; died November 21, 1987, Raleigh, North Carolina; Philadelphia Phillies, July 11, 1948–July 27, 1948

Dusty Cooke was a reserve outfielder on some of the great Yankee teams of the early 1930s, a teammate of Babe Ruth and Lou Gehrig. He also saw some time with the Boston Red Sox and Cincinnati Reds. When the Phillies fired Ben Chapman, they called on Cooke to be their interim manager until Eddie Sawyer came on board. He managed Philadelphia for 11 games and "retired" with a 6–5 record.

Year	Team	Record	Pct.	Standing
1948	Phil (N)	6–5	.545	Seventh

Jack Coombs

Born November 18, 1882, LeGrand, Iowa; died April 15, 1957, LeGrand; Philadelphia Phillies, October 8, 1918–June 8, 1919

Jack Coombs was a great pitcher with Connie Mack's Philadelphia A's, winning 31 games in 1910 and 28 games in 1911. When Mack broke up the ball club after failing to win the 1914 World Series, Coombs went to the Dodgers. The Phillies called on him to manage their club in 1919. Coombs found managing a lot harder than pitching. He lasted 62 games, winning only 18 of them. In 1920, he was back in more comfortable territory, pitching for the Detroit Tigers. He won 159 games in his career and lost only 110 in 14 years.

Year	Team	Record	Pct.	Standing
1919	Phil (N)	18–44	.290	Eighth

John Walter Cooney

Born March 18, 1901, Cranston, Rhode Island; died July 8, 1986, Sarasota, Florida; Boston Braves, August 15, 1949–September 30, 1949

Johnny Cooney's managerial career was brief and uneventful, and his listing is omitted from some early editions of the *Baseball Encyclopedia* (though not from *Total Baseball*). Less than a year after winning the National League championship, Billy Southworth faced dissention in the Boston Braves clubhouse, a lot of it caused by Southworth's drinking, according to some of his players. Owner Lou Perini was made aware of the problem and gave Southworth a leave of absence. Cooney took over, closed out the 1949 season at 20–25 and never managed again. He later coached for the Chicago White Sox.

Year	Team	Record	Pct.	Standing
1949	Bos (N)	20–25	.444	Fourth

Patrick Corrales

Born March 20, 1941, Los Angeles, California; Texas Rangers, October 2, 1978–October 5, 1980; Philadelphia Phillies, November 4, 1981–July 18, 1983; Cleveland Indians, July 31, 1983–July 15, 1987

Pat Corrales was a major league catcher for 10 years with the Phillies, Cardinals, Reds and Padres. He was brought in to manage a Texas Rangers team that finished in second place each of the two preceding years. Corrales managed the Rangers to a third place finish in 1979. After they came in fourth in 1980, he was dismissed. He resurfaced with the Philadelphia Phillies in 1982 after Dallas Green left to become general manager of the Chicago Cubs. Corrales brought the Phillies home in second place with an 89–73 record. In 1983, with the Phillies at 43–42, Corrales left Philadelphia to manage the struggling Cleveland Indians. The Phillies went on to win the National League championship. The Tribe was 40–60 when Corrales took over and in last place. Though they improved in winning percentage with a 30–32 record, the Indians finished last. They improved to 75–87 in 1984 but fell to 60–102 in 1985. They rebounded to their best season since 1968, 84–78 in 1986, good for fifth place. In 1987, the roller coaster ride was on the downswing again, and Corrales was fired with his team at 31–56, buried in seventh place in the American League East.

Year	Team	Record	Pct.	Standing
1978	Tex	1–0	1.000	Second
1979	Tex	83–79	.512	Third
1980	Tex	76–85	.472	Fourth
1982	Phil	89–73	.549	Second
1983	Phil	43–42	.506	First
1983	Cleve	30–32	.484	Seventh
1984	Cleve	75–87	.463	Sixth
1985	Cleve	60–102	.370	Seventh
1986	Cleve	84–78	.519	Fifth
1987	Cleve	31–56	.356	Seventh
9 years		**572–634**	**.474**	

John Michael "Red" Corriden, Sr.

Born September 4, 1887, Logansport, Indiana; died September 28, 1959, Indianapolis, Indiana; Chicago White Sox, May 26, 1950–October 10, 1950

Red Corriden was a shortstop with the St. Louis Browns, Detroit Tigers and Chicago Cubs between 1910 and 1915. Thirty-five years after he quit playing, Corriden got a shot at managing a Chicago White Sox team that won only eight of its first 30 games in the 1950 season. Corriden fared a little better, bringing the club home in sixth place — but not well enough to keep his job. Paul Richards was hired for the 1951 season. Corriden, who was 62 when he was hired as Chicago's manager, died on September 28, 1959, six days after the White Sox clinched their only pennant since 1919.

Year	Team	Record	Pct.	Standing
1950	Chi (A)	52–72	.419	Sixth

Charles Keith Cottier

Born January 8, 1936, Delta, Colorado; Seattle Mariners, September 1, 1984–May 8, 1986

Chuck Cottier, a second baseman for four major league teams, was brought on to manage a struggling Seattle Mariner team in 1984. Seattle was 59–76, and headed for last place when Cottier took over. Under their new manager, the Mariners won 15 and lost 12 but remained in last place. They finished sixth again in 1985, and when they lost 19 of their first 28 games in 1986, Cottier lost his job.

Year	Team	Record	Pct.	Standing
1984	Sea (A)	15–12	.556	Sixth
1985	Sea	74–88	.457	Sixth
1986	Sea	9–19	.321	Sixth
3 years		**98–119**	**.452**	

Robert Joe Cox

Born May 21, 1941, Tulsa, Oklahoma; Atlanta Braves, October 24, 1977–October 7, 1981; Toronto Blue Jays, October 15, 1981–October 25, 1985; Atlanta Braves, June 22, 1990

Bobby Cox has a chance to be rated with baseball's greatest managers. Manager of the Atlanta Braves in two different stints (1978–1981 and 1990–present), Cox also managed the Toronto Blue Jays for four seasons in the early 1980s. He was the Braves general manager from October 1985 to June 22, 1990, when he stepped back into the dugout. He has a reputation for getting the most he could out of bad teams he managed and helping good teams rise to the top with steady leadership and good pitching staffs.

His Braves teams of the 1990s were a near-dynasty, winning seven Western Division championships and playing in five World Series. The only rap against Cox: With all of those opportunities, he was able to win only one World Series.

When he came to the Braves in 1978, he took over a team that lost 101 games in 1977 and had a team earned run average of 4.65 — extremely high for that era of baseball. Phil Niekro was 16–20. No other Braves pitcher won more than seven. His 1978 Braves finished last, but Atlanta won 69, an increase of eight wins. The team earned run average was down to 4.08 but Niekro, with a 19–18 record, was still the only pitcher with more than 10 wins. The next year, 1979, was almost a repeat of 1978, with Niekro at 21–20, no other pitcher with 10 wins and the team as a whole winning 66. But in 1980, the patient Cox had his team in fourth place at 81–80, a 15-game improvement, with Niekro winning 15, Doyle Alexander winning 14, Tommy Boggs 12 and Ron Matula 11. The team ERA was 3.77. In 1981, there was a split season and Atlanta finished fifth, but once again the team ERA was down to 3.45 — an improvement of about 1.5 runs per nine innings over 1977.

In 1982, Cox went to Toronto to manage the Blue Jays. The team he left for Joe Torre to manage in Atlanta won the division championship. At Toronto, Cox worked his pitching magic again. The Blue Jays, 11th in the league in earned run average in 1981, moved up to fifth in 1982. They were third in 1984 and first in 1985, Cox's final year with the club. And more important, they moved from sixth place in 1982 to division champions in 1985.

When he returned to manage Atlanta in 1990, the Braves had Tom Glavine, Steve Avery and John Smoltz. All flourished under Cox. Then they picked up Greg Maddux from the Cubs. The Braves had developed a formula for winning. Rather than fighting the free agent wars year after year, they chose to sign their starting pitchers to long-term contracts and then concentrate on filling in the gaps in the rest of the roster.

At the end of 1999, the Braves still had Glavine, Smoltz and Maddux. They also had the seven Western Division championships, the five league championships and the one World Series championship.

As successful as he has been during the regular season, however, Cox and the Braves have faltered in the post-season.

In 1991, with Glavine and Smoltz each available, Cox started left-hander Charlie Liebrandt against the Twins in the first game of the World Series. The Twins had always hit Liebrandt hard when he was in the American League, and they beat him in Game One. In Game Six, with the Braves up three games to two, the left-handed Liebrandt came on in relief in the 10th inning, even though right-handed slugger Kirby Puckett was coming to bat. Puckett homered to win the game. The Braves lost the Series in seven games.

In 1996, the Braves won the first two games of the World Series against the Yankees — and both wins were at Yankee Stadium. They went home and lost Game Three. They had a 6–3 lead in the eighth inning of Game Four when Cox went against his usual strategy. He decided to bring in closer Mark Wohlers to face Jim Leyritz with two men on. During the season, Wohlers worked almost exclusively in the ninth inning or extra innings as a closer. Using Wohlers early had backfired: Leyritz hit a three-run homer to tie the game.

The Yankees won in nine innings and won the next two games to take the Series. (Incidentally, had the game gone extra innings, Cox would have been without his number one relief pitcher.)

In 1998, the Yankees won the first two games of the World Series against the Braves. Tom Glavine had Game Three well in hand for the Braves, working on a one-hitter. But Cox chose to remove his ace in the seventh inning and let the bullpen mop up. The Yankees came back to win Game Three, then completed the sweep the following day.

So his fortune has not been good in the short seasons of playoff series. But in the 162-game regular seasons, Cox is achieving numbers associated with some of the greatest managers of all time.

Year	Team	Record	Pct.	Standing
1978	Atl	69–93	.426	Sixth
1979	Atl	66–94	.413	Sixth
1980	Atl	81–80	.503	Fourth
1981	Atl	25–29	.463	Fourth
1981	Atl	25–27	.481	Fifth
1982	Tor	78–84	.481	Sixth
1983	Tor	89–73	.549	Fourth
1984	Tor	89–73	.549	Second
1985	Tor	99–62	.615	First
1990	Atl	40–57	.412	Sixth
1991	Atl	94–68	.580	First
1992	Atl	98–64	.605	First
1993	Atl	104–58	.640	First
1994	Atl	68–46	.590	Third
1995	Atl	90–54	.620	First
1996	Atl	96–66	.590	First
1997	Atl	101–61	.620	First
1998	Atl	106–56	.650	First
1999	Atl	103–59	.630	First
2000	Atl	95–67	.586	First
20 years		**1616–1271**	**.574**	

DIVISION CHAMPIONSHIP SERIES

Year	Team	Record	Pct.
1995	Atl	3–1	.750
1996	Atl	3–0	1.000
1997	Atl	3–0	1.000
1998	Atl	3–0	1.000
1999	Atl	3–1	.750
2000	Atl	3–1	.750
6 years		**18–3**	**.857**

LEAGUE CHAMPIONSHIP SERIES

Year	Team	Record	Pct.
1985	Tor	3–4	.429
1991	Atl	4–3	.571
1992	Atl	4–3	.571
1993	Atl	3–4	.429
1995	Atl	4–0	1.000
1996	Atl	4–3	.571
1997	Atl	2–4	.333
1998	Atl	2–4	.333
1999	Atl	4–2	.667
2000	Atl	2–4	.333
10 years		**32–31**	**.508**

WORLD SERIES

Year	Team	Record	Pct.
1991	Atl	3–4	.429
1992	Atl	2–4	.333
1995	Atl	4–2	.667
1996	Atl	2–4	.333
1999	Atl	0–4	.000
5 years		**11–18**	**.379**

Harry Francis Craft

Born April 19, 1915, Ellisville, Mississippi; died August 3, 1995, Conroe, Texas; Kansas City Athletics, August 6, 1957–September 28, 1959; Chicago Cubs (one of several head coaches), 1961; Houston Astros, September 19, 1961–September 19, 1964

Harry Craft was an outfielder for Bill McKechnie's Cincinnati Reds for part of his major league career and adopted McKechnie's steady style as a major league manager. But Craft lacked the talented teams that McKechnie often had.

Craft took over a Kansas City A's team that struggled so badly in 1957 that none of its pitchers threw enough innings to qualify for inclusion in official league statistics. The A's were 36–67 when Craft replaced Lou Boudreau. They went 23–27 the rest of the way, a remarkable turn-around in a short period of time. The A's had lost 102 games the year before and were a sure bet for another 100-loss season until Craft rescued them. Then in 1958, the A's won 73 games, a 14-game improvement over the previous year and a franchise record in Kansas City. They slipped to 66–88 in 1959, Craft's last year with the club.

Another exercise in futility occurred in 1962 when Chicago Cubs owner Philip K. Wrigley decided to use rotating coaches to lead the ball club instead of a manager. The Cubs finished at 64–90. During Craft's tenure the club was 7–9.

During his experiences in Kansas City and Chicago he came to be known as a man who could handle difficult challenges. This reputation doubtless landed Craft his next job, first manager of the expansion Houston Colt .45s. Using a club made up entirely of rookies and cast-offs from other teams, Houston won 64 games and finished eighth, ahead of the New Mets, the other expansion team, and also ahead of the Cubs. He spent two more years at Houston and finished higher than the Mets both years.

Craft stressed fundamentals and some players found him to be too much of a drill sergeant. Once, according to Vic Power, after the A's had been shut out on two hits in the second game of a doubleheader, Craft ordered his players out of their locker room and back onto the field for extra batting practice. After another game in which infielder Hector Lopez had dropped a pop-up, Craft had him out catching pop-ups for an hour while his teammates showered and dressed in the clubhouse.

If that style was a little too strict for the struggling A's, it apparently was appropriate to the expansion team in Houston. Veteran pitcher Hal Woodeshick, one of the old-timers on the roster, said Craft's attention to detail was just the right touch for a young, inexperienced team.

In the minor leagues, Craft managed Mickey Mantle on two different teams, helping to groom him for the major leagues. In Kansas City, he had a young outfielder named Roger Maris who hit 61 home runs for the New York Yankees two years after leaving Craft's A's.

His lifetime won-loss percentage of .426 is deceiving because it fails to show that every team Craft managed improved under his direction.

Year	Team	Record	Pct.	Standing
1957	KC	23–27	.460	Eighth
1958	KC	73–81	.474	Seventh
1959	KC	66–88	.429	Seventh
1961	Chi (N)	7–9	.437	Seventh
1962	Hous	64–96	.400	Eighth
1963	Hous	66–96	.407	Ninth
1964	Hous	61–88	.409	Ninth
7 years		**360–485**	**.426**	

Roger Lee Craig

Born February 17, 1931, Durham, North Carolina; San Diego Padres, March 21, 1978–September 30, 1979; San Francisco Giants, September 18, 1985–December 1, 1992

Roger Craig was a major league pitcher who experienced both the glory days, with the Brooklyn Dodgers' "Boys of Summer" in the 1950s, as well as the depths of losing more than 20 games two years in a row for the lowly York Mets in the 1960s.

His managerial career had ups and downs as well. He took over the San Diego Padres in 1978 and brought them home in fourth place, a respectable showing for a team accustomed to being below .500. They slipped well below .500 in 1979 and Craig was fired. He reappeared in 1985 as manager of a struggling San Francisco Giants team and lost 12 of 18 games to end the season. The following year, the Giants were back on track, finishing third. They won the Western Division championship in 1987 but lost to the St. Louis Cardinals, four games to three, in the league championship series. In 1989, they won their division again, beat the Chicago Cubs in the LCS but lost four straight to the Oakland A's in a World Series that was interrupted by an earthquake that hit the Bay Area.

Part of Craig's impact on a ball club was his ability to get the most out of a pitching staff. He was helped in San Diego when the Padres acquired future Hall of Famer Gaylord Perry, and they already had future Hall of Famer Rollie Fingers in the bullpen. The problem was, they didn't have much else. In San Francisco, tragedy struck when young left-hander Dave Dravecky developed cancer in his pitching arm. (Dravecky, after attempting a comeback, would have the arm amputated, ending a promising career.)

Between his stints with San Diego and San Francisco, Craig served as Sparky Anderson's pitching coach in Detroit and is credited with a big part in helping the Tigers win the pennant in 1984. In Detroit, one of the pitchers who developed under Craig's watchful eye was Jack Morris, who was to become the winningest pitcher in the 1980s.

Craig said pitching was the cornerstone of most championship teams, and over the years, he developed some theories that he passed on to his pitching staffs. For instance, he believed the best way to get a batter out was for the pitcher to think along with the hitter so that he'd be able to fool him. Also, he believed that when a game got out of hand, either because of a big lead or big deficit, a pitcher should alter his normal pitching pattern so as not to give away any clue about himself that might someday be important in a close game.

Year	Team	Record	Pct.	Standing
1978	SD	84–78	.519	Fourth
1979	SD	68–93	.422	Fifth
1985	SF	6–12	.333	Sixth
1986	SF	83–79	.512	Third
1987	SF	90–72	.556	First
1988	SF	83–79	.512	Fourth
1989	SF	92–70	.568	First
1990	SF	85–77	.525	Third
1991	SF	75–87	.463	Fourth
1992	SF	72–90	.444	Sixth
10 years		**738–737**	**.501**	

LEAGUE CHAMPIONSHIP SERIES

Year	Team	Record	Pct.
1987	SF	3–4	.429
1989	SF	4–1	.800
2 years		**7–5**	**.583**

WORLD SERIES

Year	Team	Record	Pct.
1989	SF	0–4	.000

Delmar Wesley Crandall

Born March 5, 1930, Ontario, California; Milwaukee Brewers, May 28, 1972–September 28, 1975; Seattle Mariners, June 25, 1983–September 1, 1984

Del Crandall, a catcher who played on the Milwaukee Braves National League championship teams in 1957 and 1958, got his first shot at managing in Milwaukee, with the American League Brewers in 1972. Crandall's career is like that of many managers: He took over a team and steadily improved the record, but not enough to satisfy ownership.

The Brewers of the early 1970s are a prime example. The latest Milwaukee franchise came into being when the Seattle Pilots moved there after one year in Seattle. Dave Bristol managed the Brewers for two seasons but was let go after they started the 1972 season at 10–20. Roy McMillan filled in for two games, splitting them, and then Crandall came on to guide them the rest of the way. The Brewers' win/loss percentage was .344 when Crandall took over. They finished sixth, but their percentage under Crandall rose to .435. It was .457 in 1973 and .469 in 1974, steadily inching up. But in 1975, the Brewers retreated to 67–94, a drop of nine wins from the previous year, lowering their winning percentage to .416. Crandall was fired.

He had a similar experience in Seattle. Crandall became the Mariners' manager in 1983, taking over for Rene Lachemann with the club in seventh place at 26–47, a .356 winning percentage. Crandall's record was about the same. The Mariners finished seventh. The following year saw only a slight improvement, and the Mariners were again in seventh place. After 135 games, Crandall was fired and replaced, ironically enough, by Lachemann.

Year	Team	Record	Pct.	Standing
1972	Mil	54–70	.435	Sixth
1973	Mil	74–88	.457	Fifth
1974	Mil	76–86	.469	Fifth
1975	Mil	67–94	.416	Fifth
1983	Sea	34–55	.382	Seventh
1984	Sea	59–76	.437	Seventh
6 years		**364–469**	**.437**	

Samuel Newhall Crane

Born January 2, 1854, Springfield, Massachusetts; died June 26, 1925, New York, New York; Buffalo Bisons, 1880; Cincinnati Outlaw Reds, 1884

Sam Crane was another of the numerous 19th century managers who bounced around from team to team and whose careers were short-lived. Crane's situation is unusual in that he had tremendous success with the Cincinnati team he managed in 1884 but did not hang around long enough to enjoy it. He began his managerial stints with Buffalo in 1880 and was 20–45 when he departed. Four years later, as manager of the Cincinnati ball club in the Union Association in 1884, he took over for Dan O'Leary on a team with a 33–29 record. Crane won 36 and lost only 7 but never managed again.

Year	Team	Record	Pct.	Standing
1880	Buff (N)	20–45	.308	Eighth
1884	Cin (U)	36–7	.837	Third
2 years		**56–52**	**.519**	

Clifford Carlton "Gavvy" Cravath

Born March 23, 1881, Escondido, California; died May 23, 1963, Laguna Beach, California; Philadelphia Phillies, July 8, 1919–December 18, 1920

Gavvy Cravath was a power-hitting outfielder for the Boston Red Sox, Chicago White Sox and Philadelphia Phillies in an 11-year career. In 1919, when Babe Ruth set the single-season home run record with 29, he broke the record set by Cravath, who hit 24 for the Phillies in 1915.

Cravath joined the Phillies in 1912 and had eight good seasons with them. During his last two seasons, he was player-manager. He took over the Phillies at a time when owner William F. Baker discovered that he could sell some of his best players, still field a team that fans would come to see, and he would come out of it with a profit. So he made a deal with the New York Giants in which he traded future Hall of Fame shortstop Dave Bancroft for 35-year-old infielder Art Fletcher and $100,000. He also got a pitcher named Hubbell from the Giants, but it wasn't Carl. It was Bill Hubbell, who turned in a 9–9 record.

Cravath had a bad ball club. Research on his tenure produced one interesting element to the challenge he faced: how to handle a cocky outfielder named Casey Stengel. An example of Stengel's antics: Arriving late for a game, Stengel decided to sit in the stands and watch awhile. He began needling some of the Phillies players, who went along with the gag. One of his teammates shouted that if he thought he could do any better, Stengel should come on down and suit up. He did, and hit a home run later in that same game. Meanwhile, the Phillies continued to lose. Cravath was fired at the end of the season. He played minor league baseball for a couple of years and then retired to California where he entered politics and became a justice of the peace, a fitting job title for someone who managed the rowdy Phillies of 1919 and 1920.

Year	Team	Record	Pct.	Standing
1919	Phil (N)	29–46	.387	Eighth
1920	Phil (N)	62–91	.405	Eighth
2 years		**91–137**	**.399**	

William H. Craver

Born June 1844, Troy, New York; died June 17, 1901, Troy; Troy Haymakers, 1871; Baltimore Lord Baltimores, 1872; Philadelphia Athletics, 1874–1875

Bill Craver is best remembered as one of the first players to be banished from baseball for throwing games. In 1877, when he was playing for the Louisville Colonels, Craver and three other Colonels players were expelled by National League president William Hulbert after an anonymous whistleblower predicted a number of Louisville losses. It had not been Craver's first run-in with league officials. Against the Cincinnati Red Stockings in 1869, Craver pulled his team, the Troy (NY) Haymakers, off the field after a dispute over a foul tip. The game ended in a tie and was the only blemish of Cincinnati's record.

Craver had an otherwise mediocre seven-year playing career, including two years in the National League, in which he played every position but pitcher. He managed parts of four years. His best year as manager was with Baltimore in 1872 when his team won 27 and lost only 13.

Year	Team	Record	Pct.	Standing
1871	Troy	12–12	.500	Sixth
1872	Balt	27–13	.675	Second
1874	Phil	29–29	.500	Fourth
1875	Phil	2–12	.143	Eleventh
4 years		**70–66**	**.515**	

George W. Creamer

Born in 1855, Philadelphia, Pennsylvania; died June 27, 1886, Philadelphia; Pittsburgh Pirates, 1884

George Creamer was one of five men to manage the Pittsburgh team of the American Association in one year. Creamer lasted only nine games and never managed again. He didn't have the shortest tenure with the team that year. Joe Battin, who preceded him, was gone after four games.

Year	Team	Record	Pct.	Standing
1884	Pitt (AA)	2–7	.222	Eleventh

Joseph Edward Cronin

Born October 12, 1906, San Francisco, California; died September 7, 1984, Osterville, Massachusetts; Washington Senators, October 8, 1932–November 13, 1934; Boston Red Sox, December 21, 1934–September 29, 1947

Joe Cronin had a distinguished career in major league baseball that included being a Hall of Fame ballplayer, a highly successful manager, general manager and president of the American League. He was also the son-in-law of Washington Senator owner Clark Griffith. After the 1934 season, Griffith, experiencing big money problems, had the chance to sell his son-in-law to the Red Sox for $100,000. Before making the deal, Griffith contacted Cronin, who encouraged him to follow through with it.

In his first season as player-manager of the Senators, 1933, Washington won the American League pennant, winning 99 games. Cronin was back in the World Series 13 years later as manager of the Red Sox. In between, his teams finished second four times, third once and fourth three times. His teams finished in the first division in 10 of his 15 years of managing. Cronin was the Red Sox player-manager through 1945. In 1946, his first year at the helm after his retirement as a player, the Red Sox won 104 games and won the American League pennant.

Cronin's teams emphasized hitting. He had lineups with hitters who could spray the ball all over and he had Ted Williams and others to drive them in. Cronin's teams led the American League in batting eight times and in hits seven times. None of his teams struck out a lot, they made contact, and they knew how to move runners into scoring position. Teams managed by Cronin are among the best bunting teams in baseball history. They led the league in number of bunts in five out of his first six years as a manager. Even playing in cozy Fenway Park, Cronin's Red Sox never led the league in home runs, but led in doubles four times. They never led the league in striking out.

The Cronin formula for winning: get on base, move 'em around, drive 'em in.

Year	Team	Record	Pct.	Standing
1933	Wash	99–53	.651	First
1934	Wash	66–86	.434	Seventh
1935	Bos (A)	78–75	.510	Fourth
1936	Bos	74–80	.481	Sixth
1937	Bos	80–72	.526	Fifth
1938	Bos	88–61	.591	Second
1939	Bos	89–62	.589	Second
1940	Bos	82–72	.532	Fourth
1941	Bos	84–70	.545	Second
1942	Bos	93–59	.612	Second
1943	Bos	68–84	.447	Seventh

Year	Team	Record	Pct.	Standing
1944	Bos	77–77	.500	Fourth
1945	Bos	71–83	.461	Seventh
1946	Bos	104–50	.675	First
1947	Bos	83–71	.539	Third
15 years		**1236–1055**	**.540**	

WORLD SERIES

Year	Team	Record	Pct.
1933	Wash	1–4	.200
1946	Bos	3–4	.429
2 years		**4–8**	**.333**

John Charles Crooks

Born November 9, 1865, St. Paul, Minnesota; died February 2, 1918, St. Louis, Missouri; St. Louis Cardinals, 1892

Jack Crooks was a catcher, outfielder and infielder for several teams in his eight-year playing career and served as player-manager for the St. Louis Cardinals for 60 games in the 1892 season before resuming his career solely as a player.

Year	Team	Record	Pct.	Standing
1892	StL (N)	27–33	.450	Eleventh

Lafayette Napoleon Cross

Born May 11, 1867, Milwaukee, Wisconsin; died September 4, 1927, Toledo, Ohio; Cleveland Spiders, 1899

Lave Cross managed Cleveland when the team was in the National League, but he didn't manage for long. Cross left after winning only eight of 38 games. He never managed again.

Year	Team	Record	Pct.	Standing
1899	Cleve (N)	8–30	.211	Twelfth

Michael Lee Cubbage

Born July 21, 1950, Charlottesville, Virginia; New York Mets, September 29, 1991–October 11, 1991

Mike Cubbage, a former major league infielder, served as interim manager of the New York Mets in 1991 and posted a 3–4 record, taking over for Bud Harrelson, who was fired at the end of his second year with the club. Cubbage never managed again.

Year	Team	Record	Pct.	Standing
1991	NY (N)	3–4	.429	Fifth

Edwin R. Curtis

No biographical data available; Altoona Pride, 1884

As organized baseball became more popular in the 19th century, teams were cropping up all over. One of them was in Altoona, Pennsylvania, and Ed Curtis was the manager for 25 games. His career was cut short perhaps because he won only six of them.

Year	Team	Record	Pct.	Standing
1884	Alt (U)	6–19	.240	Tenth

Charles H. Cushman

Born May 25, 1850, New York, New York; died June 29, 1909, Milwaukee, Wisconsin; Cincinnati-Milwaukee, 1891

Before the turn of the 20th century, the American Association fielded many professional teams, and sometimes two cities would share a team. Such was the case with the Cincinnati-Milwaukee ball club in 1891.

Charlie Cushman managed the team in the second half of the season and took them from seventh to fifth place in the span of 36 games, the extent of his managerial career.

Year	Team	Record	Pct.	Standing
1891	C–M (AA)	21–15	.583	Fifth

Edgar Edward "Ned" Cuthbert

Born June 20, 1845, Philadelphia, Pennsylvania; died February 6, 1905, St. Louis, Missouri; St. Louis Brown Stockings, 1882

Ned Cuthbert was one of the pioneer players in baseball, beginning his career in 1865, 11 years before the formation of the National League. He became the playing manager for the St. Louis ball club in 1882. His troops won 27 and lost 32 which turned out to be his lifetime record as a manager.

Year	Team	Record	Pct.	Standing
1882	StL (AA)	27–32	.458	Fifth

William Frederick Dahlen

Born January 5, 1870, Nelliston, New York; died December 5, 1950, Brooklyn, New York; Brooklyn Dodgers, 1910–1913

Bill Dahlen presided over a Brooklyn bunch that provided a lot of entertainment but did not win. One of the highlights of Dahlen's tenure was the debut of a feisty young outfielder named Casey Stengel who got four hits in his first four major league at-bats. Dahlen left after four seasons, getting his team no higher than sixth place.

Year	Team	Record	Pct.	Standing
1910	Brklyn	64–90	.416	Sixth
1911	Brklyn	64–86	.427	Seventh
1912	Brklyn	58–95	.379	Seventh
1913	Brklyn	65–84	.376	Sixth
4 years		251–355	.414	

Alvin Ralph Dark

Born January 7, 1922, Comanche, Oklahoma; San Francisco Giants, November 1, 1960–October 4, 1964; Kansas City Athletics, November 28, 1965–August 20, 1967; Cleveland Indians, October 2, 1967–July 30, 1971; Oakland Athletics, February 19, 1974–October 17, 1975; San Diego Padres, May 30, 1977–March 21, 1978

Alvin Dark managed two pennant winners in his 13-year managerial career: the San Francisco Giants in 1962 and the Oakland A's in 1974. The A's won the Western Division championship in 1975 but lost to Boston in the League Championship Series.

Alvin Dark

Dark was the first man to be manager of both a National League and American League All-Star team.

He was a star shortstop during his playing career with the Giants, Cubs, Cardinals, Braves and Phillies and was a student of the game. He was known for having a quick hook — except when the starter was Juan Marichal (for the Giants) or Catfish Hunter (for the A's). Dark believed that if a starting pitcher began to get into trouble, it was best to get him out, even with a big lead, and that the innings he saved that way would pay off later in the season. His winning teams always had a bullpen ace: Stu Miller with the Giants and Rollie Fingers with the A's.

His losing teams made the quick hook an easy decision. Dark's 1977 San Diego Padres set the major league record for most relief appearances in a season — 382 — a record that has been broken many times with the proliferation of specialty relief pitchers. That same Padre team, managed by Dark and then by John McNamara, had the second-most intentional walks in a season, 106. Dark managed Hall of Famers Willie Mays, Willie McCovey, Orlando Cepeda, Reggie Jackson, Juan Marichal, Gaylord Perry, Hunter and Rollie Fingers.

His players said Dark always liked to try to outthink the opposing manager. It is said that when he went up against Gene Mauch of the Phillies, another strategist, the games were always long because the two would make many changes on the field, trying to outmaneuver each other.

Dark liked his players to bunt and to hit and run, and he wasn't afraid to try unusual strategies in key situations. In 1962, the Giants and Dodgers tied for first and engaged in a best-of-three playoff. Each team won a game. In the deciding game, the Dodgers took a 4–2 lead into the ninth inning. Dark called on Matty Alou to pinch hit, and Alou bunted his way on. The Giants went on to score four runs in the ninth to take a 6–4 lead. In the bottom of the ninth inning, instead of using his relief ace, Miller, Dark rolled the dice again and brought in starter Billy Pierce, who got the save.

A few days later, in the World Series against the Yankees, Dark brought in Miller to pitch and also inserted catcher Johnny Orsino in the lineup. Miller was due to bat second when the Giants came up — and Dark didn't want to pinch hit for him so soon. So when Miller and Orsino entered the game, he flip-flopped them in the batting order. That is a common practice now, but on October 4, 1962, it was the first double-switch in World Series history.

Dark later acquired a reputation for racism, largely because a New York newspaper article published some of his doubts on the prospects of blacks managing in the major leagues. His work as a player and as a manager belie the reputation. Billy O'Dell, a Southern white pitcher Dark had at San Francisco, said Dark did a marvelous job of blending three cliques — whites, blacks and Latins — into a pennant winner.

Year	Team	Record	Pct.	Standing
1961	SF	85–69	.562	Third
1962	SF	103–62	.624	First
1963	SF	88–74	.543	Third
1964	SF	90–72	.556	Fourth
1966	KC	74–86	.463	Seventh
1967	KC	52–69	.430	Tenth
1968	Cleve	86–75	.534	Third
1969	Cleve	62–99	.385	Sixth
1970	Cleve	76–86	.469	Fifth
1971	Cleve	42–61	.408	Sixth
1974	Oak	90–72	.556	First
1975	Oak	98–64	.605	First
1977	SD	48–65	.425	Fifth
13 years		**994–954**	**.510**	

LEAGUE CHAMPIONSHIP SERIES

Year	Team	Record
1974	Oak	3–1
1975	Oak	0–3
2 years		**3–4**

WORLD SERIES

Year	Team	Record
1962	SF	3–4
1974	Oak	4–1
2 years		**7–5**

James Houston Davenport

Born August 17, 1933, Siluria, Alabama; San Francisco Giants, October 30, 1984–September 18, 1985

Jim Davenport was a major league third baseman for 13 years with the San Francisco Giants. In the early 1980s, the Giants shuffled their managerial deck many times and had four managers in less than two years in 1984 and 1985. The third of these was Davenport, who took over for Danny Ozark at the start of the 1985 season. After 144 games, and with the Giants buried in sixth place, Davenport was replaced by Roger Craig.

Year	Team	Record	Pct.	Standing
1985	SF	56–88	.380	Sixth

Mordecai H. Davidson

Born November 30, 1846, Port Washington, Ohio; died September 6, 1940, Louisville, Kentucky; Louisville Colonels, 1888

Mordecai Davidson took over the Louisville team in the American Association for part of the 1888 season. He lasted less than 100 games but stayed in Louisville for the rest of his life. He died there 52 years after his one shot at managing.

Year	Team	Record	Pct.	Standing
1888	Lou	37–55	.402	Eighth

George Stacey Davis

Born August 23, 1870, Cohoes, New York; died October 17, 1940, Philadelphia, Pennsylvania; New York Giants, 1895, 1901–1902

George Davis was a shortstop for Cleveland and the New York Giants for 22 years. He managed the Giants for a brief time in 1895 and then became their player-manager in 1900. He was unable to lift them higher than seventh place. In 1902, he gave up managing and went back to playing full-time and ended his career with the Chicago White Sox in 1909.

Year	Team	Record	Pct.	Standing
1895	NY (N)	17–17	.500	Eighth
1900	NY	39–37	.513	Eighth
1901	NY	52–85	.380	Seventh
3 years		**108–139**	**.437**	

Harry H. "Jasper" Davis

Born July 10, 1873, Philadelphia, Pennsylvania; died August 11, 1947, Philadelphia; Cleveland Naps, May 27, 1912–August 15, 1912

To understand the managerial career of Harry "Jasper" Davis, it is necessary to look at his two predecessors. Jim "Deacon" McGuire managed the Cleveland Naps from 1909 into the 1911 season. When the Naps started 1911 at 6–17, owner Charlie Somers looked for some help. He got it from his friend Connie Mack in Philadelphia. The two made a deal in which the A's sent aging first baseman George Stovall to Cleveland. After the Naps' slow start, Somers fired McGuire and named Stovall player-manager, an interim move until a full-time manager could be found. Stovall rallied the troops and the Indians finished third with an 80–73 record. Despite the surprising strong showing, Somers carried out his original plan and replaced Stovall with Davis. The players and fans were furious.

Davis was much more of a disciplinarian than Stovall had been, and he was soundly criticized by fans and the newspapers. Had the Naps won, Davis might have survived. But they didn't, and in August he quit, with the Indians in sixth place. Davis never managed again.

Year	Team	Record	Pct.	Standing
1912	Cleve	54–71	.532	Sixth

Virgil Lawrence "Spud" Davis

Born December 20, 1904, Birmingham, Alabama; died August 14, 1984, Birmingham; Pittsburgh Pirates, September 27–30, 1946

Spud Davis was one of Frankie Frisch's coaches with the Pittsburgh Pirates. When Frisch was fired at the end of the 1946 season, Davis took over for three games and lost two of them. Frisch, who had previously managed the Cardinals and had managed the Pirates for seven years, later managed the Cubs. Davis's managerial career consisted of those three games for the Pirates.

Year	Team	Record	Pct.	Standing
1946	Pitt	1–2	.333	Seventh

John B. Day

Born September 3, 1847, Colchester, Massachusetts; died January 25, 1925, Cliffside, New Jersey; New York Giants, 1899

John B. Day

John B. Day was not your typical baseball player or manager. He was a cigar manufacturer who was thought to be a millionaire when he began playing baseball professionally. Later he owned the Giants franchise, but money problems forced him to sell his stock. His cigar factories also began to fail and, in desperation, Day agreed to manage the Giants in 1899, not for the love of the game but because this once rich man needed the money. He quit halfway into the season with his team in ninth place. He then got a job as an inspector of umpires until ill health forced him to quit. He died in poverty in 1925.

Year	Team	Record	Pct.	Standing
1899	NY (N)	30–40	.429	Ninth

John Henry Deane

Born May 6, 1846, Trenton, New Jersey; died May 31, 1925, Indianapolis, Indiana; Fort Wayne Kekiongas, 1871

John Henry "Harry" Deane played parts of two seasons as an outfielder and infielder in the National Association. He managed the Fort Wayne team in that league for five games in 1871, losing one more than he won.

Year	Team	Record	Pct.	Standing
1874	Ft. Wyne	2–3	.400	Eighth

Herman J. Dehlman

Born in 1850, Catassauqua, Pennsylvania; died March 13, 1885, Wilkes-Barre, Pennsylvania; St. Louis Brown Stockings, 1876

Herman Dehlman was the first baseman and manager on the St. Louis ball club that was a charter member of the National League. Dehlman was the captain and directed the players on the field. And the players did well. Only Al Spalding's Chicago team finished with a better record. The next season, club president John Lucas started the season as manager, followed by George McManus. St. Louis finished fourth with a record of 28–32. Dehlman, despite his success, was done as a manager — with a lifetime winning percentage of .703.

Year	Team	Record	Pct.	Standing
1876	StL (N)	45–19	.703	Second

Russell Earl "Bucky" Dent

Born November 25, 1951, Savannah, Georgia; New York Yankees, August 18, 1989–June 6, 1990

Bucky Dent experienced both ends of the baseball spectrum with the New York Yankees. In 1978, Dent's home run against the Boston Red Sox in a one-game playoff helped propel the Yankees into the playoffs. Then he got 10 hits in 24 at-bats and was named the Most Valuable Player in that year's World Series. Eleven years later, owner George Steinbrenner named Dent to manage the Yankees, replacing Dallas Green. He guided them to an 18–22 finish (for an overall record of 74–87 that year), better than they had done under Green. But when the Yankees got out of the gate in 1990 with an 18–31 mark, Dent was fired. He has not managed again in the major leagues.

Year	Team	Record	Pct.	Standing
1989	NY (A)	18–22	.450	Fifth
1990	NY	18–31	.360	Seventh
2 years		**36–53**	**.404**	

William Malcolm Dickey

Born June 6, 1907, Bastrop, Louisiana; died November 12, 1993, Little Rock, Arkansas; New York Yankees, May 24, 1946–September 12, 1946

Bill Dickey was a Hall of Fame catcher for the New York Yankees who had a lifetime batting average of .313 over a 17-year career and handled a pitching staff that included Lefty Gomez, Red Ruffing, Spud Chandler and other greats.

He took over as manager of the Yankees when Joe McCarthy resigned for health reasons, ending a 16-year run as the Yankee skipper. Dickey remained as the club's catcher. McCarthy left with the Yankees in second place with a 22–13 record. The Yankees were 57–48 under Dickey when he was relieved of his duties and replaced by coach Johnny Neun. The Yankees finished third. After the season, the Yankees named Bucky Harris their manager for 1947. Neun left to manage Cincinnati. Dickey never managed again but was a Yankee coach for many years. Had he remained as manager, he might not have had the time he did as coach to work with a young Yankee catcher who succeeded him behind the plate — Yogi Berra.

Bill Dickey

Year	Team	Record	Pct.	Standing
1946	NY (A)	57–48	.543	Third

Henry H. Diddlebock

Born June 27, 1854, Philadelphia, Pennsylvania; died February 5, 1900, Philadelphia; St. Louis Cardinals, 1896

Harry Diddlebock was a sportswriter for the *Philadelphia Inquirer* and a drinking buddy of one of the owners of the St. Louis Cardinals. In 1896, he was asked to manage St. Louis as a favor for his friend. He had no managerial experience. He did the best he could for 18 games and actually won seven of them. Five other managers followed him. Together they compiled a record of 40–90.

Year	Team	Record	Pct.	Standing
1896	StL (N)	7–11	.389	Tenth

Lawrence Edward Dierker

Born September 22, 1946, Hollywood, California; Houston Astros, October 4, 1996–November 1, 2001

Larry Dierker pitched 13 years for the Houston Astros and still holds many of the team's pitching records. After his playing days passed, he spent several years as an Astro broadcaster before he was lured out of the radio booth to become the team's manager in 1997. Dierker is an example of a popular player who also became a popular and successful manager in the city where he played. The Astros won the Central Division championship in the National League in each of Dierker's first three seasons but were eliminated in the playoffs each year. In 1999, Dierker suffered a serious seizure in the Houston dugout and had to undergo brain surgery. He returned to the team a month later and managed without incident another two years.

Year	Team	Record	Pct.	Standing
1997	Hous	84–78	.510	First
1998	Hous	102–60	.620	First
1999	Hous	97–65	.590	First
2000	Hous	72–90	.444	Fourth
2001	Hous	93–69	.574	First
5 years		**448–362**	**.553**	

DIVISIONAL PLAYOFFS

Year	Team	Record	Pct.
1997	Hous	0–3	.000
1998	Hous	1–3	.250
1999	Hous	1–3	.250
3 years		**2–9**	**.181**

Lawrence Eugene Doby

Born December 13, 1923, Camden, New Jersey; Chicago White Sox, June 30, 1978–October 19, 1978

Larry Doby was the first African American to play in the American League, beginning his big league career mere months after the National League's Jackie Robinson. He was the second African American to manage in the major leagues. Cleveland Indians owner Bill Veeck brought him up in 1947, the color barrier freshly breached; thirty-one years later, Veeck, as owner of the Chicago White Sox, tabbed Doby to succeed Bob Lemon as Chicago's manager. The only other black manager had been Frank Robinson whom the Cleveland Indians hired in 1975.

Lemon's team had finished third in 1977 with Oscar Gamble and Richie Zisk hitting 31 and 30 home runs, respectively. But in 1978, free agents Gamble and Zisk were gone and at mid-season, so was Lemon. He succeeded Billy Martin as New York Yankee manager and ended up in the World Series after the famous playoff game with the Red Sox in which Bucky Dent hit the game-winning home run.

Meanwhile, Doby took over a Chicago team that had little power and a pitching staff led by Steve Stone in his pre–Cy Young Award winning days. Stone led the staff with 12 wins. Chicago slipped to fifth place and Doby was not invited back as manager.

Year	Team	Record	Pct.	Standing
1978	Chi (A)	37–50	.425	Fifth

Patrick Joseph "Patsy" Donovan

Born March 16, 1865, County Cork, Ireland; died December 25, 1953, Lawrence Massachusetts; Pittsburgh Pirates, September 21, 1896–September 30, 1897; St. Louis Cardinals, October 1, 1900–January 18, 1904; Washington Senators, 1904; Brooklyn Dodgers, 1906–1908; Boston Red Sox, 1910–1911

Patsy Donovan was one of the first managers in baseball history to discover the benefits of relief pitching. His 1899 Pittsburgh Pirate team used relief pitchers 39 times, the most ever at that time. (Baseball strategies change over the years. The 1995 Colorado Rockies used relief pitchers 456 times.)

Donovan, a native of Ireland, managed five major league teams in an 11-year career. His 1901 St. Louis Cardinal team finished fourth, the highest any of his teams ever placed. His career winning percentage, .438, is the second lowest of anyone who managed more than 10 years. (Jack Chapman had a .417 percentage.)

Donovan's problems were not of his own making. He took over the Cardinals just as the fledgling American League was coming into being, and many great players jumped leagues. Donovan lost John McGraw, his star infielder, Wilbert Robertson, his catcher, and Cy Young, one of baseball's best pitchers, to the American League. In an effort to shore up the weaknesses, St. Louis traded an unproven youngster, Mordecai "Three Finger" Brown, to the Cubs for some veteran players. Brown developed into one of the game's best pitchers and led Chicago to several National League championships. Had Donovan been able to field a Cardinal team featuring McGraw, Robinson, Young and Brown, all in their prime, he might have been one of baseball's winningest managers.

Donovan's biggest skill, and perhaps the thing that kept him in the major leagues as long as he lasted, was his ability to identify young talent. As chief scout for the Boston Red Sox, he urged the team to sign Babe Ruth, a pitcher who could also hit. As a Yankee scout, he signed Herb Pennock, a pitcher who had many great years. Billy Rogell was a struggling

Patsy Donovan

ballplayer at Jersey City when he crossed paths with Donovan. Rogell later played in the major leagues. Though he never became a star, he did play on a Detroit Tiger team that made it to the World Series. Rogell was so appreciative of the advice and encouragement Donovan gave him that he sent Donovan his commemorative World Series watch as a gift.

Donovan had a 17-year major league playing career with six teams and then managed for 25 years, 14 of which were in the minor leagues. Donovan continued to scout until 1946. He died on Christmas Day, 1953, at the age of 88.

Year	Team	Record	Pct.	Standing
1897	Pitt	60–71	.458	Eighth
1899	Pitt	68–57	.544	Seventh
1901	StL (N)	76–64	.543	Fourth
1902	StL	56–78	.418	Sixth
1903	StL	43–94	.314	Eighth
1904	Wash	37–97	.276	Eighth
1906	Brklyn	66–86	.434	Fifth
1907	Brklyn	65–83	.439	Fifth
1908	Brklyn	53–101	.344	Seventh
1910	Bos (A)	81–72	.529	Fourth
1911	Bos	78–75	.510	Fifth
11 years		**683–878**	**.438**	

William Edward "Wild Bill" Donovan

Born October 13, 1876, Lawrence, Massachusetts; died December 9, 1923, Forsyth, New York; New York Yankees, 1915–1917; Philadelphia Phillies, 1921

There are two things that distinguish Wild Bill Donovan's tenure as manager of the New York Yankees: 1) New York began wearing their now familiar pinstripes in 1915, Donovan's first year with the club; 2) when he was dismissed after his third straight losing season in 1918, he was replaced by Miller Huggins, who had not distinguished himself as manager of the St. Louis Cardinals but would soon create a dynasty in the Bronx.

Donovan was later hired to manage the Philadelphia Phillies but won only 31 of 102 games and was gone after one season.

Year	Team	Record	Pct.	Standing
1915	NY (A)	69–83	.454	Fifth
1916	NY	80–74	.519	Fourth
1917	NY	71–82	.464	Sixth
1921	Phil (N)	31–71	.304	Eighth
4 years		**251–310**	**.447**	

Charles Sebastian "Red" Dooin

Born June 12, 1879, Cincinnati, Ohio; died May 14, 1952, Rochester, New York; Philadelphia Phillies, February 22, 1910–February 2, 1915

Red Dooin managed the Philadelphia Phillies for five years and had them over .500 for four of those years. He had been the regular catcher for the club since 1902 and was promoted to player-manager in 1910. He immediately showed some of his knowledge of hitters and pitchers, plus his sense of strategy, by sending 107 relief pitchers into ball games, the first time in the major leagues that more than 100 relief appearances had been registered by a team.

One of his pitchers didn't need much relief. Grover Cleveland Alexander won 28 games in his rookie year of 1911, and then won 19, 22 and 27 in his next three years. Dooin brought the club home in second place in 1913 but after a dismal sixth-place finish in 1914, he was replaced by Pat Moran.

Year	Team	Record	Pct.	Standing
1910	Phil (N)	78–75	.510	Fourth
1911	Phil	79–73	.520	Fourth
1912	Phil	73–79	.480	Fifth
1913	Phil	88–63	.583	Second
1914	Phil	74–80	.481	Sixth
5 years		**392–370**	**.514**	

Michael Cornelius Dorgan

Born October 2, 1853, Middletown, Connecticut; died April 26, 1909, Hartford, Connecticut; Syracuse Stars, 1879

Mike Dorgan was a hard-hitting catcher who is credited with teaching Harry McCormick, one of baseball's earliest pitching stars, how to throw a curveball.

He was a successful player-manager in what would be considered the minor leagues of his era, and managed the Syracuse Stars in the National League for one year.

Year	Team	Record	Pct.	Standing
1879	Syr (N)	22–48	.314	Seventh

Thomas Jefferson "Buttermilk Tommy" Dowd

Born April 20, 1869, Holyoke, Massachusetts; died July 2, 1933, Holyoke; St. Louis Browns, 1896–1897

Tommy Dowd was a pretty good outfielder on a pretty bad team, the St. Louis Browns that would one day become the St. Louis Cardinals. In 1896, the Browns went through six managers, with Dowd the sixth. They finished eleventh. In 1897, they had two managers, with Dowd being the first. They finished twelfth. Dowd resumed his playing career full-time and never managed again.

Year	Team	Record	Pct.	Standing
1896	StL (N)	24–38	.387	Eleventh
1897	StL	6–25	.194	Twelfth
2 years		**30–63**	**.323**	

John Joseph Doyle

Born October 25, 1869, Killorgin, England; died December 31, 1958, Holyoke, Massachusetts; New York Giants, 1895; Washington Senators, 1898

John Doyle earned the nickname "Dirty Jack" because of his aggressive style of play. He was one of the best baserunners of his day, and he often slid into a base with his spikes high. Doyle brawled with opposing players, umpires and fans and was actually arrested several times for his actions.

He was a natural leader and was named team captain when he played for New York, Brooklyn and Chicago. His two brief stints at managing were both on an interim basis, and he performed adequately, hovering around the .500 mark over 106 games.

After his playing and managing days were over, he umpired and scouted. He was a scout for 38 years for the Chicago Cubs and is credited with discovering such future stars as Gabby Hartnett, Charlie Root, Stan Hack and Phil Cavarretta. He also recommended that the Cubs sign Hack Wilson when Wilson was left unprotected by the Giants.

Year	Team	Record	Pct.	Standing
1895	NY (N)	31–31	.500	Ninth
1898	Wash (N)	20–24	.455	Eleventh
2 years		**51–55**	**.481**	

Joseph J. Doyle

Born April 9, 1938, New York, New York; died January 7, 1906, White Plains, New York; Brooklyn Trolley Dodgers, 1885

Joseph J. Doyle was one of three businessmen who put their heads together, as well as their money, and formed what was to become one of baseball's most storied franchises. Called the Trolley Dodgers for people who had to jump out of the way of horse-drawn trolleys on Brooklyn's busy streets, the club would later be known simply as the Dodgers. Doyle, who according to the *Cultural Encyclopedia of Baseball* earned a share of a gambling establishment (as did Ferdinand Abel, another of the Dodgers' original financiers), had the distinction of being manager of the team, but only for a little while, "retiring" with a 13–20 record.

Year	Team	Record	Pct.	Standing
1883	Brklyn	13–20	.394	Seventh

Charles Walter Dressen

Born September 20, 1898, Decatur, Illinois; died August 10, 1966, Detroit, Michigan; Cincinnati Reds, July 28, 1934–September 13, 1937; Brooklyn Dodgers, November 28, 1950–October 14, 1953; Washington Senators, September 28, 1954–May 6, 1957; October 23, 1959–September 2, 1961; Detroit Tigers, June 17, 1963–March 7, 1965; May 19, 1965–May 16, 1966

Charlie Dressen's style of managing didn't change in 30 years. He was smart, brash, confident and knew a great deal about the game. And he was always thinking two innings ahead. Many managers with these qualities are in the Hall of Fame. Dressen is not because he had an uncanny knack for taking his strengths and turning them into weaknesses — particularly the confidence he had in himself. One of his most repeated quotes is the answer he once gave his ballplayers when they were losing badly in a ball game: "Don't worry, boys. I'll think of something."

Dressen was an infielder for the Cincinnati Reds for seven years and the New York Giants for one year, 1932. He was on the roster when they went to the World Series that year, and though he didn't play he may have had a hand in the Series' outcome. In the 11th inning of Game Four, the Giants were winning, 2–1, when Washington mounted a challenge by loading the bases with one out. Manager Bill Terry was about to move the infield in to try for a play at the plate. Dressen talked him out of it, saying he knew the hitter, Cliff Bolton, from his minor league days, and that Bolton could be induced into hitting into a double play. Terry followed his reserve infielder's advice, Bolton hit into the double play and Dressen's reputation began to grow.

Larry MacPhail hired Dressen to manage the Reds the following year. They had finished last three years in a row. They finished last in Dressen's first year, too. He got them as high as fifth in 1936, but they slumped back to eighth in 1937 and Dressen was fired. By this time MacPhail had moved on to the Dodgers and hired Dressen as a coach. Once again, Dressen demonstrated great skill at anticipating what would happen in a game and became manager Leo Durocher's most trusted adviser. Later on, MacPhail moved once again, this time to the Yankees, and once again Dressen hooked on as a coach. When the Yankees decided to make a managerial change at the end of the 1948 season, Dressen was on the short list of prospects. Instead, he was assigned to manage the Yankee farm team in Oakland; Oakland's manager, Casey Stengel, was brought to New York to manage the Yankees. While no reason was given for Dressen's snubbing, many believed his ego and sense of self-importance spelled his doom.

Dressen got his big break in 1951 when the Dodgers hired him as their manager, 14 years after he had last managed in the major leagues. Brooklyn blew a big lead in the standings and then lost the pennant to the Giants on Bobby Thomson's home run in the third game of a playoff series. But the Dodgers won National League championships in 1952 and 1953, winning 105 games in '53. Those Dodger teams featured four Hall of Famers in the starting lineup: Jackie Robinson at second, PeeWee Reese at shortstop, Duke Snider in centerfield and Roy Campanella catching. Within a few years they would have Hall of Famers Don Drysdale and Sandy Koufax as mainstays on their pitching staffs. They would win pennants again in 1955, 1956, 1959, 1963 and 1965, but Dressen would not be with them. Once again, his ego got the best of him.

Dodger owner Walter O'Malley was in the habit of giving his managers one-year contracts. After the great 1953 season, Dressen asked for a multi-year contract and even had his wife, Ruth, write a letter to O'Malley in his behalf. The result was that O'Malley shocked the baseball world by firing Dressen, who had won pennants the past two years. Dressen's successors, Walter Alston and Tom Lasorda, are both in the Hall of Fame. Had Dressen agreed to one-year contracts, he too might be in the Hall of Fame.

Dressen went to Washington, where no amount of a manager's self-confidence could boost the lowly Senators. After finishing eighth and seventh, and heading for another eighth-place finish in his third season, he was fired. He then managed Milwaukee for two years and was in his fourth year as manager of the Tigers when ill health forced him to resign. He died later that same year.

Year	Team	Record	Pct.	Standing
1934	Cin	25–41	.378	Eighth
1935	Cin	68–85	.444	Sixth
1936	Cin	74–80	.481	Fifth
1937	Cin	51–78	.395	Eighth
1951	Brklyn	97–60	.618	Second
1952	Brklyn	96–57	.627	First
1953	Brklyn	105–49	.682	First
1955	Wash	53–101	.344	Eighth
1956	Wash	59–95	.383	Seventh
1957	Wash	5–16	.238	Eighth
1960	Mil	88–66	.571	Second

Year	Team	Record	Pct.	Standing
1961	Mil	71–58	.550	Third
1963	Det	55–47	.539	Fifth
1964	Det	85–77	.525	Fourth
1965	Det	89–73	.549	Fourth
1966	Det	16–10	.615	Third
16 years		**1037–993**	**.511**	

WORLD SERIES

Year	Team	Record
1952	Brklyn	3–4
1953	Brklyn	2–4
2 years		**5–8**

Hugh Duffy

Born November 26, 1866, Cranston, Rhode Island; died October 19, 1954, Boston, Massachusetts; Milwaukee Brewers, 1901; Philadelphia Phillies, March 3, 1904–1906; Chicago White Sox, May 6, 1910–1911; Boston Red Sox, October 29, 1920–1922

Hugh Duffy was a little man who was one of the greatest hitters of the 19th century. In 1894, he hit .438, still the highest single-season batting average in the history of baseball. Duffy was the victim of one of baseball's greatest zingers. When he reported to the Chicago White Stockings in 1888, Chicago manager Cap Anson looked at the 5'7" outfielder and said, "Where's the rest of you?" Duffy finished his 21-year career with a lifetime batting average of .340.

He had an unusual managing career in that he managed four teams for a total of eight seasons, but over a span of 21 years. He was a player-manager for the ill-fated Milwaukee Brewers in 1901 and for the Philadelphia Phillies from 1904 to 1906. After his playing days were over, he managed the Chicago White Sox and Boston Red Sox. He had much greater success as a player than he did as a manager. His teams never finished higher than fourth and finished dead last in three of his eight years.

After his managerial career was over, he scouted for many years for the Red Sox.

Year	Team	Record	Pct.	Standing
1901	Mil (A)	48–89	.350	Eighth
1904	Phil (N)	52–100	.342	Eighth
1905	Phil	83–69	.546	Fourth
1906	Phil	71–82	.464	Fourth
1910	Chi (A)	68–85	.444	Sixth
1911	Chi	77–74	.510	Fourth
1921	Bos (A)	75–79	.487	Fifth
1922	Bos	61–93	.396	Eighth
8 years		**535–671**	**.444**	

Frederick C. Dunlap

Born May 21, 1859, Philadelphia, Pennsylvania; died December 1, 1902, Philadelphia; Pittsburgh Pirates, 1889

Fred Dunlap managed the Pittsburgh franchise in the National League for 16 games in 1889, winning seven of them. He was the second of three managers for Pittsburgh that year. The third manager, Dunlap's successor, Ned Hanlon, then began his brilliant managerial career that lasted 19 years and more than 2,500 games. Dunlap never managed again.

Year	Team	Record	Pct.	Standing
1889	Pitt (N)	7–9	.438	Seventh

Leo Ernest Durocher

Born July 27, 1905, West Springfield, Massachusetts; died October 7, 1991, Palm Springs, California; Brooklyn Dodgers, October 13, 1938–April 12, 1947; April 21, 1948–July 16, 1948; New York Giants, July 16, 1948–September 24, 1955; Chicago Cubs, October 25, 1965–July 24, 1972; Houston Astros, August 26, 1972–October 1, 1973

Leo Durocher was a colorful and controversial player and manager whose 2,010 wins rank him seventh among managers for all-time wins.

When he was manager of the Brooklyn Dodgers in the 1940s, says Durocher in *Nice Guys Finish Last*, newspaperman Frank Graham asked him why he stuck by the Dodgers' modestly talented Eddie Stanky. The reply amounts to "scrappiness"; but his roundabout answer was gotten at by illustration. Watching the starters of the opposing nine file onto the field, he pointed at one after another and said, "All nice guys. They'll finish last. Nice guys. Finish last." The opposing manager was Mel Ott, a reputed gentleman. By transference, Ott has become, quite wrongly, the presumed target of Durocher's wit.

Durocher managed for 24 years, all in the National League, with the Dodgers for a slight majority of that time. He won pennants with the 1941 Dodgers, 1951 Giants and 1954 Giants. His 1942 Dodgers won 104 games but finished second to the St. Louis Cardinals. His 1969 Cubs were in first place for five months but were overtaken by the New York Mets in the final weeks of the season. His 1951 Giants team won the pennant by beating Brooklyn in a playoff series in which Bobby Thomson hit a three-run homer in the ninth inning of the final game. His 1954 Giants won the World Series by sweeping a Cleveland Indian team that had set an American League record for wins with 111.

Durocher's managerial style had three distinct characteristics: He preferred a set lineup to platoons; he strongly favored experienced players, to the point where young players felt they had to be sensational even to be noticed; yet he always seemed to pin some hope on a sensational young player — Pete Reiser with the Dodgers,

Leo Durocher

Willie Mays with the Giants, Ferguson Jenkins with the Cubs and Cesar Cedeno with the Astros.

As for using a set lineup: Durocher's 1941 Dodger pennant winner featured shortstop PeeWee Reese, who played 152 games in a 154-game schedule; first baseman Dolf Camilli, who played 149; second baseman Billy Herman, who played 144; and outfielder Pete Reiser, who played 137 and would have played more had it not been for injuries.

In 1954, his shortstop with the Giants, Alvin Dark, played in all 154 games. In addition, outfielder Don Mueller played in 153, Willie Mays 151, first baseman Whitey Lockman 148, second baseman Davey Williams 142 games. Those five players played in an average of 150 games that season. Outfielder Monte Irvin played in 135 and third baseman Hank Thompson played in 136. The only position that was truly shared was catcher, where Ray Katt and Wes Westrum were rotated.

A look at Durocher's 1969 Cubs shows the same preference for a set lineup. First baseman Ernie Banks, at age 38, played in 155 games. Catcher Randy Hundley appeared in 151 games. Shortstop Don Kessinger played in 158. Third baseman Ron Santo was in 160. Outfielder Billy Williams played in 163 games. That's an average of 157 games for a team that played half its games in the bright sunshine of Wrigley Field in Chicago.

Years later, reflecting on that 1969 team, Kessinger said he wilted in August and September and simply did not have the strength that he had earlier in the year. He acknowledged that Durocher was criticized for not resting his players, but Kessinger maintained that none of them wanted to come out of the lineup. Durocher also had a "set lineup" in his bullpen, relying on veteran Phil Regan who appeared in 71 games and won 12, the fourth most on the staff in 1969.

While Durocher's years with the Cubs were the most successful that the club had experienced since its 1945 pennant winner, his disregard for younger players who did not impress him wound up hurting the Cubs in the long run. Joe Niekro was traded to San Diego and went on to win 210 games in his career. A few years later, Larry Gura was traded to Texas. He later became the winningest pitcher for the Kansas City Royals.

Durocher's career was marred by controversy. In 1947, commissioner Happy Chandler suspended him for a year because of his alleged association with gamblers. He returned to manage the Dodgers in 1948 and was fired, setting the stage for his move over to the Giants. Had he not been suspended, Durocher would have been Jackie Robinson's manager when Robinson broke the racial barrier in the major leagues.

Durocher was regarded as someone who did an ordinary job with an ordinary team but was great when his team had a chance to be the champion. He proved that repeatedly in his long career, the '69 Cubs notwithstanding. Despite more than 2,000 wins, Durocher was not elected to the Hall of Fame until 1994, three years after his death. Many believe the delay in his induction was due in part to the stormy relationship he had with opposing players and managers, the press and the public.

Year	Team	Record	Pct.	Standing
1939	Brklyn	84–69	.549	Third
1940	Brklyn	88–65	.575	Second
1941	Brklyn	100–54	.649	First
1942	Brklyn	104–50	.675	Second
1943	Brklyn	81–72	.529	Third
1944	Brklyn	63–91	.409	Seventh

Year	Team	Record	Pct.	Standing
1945	Brklyn	87–67	.565	Third
1946	Brklyn	96–60	.615	Second
1948	Brklyn	37–38	.493	Fifth
1948	NY (N)	41–38	.519	Fifth
1949	NY	73–81	.474	Fifth
1950	NY	86–68	.558	Third
1951	NY	98–59	.624	First
1952	NY	92–62	.597	Second
1953	NY	70–84	.455	Fifth
1954	NY	97–57	.630	First
1955	NY	80–74	.519	Third
1966	Chi (N)	59–103	.364	Tenth
1967	Chi	87–74	.540	Third
1968	Chi	84–78	.519	Third
1969	Chi	92–70	.568	Second
1970	Chi	84–78	.519	Second
1971	Chi	83–79	.512	Third
1972	Chi	46–44	.511	Fourth
1972	Hous	16–15	.516	Second
1973	Hous	82–80	.506	Fourth
24 years		**2008–1710**	**.540**	

WORLD SERIES

Year	Team	W–L
1941	Brklyn	1–4
1951	NY (N)	2–4
1954	NY	4–0
3 years		**7–8**

John Francis "Frank" Dwyer

Born March 25, 1868, Lee, Massachusetts; died February 4, 1953, Pittsfield, Massachusetts; Detroit Tigers, 1902

Frank Dwyer was a better than average pitcher in the 19th century who won more than 20 games twice and had 176 wins in a 13-year career. In 1902, he managed the Detroit ball club in the American League's second year, a tumultuous time in which the new league was trying to establish itself, new teams were raiding players from the well-established National League, and new stars were emerging. Dwyer lasted one year, a year in which his Tigers finished seventh. Twenty-two years later, he went to spring training to help manager John McGraw get his New York Giants ready for a new season, becoming one of the first pitching coaches in the major leagues.

Year	Team	Record	Pct.	Standing
1902	Det	52–83	.385	Seventh

Edwin Hawley Dyer

Born October 11, 1900, Morgan City, Louisiana; died April 20, 1964, Houston, Texas; St. Louis Cardinals, November 6, 1945–October 16, 1950

Eddie Dyer had one of the most successful five-year managerial runs in history. The St. Louis Cardinals had dominated the National League in the 1940s, winning pennants in 1942, 1943 and 1944 under Billy Southworth. In 1945, the Chicago Cubs overtook the Cardinals. Dyer was brought on for the 1946 season, and the Cardinals returned to the top. They finished second in each of the next three years. Then in 1950, they slipped to fifth place and Dyer was relieved of his duties.

Dyer had a tough act to follow when he took over the Cardinals. St. Louis had been only the third team in baseball history to win three consecutive National League championships. Early in 1945, Southworth's son, a pilot, was killed in a plane crash in New York, an event that obviously devastated the manager and had an impact on the entire team. At the end of the season, Southworth asked to be let out of his contract because of a lucrative offer made to him by the Boston Braves. Cardinal owner Sam Breadon agreed and plucked Dyer out of his Houston oil business to run the team.

Dyer had worked for the Cardinals for 25 years before retiring to the oil fields of Houston. He had been director of the farm system at the time he retired so he was familiar with most of the club's young ballplayers.

In 1945, St. Louis had a good team that almost won the pennant. When in 1946 the Cardinals had stars such as Stan Musial, Terry Moore, Howie Pollet, Max Lanier, Enos Slaughter and Harry Walker back from the war, the club was even better. They were the heavy favorite to return to the top, but that was a big challenge for a new manager. Second place would have seemed like a failure.

Dyer was not a platooner but he did shift players around until he got the combination he liked. His first baseman was rookie Dick Sisler, son of the great Hall of Famer George Sisler. The young Sisler did not live up to his advance billing, and Dyer made a change that he thought would work. He moved Musial, who had never before played anywhere but in the outfield for the Cardinals, to first base, where he played the majority of the time for the next two seasons. Dyer had to make many other changes because several of the longtime Cardinals, including veteran pitcher Mort Cooper, wound up in Boston with Southworth. So many ex–Redbirds played for the Braves that they were sometimes referred to as the Cape Cod Cardinals.

Dyer shuffled the deck enough to finish in a tie with Brooklyn. The Cardinals then won a best-of-three playoff and went on to beat the Boston Red Sox in the World Series.

Year	Team	Record	Pct.	Standing
1946	StL (N)	98–58	.628	First
1947	StL	89–65	.578	Second
1948	StL	85–69	.552	Second
1949	StL	96–58	.623	Second
1950	StL	78–75	.510	Fifth
5 years		**446–325**	**.57**	

WORLD SERIES

Year	Team	Record
1946	StL (N)	4–3

James Joseph Dykes

Born November 10, 1896, Philadelphia, Pennsylvania; died June 15, 1976, Philadelphia; Chicago White Sox, May 8, 1934–May 24, 1946; Philadelphia Athletics, October 18, 1950–November 4, 1953; Baltimore

Orioles, November 11, 1953–September 14, 1954; Cincinnati Reds, August 14, 1958–September 29, 1958; Detroit Tigers, May 3, 1959–August 3, 1960; Cleveland Indians, August 3, 1960–September 30, 1961

Jimmy Dykes managed for 21 years and never got a team higher than third place. One of the reasons was that he was always called on to try to improve teams that were well shy of pennant-winning talent. He managed the Chicago White Sox for 13 years and was able to bring them home in third place three times and fourth place three times. The other six years they were in the second division. He later said that in all his years with the White Sox, he never had a power hitter. A check of the record shows that first baseman Zeke Bonura hit 27 home runs in 1934 and 21 in 1935. Other than that, only one player, Joe Kuhel, hit more than 20—he hit 27 in 1940—and in 1942 and 1943, the White Sox home run leaders were Wally Moses with seven and Kuhel with five.

Dykes' next managerial assignment was to take over for Connie Mack with the lowly Philadelphia A's as Mack ended his half-century career as the A's manager. Dykes took a poor team and finished sixth, fourth and seventh before taking on another tough chore, managing the Baltimore Orioles in their first year after moving from St. Louis. The Orioles finished seventh, ahead of the A's. That team had a young pitcher named Don Larsen who suffered through one of the worst seasons ever for a pitcher. He was 3–21. Two years later, he pitched a perfect game for the New York Yankees in the World Series.

In 1958, Dykes did his best short-term task of turning a team around. He took over the Cincinnati Reds in mid-season after Birdie Tebbetts was fired. The Reds were 52–61 and in seventh place. In the remaining 41 games, Dykes guided them to a 24–17 record and fourth-place finish. That team had offensive power in Frank Robinson, Gus Bell and Jerry Lynch, the best double play combination in baseball in Roy McMillan and Johnny Temple, and a pitching staff led by right-hander Bob Purkey and left-hander Joe Nuxhall. Dykes' philosophy was to let them play. He said his success with the Reds was proof that sometimes "undermanaging" is the best approach.

The Reds were shuffling the deck, trying to find the right combination, and decided to go with a younger manager, Mayo Smith, in 1959. Halfway through the season, Smith was fired and Fred Hutchinson came aboard. Two years later, the Reds won the pennant under Hutchinson.

Meanwhile, the Detroit Tigers called on Dykes after they started the 1959 season with a 2–15 mark under Bill Norman. Dykes, once again using an "undermanaging" style, got the most out of a team that featured future Hall of Famer Al Kaline, batting champion Harvey Kuenn and power hitter Charley Maxwell, as well as a pitching staff led by future Hall of Famer Jim Bunning. The Tigers marched from seventh to fourth by the end of the year.

In 1960, Dykes was involved in a most unusual trade. The Tigers and Cleveland Indians swapped managers, with Joe Gordon moving from Cleveland to Detroit to lead the Tigers. Dykes retired after the 1961 season with the Indians.

As he demonstrated many times in his career, Dykes believed in a low-key approach in dealing with his ballplayers, but was fairly set in his ways regarding strategy. He believed a manager could be responsible for winning as many as 15 games a year by knowing the capabilities of his pitching staff. "The manager who knows when a starter is weakening—and which reliever to bring in—has the advantage," he said. He did not believe in platooning; in fact, he thought it hurt teams because it prevented young players from getting enough playing time. "I am a firm believer in the idea that the best eight players belong in the game every day, whether they're lefties, righties or ambidextries," said Dykes.

Year	Team	Record	Pct.	Standing
1934	Chi (A)	49–86	.383	Eighth
1935	Chi	74–78	.487	Fifth
1936	Chi	81–70	.536	Third
1937	Chi	86–68	.558	Third
1938	Chi	65–83	.439	Sixth
1939	Chi	85–69	.552	Fourth
1940	Chi	82–72	.532	Fourth
1941	Chi	77–77	.500	Third
1942	Chi	66–82	.446	Sixth
1943	Chi	82–72	.532	Fourth
1944	Chi	71–83	.461	Seventh
1945	Chi	71–78	.477	Sixth
1946	Chi	10–20	.333	Eighth
1951	Phil (A)	70–84	.455	Sixth
1952	Phil	79–75	.513	Fourth
1953	Phil	59–95	.383	Seventh
1954	Bal	54–100	.351	Seventh
1958	Cin	24–17	.585	Fourth
1959	Det	74–63	.540	Fourth
1960	Det	44–52	.458	Sixth
1960	Cleve	26–32	.448	Fourth
1961	Cleve	78–82	.488	Fifth
21 years		**1407–1538**	**.478**	

John F. Dyler

Born in 1852, Louisville, Kentucky; date of death unknown; Louisville Colonels, 1882

Like so many of his contemporaries in the early days of baseball, John Dyler's managerial career was short and uneventful. It consisted of 13 games with Louisville in the old American Association.

Year	Team	Record	Pct.	Standing
1882	Lou (AA)	6–7	.462	Fourth

Charles Hercules Ebbets

Born October 29, 1859, New York, New York; died April 18, 1925, New York; Brooklyn Dodgers, 1898

Charlie Ebbets became one of the owners of the Brooklyn baseball franchise at the age of 31 and, mostly through the deaths of other owners and stockholders, became president of the club in 1897 at age 38. The Dodgers were floundering on the field and having trouble making ends meet off the field. Ebbets, convinced the team needed a new ballpark, built what eventually became Ebbets Field. With a new ballpark and fresh enthusiasm, the Dodgers looked forward to a great 1898 season. It didn't happen. Veteran manager Bill Barnie was fired and Ebbets replaced him with one of his outfielders, Mike Griffin. When that didn't seem to work, Ebbets installed himself as manager. He sat in the dugout and directed his team while wearing a top hat, the usual attire for owners in those days. He finished out the season and then returned to the front office, where he was much more successful.

Year	Team	Record	Pct.	Standing
1898	Brklyn	38–68	.358	Tenth

Howard Rodney "Doc" Edwards

Born December 10, 1937, Red Jacket, West Virginia; Cleveland Indians, July 15, 1987–September 12, 1989

Doc Edwards caught in the major leagues for parts of five seasons and became manager of the Cleveland Indians in 1987, replacing Pat Corrales. Under Edwards, the Indians won 30 of their remaining 75 games, about par for the course for Cleveland in those days. In 1988, the typically lethargic Indians got off to a great start and were among the league leaders through the end of May. But they faltered and finished sixth. They were in sixth place after 143 games in the 1989 season when Edwards was fired.

Year	Team	Record	Pct.	Standing
1987	Cleve	30–45	.400	Seventh
1988	Cleve	78–84	.480	Sixth
1989	Cleve	65–78	.450	Sixth
3 years		**173–207**	**.455**	

Norman Arthur "Kid" Elberfeld

Born April 13, 1875, Pomeroy, Ohio; died January 13, 1944, Chattanooga, Tennessee; New York Yankees, June 24, 1908–October 8, 1908

Kid Elberfeld has the distinction of being the manager of the worst team in New York Yankee history. He had double trouble when he took over. Clark Griffith, who had been the club's only manager since its American League debut in 1901, quit after getting into a dispute with owner Frank Farrell and watching his team struggle to a 24–32 record. Elberfeld, an infielder, was installed as manager, and that infuriated star first baseman Hal Chase, who thought he should have gotten the job. The temperamental Chase abandoned the team to play with Stockton in the California State League. Adding to his troubles, Elberfeld was injured most of the year and played in only 19 games after becoming manager. The Yankees finished last with a record of 51–103, 39½ games out of first place — and 17 games out of seventh place.

Year	Team	Record	Pct.	Standing
1908	NY (A)	27–71	.276	Eighth

Lee Constantine Elia

Born July 16, 1937, Philadelphia, Pennsylvania; Chicago Cubs, October 22, 1981–August 22, 1983; Philadelphia Phillies, June 18, 1987–September 23, 1988

Lee Elia played in 95 major league games as an infielder for the Chicago White Sox in 1966 and Chicago Cubs in 1968. He retired with a .203 lifetime batting average and began a new career as a minor league coach and manager. He became manager of the Cubs in 1982. Chicago finished a distant fifth. In 1983, the Cubs were headed for another dismal finish while the White Sox, on the other side of Chicago, were winning their division. When fans and media began to heckle Elia, he responded by saying Cub fans were uneducated and unemployed (a reference to the crowds at day games). Elia was fired after 123 games but resurfaced four years later to manage the Phillies.

Year	Team	Record	Pct.	Standing
1982	Chi (N)	73–89	.451	Fifth
1983	Chi	54–69	.439	Fifth
1987	Phil	51–50	.505	Fourth
1988	Phil	60–92	.395	Sixth
4 years		**238–300**	**.442**	

Joseph J. Ellick

Born April 3, 1854, Cincinnati, Ohio; died April 21, 1923, Kansas City, Missouri; Chicago-Pittsburgh, 1884

Joe Ellick's managerial career in professional baseball lasted 12 games, but his percentage was at .500 better than those of the majority of major league managers. Ellick managed the Chicago-Pittsburgh entry in the Union League and split 12 games.

Year	Team	Record	Pct.	Standing
1884	Chi–Pitt (U)	6 –6	.500	Sixth

Robert Irving Elliott

Born November 16, 1916, San Francisco, California; died May 4, 1966, San Diego, California; Kansas City Athletics, October 2, 1959–October 4, 1960

Bob Elliott took over a Kansas City team that had finished seventh three years in a row and eighth the year before that. Elliott, who had a 15-year major league career, a .289 lifetime batting average and 2,061 hits, didn't have anybody on the 1960 A's who could hit as well as he could. Norm Siebern hit .279 with 19 home runs to lead the club. Ray Herbert won 14 games, Buddy Daley won 16, and the rest of the staff won 28. The A's returned to last place and Elliott was out after one year.

Year	Team	Record	Pct.	Standing
1960	KC	58–96	.377	Eighth

Jewel Willoughby Ens

Born August 24, 1889, St. Louis, Missouri; died January 17, 1950, Syracuse, New York; Pittsburgh Pirates, September 4, 1929–October 27, 1931

Jewel Ens was a coach for the Pittsburgh Pirates who was out of the Bill McKechnie mold: he was a former utility infielder with a reputation for a good head for the game. He worked for Pittsburgh owner Barney Dreyfus, who had a knack for shuffling players around for a variety of reasons. The Pirates had won the National League pennant in 1927 and were in the pennant race most of 1928 until they hit a late-season slump. Dreyfus removed his pennant-winning manager, Donie Bush, and moved Ens up to finish the season. Under the mild-mannered tactician, the Pirates finished at 21–14 and secured second place. Burleigh Grimes was the Pirates' leading pitcher at 17–7, a great record but short of his 25–14 record the year before. When Dreyfus cut his pay, Grimes refused to sign, and he was promptly traded to the Boston Braves. The Braves later traded him to the St. Louis Cardinals where he helped St. Louis win the pennant. Meanwhile, the Pirates slipped to fifth place each of the next two years. Dreyfus made another change, replacing Ens, who never managed again.

Year	Team	Record	Pct.	Standing
1928	Pitt	21–14	.600	Second
1929	Pitt	80–74	.519	Fifth
1930	Pitt	75–79	.487	Fifth
3 years		**176–167**	**.513**	

Calvin Coolidge Ermer

Born November 10, 1923, Baltimore, Maryland; Minnesota Twins, June 9, 1967–September 30, 1968

Cal Ermer, a Minnesota Twins coach, took over for highly successful manager Sam Mele 50 games into the 1967 season. Minnesota sat in sixth place with a 25–25 record. Ermer steadied the ship and guided the Twins to a 66–46 record the rest of the way as they crept back into a second-place tie in one of the wildest races in American League history. Going into the last weekend of the season, Boston, Detroit, Chicago and Minnesota all had a chance at the championship. At season's end, Boston was ahead of both Detroit and Minnesota by one game and by three games over Chicago. The following year, the Twins dropped to 79–83, a seventh-place finish despite being just four games below .500. Ermer was not invited back to manage in 1969.

Year	Team	Record	Pct.	Standing
1967	Minn	66–46	.589	Second
1968	Minn	79–83	.488	Seventh
2 years		**145–129**	**.529**	

James Sarkin Essian

Born January 2, 1951, Detroit, Michigan; Chicago Cubs, May 22, 1991–October 18, 1991

Jim Essian, who caught in the major leagues for 12 years, was a successful minor league manager and was piloting the Chicago Cubs' Triple-A farm team in Des Moines when Cubs manager Don Zimmer was fired in 1991. Chicago ended up four games under .500 under Essian and he was not rehired.

Year	Team	Record	Pct.	Standing
1991	Chi (N)	59–63	.480	Fourth

Thomas Jefferson "Dude" Esterbrook

Born June 20, 1860, Staten Island, New York; died April 30, 1901, Middletown, New York; Louisville Colonels, 1889

Dude Esterbrook played most of his major league career with the New York teams in the 1880s. He was a catcher and infielder. In 1884, he led the league in both batting percentage and fielding percentage. Esterbrook was a colorful player and quite the ladies' man, which earned him his nickname. His managerial career was brief and uneventful.

Esterbrook's stint lasted just 10 games with Louisville, perhaps because he won only two of them. The team didn't do much better without him, losing 111 games for the season.

When Esterbrook's career was over, he developed a type of mental illness in which he fell into trances. His brother accompanied him on a train to take him to a mental hospital in 1901 when Esterbrook excused himself to use a lavatory. Locking the door behind him, he then jumped out a window and died of a skull fracture at the age of 40.

Year	Team	Record	Pct.	Standing
1889	Lou (AA)	2–8	.200	Eighth

Ford J. Evans

Date of birth unknown; died October 14, 1884, Akron Ohio; Cleveland Blues, 1882

In 19th century baseball, managers sometimes didn't last more than a week or two. Ford Evans lasted half a season and won more than he lost. His Cleveland team was 42–40 under his direction, but that was the extent of his managerial career.

Year	Team	Record	Pct.	Standing
1882	Cleve (N)	42–40	.512	Fifth

John Joseph Evers

Born July 21, 1881, Troy, New York; died March 28, 1947, Albany, New York; Chicago Cubs 1913, 1921; Chicago White Sox, 1924

Johnny Evers was a solid second baseman for the Chicago Cubs during their glory years in the early 1900s. He played on Cub pennant winners in 1906, 1907 and 1908 and was Chicago's player-manager in 1913, succeeding the great Frank Chance. The Cubs finished third that year and Evers was traded to Boston, where he helped the "Miracle Braves" of 1914 win the pennant and beat Connie Mack's Philadelphia Athletics in the World Series. Evers also managed the White Sox in 1921 and 1924.

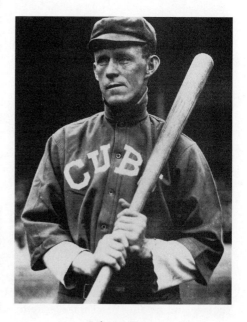

He did well managing a good Cubs team, but his White Sox teams were reeling from the scandal of 1919 and the subsequent banishment of eight star players for their alleged roles in conspiring with gamblers to fix the 1919 World Series.

Evers said his biggest problem as a manager was that he always wanted to be on the field, in the middle of the action. He said he admired how Pittsburgh manager Fred Clarke could stay in the dugout just sitting and watching the action. Evers eventually went back to playing full-time, retiring in 1929 — five years after he had finished managing.

Johnny Evers

There is ample evidence that Evers was a thinker on the field. In 1908, he instigated the controversial events that would secure Fred Merkle's unenviable place in baseball history. In a late-season game between the Cubs and Giants, New York had two runners on base in the ninth inning of a tie game. On a base hit, the apparent winning run scored. Merkle, a rookie who'd just come through with a big hit, started for second base. When he saw the ball go through to the outfield and the winning run score, he turned and headed for the clubhouse. Evers quickly called for the ball — which some say had been thrown into the stands and lost — ran over and touched second base for a force out of Merkle. The ball, Evers claimed, was live, the force play at second still in order; no run may score, he reminded the umps, on a forced third out. The game ended in a tie, called because of darkness. When it was replayed later, the Cubs won the game and the pennant.

Perhaps Evers is best remembered for the Franklin P. Adams poem "Baseball's Sad Lexicon," which lauds the Cubs double-play combination of Tinker to Evers to Chance.

Year	Team	Record	Pct.	Standing
1913	Chi (N)	88–65	.575	Third
1921	Chi (A)	42–56	.529	Seventh
1924	Chi (A)	66–87	.431	Eighth
3 years		196–208	.485	

William "Buck" Ewing

Born October 17, 1859, Hoaglands, Ohio; died October 20, 1906, Cincinnati, Ohio; New York Giants, 1890; Cincinnati Reds, 1895–1899; New York Giants, 1900

Buck Ewing has been described as the best all-around player of the 19th century. He was primarily a catcher but played many other positions and played them all well. He was the team captain of a New York Giants team that won consecutive championships in 1888 and 1889. He managed the Giants in 1890. From 1895 to 1899, he managed his hometown Cincinnati ball club and then managed the Giants again for part of the 1900 season. Ewing was well known for not letting all of his fame and glory go to his head. One sportswriter wrote of how well he handled the "the platitudes of the multitudes." As a manager, Ewing was intense but not overbearing, choosing instead to point out players' mistakes good naturedly. He died of Bright's Disease in 1906 at the age of 45.

Year	Team	Record	Pct.	Standing
1890	NY (P)	74–57	.565	Third
1895	Cin	66–64	.508	Eighth
1896	Cin	77–50	.606	Fifth
1897	Cin	76–56	.576	Fourth
1898	Cin	92–60	.605	Third
1899	Cin	83–67	.553	Sixth
1900	NY (N)	21–41	.339	Eighth
7 years		489–395	.553	

Jayson S. Faatz

Born October 24, 1860, Weedsport, New York; died April 10, 1923, Syracuse, New York; Cleveland Infants, 1890

Buck Ewing and Jayson Faatz made their managerial debuts in the same league, the Players League, in the same year, 1890, Ewing with New York, Faatz with Cleveland. While Ewing went on to a successful seven-year managerial career, Faatz lasted just 25 games with Cleveland, winning only 10 of them.

Year	Team	Record	Pct.	Standing
1890	Cleve (P)	10–25	.286	Seventh

Bibb August Falk

Born January 27, 1899, Austin, Texas; died June 8, 1989, Austin, Texas; Cleveland Indians, June 10, 1933

Bibb Falk filled in for the Cleveland Indians in 1933 after Roger Peckinpaugh was fired and before Walter Johnson had arrived from his farm to take over the ball club. Two years earlier, he retired after 12 years as a major league outfielder, most of those years with the Indians. Falk won the only game he managed.

Year	Team	Record	Pct.	Standing
1933	Cleve	1–0	1.000	Fifth

William James "Jim" Fanning

Born September 14, 1927, Chicago, Illinois; Montreal Expos, September 8, 1981–October 3, 1982; August 30, 1984–November 14, 1984

Jim Fanning was a second-string catcher for the Chicago Cubs in the 1950s who saw action in only 64 major league games. After retiring as a player, he joined the Montreal Expos organization and eventually served as coach, manager and general manager. He managed the Expos during one of their most unusual and exciting seasons. Fanning took over for Dick Williams in the second half of the strike-shortened 1981 season. The decision was made to split the season and to have the winners of each half-season engage in divisional playoffs to determine who would be in the league championship series. The Phillies won the first-half championship in the Eastern Division. In the second half, the Expos were 14–12 when Fanning took over. He guided them to a 16–11 finish, and that was good enough to move them into first place. Then the surprising Expos beat the Phillies in the divisional playoff but lost to the Dodgers, three games to two, in the league championship series. That is as close as the Expos have ever come to winning a championship. In 1982, the Expos slipped to third place and Fanning was removed in favor of Bill Virdon. Virdon lasted until the last month of the 1984, when Fanning took over for the last 30 games, strictly on an interim basis.

Year	Team	Record	Pct.	Standing
1981	Mont	16–11	.593	First
1982	Mont	86–76	.531	Third
1984	Mont	14–16	.467	Fifth
3 years		**116–103**	**.530**	

DIVISIONAL PLAYOFF SERIES

Year	Team	Record
1981	Mont	3–2

LEAGUE CHAMPIONSHIP SERIES

Year	Team	Record
1981	Mont	2–3

John A. Farrell

Born July 5, 1857, Newark, New Jersey; died February 10, 1914, Overbrook, New Jersey; Providence Grays, 1881

Jack Farrell was one of the many 19th century players who was called on to manage for a short period. For Farrell, it was while he was playing for Providence in the National League. Had he won two more games, his lifetime managerial record — for 51 games — would have shown more wins than losses.

Year	Team	Record	Pct.	Standing
1881	Prov	24–27	.471	Fourth

Major Kerby Farrell

Born September 3, 1913, Leapwood, Tennessee; died December 17, 1975, Nashville, Tennessee; Cleveland Indians, September 30, 1956–September 27, 1957

If anyone had a tough act to follow, it was Kerby Farrell. Al Lopez had managed the Indians for six years and had one pennant and five second-place finishes when he left to manage the Chicago White Sox. Lopez had averaged 95 wins with the Indians. On May 10, 1957, a tragic injury set the tone for the rest of Farrell's one season with the Indians. Star pitcher Herb Score, who was 16–10 in his rookie year in 1955 and 20–9 in 1956, was struck in the eye by a line drive hit by the Yankees' Gil McDougald. Score was out for the year and never regained the form that had made him one of the American League's best southpaws. As for the Indians, they missed those 20 potential wins from Score and finished sixth. Farrell was fired at the end of the season and never managed again.

Year	Team	Record	Pct.	Standing
1957	Cleve	76–77	.497	Sixth

John Felske

Born May 30, 1942, Chicago, Illinois; Philadelphia Phillies, September 30, 1984–June 18, 1987

John Felske had three up-and-down years as manager of the Philadelphia Phillies. They improved from a fifth-place finish in his first year to a second-place finish in 1986. In 1987, with the team nine games below .500 after the first third of the season, Felske was replaced.

Year	Team	Record	Pct.	Standing
1985	Phil	75–87	.463	Fifth
1986	Phil	86–75	.534	Second
1987	Phil	29–32	.475	Fifth
3 years		**190–194**	**.495**	

Robert B. Ferguson

Born January 31, 1845, Brooklyn, New York; died May 3, 1894, Brooklyn; New York Mutuals, 1871; Brooklyn Atlantics, 1872–1874; Hartford Dark Blues, 1876–1877; Chicago White Stockings, 1878; Troy Trojans, 1879–1882; Philadelphia Phillies, 1883; Pittsburgh Alleghenys, 1884; New York Metropolitans, 1886–1887

Bob Ferguson was known as a smart manager but also an intense man who was often hard to get along with. He managed six teams in parts of 11 seasons, but in four of those seasons, he managed in 30 games or less. When he took the field with his Hartford team in 1876, he helped inaugurate National League baseball and had his best season. Ferguson won more than twice as many as he lost that year, and still finished only third.

Year	Team	Record	Pct.	Standing
1871	NY	16–17	.485	Fourth
1872	Brklyn	9–28	.243	Sixth
1873	Brklyn	17–37	.315	Sixth
1874	Brklyn	22–33	.400	Sixth
1876	Hart	47–21	.691	Third
1877	Hart	31–27	.534	Third
1878	Chi (N)	30–30	.500	Fourth
1879	Troy	7–10	.412	Eighth
1880	Troy	41–42	.494	Fourth
1881	Troy	39–45	.464	Fifth
1882	Troy	35–48	.422	Seventh
1883	Phil (N)	4–13	.235	Eighth
1884	Pitt (AA)	5–21	.192	Fifth
1886	NY (AA)	47–70	.402	Seventh
1887	NY	6–24	.200	Seventh
15 years		**417–516**	**.447**	

Mike Ferraro

Born August 14, 1944, Kingston, New York; Cleveland Indians, November 4, 1982–July 29, 1983; Kansas City Royals, July 18, 1986–September 30, 1986

Mike Ferraro became manager of the Cleveland Indians at a time when the team was one of the American League's perpetual losers. He took over for Dave Garcia, and came from the Yankees where he had been a successful third base coach except for one unfortunate incident in the 1980 playoffs. Ferraro waved Willie Randolph home and Randolph was thrown out at the plate as a result of two perfect Kansas City throws. It was a crucial play in a game the Royals eventually won, and Yankee owner George Steinbrenner publicly berated his coach. When Ferraro took over the Cleveland job, it was hoped the Yankee winning tradition would rub off on the Indians. It didn't. Ferraro was fired after 100 games. He resurfaced two years later as an interim manager for the Royals.

Year	Team	Record	Pct.	Standing
1983	Cleve	40–60	.400	Seventh
1986	KC	46–38	.497	Third

Wallace Fessenden

No biographical data available; Syracuse Stars, 1890

Not much information is available on Wallace Fessenden, who managed the 1890 Syracuse ball club that lost seven of 11 games under his direction.

Year	Team	Record	Pct.	Standing
1890	Syr (AA)	4–7	.364	Seventh

Frederick Landis Fitzsimmons

Born July 28, 1901, Mishawauka, Indiana; died November 18, 1979, Yucca Valley, California; Philadelphia Phillies, July 28, 1943–June 29, 1945

Freddie Fitzsimmons was a highly successful major league pitcher, winning 217 games with the New York Giants and Brooklyn Dodgers. At age 42, he was 3–4 with the Dodgers in 1943 when he was hired to replace Bucky Harris as manager of the Philadelphia Phillies. In making the move, he went from one of baseball's best teams to one of its worst. And that wasn't the worst of it. Phillie players, upset that Harris was fired, threatened to go on strike. Harris went into their locker room the day after he was let go and pursuaded them to take the field. That's how Fitzsimmons' tenure began with the Phillies. It ended three years later after a seventh place finish, an eighth place finish and a 17–50 start to the 1945 season. Fitzsimmons made a major contribution to a winning team 10 years later when he was Leo Durocher's pitching coach with the great Giant teams of the early 1950s. Durocher was well aware of Fitzsimmons' knowledge of pitching; he had hurled his way to a 16–2 record for Durocher's 1940 Dodgers.

Year	Team	Record	Pct.	Standing
1943	Phil (N)	24–37	.393	Seventh
1944	Phil	61–92	.399	Eighth
1945	Phil	17–50	.254	Eighth
3 years		**102–179**	**.363**	

Arthur Fletcher

Born January 5, 1885, Collinsville, Illinois; died February 6, 1950, Los Angeles California; Philadelphia Phillies, 1923–September 16, 1926; New York Yankees, September 25, 1929–October 23, 1929

Art Fletcher began his major league managing career with the Philadelphia Phillies and won fewer than 60 games in three of his four seasons there. He was fired after the 1926 season. His only other managerial stint was with the New York Yankees after the death of Miller Huggins in 1929. Under his direction, the Yankees won six, lost five and finished in second place.

With the hapless Phillies, Fletcher's personality was totally different on the field from off it. He was known as a soft-spoken, kind man — until he put on the uniform. As manager of the Phillies, he tried to ignite the club's spirit by showing them a fighting spirit of his own. The result? Fletcher, thrown out of many games, was eventually suspended by league president John Heydler. And the Phillies continued to lose.

When he left Philadelphia, he was offered managerial jobs by several other clubs and turned them all down. He agreed to fill in as Yankees manager after Huggins died but turned down an offer to manage them full-time. He remained for many years as a Yankee coach but never wanted to manage again after his four long years with Philadelphia.

Year	Team	Record	Pct.	Standing
1923	Phil (N)	50–104	.325	Eighth
1924	Phil	55–96	.364	Seventh
1925	Phil	68–85	.444	Sixth
1926	Phil	58–93	.384	Eighth
1929	NY (A)	6–5	.545	Second
5 years		**237–383**		

Frank Sylvester "Silver" Flint

Born August 3, 1855, Philadelphia, Pennsylvania; died January 14, 1892, Chicago, Illinois; Chicago White Stockings, 1879

Silver Flint was a catcher for the Chicago White Stockings during the earliest days of the National League and won four out of nine games in his brief stints as a player-manager in 1879. His tenure was unusual because he managed during two different parts of the year. In his debut, he was 1–0 in an interim role. Later, again the interim manager, he was 3–5.

Year	Team	Record	Pct.	Standing
1879	Chi (N)	4–5	.444	Fourth

James G. Fogarty

Born February 12, 1864, San Francisco, California; died May 20, 1891, Philadelphia, Pennsylvania; Philadelphia Athletics, 1890

Jim Fogarty had been an outfielder, one of the greatest defensive players of the 19th century. He played for Philadelphia in the National League and then jumped to the Players League in 1890 where, at age 26, he became player-manager. But Fogarty became angry at the interference of club president H.M. Love, who berated the players with language Fogarty thought was objectionable. He filed a grievance with the team's board of directors, demanding a formal apology from Love. The board formed a committee to investigate the matter, but Fogarty resigned. The next year, he agreed to manage Philadelphia of the National League but became ill before the season started and died of tuberculosis at the age of 27.

Year	Team	Record	Pct.	Standing
1890	Phil (P)	30–19	.612	Fifth

Horace S. Fogel

Born March 2, 1861, Macungie, Pennsylvania; died November 15, 1928, Philadelphia, Pennsylvania; Indianapolis Hoosiers, 1887; New York Giants, 1902

Horace Fogel was a Philadelphia sportswriter who never played major league baseball but managed two different teams and eventually owned the Philadelphia Phillies. His antics as an owner tarnished the reputations of at least two Hall of Fame managers and eventually led to his expulsion from the game.

Fogel managed the Indianapolis franchise in 1887 but could win only 20 of 69 games. Fifteen years later, the New York Giants hired him — and then fired him after 42 games.

One of the managers who followed him was John McGraw, who became one of the greatest managers of all time. In 1909, Fogel, who had gone back to sportswriting, was the major partner in a group that bought the Philadelphia Phillies for $350,000. In 1912, Fogel accused St. Louis manager Roger Bresnahan and his Cardinals of "taking it easy" in games against McGraw's Giants. (Bresnahan was a former Giant catcher and a friend of McGraw's.) Later, Fogel alleged that some National League umpires had also conspired to have the Giants win the pennant. After an investigation, Fogel's accusations were found to be without merit and he was banned from the National League for life. But the scandal had an effect on Bresnahan. He was fired by the Cardinals and replaced by a St. Louis infielder who began a Hall of Fame career as a manager. The new skipper was Miller Huggins.

Year	Team	Record	Pct.	Standing
1887	Ind (N)	20–49	.290	Eighth
1902	NY (N)	18–23	.439	Fourth
2 years		**38–72**	**.345**	

Leo Alexander "Lee" Fohl

Born November 28, 1876, Lowell, Ohio; died October 30, 1965, Cleveland Ohio; Cleveland Indians, 1915–1919; St. Louis Browns, 1921–1923; Boston Red Sox, 1924–1926

Lee Fohl, an ex-catcher, joined the Cleveland Naps as a coach in 1914. He was named manager in 1915, the same year that the Indians' popular star, Nap Lajoie, was sent to Philadelphia. (The "Naps" nickname was in honor of Lajoie. After he left, the club was renamed the Indians.) That same year, another star, Joe Jackson, was sold to the White Sox. So Fohl took over but did not have the two best players from the previous year. Nonetheless, Fohl moved the Indians up from eighth to seventh place in his first year. In 1916, the Indians acquired the great outfielder Tris Speaker. He and Fohl had a strong relationship, and Fohl's managerial style with the Indians involved Speaker directly. The two, who talked strategy before and after games, would exchange signals when Fohl was in the dugout and Speaker was in center field. Speaker was a great hitter and Fohl, the old catcher, had been known as a good handler of pitchers.

When several star Indian players returned from World War I, the team, league doormat for years, was expected to contend for the 1919 American League pennant. But things took a fateful turn — for Fohl, at least — on July 18, 1919, when the Indians played the Boston Red Sox in Cleveland. The home team had taken a 7–3 lead late into the game. In the top of the ninth, however, the Red Sox scored a run and loaded the bases with two out and Babe Ruth coming to bat. Fohl signaled Speaker from the dugout. Bring in a right-hander, Speaker signed. But Fohl brought in left-hander Fritz Coombe. Ruth hit a grand-slam home run. Boston won, 8–7. After the game, a dejected Fohl resigned and Speaker was named to replace him as manager. Under Speaker, the Indians won the pennant the following year. Had they won it in 1919, baseball's greatest scandal would have been prevented. Instead, Black Sox (née White Sox) conspired with gamblers to hand the World Series to Cincinnati in exchange for a grand payout.

In 1921, Fohl began a three-year stint as manager of the St. Louis Browns — and the Browns had three consecutive winning seasons. Then he finished his managerial career with three losing seasons with poor Red Sox ball clubs that won only 160 and lost 299 —

an average of about 100 losses a year. His 1924 club finished seventh — the last Red Sox team in the 1920s to finish out of the cellar. His tenure with the Red Sox cost him the distinction of a career winning percentage above .500.

Year	Team	Record	Pct.	Standing
1915	Cleve	45–79	.363	Seventh
1916	Cleve	77–77	.500	Sixth
1917	Cleve	88–66	.571	Third
1918	Cleve	73–54	.575	Second
1919	Cleve	45–34	.570	Second
1921	StL (A)	81–73	.526	Third
1922	StL	93–61	.604	Second
1923	StL	51–49	.510	Fifth
1924	Bos (A)	67–87	.435	Seventh
1925	Bos (A)	47–105	.309	Eighth
1926	Bos	46–107	.301	Eighth
11 years		**713–792**	**.474**	

Lewis Albert Fonseca

Born January 21, 1899, Oakland, California; died November 26, 1989, Ely, Iowa; Chicago White Sox, October 27, 1931–May 8, 1934

Lew Fonseca had a lifetime batting average of .316 in a 12-season career with Cincinnati, Philadelphia, Cleveland and the Chicago White Sox. He came to the White Sox in 1931 and was player-manager in 1932 and 1933, though he played sparingly. He took over a team that had finished eighth in 1931. Though the White Sox won only 49 games in 1932, they managed to finish seventh, ahead of the hapless Boston Red Sox. They climbed to sixth place in 1933 but started horribly in 1934. Fonseca was fired after the White Sox won only four of their first 17 games.

Lew Fonseca

Year	Team	Record	Pct.	Standing
1932	Chi (A)	49–102	.325	Seventh
1933	Chi	67–83	.447	Sixth
1934	Chi	4–13	.235	Eighth
3 years		**120–198**	**.377**	

David Luther Foutz

Born September 7, 1856, Carroll County, Maryland; died March 5, 1897, Waverly, Maryland; Brooklyn Dodgers, 1893–1896

Dave Foutz was ill much of the time he managed Brooklyn and often was manager in name only, leaving the on-the-field duties to others. He was fired after his fourth season and died six months later.

Year	Team	Record	Pct.	Standing
1893	Brklyn	65–63	.508	Sixth
1894	Brklyn	70–61	.534	Fifth
1895	Brklyn	71–60	.542	Fifth
1896	Brklyn	58–73	.443	Ninth
4 years		**264–257**	**.507**	

Charles Francis Fox

Born October 7, 1921, New York, New York; San Francisco Giants, May 23, 1970–June 27, 1974; Montreal Expos, September 3, 1976–October 5, 1976; Chicago Cubs, August 22, 1983–October 6, 1983

Charlie Fox took over a San Francisco Giant team in fifth place in 1970, guided the Giants to 67–51 mark the rest of the way as San Francisco finished third. The following year, Fox's first full season as a major league manager, the Giants won the Western Division championship with a team that featured four future Hall of Famers: Willie Mays, Willie McCovey, Juan Marichal and Gaylord Perry. The Giants lost to Pittsburgh in the playoffs. Fox managed six more years, including stints as interim managers with the Montreal Expos and Chicago Cubs. After 1971, his teams never finished higher than third.

His career as a player amounted to three games as a catcher for the New York Giants in 1942. He got up seven times and had three hits.

Year	Team	Record	Pct.	Standing
1970	SF	67–51	.568	Third
1971	SF	90–72	.556	First
1972	SF	69–86	.445	Fifth
1973	SF	88–74	.543	Third
1974	SF	34–42	.447	Fifth
1976	Mont	12–22	.353	Sixth
1983	Chi (N)	17–22	.436	Fifth
7 years		**377–369**	**.505**	

LEAGUE CHAMPIONSHIP SERIES

Year	Team	Record
1971	SF	1–3

Terry Francona

Born April 22, 1959, Aliquippa, Pennsylvania; Philadelphia Phillies, October 30, 1996–October 12, 2000

Terry Francona, son of major league outfielder Tito Francona, had a 10-year big league career himself, playing for Montreal, Chicago Cubs, Cincinnati, Cleveland and Milwaukee. As manager, Francona demonstrated a distaste for substitution, often foregoing late-inning defensive replacement and allowing his starting pitchers to work beyond the 120-pitch mark. After four straight seasons of sub-.500 baseball, he was fired by the Philadelphia Phillies.

Year	Team	Record	Pct.	Standing
1997	Phil	68–94	.420	Fifth
1998	Phil	75–87	.463	Third
1999	Phil	77–85	.475	Fifth
2000	Phil	65–97	.401	Fifth
4 years		**285–363**	**.440**	

Herman Louis Franks

Born January 4, 1914, Price, Utah; San Francisco Giants, October 4, 1964–October 11, 1968; Chicago Cubs, November 24, 1976–September 24, 1979

Herman Franks had his greatest success managing the San Francisco Giants to four consecutive second-place finishes, behind the Los Angeles Dodgers twice and St. Louis Cardinals twice between 1965 and 1968. But it was as manager of the Chicago Cubs that Franks made a strategy move that changed the way the game is played.

Franks had the best relief pitcher in the major leagues, Bruce Sutter, whose bread and butter pitch was the "split-finger fastball." (Years later, Elroy Face, the Pirate ace relief pitcher in the 1950s and '60s was asked the difference between his fork ball and the split-finger fastball. "About $3 million," he said.) Franks had the kind of team with the Cubs in which a relief pitcher was used often. In 1977, Sutter pitched in 62 games, had a 1.35 earned run average, a 7–3 record and 31 saves. In 1978, he appeared in 64 games, had an 8–10 record, 27 saves and an earned run average that had climbed to 3.18. Franks came to the conclusion that he was pitching Sutter too often. Statistics showed that the pitcher was less effective in the second half of the season than in the first half— but that he was almost always effective when he was first brought in to a ball game. So Franks decided to use Sutter only when one or two outs would save a ball game (though "save" had been coined years before, "save situation" was still a scenario recognized by only the baseball cognoscenti.) The result was that Sutter returned to form in 1979 with a league-leading 37 saves and a 2.23 earned run average to go with a 6–6 record. Nearly every successful major league manager since 1979 reserved his best relief pitcher for save situations — the practice started by Franks with Sutter. The irony is that Franks didn't last the season with the Cubs and never managed again in the major leagues.

Year	Team	Record	Pct.	Standing
1965	SF	95–67	.586	Second
1966	SF	93–68	.568	Second
1967	SF	91–71	.562	Second
1968	SF	88–74	.543	Second
1977	Chi (N)	81–81	.500	Fourth
1978	Chi	79–83	.488	Third
1979	Chi	78–77	.503	Fifth
7 years		**605–521**	**.537**	

George Kasson Frazer

Born January 7, 1861, Syracuse, New York; died February 13, 1913, Philadelphia, Pennsylvania; Syracuse Stars, 1890

Like so many of his contemporaries before the 20th century, George Frazer got one shot at managing. His came with the American Association Syracuse Stars in 1890 and lasted most of one season in which Syracuse was only able to win 55 of 127 games.

Year	Team	Record	Pct.	Standing
1890	Syr	55–72	.433	Sixth

Joseph Filmore Frazier

Born October 6, 1922, Liberty, North Carolina; New York Mets, October 3, 1975–May 31, 1977

Joe Frazier became manager of the New York Mets at a time when the ball club was trying to regroup after the Yogi Berra era. Berra had won a pennant with the club in 1973 but was fired when the Mets were struggling at 56–53 midway through the 1975 season. Roy McMillan took over the club and finished at 26–27 (82–80 for the year.) That wasn't good enough and coach Joe Frazier got his chance. Frazier, who played in 217 major league games as an outfielder, had a good run in 1976 as Jerry Koosman won 21 games and Jon Matlack won 17. But ace Tom Seaver slipped to 14–11, and the Mets finished third behind Philadelphia and Pittsburgh. In 1977, the Mets got off to a disastrous start, losing 30 of their first 45 games. Frazier was replaced by Joe Torre and never managed again in the major leagues.

Year	Team	Record	Pct.	Standing
1976	NY (N)	86–76	.531	Third
1977	NY (N)	15–30	.333	Sixth
2 years		**101–106**	**.488**	

James Louis Fregosi

Born April 4, 1942, San Francisco, California; California Angels, June 1, 1978–May 28, 1981; Chicago White Sox, June 22, 1986–October 7, 1988; Philadelphia Phillies, April 23, 1991–September 30, 1996; Toronto Blue Jays, March 19, 1999–October 10, 2000

Jim Fregosi is a journeyman major league manager who took the helm of his fourth team when he became the skipper of the Toronto Blue Jays in 1999. In his playing days, he was a six-time All-Star third baseman for the Los Angeles and California Angels and was involved in one of baseball's most famous trades. He was the key man in a trade on December 10, 1971, that sent him to the New York Mets for four young players: catcher Francisco Estrada, outfielder Leroy Stanton, pitcher Don Rose and a fireballing young right-handed pitcher named Nolan Ryan. Fregosi played one year with the Mets and was a fringe player for several teams for the next few years. Ryan went on to a Hall of Fame career with the Angels, Houston Astros and Texas Rangers. Eight years after the big trade, Fregosi, in his first full season as manager of the Angels, guided them to the Western Division championship in the American League. One of his top pitchers was the veteran Ryan, who won 16 games and led the league in strikeouts with 223. The Angels lost to Baltimore, three games to one, in the playoffs. Fregosi had replaced Dave Garcia as manager on June 1, 1978, and compiled a 62–54 record as the Angels finished second. Then came the division title in 1979.

He succeeded Tony LaRussa as manager of the Chicago White Sox on June 22, 1986, but could not move them above the .500 level in three seasons. He was released after the 1988 season and hired by the Phillies to take over for Nick Leyva in April of 1991.

In 1993, Fregosi's Phillies were in the World Series. They lost to the Toronto Blue Jays, who won on Joe Carter's game-winning homer off reliever Mitch Williams.

Early in his managerial career, Fregosi platooned frequently. And he made frequent substitutions on his 1993 Phillie championship team. By contrast, in 1996, though he tinkered with the starting lineup frequently, he took more the *laizzez-faire* approach once the game started. Bill James, in his *The Bill James Guide to Baseball Managers*, reads this radical change in Frogosi's maneuvering — his defensive substitutions went from a league high 73 in 1993 to a league low 6 in 1996 — as manifest lost confidence in his reserves. So this doesn't reflect a change in style so much as a change in the depth of the ball club. The 1993 team won 97, the 1996 team won 67. One sign of a durable manager is the accounting for talent in developing team strategy — the season-by-season accounting of the manager's stocklist of moves and countermoves. Fregosi has proven his adaptability over the years.

Fregosi once summed up his managerial philosophy this way: "Me and my owners think exactly alike. Whatever they're thinking, that's what I think."

Year	Team	Record	Pct.	Standing
1978	Cal	62–55	.530	Second
1979	Cal	88–74	.543	First
1980	Cal	65–95	.406	Sixth
1981	Cal	22–25	.468	Fourth
1986	Chi (N)	45–51	.469	Fifth
1987	Chi	77–85	.475	Fifth
1988	Chi	71–90	.441	Fifth
1991	Phil	74–75	.490	Third
1992	Phil	70–92	.430	Sixth
1993	Phil	97–65	.590	First
1994	Phil	54–61	.460	Third
1995	Phil	69–75	.470	Third
1996	Phil	67–95	.410	Fifth
1999	Tor	84–78	.510	Third
2000	Tor	83–79	.512	Third
15 years		**1028–1095**	**.484**	

LEAGUE CHAMPIONSHIP SERIES

Year	Team	Record
1979	California	1–3
1993	Phil	4–2

WORLD SERIES

Year	Team	Record
1993	Phil	2–4

James Gottfried Frey

Born May 26, 1931, Cleveland, Ohio; Kansas City Royals, October 24, 1979–August 31, 1981; Chicago Cubs, October 6, 1983–June 12, 1986

Not many managers get the chance to be the man of the moment, the man who comes into a situation and is exactly the right fit. It happened twice in Jim Frey's managerial career — and he managed only five seasons.

Frey, who never played in the major leagues, took the reins of the Kansas City Royals in 1980 and guided them to the American League championship. The Royals lost the World Series to the Philadelphia Phillies, four games to two. Then in 1984, Dallas Green hired Frey to manage the Chicago Cubs. Green had been the general manager of the 1980 Phillies team. When he took a similar position with the Cubs, he traded for several Phillie players, including left fielder Gary Mathews, center fielder Bob Dernier, shortstop Larry Bowa, and young, unproven infielder (he was not yet settled at second) Ryne Snadberg. The Cubs also acquired veteran third baseman Ron Cey from the Dodgers and, in mid-season, right-hander Rick Sutcliffe from the Cleveland Indians. Sutcliffe went 16–1 with the Cubs, who won the Eastern Division championship.

So Frey had the distinction for winning championships his first year with a team in each league. The Cubs won the first two games of the league championship series at Wrigley Field but then lost three in a row to the Padres at San Diego, missing their best chance at a World Series appearance since 1945.

Frey had the reputation of being a good handler of pitchers. At Kansas City, he inherited Whitey Herzog's second-place team of 1979 and led them to the championship in 1980 with a staff anchored by Larry Gura (18–10), Dennis Leonard (20–11), Paul Splittorf (14–11) and Rich Gale (13–9). Dan Quisenberry appeared in 75 games, winning 12 and saving 33. Frey also had Hall of Fame third baseman George Brett, who hit .390. Frey was asked if he gave Brett any batting tips that year. Frey replied, "I said, 'Atta boy, George.'"

The 1984 Cubs had a pitching staff that included Sutcliffe (16–1), Steve Trout (13–7), Dennis Eckersley (10–8) and Scott Sanderson (8–5). Lee Smith had 33 saves and nine wins in 69 appearances. In later years, Eckersley became one of baseball's great relief pitchers but he was starter with the '84 Cubs.

A manager's stability is dependent not only on the ability of his players but also their health. In 1985, all four Chicago starting pitchers went on the disabled list. The Cubs finished fourth, winning 19 fewer games than they did in 1984. Frey was fired 56 games into the 1986 season with the Cubs headed for yet another down year.

Year	Team	Record	Pct.	Standing
1980	KC	97–65	.590	First
1981	KC	20–30	.400	Fifth
1981	KC	10–10	.500	First
1984	Chi (N)	96–65	.590	First
1985	Chi	77–84	.470	Fourth
1986	Chi	23–33	.410	Fifth
5 years		**323–287**	**.530**	

LEAGUE CHAMPIONSHIP SERIES

Year	Team	Record
1980	KC	3–0
1984	Chi	2–3
2 years		**5–3**

WORLD SERIES

Year	Team	Record
1980	KC	2–4

Frank Francis Frisch

Born September 9, 1898, Queens, New York; died March 12, 1973, Wilmington, Delaware; St. Louis Cardinals, July 24, 1933–September 10, 1938; Pittsburgh Pirates, October 3, 1939–September 27, 1946; Chicago Cubs, June 10, 1949–July 22, 1951

Frankie Frisch was a disciple of John McGraw but managed like him only in intensity. McGraw liked to develop young ballplayers: Frisch, particularly in his later years, didn't like inexperienced players. McGraw's early teams bunted often. Frisch's teams hardly ever bunted and twice led the league in fewest bunts. McGraw was a stern, humorless man on the field. Frisch was a prankster who liked to bait umpires. He once came out of the dugout holding an open umbrella — a hint to umpires that it was raining too hard to continue the game.

Frisch was the second baseman on McGraw's New York Giant dynasty that won pennants from 1921 through 1924. He later played on four St. Louis Cardinal championship teams including one he managed in 1934. Frisch was a member of and mentor to the famed Gas House Gang of the early 1930s that also included Dizzy and Paul Dean, Joe Medwick, Leo Durocher, and Pepper Martin. But Frisch's teams were more successful in folklore than

they were on the field: in six years the Cardinals won the pennant once, finished second twice, and fourth, fifth and sixth once each. He then managed seven years at Pittsburgh, finishing second once and no higher than fourth the rest of the time. His three Chicago Cub teams finished eighth twice and seventh once.

Frisch had a reputation for little patience with bad ball clubs. He was reportedly fired by Cubs owner Phil Wrigley when he was spotted reading a book in the dugout during a game.

In his autobiography, Frisch is candid about what it takes to be a good manager. "The ballplayers make the ball club and they make the manager," writes Frisch. No manager, he continues, is going to take an eighth place club and turn it around — which might explain how he lost interest in managing the Cubs. "A bad ball club is just that, no matter who is managing."

In Frisch's view, managers accept jobs not because they love the challenge but rather because they love to manage. And what they get in return are ulcers, inept front offices and too many bases on balls.

Frankie Frisch

When Frisch managed at Pittsburgh, he once let one of the regular box seat customers, a man who frequently ridiculed Frisch, help manage the ball club one day. The man and Frisch would trade signals back and forth and the customer took part in some of the decision making. The Pirates lost — not a surprising outcome no matter who was managing. After the game, Frisch approached the man and asked him what he did for a living. The man said he was a stockbroker. Frisch informed him that he and his coaches would be in the man's office the next day to tell him how to run his business.

Cub outfielder Frank Baumholtz said Frisch didn't like him and didn't play him. After Frisch left the Cubs, Baumholtz became the Cubs' regular center fielder and was a .300 hitter under Frisch's successor, Phil Cavarretta. Johnny Klippstein, a Cub pitcher, remembers Frisch leaving for the clubhouse before a game was over, saying, "I can't stand to watch minor league baseball." Third baseman Randy Jackson said he thought Frisch expected everyone to be as good as he was when he was playing. Frisch summed up a manager's life this way: "Have one good year and you can fool them for five more, because for five more years they expect you to have another good one."

Worth noting: Frisch's most successful years as a manager were when he was a playing manager, from 1933 to 1937.

Year	Team	Record	Pct.	Standing
1933	StL (N)	36–26	.581	Fifth
1934	StL	95–58	.621	First
1935	StL	96–58	.623	Second
1936	StL	87–67	.565	Second
1937	StL	81–73	.526	Fourth
1938	StL	62–72	.463	Sixth
1940	Pitt	78–76	.506	Fourth
1941	Pitt	81–73	.526	Fourth
1942	Pitt	66–81	.449	Fifth
1943	Pitt	80–74	.519	Fourth
1944	Pitt	90–63	.588	Second
1945	Pitt	82–72	.532	Fourth
1946	Pitt	62–89	.411	Seventh
1949	Chi (N)	42–62	.404	Eighth
1950	Chi	64–89	.418	Seventh
1951	Chi	35–45	.438	Seventh
16 years		**1137–1078**	**.513**	

WORLD SERIES

Year	Team	Record
1934	StL (N)	4–3

Emil Edwin Fuchs

Born April 17, 1878, New York, New York; died December 5, 1961, Boston, Massachusetts; Boston Braves, May 14, 1929–November 3, 1929

Emil Fuchs was an eccentric former New York City magistrate who purchased the Boston Braves in 1923 but knew little about baseball. For several years, Christy Mathewson was the team president.

Fuchs is remembered mainly for two decisions he made: 1) to sign Babe Ruth after the Yankees released him in 1934; 2) to step in and manage his team for a season. Fuchs reportedly led Ruth to believe that he would eventually be manager of the Braves, an apparent ruse to get him to sign. Fuchs knew Ruth would be a box-office attraction and he was right. But two months after the 1935 season started, Ruth retired. Fuchs tried managing after suffering through several years of watching others manage. The Braves finished last in 1923 under manager Frank Chance, last in 1924 under Dave Bancroft, fifth in 1925 under Bancroft, and seventh in 1926 and 1927 under Bancroft. In 1928, Fuchs hired Jack Slattery but fired him after the Braves won just 11 of their first 31 games and replaced him with Rogers Hornsby. Hornsby hit .387 as the Braves player-manager, but Boston finished with a 50–103 record and another seventh place finish.

Fuchs then installed himself as manager for the 1929 season but depended on coach Johnny Evers to make most of the decisions on the field. To everyone's surprise, the Braves got off to a 10–2 start but finished last with a 56–98 record. Bill McKechnie took over in 1930 and Boston moved up to sixth place, winning 70 games.

Year	Team	Record	Pct.	Standing
1929	Bos (N)	56–98	.364	Eighth

Charles John "Chick" Fulmer

Born February 12, 1851, Philadelphia, Pennsylvania; died February 15, 1940, Philadelphia; Louisville Grays, 1876

In the National League's first year, Chick Fulmer played shortstop and managed the Louisville club. Louisville finished fifth in the eight-team league with a 30–36 record and never managed again.

Year	Team	Record	Pct.	Standing
1876	Lou	30–36	.455	Fifth

Thomas Furniss

No biographical data available; Boston Reds, 1884

Tom Furniss had a managerial career that lasted 10 games with the Boston team in the fledgling Union League in 1884. He won four of the 10, but that was the end of his managerial career.

Year	Team	Record	Pct.	Standing
1884	Bos (U)	4–6	.400	Fifth

John H. Gaffney

Born June 29, 1855, Roxbury, Massachusetts; died August 8, 1913, New York, New York; Washington Statesmen, 1886–1887

John Gaffney was regarded as the greatest umpire of the 19th century. He umpired more games than anyone of his day and was the originator of many techniques used by future umpires. He was a good ballplayer as a youngster, but an arm injury he suffered while throwing a snowball stopped any chance of a professional career. He turned to umpiring and became one of the best. He interrupted his umpiring career briefly in 1886 and 1887 to manage the Washington Statesmen, a woefully bad team. They finished eighth his first year and seventh his second year. There was no third year. Gaffney was fired, giving him the opportunity to resume his umpiring career.

Year	Team	Record	Pct.	Standing
1886	Wash	15–26	.366	Eighth
1887	Wash	46–76	.377	Seventh
2 years		**61–192**	**.374**	

James Francis "Pud" Galvin

Born December 25, 1855, St. Louis, Missouri; died March 7, 1902, Pittsburgh, Pennsylvania; Buffalo Bisons, 1885

Pud Galvin won 361 games in a 14-year career as a pitcher, mostly with Buffalo and Pittsburgh before the 20th century. He started 682 games and completed 639 of them and had a lifetime earned run average of 2.87. In 1885, he was called on to manage Buffalo, a stint that lasted 30 games. Buffalo lost 22 of them. Galvin returned to the mound full-time and finished a career that landed him in the Hall of Fame.

Year	Team	Record	Pct.	Standing
1885	Buff	8–22	.267	Seventh

John Henry Ganzel

Born April 7, 1874, Kalamazoo, Michigan; died January 14, 1959, Orlando, Florida; Cincinnati Reds, 1908–January 15, 1909; Brooklyn Tiptops, 1915

Johnny Ganzel was a first baseman for the Cincinnati Reds when Ned Hanlon retired as manager. Owner Garry Hermann hired Ganzel to replace him but as a playing manager. Hermann had thought of Ganzel as only an interim manager, even though he hired him for the entire season. While Ganzel was bringing the Reds up one spot in the standings, from sixth to fifth, Hermann was working behind his back to find a successor. Ganzel was fired at the end of the season and was replaced by Clark Griffith. Ganzel resurfaced seven years later as manager of the Brooklyn team in the upstart Federal League but was gone after 35 games. He never managed again.

Year	Team	Record	Pct.	Standing
1908	Cin	73–81	.474	Fifth
1915	Brklyn (F)	17–18	.486	Seventh
2 years		**90–99**	**.476**	

David Garcia

Born September 15, 1920, East St. Louis, Missouri; California Angels, July 11, 1977–June 1, 1978; Cleveland Indians, July 23, 1979–October 4, 1982

Dave Garcia managed in 617 major league games with two teams over a six-year period. Had his teams won two more games, Garcia would have finished with a managerial won-loss percentage of over .500. He took over for Norm Sherry as manager of the California Angels in 1977 and did about as well as Sherry had done with them. The Angels finished fifth, 28 games behind league-leading Kansas City. In 1978, the Angels got off to a 25–20 start but Garcia was relieved of his duties and Jim Fregosi took over. Garcia hooked on with Cleveland in 1979 but could bring them home no higher than fifth in his four years there.

Year	Team	Record	Pct.	Standing
1977	Cal	35–46	.432	Fifth
1978	Cal	25–20	.556	Third
1979	Cleve	38–28	.576	Sixth
1980	Cleve	79–81	.494	Sixth
1981	Cleve	26–24	.520	Sixth
1981	Cleve	26–27	.491	Fifth
1982	Cleve	78–84	.481	Sixth
6 years		**307–310**	**.498**	

William Frederick Gardner

Born July 19, 1927, Waterford, Connecticut; Minnesota Twins, May 22, 1981–June 21, 1985; Kansas City Royals, February 23, 1987–August 27, 1987

Billy Gardner was a 10-year major league infielder who averaged four home runs a year and had a lifetime batting average of .237. He took over a woefully weak Minnesota Twins team in 1981 that had lost 25 of its first 36 games under John Goryl. That was a strike year, the year of the split season, and the Twins didn't do well in either half. Roy Smalley was their leading home run hitter with seven and Pete Redfern led the pitching staff with nine wins. Gardner stayed four years and the ball club made steady improvements. In 1984, Kirby Puckett's first and Gardner's last year, the Twins reached .500 and finished second in their division. The Twins featured, in addition to Puckett, hitters Kent Hrbek, Gary Gaetti and Tom Brunansky. Eighteen-game winner Frank Viola led the pitching staff. In three years, that would be the nucleus of the team that won the World Series championship, but by then Gardner was long gone.

Gardner played for Paul Richards and admired him greatly but he didn't follow his mentor's style of managing. Richards taught and stressed fundamentals and his teams moved players around the bases with bunts, hit-and-run plays, hitting behind the runners, sacrificing and other similar maneuvers.

A statistic that jumps out regarding Gardner's teams is that they bunted less often than most any other team in baseball, usually less than 30 times a year. One of the reasons for this difference in style can be attributed to the fact that Richards often had players such as Gardner, who were light hitting, and Gardner had players such as Hrbek, Gaetti, Puckett and Brunansky, who got the job done with power.

After leaving the Twins in 1985, Gardner was hired in 1987 to manage the Kansas City Royals. He was relieved of his duties late in the season with the Royals in second place but two games below .500 and with no chance of catching the Twins team that Gardner had nurtured just two years before.

Year	Team	Record	Pct.	Standing
1981	Minn	6–14	.300	Seventh
1981	Minn	24–29	.453	Fourth
1982	Minn	60–102	.370	Seventh
1983	Minn	70–92	.432	Fifth
1984	Minn	81–81	.500	Second

Year	Team	Record	Pct.	Standing
1985	Minn	27–35	.430	Fourth
1987	KC	62–64	.490	Second
6 years		**330–417**	**.441**	

Philip Mason Garner

Born April 30, 1949, Jefferson City, Tennessee; Milwaukee Brewers, October 31, 1991–August 11, 1999; Detroit Tigers, October 14, 1999–present

Phil Garner was a scrappy major league infielder for 16 years who was known as a tough competitor. He took over as manager of the Milwaukee Brewers in 1992 and guided them to a second place finish with 92 wins. In the next seven years, the Brewers never finished above .500 and never won more than 80 games. Garner was fired at the end of the 1999 season and was hired as manager of the Detroit Tigers for the 2000 season.

Early in his career, Garner was a manager who went with a set lineup, relying on his starters to get the job done. His teams used pinch hitters less than most other American League teams, but he used pinch runners and made late inning defensive changes as much or more than his American League counterparts.

Over time, Garner's use of starting pitchers grew more cautious, his moves more preemptive, and by 1998 he was second in the league for quick hooks. Garner had the unusual distinction of managing in both leagues without changing teams. In 1998, the Brewers were part of a realignment that shifted them from the American to the National League. The Brewers were expected to improve because they had moved out of the tough American League Central, dominated by the Cleveland Indians, and into the National League Central, where there was no dominant team. When the Brewers showed no improvement, Garner was replaced. He then served just more than two years with Detroit, losing his job six games into the 2002 season.

Year	Team	Record	Pct.	Standing
1992	Mil (A)	92–70	.560	Second
1993	Mil	69–93	.420	Seventh
1994	Mil	53–62	.460	Fifth
1995	Mil	65–79	.450	Fourth
1996	Mil	80–82	.490	Third
1997	Mil	78–83	.480	Third
1998	Mil	74–88	.450	Fifth
1999	Mil	74–87	.460	Fifth
2000	Det	79–83	.488	Third
2001	Det	66–96	.407	Fourth
2002	Det	0–6	.000	Fifth
10 years		**730–829**	**.468**	

Clarence Edwin "Cito" Gaston

Born March 17, 1944, San Antonio, Texas; Toronto Blue Jays, May 15, 1989–August 21, 1991; September 27, 1991–September 24, 1997

Cito Gaston is the winningest manager in Toronto Blue Jays history. Taking over for Jimy Williams in 1989, he directed the Blue Jays to the American League's Eastern Division championship, the first of four division championships the Blue Jays would win in Gaston's nine years as manager.

He was a major league outfielder for 12 years, most of them with the San Diego Padres. Gaston was a minor league hitting instructor for the Atlanta Braves in 1981 and then held the same position for the Blue Jays from 1982 until 1989. On May 15, 1989, he succeeded Williams as manager. The Blue Jays finished 77–49 to win the division but lost to Oakland in five games in the league championship series. In 1990, Gaston's first full season as manager, the Blue Jays finished second behind the Boston Red Sox. In 1991, the Blue Jays returned to the top but Gaston needed help from coach Gene Tenace, who was interim manager from August 21 to September 27, when Gaston was sidelined with back problems. Toronto lost to the Twins, four games to one, in the league championship series. The Blue Jays made it to their first World Series in 1992 and beat the Atlanta Braves, four games to two. In 1993, they were back in the World Series, this time beating the Philadelphia Phillies, four games to two, on Joe Carter's game-winning home run off of Mitch Williams.

Gaston was the first manager to win back-to-back World Series championships since Sparky Anderson accomplished it with Cincinnati in 1975-1976. The last American League manager to do it had been Dick Williams with Oakland in 1972-73. (Since then, Joe Torre has accomplished it with the New York Yankees.) The Blue Jays suffered their first losing year under Gaston in the strike-shortened 1994 season and struggled to reach .500 each of the next three years. Gaston was fired with five games left in the 1997 season.

Bill James, in his *The Bill James Guide to Baseball Managers*, calls Gaston "the most conservative, virtually inert manager in baseball." And, indeed, Gaston's style of managing was unique. He preferred a set lineup year after year and made few moves during a game compared to other managers in the league. Late-inning defensive substitutions were relatively infrequent, and his starting pitchers often worked past the sixth inning. His strategy was to put the best he had on the field every day and let them play, the philosophy of Jimmy Dykes a couple of generations earlier. Gaston's teams were traditionally among the lowest in the league in use of pinch hitters, pinch runners, and he seldom platooned to take advantage of the lefty-righty match-up. In 1996, he changed his lineup 87 times, Kansas City's Bob Boone changed the Royals lineup 152 times. Gaston used 23 pinch runners; Oakland's Art Howe used more than three times that many, 74.

Year	Team	Record	Pct.	Standing
1989	Tor	77–49	.610	First
1990	Tor	86–76	.530	Second
1991	Tor	72–53	.550	First
1992	Tor	96–66	.590	First
1993	Tor	95–67	.580	First
1994	Tor	55–60	.470	Fourth
1995	Tor	56–88	.380	Fifth
1996	Tor	74–88	.450	Fourth
1997	Tor	72–86	.450	Fifth
9 years		**683–637**	**.517**	

League Championship Series

Year	Team	Record
1989	Tor	1–4
1991	Tor	1–4
1992	Tor	4–2
1993	Tor	4–2
4 years		**10–12**

WORLD SERIES

Year	Team	Record
1992	Tor	4–2
1993	Tor	4–2
2 years		**8–4**

John Joseph Gerhardt

Born February 14, 1855, Washington, D.C.; died March 11, 1922, Middletown, New York; Louisville Eclipse, 1883–1884

Joe Gerhardt was a light-hitting, good-fielding second baseman who played in the earliest days of the National League. In 1883, he was named player-manager of the Louisville team but missed most of the season after being hit in the face with a pitch. Partial paralysis set in and there was concern whether he would ever play again. He returned as player-manager in 1884, but that season was marred by the illness and subsequent death of his infant child. He was replaced before season's end. He played several more years but never managed again.

Year	Team	Record	Pct.	Standing
1883	Lou	16–19	.457	Fourth
1884	Lou	39–18	.684	Third
2 years		**55–37**	**.598**	

Harry Homer "Doc" Gessler

Born December 23, 1880, Indiana, Pennsylvania; died December 26, 1924, Indiana; Pittsburgh Rebels, 1914

Doc Gessler managed the Pittsburgh team in the upstart Federal League — but not for long. He was gone after his team won only six of its first 18 games, and he never managed again. Pittsburgh finished seventh of eight teams.

Year	Team	Record	Pct.	Standing
1914	Pitt	6–12	.333	Seventh

George Gibson

Born July 22, 1880, London, Ontario, Canada; died January 25, 1967, London; Pittsburgh Pirates, February 14, 1920–1922; Chicago Cubs, September 3, 1925–September 30, 1925; Pittsburgh Pirates, November 30, 1931–June 19, 1934

George Gibson managed some good teams in his seven-year managerial career but could not put any of them over the top. In 1921, he guided the Pittsburgh Pirates to a second place finish but left when the Pirates got off to a sluggish start in the 1922 season. It was rumored that when Bill McKechnie was hired as a coach in 1921, it was done with the understanding that he would be the next manager if the Pirates slipped. They slipped from first place in the final weeks of the 1921 season. It was a heartbreaker for Gibson, and when the Pirates were 32–33 after 65 games in 1922, Gibson resigned and McKechnie replaced him. Under McKechnie, the Pirates were in the World Series by 1925.

The Cubs hired Gibson to mop up a horrible 1925 season in which they finished eighth. Gibson was their third manager that year. Chicago then hired Joe McCarthy for the 1926 season. By 1929, the Cubs had made it to the top. Gibson returned to the Pirates in 1932 and once again led the Pirates to two second place finishes. Once again, too, he was gone after the Bucs started slowly in the 1934 season.

Year	Team	Record	Pct.	Standing
1920	Pitt	79–75	.513	Fourth
1921	Pitt	90–63	.588	Second
1922	Pitt	32–33	.492	Fifth
1925	Chi (N)	12–14	.462	Eighth
1932	Pitt	86–68	.558	Second
1933	Pitt	87–67	.565	Second
1934	Pitt	27–24	.529	Fourth
7 years		**413–344**	**.546**	

James H. Gifford

Born October 18, 1845, Warren, New York; died December 19, 1901, Columbus, Ohio; Indianapolis Hoosiers, 1884; New York Metropolitans, 1885–1886

Jim Gifford managed parts of three years in the old American Association with less than impressive results. In his first year, he managed Indianapolis. His team was in eleventh place in a 12-team league with a 25–59 record when he was replaced. He turned up the next year with New York and came in seventh. When New York lost 12 of its first 18 games in his third year, Gifford was gone.

Year	Team	Record	Pct.	Standing
1884	Ind	25–59	.298	Eleventh
1885	NY (AA)	44–64	.407	Seventh
1886	NY	6–12	.333	Eighth
3 years		**75–135**	**.357**	

John Wesley Glasscock

Born July 22, 1859, Wheeling, West Virginia; died February 24, 1957, Wheeling; Indianapolis Hoosiers, 1889

Jack Glasscock took over an Indianapolis team that was buried in seventh place in 1889, 17 games below .500. Glasscock guided the team to a 34–33 record but could not get out of seventh place and was not given another chance to try. He was replaced at the end of the season.

Year	Team	Record	Pct.	Standing
1889	Ind	34–33	.507	Seventh

William J. "Kid" Gleason

Born October 26, 1866, Camden, New Jersey; died January 2, 1933, Philadelphia, Pennsylvania; Chicago White Sox, December 31, 1918–October 26, 1923

Kid Gleason will always be remembered as the manager of the 1919 White Sox, the team on which eight ballplayers were accused of conspiring with gamblers to fix the World

Series against the Cincinnati Reds. Long before that, Gleason won 138 games as a pitcher in the American Association before switching to second base and becoming one of the slickest-fielding second basemen of his time. He joined the White Sox as a coach in 1912 and became manager in 1919. The White Sox easily won the American League pennant and were heavy favorites to beat Cincinnati in the World Series. But several Chicago players were unhappy with White Sox owner Charles Comiskey for not paying them what they thought they were worth. So they were easy prey for Arnold Rothstein and other gamblers who offered them big money to throw the World Series. Pitcher Eddie Cicotte, a 29-game winner, Lefty Williams, who won 23 games, and first baseman Chick Gandil, shortstop Swede Risberg, third baseman Buck Weaver, center fielder Happy Felsch, left fielder Joe Jackson and utility infielder Fred McMullin were acquitted in court but were banned from baseball for life by commissioner Kenesaw Mountain Landis.

As the scandal was being uncovered in 1920, the White Sox won more games (96), than they had in 1919 (88), but Chicago finished second. By 1921, the eight players were banished and the White Sox nose-dived to seventh place. Gleason hung on for two more years. He then retired from baseball for two years but was lured out of retirement to coach Connie Mack's Philadelphia A's and help mold them into an American League power-house.

Gleason was fun-loving as both a player and manager. He got along well with his players and liked to keep his clubhouse loose. As a player, he was often the leading prankster on his team. As a manager, he enjoyed a good laugh as much as his players but could be earnest, giving respect as readily as he got it. During the 1919 season, in fact, he made a pitch to Comiskey to give the players the money they deserved. It was to no avail.

When Gleason died in 1933, among those attending his funeral were Landis, Mack and Giants manager John McGraw, who 30 years earlier had been a teammate.

Year	Team	Record	Pct.	Standing
1919	Chi (A)	88–52	.629	First
1920	Chi	96–58	.623	First
1921	Chi	62–92	.403	Seventh
1922	Chi	77–77	.500	Fifth
1923	Chi	69–85	.448	Seventh
5 years		**392–364**	**.519**	

Pedro Martinez "Preston" Gomez

Born April 20, 1923, Central Preston, Cuba; San Diego Padres, August 29, 1968–April 27, 1972; Houston Astros, October 1, 1973–August 19, 1975; Chicago Cubs, October 2, 1979–July 25, 1980

Preston Gomez's managerial career is proof that a manager is only as good as his players, no matter how good a manager he is. In 1969, he got his first shot at being a major league manager, with one of the National League's two expansion teams, the San Diego Padres. Tellingly, Clay Kirby (7–20) and Joe Niekro (8–17) were the ace pitchers. The rest of the staff won only 37 games as the Padres finished with a 52–110 record. The following year, Pat Dobson was the leading pitcher at 14–15 and the Padres improved to 63–99 but finished last for the second straight year. The next year was about the same, as the team finished 61–100. When the Padres started their fourth year losing seven out of their first 11, Gomez was out and Don Zimmer was in. Gomez resurfaced in 1974 with the Houston Astros, guiding them to a fourth place finish and a .500 record. But in 1975, they reverted to their losing ways and once again Gomez departed. His third managerial tenure was with the Chicago Cubs in 1980. This time he was dismissed after 90 games, when the Cubs' record stood at 38–52. "You never unpack your suitcases in this business," said Gomez.

On August 8, 1980, the Cubs won a game in the 15th inning that had been suspended earlier in the season because of darkness. Gomez was the manager when the game started, but the win went on the record of Joe Amalfitano, who had replaced Gomez in the interim.

Gomez was regarded as a good baseball man, smart, even-tempered and capable. Veteran umpire Ed Sudol said Gomez was one of the league's best managers. He just never had the players to produce much of a record.

Year	Team	Record	Pct.	Standing
1969	SD	52–110	.321	Sixth
1970	SD	63–99	.389	Sixth
1971	SD	61–100	.379	Sixth
1972	SD	4–7	.364	Sixth
1974	Hous	81–81	.500	Fourth
1975	Hous	47–80	.370	Sixth
1980	Chi (N)	38–52	.422	Sixth
7 years		**346–529**	**.395**	

Miguel Angel "Mike" Gonzalez

Born September 24, 1890, Havana, Cuba; died February 19, 1977, Havana; St. Louis Cardinals, September 10, 1938–November 6, 1938; June 7, 1940–June 12, 1940

Mike Gonzalez was the first native-born Cuban to manage in the major leagues. He managed the Cardinals for two brief interim stints in between the tenures of two legendary Cardinal managers. Gonzalez was a Cardinal coach when he was named to temporarily replace Frankie Frisch in 1938. Frisch had managed the Cardinals during the glory days of the Gas House Gang, but St. Louis was in sixth place when Gonzalez took the helm. That's where they remained, finishing 9–8 under their interim boss. Ray Blades, another coach, got the managerial assignment in 1939, and the Cardinals won 92 games for a second place finish, five games behind Cincinnati. When the Cardinals got off to a 15–24 start in 1940, impatient owner Sam Breadon fired Blades and put Gonzalez in charge, again temporarily. The Cardinals went 0–5 for Gonzalez before Breadon hired Billy Southworth to take over. Southworth's reign included three National League pennants.

Year	Team	Record	Pct.	Standing
1938	StL (N)	9–8	.529	Sixth
1940	StL	0–5	.000	Sixth
2 years		**9–13**	**.409**	

Joseph Lowell Gordon

Born February 18, 1915, Los Angeles, California; died April 14, 1978, Sacramento, California; Cleveland Indians, June 26, 1958–August 3, 1960; Detroit Tigers, August 3, 1960–October 3, 1960; Kansas City Athletics, October 4, 1960–June 19, 1961; September 9, 1968–October 8, 1969

Joe Gordon was an outstanding second baseman for the New York Yankees and Cleveland Indians for 11 years. In 1942, he won the American League's Most Valuable Player

Award, hitting .322 with 18 home runs and 103 runs batted in. That was the same year Ted Williams, never a favorite with the baseball writers, won the Triple Crown with a .356 batting average, 36 home runs and 137 runs batted in.

As a manager, Gordon was once again involved in something unusual. On August 10, 1960, while at the helm of the Cleveland Indians, he was traded to the Detroit Tigers for their manager, Jimmy Dykes. It is the only time in baseball history that managers were traded for one another. Gordon was in his third year at Cleveland. He was dismissed at the end of the 1960 season with Detroit. After that, he had two one-year stints with the Kansas City A's, just enough to pull his lifetime record under .500.

He is credited with pulling together a Cleveland ball club that had been pretty well dismantled by general manager Frank Lane. The Indians had enjoyed a great run under manager Al Lopez, finishing first in 1954 and second in 1951, 1952, 1953, 1955 and 1956. Lopez went to Chicago in 1957 (and finished second) and the Indians plunged to sixth under Kerby Farrell, who was fired at the end of the year.

Gordon entered and soon found he didn't have the players Lopez did. Future Hall of Fame pitcher Early Wynn and journeyman outfielder Al Smith had rejoined Lopez in Chicago. But Gordon did much with what he had, coaxing a career year from Calvin Coolidge McLish. McLish, who in a 15-year major league career would compile a 92–92 record, hurled his way to a 19–8 mark. He never approached such dominance again. Gary Bell, who would win 121 games in his 12-year big-league run, won 16 games under Gordon. He never won more than 14 after the 1959 season. The year after McLish won 19 games for Gordon, Lane traded him to Cincinnati where he was 4–14 for the Reds in 1960.

The Cleveland pitchers were helped by the bat of Rocky Colavito, who hit a league-leading 42 home runs, including four in one game against Baltimore, and drove in 111 runs. The following year, "Trader Lane" sent Colavito to Detroit in exchange for Harvey Kuenn, the American League batting champion. It was the only time a home run champ was ever traded for a batting champ. The Indians missed the power and dropped to fourth, winning 13 fewer games than they did in 1959. But by that time, Gordon was managing at Detroit.

Gordon had success with his hitters, too, in 1959. He convinced first baseman Tito Francona to start swinging down on the ball. Francona responded by hitting .363. He hit over .300 only one other time in his 15-year career. Shortstop Woodie Held had bounced around for a few years before settling in with Gordon's Indians. He hit 29 home runs in 1959 and 21 in 1960 for Gordon. In his 14-year career, he hit more than 20 home runs only one other time.

Statistically, Gordon was no Al Lopez. But Lopez didn't have a general manager who traded the home run champion and a 19-game winner out from under him.

Year	Team	Record	Pct.	Standing
1958	Cleve	46–40	.535	Fourth
1959	Cleve	89–65	.578	Second
1960	Cleve	49–46	.516	Fourth
1960	Det	26–31	.456	Sixth
1961	KC	26–43	.377	Eighth
1969	KC	69–93	.426	Fourth
5 years		**305–318**	**.490**	

George F. Gore

Born May 3, 1857, Saccarappa, Maine; died September 16, 1933, Utica, New York; St. Louis Browns/Cardinals, 1892

George Gore was an outfielder for 14 years with three teams before the start of the 20th century. He was a big man for his era — 5 feet, 11 inches, 195 pounds — who had the picturesque nickname of "Piano Legs." In the 1890s, St. Louis was going through two and three managers a year. Gore got his turn in a 15-game stretch at mid-season 1892. He never managed again.

Year	Team	Record	Pct.	Standing
1892	StL	6–9	.400	Twelfth

John Albert Goryl

Born October 21, 1933, Cumberland, Rhode Island; Minnesota Twins, August 24, 1980–May 22, 1981

John Goryl managed the Minnesota Twins for parts of two seasons. He had great success at the end of 1980, but the Twins faltered in the first half of 1981. For Goryl, there was no last half of 1981.

Year	Team	Record	Pct.	Standing
1980	Minn	23–13	.639	Third
1981	Minn	11–25	.306	Seventh
2 years		**34–38**	**.472**	

Charles Harvey Gould

Born August 21, 1847, Cincinnati, Ohio; died April 10, 1917, Flushing, New York; New Haven Elm Citys, 1875; Cincinnati Red Stockings, 1876

In 1876, the National League's opening season, Charlie Gould played first base and managed the Cincinnati ball club, and he established a dubious record that has withstood the test of time. No manager has had a poorer record, even for a partial season, 9–56.

Year	Team	Record	Pct.	Standing
1875	NH	2–21	.087	Eighth
1876	Cin	9–56	.138	Eighth
2 years		**11–77**	**.125**	

Henry Morgan Gowdy

Born August 24, 1889, Columbus, Ohio; died August 1, 1966, Columbus; Cincinnati Reds, September 22, 1946–November 5, 1946

Hank Gowdy was a 17-year major league veteran who caught most of the time and also played first base. He is best known as a player for two achievements. In 1914, he was the catcher for the "Miracle Braves" team that rose from last place on July 4 to win the National League pennant and then sweep Connie Mack's Philadelphia A's in the World Series. Gowdy's .545 World Series batting average remains the record for a four-game Series.

Gowdy was the first major league ballplayer to enlist in the armed services during World War I. After his playing career, he was one of Bill McKechnie's coaches with Cincinnati and helped a young Johnny Vander Meer to get over his early wildness. Gowdy called on an old friend of his, Hall of Fame pitcher Lefty Grove, to help Vander Meer. Grove, who also had been wild early in his career, watched the young pitcher and advised him to follow through more on his delivery. Vander Meer went on to become the only major league hurler to throw two consecutive no-hitters. Gowdy's only managerial opportunity came in 1946, filling in for four games and "retiring" with a 3–1 record.

Year	Team	Record	Pct.	Standing
1946	Cin	3–1	.750	Sixth

Mason Graffen

No biographical data available; St. Louis Brown Stockings, 1876

Mase Graffen has the distinction of managing the St. Louis team for 56 games in the first official year of the National League, 1876. In considering every manager before and since Graffen's stint, only two other managers who were at the helm for 10 games or more have a better percentage. George Wright, in the same era as Graffen, had a 59–25 record for a .702 percentage. Heinie Groh is second with a .700 percentage, having managed exactly 10 games. Graffen is third at 39–17, for a .696 percentage. His record may be a dubious distinction since historians say first baseman Herman Dehlman actually directed play and some books even list him as manager, though he was what would be known today as team captain.

Year	Team	Record	Pct.	Standing
1876	StL	39–17	.696	Second

Alexander Peter Grammas

Born April 3, 1926, Birmingham, Alabama; Pittsburgh Pirates, September 26, 1969–October 9, 1969; Milwaukee Brewers, November 7, 1975–November 19, 1977

Alex Grammas was a major league infielder for 10 years who got his first shot at managing at the end of the 1969 season when he took over for Larry Shepard with the Pittsburgh Pirates and won four out of five games. Seven years later, he managed the Milwaukee Brewers. In two seasons with Milwaukee, the Brewers were consistent but were not successful. Grammas was relieved of his duties after the 1977 season.

Year	Team	Record	Pct.	Standing
1969	Pitt	4–1	.800	Third
1976	Mil	66–95	.410	Sixth
1977	Mil	67–95	.414	Sixth
3 years		**137–191**	**.418**	

George Dallas Green

Born August 4, 1934, Newport, Delaware; Philadelphia Phillies, August 31, 1979–October 15, 1981; New York Yankees, October 7, 1988–August 18, 1989; New York Mets, May 19, 1993–August 26, 1996

Dallas Green was a hard-nosed, no-nonsense player, manager and executive who built two losing franchises — the Philadelphia Phillies and the Chicago Cubs — into winners, at least temporarily.

As a player, he was a relief pitcher for a few seasons, including 1964, when as a member of the Philadelphia Phillies, he watched his team lose a 6½ game lead by losing 11 of their last 12 games. In the early 1970s, working in the front office for the Phillies, he helped build up their farm system and was involved in trades and free-agent signings that helped produce a Phillies division championship in 1978 under manager Danny Ozark. The Phillies stumbled in 1979 and Green took over as manager with the team at 65–67. They went 19–11 the rest of the way and finished fourth. In 1980, led by veterans Pete Rose, Larry Bowa, Mike Schmidt, Bake McBride and Greg Luzinski, and a pitching staff that could start 24-game winner Steve Carlton and finish with Tug McGraw, the Phillies were back on top. Philadelphia won the World Series, beating Kansas City in six games.

In 1981, the season was split by the players' strike. The Phillies finished first in the first half of the season, with Montreal topping the second half. The Expos then beat the Phillies in a divisional playoff.

Green left Philadelphia to become vice president and general manager of the Chicago Cubs, a franchise that had not been in postseason play since 1945. In 1984, with Green pulling the strings off the field, the Cubs won the Eastern Division championship, led by the efforts of left fielder Gary Mathews, center fielder Bob Dernier, catcher–right fielder Keith Moreland and shortstop Larry Bowa—all ex–Phillies. Green had also gleaned an untested Ryne Sandberg from his old organization, and plucked third baseman Ron Cey from the Dodgers two years earlier. The crowning touch in 1984, however, was Green's mid-season acquisition of pitcher Rick Sutcliffe from the Cleveland Indians. Sutcliffe went 16–1 for the Cubs, who lost to the San Diego Padres in the league Championship series.

Green's next managerial challenge came when he was hired to take over the New York Yankees in 1989. The combination of George Streinbrenner and Green, each with one hand on the reins, made rough going a certainty. But when the Yankees didn't produce on the field, Green's short, noisy tenure was ended, a mere 121 games into the season. He took over a struggling Mets team in 1993 and was moving them in the right direction when the players' strike cut off the 1994 season. He stayed with the Mets two more years before retiring to his farm in Pennsylvania. He still does some scouting for the Phillies.

Green's strength as a manager was finding the right players to fit his situation. When he managed the great Phillie teams, he went with a set lineup and would make defensive replacements such as getting Luzinski out of the outfield when his bat was no longer needed in the game. When he managed the Mets, where the talent wasn't what it had been in Philadelphia, he platooned more than any other manager in the National League.

Year	Team	Record	Pct.	Standing
1979	Phil	19–11	.630	Fourth
1980	Phil	91–71	.560	First
1981	Phil	34–21	.610	First
1981	Phil	25–27	.480	Third
1989	NY (A)	56–65	.460	Fifth
1993	NY (N)	46–78	.370	Seventh
1994	NY	55–58	.480	First
1995	NY	69–75	.470	Second
1996	NY	59–72	.450	Fourth
8 years		**454–478**	**.487**	

Michael Joseph Griffin

Born March 20, 1865, Utica, New York; died April 10, 1908, Utica; Brooklyn Dodgers, June 10–June 13, 1898

Mike Griffin was an outfielder with Charlie Ebbets' Brooklyn ball club. In 1898, Ebbets became impatient with the team's progress, firing Bill Barnie and installing Griffin as the manager. Brooklyn lost three out of four games under Griffin before the perplexed Ebbets relieved Griffin and took over the managerial duties himself. The Dodgers were 38–68 under Ebbets — with Griffin back in the outfield.

Year	Team	Record	Pct.	Standing
1898	Brklyn	1–3	.250	Tenth

Tobias Charles "Sandy" Griffin

Born July 19, 1858, Fayetteville, New York; died June 5, 1926, Fayetteville, New York; Washington States-men, 1891

Sandy Griffin managed the Washington club in the fledgling American Association for 17 games in 1891. His team won only four of them, putting an end to Griffin's managerial career.

Year	Team	Record	Pct.	Standing
1891	Wash	4–13	.235	Eighth

Clark Calvin Griffith

Born November 20, 1869, Stringtown, Missouri; died October 27, 1955, Washington D.C.; Chicago White Sox, 1901–1902; New York Highlanders, August 25, 1902–June 24–1908; Cincinnati Reds, 1909–1911; Washington Senators, October 30, 1911–December 18, 1920

Clark Griffith was successful, seemingly in everything he did. As a pitcher, he won 20 or more games for six straight seasons. Later, he helped form the American League, and then managed in the league for the better part of 20 years before turning baseball executive for 30 years more. For any one of these accomplishments, Griffith could have been elected to the Hall of Fame. He was elected on the basis of all of them in 1946.

When Ban Johnson decided to form the American League in 1901, he needed someone to spearhead the effort, to give the league some instant credibility. He found Griffith, who had been a highly successful pitcher for Cap Anson's Chicago Colts. Griffith managed the Chicago White Sox in the Junior Circuit, and the club won the pennant in its first year of existence. Unfortunately for Griffith, it was two years before any World Series was played — and it was his only championship club. Griffith managed Chicago for two years, then managed the New York Highlanders, forerunners of the Yankees for six years. He moved on to Cincinnati for a three-year stay before taking over the Washington Senators, a club he eventually owned.

Griffith was an intelligent baseball man. Chicago sportswriter Hugh Fullerton wrote that "no brainier pitcher ever lived." As a pitcher and later as a manager, Griffith often sat in the dugout and predicted what pitches would be coming. He was accurate 90 percent of time, according to his players and coaches.

Griffith was one of the first managers to use scouts, both to do advance work on teams and to look for ballplayers, young and old, who could fill gaps on the ball club.

Griffith was also a pioneer in the use of relief pitchers. In 1905, with the Highlanders, Griffith went to the bullpen 75 times — a major league record almost doubling the previous mark. Later, as manager of the Senators, Griffith used his star pitcher Walter Johnson in relief in key situations. And the first great relief pitcher in the major leagues was Firpo Marberry, who helped Griffith's Senators win pennants in 1924 and 1925. By then Bucky Harris was the manager, but Griffith's influence was apparent in the makeup, style and strategy of the team.

Griffith had some good years and some so-so years as New York manager and when the Highlanders fired him after the 1908 season, it led to Griffith's lifelong dislike of the New York ball club. After three unremarkable seasons in Cincinnati, Griffith's old friend Ban Johnson asked him to help out with the struggling Washington franchise in the American League. The Senators finished second in each of Griffith's first two years there, their highest standing ever at the time. He remained the manager through 1920 when he bought a controlling interest in the team.

Griffith remained an innovator. It was his connections in Washington that led to the tradition of the president of the United States throwing out the first ball to start the season. He often found himself in financial trouble with the Senators and would have to pull off slick deals to make ends meet. One of them was the sale of his best ballplayer, Joe Cronin, to the Boston Red Sox for some quick cash — $175,000. Cronin was his son-in-law.

Year	Team	Record	Pct.	Standing
1901	Chi (A)	83–53	.610	First
1902	Chi	74–60	.562	Fourth
1903	NY (A)	72–62	.537	Fourth
1904	NY	92–59	.609	Second
1905	NY	71–78	.477	Sixth
1906	NY	90–61	.596	Second
1907	NY	70–78	.473	Fifth
1908	NY	24–32	.429	Sixth
1909	Cin	77–76	.503	Fourth
1910	Cin	75–79	.487	Fifth
1911	Cin	70–83	.458	Sixth
1912	Wash	91–61	.599	Second
1913	Wash	90–64	.584	Second
1914	Wash	81–73	.526	Third
1915	Wash	85–68	.556	Fourth
1916	Wash	76–77	.497	Seventh
1917	Wash	74–79	.484	Fifth
1918	Wash	72–56	.563	Third
1919	Wash	56–84	.400	Seventh
1920	Wash	68–84	.447	Sixth
20 years		**1491–1367**	**.522**	

Burleigh Arland Grimes

Born August 18, 1893, Clear Lake, Wisconsin; died December 6, 1985, Clear Lake; Brooklyn Dodgers, November 5, 1936–October 10, 1938

Burleigh Grimes won 270 games in a 19-year major league career. He took over as manager of the Brooklyn Dodgers in 1937, replacing Casey Stengel, whose team had finished seventh in 1936. Under Grimes, the Dodgers moved up to sixth in 1937 but slipped back to seventh in 1938, ending Grimes' managerial career. The following year, Brooklyn was led by Leo Durocher, beginning a managerial career that would lead to his induction into the Hall of Fame. Grimes too would make it to Cooperstown, but on the strength of his brilliant pitching.

Year	Team	Record	Pct.	Standing
1937	Brklyn	62–91	.405	Sixth
1938	Brklyn	68–80	.459	Seventh
2 years		**130–171**	**.432**	

Charles John Grimm

Born August 28, 1898, St. Louis, Missouri; died November 15, 1983, Scottsdale, Arizona; Chicago Cubs, August 2, 1932–July 20, 1938; May 5, 1944–June 10, 1949; Boston/Milwaukee Braves, May 31, 1952–June 17, 1956; Chicago Cubs, September 28, 1959–May 4, 1960

"Every time we call on Charlie, we win a pennant," said Chicago Cubs owner Philip K. Wrigley. He was almost right. Charlie Grimm was one of the most successful managers in Chicago Cubs history and has the distinction of managing the Cubs' last team to make it to the World Series in 1945. Prior to that, he managed Cub pennant winners in 1932 and 1935. Grimm played for 20 years, the majority of the time with the Cubs, and was a player-manager from 1932 to 1936. He had a lifetime batting average of .290.

In 1932, Chicago was in second place but weakened by the bickering of hard-nosed manager Rogers Hornsby. Grimm, who was loose and easy-going and liked to play his banjo at team parties, replaced Hornsby. The Cubs went on to be National League champions. It marked the first time in baseball history that a manager who took over a team in mid-season won a pennant. The second time it occurred was in 1938, when Gabby Hartnett replaced Grimm and the Cubs won.

Chicago lost the 1932 World Series to the New York Yankees, but in one of the games, Babe Ruth is said to have pointed to the bleachers, calling his shot before homering off of Cub right-hander Charlie Root. The Cubs won again under Grimm in 1935. In 1938, the Cubs were in third place, nine games over .500 when Grimm was replaced as manager by Hartnett, the catcher. The Cubs were on a seven-game winning streak when Grimm was replaced.

Wrigley had a habit of rewarding players he liked by giving them an opportunity to manage. Cub history is filled with such examples — Grimm, Hartnett, Phil Cavarretta, Stan Hack. Grimm actually had three chances. He was brought back to manage in 1944 and directed the 1945 pennant winner. After managing five years with the Braves in Boston and Milwaukee, Wrigley brought Grimm back to Chicago one more time, for an abbreviated stint in 1960.

Grimm was a colorful player and manager, earning the nickname "Jolly Cholly" for his antics on and off the field. On one occasion, while coaching third base for the Cubs, Marty Marion of the Cardinals made two great plays in a row, robbing two Cubs of hits. After the second one, Grimm keeled over backwards in the coaching box as if he fainted. Another time, while in the Cub dugout, Grimm watched as one Cub hitter after another failed to get a hit. Grimm dug a hole in front of the dugout and buried his lineup card.

Grimm's teams were seldom powerhouses — the exception being Milwaukee with Henry Aaron, Eddie Mathews and Joe Adcock. But his teams were usually fundamentally sound.

Six of Grimm's teams led the National League in fielding percentage and four times had the fewest errors. In five different seasons, Grimm's teams led the league in complete games. When the pitching and defense are solid, teams can win a lot of games by pushing runners around the bases rather than bringing them home with the long ball — and that's what Grimm's best teams did. The Cubs led the National League in sacrifice bunts in 1932, 1935, 1936 and 1937. His Milwaukee teams also led the league in sacrifice bunts in 1954 and 1956. Even slugger Joe Adcock, who hit 38 home runs in 1956, had 11 successful sacrifice bunts.

Grimm's 1945 Cub team was coming off a fourth-place finish in 1944, 30 games behind the St. Louis Cardinals. The 1945 pitching staff had young Hank Wyse, who won 22 games, and veteran Claude Passeau, who won 17. In mid-season, the Cubs acquired pitcher Hank Borowy from the Yankees. He went 11–2 for the Cubs, giving him a 21–7 season. Nobody had better pitching than the Cubs that year, and Grimm seemed to make the right moves at the right time. The Cubs swept 20 doubleheaders that year, a major league record.

In the World Series against Detroit, Grimm's ability to make the right moves was put to a severe test in the sixth game. The Cubs were down, three games to two, and had lost Game Five with their ace, Borowy, on the mound. In game six, Passeau, who had thrown a one-hitter in Game Three, went into the seventh inning with a 5–1 lead. But he was hit on the index finger of his pitching hand with a line drive and had to leave the game. Grimm called on Wyse and on another starter, Ray Prim, to try to hold back the Tigers, but both faltered. With the game at a 7–7 tie in the ninth inning, Grimm called on Borowy. He pitched four scoreless innings and the Cubs won, 8–7, in 12 innings. But Grimm had used all four of his starters to salvage the win. In Game Seven, he decided to go with his ace, Borowy, who would be pitching in his third straight game. This time the move didn't work. Borowy couldn't get anybody out in the first inning and the Cubs lost, 9–3.

When Wrigley called on Grimm for a third time, at the start of the 1960 season, Grimm stayed with it for 17 games, winning only six before switching places with radio announcer Lou Boudreau.

Jolly Cholly, whose managerial style was once described by pitcher Bob Buhl as "Boys, here's a bat, ball and glove — go get 'em," managed in 2,370 major league games. His winning percentage of .546 is among baseball's best.

Year	Team	Record	Pct.	Standing
1932	Chi (N)	37–20	.649	First
1933	Chi	86–68	.558	Third
1934	Chi	86–65	.570	Third
1935	Chi	100–54	.649	First
1936	Chi	87–67	.565	Second
1937	Chi	93–61	.604	Second
1938	Chi	45–36	.556	Third
1944	Chi	74–69	.517	Fourth
1945	Chi	98–56	.636	First
1946	Chi	82–71	.536	Third
1947	Chi	69–85	.448	Sixth
1948	Chi	64–90	.416	Eighth
1949	Chi	19–31	.380	Eighth
1952	Bos (N)	51–67	.432	Seventh
1953	Mil	92–62	.597	Second
1954	Mil	89–65	.578	Third

Year	Team	Record	Pct.	Standing
1955	Mil	85–69	.552	Second
1956	Mil	24–22	.522	Fifth
1960	Chi	6–11	.353	Eighth
19 years		**1287–1069**	**.546**	

WORLD SERIES

Year	Team	Record
1932	Chi (N)	0-4
1935	Chi	2-4
1945	Chi	3-4
3 years		**5-12**

Henry Knight "Heinie" Groh

Born September 18, 1889, Rochester, New York; died August 22, 1968, Cincinnati, Ohio; Cincinnati Reds, 1918

Third baseman Heinie Groh took over for Christy Mathewson as manager of the Cincinnati Reds for the last 10 games of the 1918 season and won seven of them, moving the Reds up a notch, from fourth to third place in that stretch. It was not enough for Groh to win a full-time managerial job. The Reds hired Pat Moran to manage the 1919 Reds who won the National League pennant with Groh at his familiar third base position.

Year	Team	Record	Pct.	Standing
1918	Cin	7–3	.700	Third

Donald Joseph Gutteridge

Born June 19, 1912, Pittsburg, Kansas; Chicago White Sox, May 2, 1969–September 3, 1970

Don Gutteridge had been a longtime coach with the Chicago White Sox when he got his chance to manage the club. Eddie Stanky gave up the reins in 1968 after several near misses at a championship. The White Sox brought Al Lopez out of retirement to take over. Lopez had managed the White Sox to an American League championship in 1959, but didn't have Early Wynn or Nelson Fox or Luis Aparacio this time around. He finished the 1968 season at 33–48. When Chicago started 1969 at 8–9, he retired and Gutteridge took over. After parts of two lackluster seasons in which Chicago finished fifth and sixth, Gutteridge was fired.

Year	Team	Record	Pct.	Standing
1969	Chi (A)	60–85	.414	Fifth
1970	Chi	49–87	.360	Sixth
2 years		**109–172**	**.388**	

George Edwin Haas

Born May 26, 1935, Paducah, Kentucky; Atlanta Braves, October 1, 1984–August 26, 1985

Eddie Haas replaced Joe Torre as manager of the Atlanta Braves for the 1985 season — but not for all of it. Haas was replaced by Chuck Tanner after 121 games, with the Braves 21 games under .500 and buried in fifth place.

Year	Team	Record	Pct.	Standing
1985	Atl	50–71	.413	Fifth

Stanley Camfield Hack

Born December 6, 1909, Sacramento, California; died December 15, 1979, Dixon, Illinois; Chicago Cubs, March 29, 1954–October 11, 1956; St. Louis Cardinals, September 17, 1958–September 29, 1958

Stan Hack

Stan Hack, a left-handed hitting third baseman, was one of the most popular players on the Chicago Cubs. He delivered the winning hit in the sixth game of the 1945 World Series against the Detroit Tigers that forced a seventh game.

In spring training of 1954, Cubs owner Philip K. Wrigley became angry when manager Phil Cavarretta told the media he didn't expect the Cubs to do well. Wrigley fired him and hired Hack, continuing the custom of hiring popular players as managers. Hack managed three years and could get the Cubs no higher than sixth. In 1958, he finished out the last 10 games of the season with the St. Louis Cardinals but never managed again after that.

Hack's legacy with the Cubs is that he was a nice guy, much nicer to the players than Cavarretta. It was similar to the transition 22 years earlier when Charlie Grimm replaced Rogers Hornsby. Only the results weren't similar. Grimm won a pennant his first year and two more during his tenure with the Cubs. In Hack's best year, the Cubs won 72 games.

Year	Team	Record	Pct.	Standing
1954	Chi (N)	64–90	.416	Seventh
1955	Chi	72–81	.471	Sixth
1956	Chi	60–94	.390	Eighth
1958	StL	3–7	.300	Fifth
4 years		**199–272**	**.423**	

Charles M. Hackett

Born in Holyoke, Massachusetts; died August 1, 1898, Holyoke; Cleveland Blues, 1884; Brooklyn Trolley Dodgers, 1885

Not much is recorded about the managerial career of Charlie Hackett. He managed two teams — Cleveland in 1884 and Brooklyn in 1885 — in two leagues — the National League and the American Association — over a period of two years. He could get neither team higher than seventh place.

Year	Team	Record	Pct.	Standing
1884	Cleve	35–77	.313	Seventh
1885	Brklyn	15–25	.325	Seventh
2 years		**50–102**	**.329**	

William Wilson Hallman

Born March 30, 1867, Pittsburgh, Pennsylvania; died September 11, 1920, Philadelphia; St. Louis Cardinals, 1897

Bill Hallman managed the forebear of today's St. Louis Cardinals in 1897. He was the third of four St. Louis managers that year and won only 13 of 59 games, bringing an abrupt end to his managerial career. The team suffered through a 29–102 season.

Year	Team	Record	Pct.	Standing
1897	StL (N)	13–46	.220	Twelfth

Frederick Girard Haney

Born April 25, 1898, Albuquerque, New Mexico; died November 9, 1977, Beverly Hills, California; St. Louis Browns, November 7, 1938–June 5, 1941; Pittsburgh Pirates, December 11, 1952–November 2, 1955; Milwaukee Braves, June 17, 1956–October 3, 1959

Fred Haney managed two teams that weren't very competitive and then managed a great team to cap off his career. Haney managed the St. Louis Browns in 1939 and 1940 and was fired early in the 1941 season. He didn't get another major league managerial chance for 12 years. He took over a Pittsburgh Pirate team that was 42–112 in 1952. Under Haney, the Pirates won 50 in 1953, 53 in 1954 and 60 in 1955. So while the improvement was steady, Haney's lifetime statistics showed that his teams had lost 100 games or more in three out of his first five years and 94 in the sixth year. Nonetheless, when the Milwaukee Braves started too slowly for management's liking in 1956, the Braves chose Haney to take over. Milwaukee immediately won seven in a row and had a 68–40 record under Haney. It wasn't good enough to catch the Brooklyn Dodgers, but it was good enough for second place. The Braves won the pennant the next two years. They beat New York Yankees in the 1957 World Series and lost to them in 1958. The Braves tied the Dodgers for first place in 1959 but lost a playoff to them and finished second. It was Haney's last year as a major league manager.

Haney had great talent at Milwaukee, so great in fact that the Braves almost won championships in 1956 and 1959. Had they done that, to go along with the 1957 and 1958 titles, the Braves would be compared to the great Yankee teams and Haney would have become another Casey Stengel. Haney became general manager of the Los Angeles Angels, one of the American League's expansion teams, in 1961.

Former players praise Haney as a shrewd baseball man and a player's manager. Frank Thomas credits him with giving him the confidence to play at the major league level. Dick Groat said Haney was a good manager with a bad team in Pittsburgh. Bob Buhl said Haney put some spark into a Braves club that had fizzled a little under his predecessor, Charlie Grimm.

Despite the dismal statistics for the first six years of his managerial career, Haney came within four wins of being ranked among baseball's all-time great managers — two in the 1956 season that would have given them the championship over the Dodgers and two in the 1959 playoff with the Dodgers. Those four wins would have given the Braves four straight championships.

Year	Team	Record	Pct.	Standing
1939	StL (A)	43–111	.279	Eighth
1940	StL	67–87	.435	Sixth
1941	StL	15–29	.341	Seventh
1953	Pitt	50–104	.325	Eighth
1954	Pitt	53–101	.344	Eighth
1955	Pitt	60–94	.390	Eighth
1956	Mil	68–40	.630	Second
1957	Mil	95–59	.617	First
1958	Mil	92–62	.597	First
1959	Mil	86–70	.551	Second
10 years		**629–757**	**.454**	

WORLD SERIES

Year	Team	Record
1957	Mil	4–3
1958	Mil	3–4
2 years		**7–7**

Edward Hugh Hanlon

Born August 27, 1857, Montville, Connecticut; died April 14, 1937, Baltimore, Maryland; Pittsburgh Alleghenys, 1889–1891; Baltimore Orioles, 1892–1898; Brooklyn Superbas, 1899–1905; Cincinnati Reds, 1906–1907

Ned Hanlon was the most innovative manager of the 1890s and early 1900s and was the mentor of many players who went on to be great major league managers. Hanlon's greatest asset as a ballplayer was his intensity. He rarely hit for high average and bounced between several positions in the field, mostly in an effort to find the one where he would do the least harm. But he learned the game well, and when it came time for him to manage, he set some standards that others followed for the next century. In one nine-year period, Hanlon's teams finished first five times, second three times and third once. At the end of his 19-year career, Hanlon's teams had won 1,315 games and lost 1,165, a winning percentage of .530.

His first managerial assignment was at Baltimore, with a team that finished twelfth in 1892. They improved to eighth in 1893, but that was only the beginning of moving up and doing things a little differently. Before the 1894 season officially began, Hanlon had his team go south to practice for a few weeks before the season started. He was roundly criticized, but the training time gave his team ample time to work together as a unit, getting into shape and practicing for the coming season. Today, every major league team follows Hanlon's then bizarre practice. Spring training is a part of the baseball tradition.

Hanlon was also the first to use right-handed hitters against left-handed pitchers and vice versa. He also taught his fielders to cover for one another when one of them got caught out of position. When Baltimore was at bat, Hanlon often had a base runner take off while the batter was swinging at a pitch — the birth of the "hit and run." Hanlon also understood home field advantage. He hired a groundskeeper to keep his field in shape. It is believed that Hanlon had a cement block embedded just below the ground and just in front of home plate in Baltimore. He instructed his players to swing down on the ball. When they did, the ball would hit the surface just above the cement and bounce high in the air, allowing base runners a chance to beat out the hit. There are no cement blocks under infields today, but a ball that is hit down and then bounces high is still called a "Baltimore chop."

In addition to all of the gimmickry, trickery and generally rowdy play, the Orioles had talent. The 1894 Baltimore team had six future Hall of Famers in its starting lineup: John McGraw, Hughie Jennings, Dan Brouthers, Willie Keeler, Joe Kelley and Wilbert Robinson.

Hanlon left the Orioles after the 1898 season and took over as manager of the Brooklyn Dodgers — and finished first his first two seasons there. He ended his career managing the Cincinnati Reds for two years.

Connie Mack, Hugh Jennings, John McGraw, Miller Huggins, Kid Gleason and Wilbert Robinson are among those who played for Hanlon who later managed in the major leagues.

Year	Team	Record	Pct.	Standing
1889	Pitt (N)	26–19	.578	Fifth
1890	Pitt	60–68	.469	Sixth
1891	Pitt	31–47	.397	Eighth
1892	Bal	45–85	.346	Twelfth
1893	Bal	60–70	.462	Eighth
1894	Bal	89–39	.695	First
1895	Bal	87–43	.669	First
1896	Bal	90–39	.698	First
1897	Bal	90–40	.692	Second
1898	Bal	96–53	.644	Second
1899	Brklyn	101–47	.682	First
1900	Brklyn	82–54	.603	First
1901	Brklyn	79–57	.581	Third
1902	Brklyn	75–63	.543	Second
1903	Brklyn	70–66	.515	Fifth
1904	Brklyn	56–97	.366	Sixth
1905	Brklyn	48–104	.316	Eighth
1906	Cin	64–87	.424	Sixth
1907	Cin	66–87	.431	Sixth
19 years		**1315–1165**	**.530**	

Melvin Leroy Harder

Born October 15, 1909, Beemer, Nebraska; Cleveland Indians, September 22–24, 1961; September 29, 1961

Former big league hurler, Mel Harder, at the time a pitching coach for the Cleveland Indians, was called on to be the Indians interim manager for one game in the 1961 season. He was tapped for two more games in the 1962 season. The result is that Harder has the distinction of having the highest lifetime percentage of anyone who has ever managed in the major leagues. He retired undefeated at 3–0.

Year	Team	Record	Pct.	Standing
1961	Cleve	1–0	1.000	Sixth
1962	Cleve	2–0	1.000	Sixth
2 years		**3–0**	**1.000**	

Dudley Michael Hargrove

Born October 26, 1949, Perrytown, Texas; Cleveland Indians, July 6, 1991–October 15, 1999; Baltimore Orioles, November 3, 1999–present

Mike Hargrove won five consecutive division championships as manager of the Cleveland Indians and led them to the World Series twice. The Indians averaged 94 wins in those five years. His squads spent millions of dollars during Hargrove's tenure, at first signing good young ballplayers like slugger Jim Thome and catcher Sandy Alomar to long-term contracts and then picking up valuable free agents such as Matt Williams, Roberto Alomar (Sandy's brother), plus pitchers such as Orel Hershiser and Dwight Gooden. But shortly after the New York Yankees eliminated the Indians in the 1999 League Championship Series, Hargrove was fired.

Once he got the players he wanted, Hargrove hardly ever fooled with his starting lineup. Opponents knew who they were going up against. Yet he made a lot of defensive substitutions, leading the league in that category in 1993 and 1994. His 1993 team led the league in use of pinch hitters — an indication of a good bench as much as it is a managerial style. His 1995 Indians team led the league in stolen base attempts, largely due to the running of Kenny Lofton.

He is the only manager in baseball history to win five consecutive division championships and then be fired. Within two weeks of his dismissal by the Indians, Hargrove was hired to manage the Baltimore Orioles.

Year	Team	Record	Pct.	Standing
1991	Cleve	32–53	.370	Seventh
1992	Cleve	76–86	.460	Fourth
1993	Cleve	76–86	.460	Sixth
1994	Cleve	66–47	.580	Second
1995	Cleve	100–44	.690	First
1996	Cleve	99–62	.610	First
1997	Cleve	86–75	.530	First
1998	Cleve	89–73	.540	First
1999	Cleve	97–65	.590	First
2000	Bal	74–88	.457	Fourth
2001	Bal	63–98	.391	Fourth
11 years		**858–777**	**.525**	

DIVISION PLAYOFFS

Year	Team	Record	Pct.
1996	Cleve	1–3	.250
1997	Cleve	3–1	.750
1998	Cleve	3–1	.750
1999	Cleve	1–3	.250
3 years		**8–8**	**.500**

LEAGUE CHAMPIONSHIP SERIES

Year	Team	Record	Pct.
1995	Cleve	4–2	.667
1997	Cleve	4–2	.667
1998	Cleve	2–4	.333
4 years		**10–10**	**.500**

WORLD SERIES

Year	Team	Record	Pct.
1995	Cleve	2–4	.333
1997	Cleve	3–4	.429
2 years		**5–8**	**.385**

Toby Harrah

Born October 26, 1948, Sissonville, West Virginia; Texas Rangers, July 9, 1992–October 5, 1992

Toby Harrah was a shortstop and third baseman for several major league teams, including the Texas Rangers. He got a chance to manage the Rangers in 1992, but his tenure lasted only 76 games.

Year	Team	Record	Pct.	Standing
1992	Tex	32–44	.421	Fourth

Derrel McKinley "Bud" Harrelson

Born June 6, 1944, Niles, California; New York Mets, May 29, 1990–September 29, 1991

Bud Harrelson was a New York Mets shortstop for 13 of his 16 years in the major leagues and was known for his fiery attitude. Harrelson played on two pennant winners, the 1969 "Miracle Mets" and the Mets who snuck into first place with an 83–79 record in 1973. He was named manager of the Mets in 1990 and had a terrific run — 71–49 — as the Mets finished second. The next year was not terrific (74–80), and Harrelson was finished before the season was.

Year	Team	Record	Pct.	Standing
1990	NY (N)	71–49	.592	Second
1991	NY	74–80	.481	Third
2 years		**145–129**	**.529**	

Stanley Raymond "Bucky" Harris

Born November 8, 1896, Port Jervis, New York; died November 8, 1977, Bethesda, Maryland; Washington Senators, February 10, 1924–October 17, 1928, November 13, 1934–1942, 1950–September 26, 1954; Detroit Tigers, October 17, 1928–September 24, 1933, September 30, 1954–October 1, 1956; Boston Red Sox, November 24, 1933–1934; Philadelphia Phillies, 1943; New York Yankees, February 27, 1947–1948.

Bucky Harris was an innovative manager who surprised even opposing managers with some of his moves. In the seventh game of the 1924 World Series, Harris, then a green, 27-year-old player-manager of the Washington Senators, tried to outsmart legendary Giants manager John McGraw.

Bill Terry, the Giants great first baseman, had been wearing out right-handers but had difficulty with the Senator left-handed pitchers. George Mogridge, a left-hander, was the scheduled Washington starter. After conferring with Senators owner Clark Griffith about his plan, young Harris announced that his starter would be Curly Ogden, a right-hander. McGraw started Terry at first base and inserted other left-handed batters into his lineup. Ogden pitched to one batter. Then Harris went to the bullpen and brought in

Mogridge to face the rest of the Giant lineup. The Senators won the game, 4–3, in 12 innings, with Harris using Firpo Marberry and Hall of Fame starter Walter Johnson in relief. Marberry was baseball's first true relief pitcher, another Griffith-Harris innovation. The veteran Johnson had lost two previous games in the Series. Harris played a hunch and gave the Big Train one more chance.

Washington won the pennant in Harris' second year at the helm, too, but lost to an awesome Pittsburgh Pirate team led by Pie Traynor, KiKi Cuyler and Paul and Lloyd Waner. In the seventh game of that Series, Harris started Johnson and left him in even after the old veteran squandered leads of 4–0 and 6–3. Curiously, as Johnson was getting hammered, Harris did not go to the bullpen for Marberrry. When the Series was over, Harris received a letter from American League president Ban Johnson accusing him of leaving Johnson in the game for sentimental reasons rather than sound baseball judgment. Harris never publicly explained his reasoning.

Harris is the only man in baseball history to lead two different teams to pennants in his first year managing them: the Senators in 1924 and the New York Yankees in 1947. Both the 1924 Senators and 1947 Yankees won the World Series too, putting Harris in the record books for that as well.

Harris managed the Senators from 1924 to 1928, from 1935 to 1942 and from 1950 to 1954. He managed Detroit from 1929 to 1933 and from 1955 through 1956. He managed the Boston Red Sox and Philadelphia Phillies briefly.

After winning the pennant and World Series with the Yankees in 1947, his 1948 New York club was eliminated in the last weekend of the season as Cleveland won the championship. The Yankees responded by firing Harris and hiring Casey Stengel to replace him.

Harris' teams didn't bunt much. Three of his Detroit Tiger teams, three of his Senator teams and his Boston Red Sox ball club all were last in the American League in sacrifice bunts. Though he created the relief specialist, he dropped the idea for more than 20 years — or perhaps he didn't feel he ever had the right person. Then, in 1947, Joe Page was instrumental in helping the Yankees win the pennant after Harris pulled him out of the starting rotation and made him his ace relief pitcher. The success of Page prompted other managers to develop short relievers.

Only three other managers, John McGraw, Connie Mack and Sparky Anderson, won more games in their careers than Harris, whose teams won 2,159. But because of the caliber of teams he was called on to try to salvage over the years, he also ranks second in losses with 2,219, behind only Connie Mack.

Year	Team	Record	Pct.	Standing
1924	Wash	92–62	.597	First
1925	Wash	96–55	.636	First
1926	Wash	81–69	.540	Fourth
1927	Wash	85–69	.552	Third
1928	Wash	75–78	.487	Fourth
1929	Det	70–84	.455	Sixth
1930	Det	75–79	.487	Fifth
1931	Det	61–93	.396	Seventh
1932	Det	76–75	.503	Fifth
1933	Det	73–79	.480	Fifth
1934	Bos (A)	76–76	.500	Fourth
1935	Wash	67–86	.438	Sixth

Year	Team	Record	Pct.	Standing
1936	Wash	82–71	.536	Fourth
1937	Wash	73–80	.477	Sixth
1938	Wash	75–76	.497	Fifth
1939	Wash	65–87	.428	Sixth
1940	Wash	64–90	.416	Seventh
1941	Wash	70–84	.455	Sixth
1942	Wash	62–89	.411	Seventh
1943	Phil	40–53	.430	Fifth
1947	NY (A)	97–57	.630	First
1948	NY	94–60	.610	Third
1950	Wash	67–87	.435	Fifth
1951	Wash	62–92	.403	Seventh
1952	Wash	78–76	.506	Fifth
1953	Wash	76–76	.500	Fifth
1954	Wash	66–88	.429	Sixth
1955	Det	79–75	.513	Fifth
1956	Det	82–72	.532	Fifth
29 years		**2159–2219**	**.493**	

WORLD SERIES

Year	Team	Record
1924	Wash	4–3
1925	Wash	3–4
1947	NY (A)	4–3
3 years		**11–10**

Chalmer Luman Harris

Born January 17, 1915, New Castle, Alabama; Baltimore Orioles, September 1, 1961–October 10, 1961; Houston Colt 45s, September 19, 1964–December 12, 1965; Atlanta Braves, October 7, 1967–August 7, 1972

Lum Harris took over a good Baltimore Oriole team in 1961 when Paul Richards resigned to become general manager of the new expansion franchise in the National League, the Houston Astros. When Richards resigned, the Orioles were in third place with a 78–57 record. Harris guided them to a 17–10 record the rest of the way, which kept them in third place, behind the Maris-Mantle Yankee brigade and the Detroit Tigers. Harris was replaced by Billy Hitchcock in 1962. But in 1964, Richards brought him to Houston to close out the 1964 season, and he was 5–8 for a club that finished ninth. In 1965, he had the team for the entire season and again they finished ninth. Harris was replaced by Grady Hatton. Harris had his best success with Atlanta and won the Western Division championship with the Braves in 1969. He had Hall of Famer Phil Niekro, who turned in one of his best years at 23–13, and three lesser names — Ron Reed, Pat Jarvis and George Stone — who all won in double figures. Henry Aaron and Orlando Cepeda led the offense with 44 and 22 home runs, respectively, but Aaron was the only .300 hitter in the lineup (and he hit exactly .300). Nobody drove in 100 runs. Harris learned from Richards, his mentor, about taking care of the fundamentals. The Braves made the fewest errors of any team in the league that year and led the league in fielding percentage.

Harris probably never got the full credit he deserved for bringing in a winner with the '69 Braves because elsewhere in the National League that year, the "Miracle Mets" were putting on a furious late-season charge to overtake the Cubs. The Mets then swept the Braves in the League Championship Series.

Year	Team	Record	Pct.	Standing
1961	Bal	17–10	.630	Third
1964	Hous	5–8	.385	Eighth
1965	Hous	65–97	.401	Ninth
1968	Atl	81–81	.500	Fifth
1969	Atl	93–69	.574	First
1970	Atl	76–86	.469	Fifth
1971	Atl	82–80	.506	Third
1972	Atl	47–57	.452	Fifth
8 years		**466–488**	**.488**	

LEAGUE CHAMPIONSHIP SERIES

Year	Team	Record
1969	Atl	0–3

James Aristotle Hart

Born July 10, 1855, Fairview, Pennsylvania; died July 18, 1919, Chicago, Illinois; Louisville Colonels, 1885–1886; Boston Beaneaters, 1889

Jim Hart survived longer than many of his contemporaries as a 19th-century baseball manager. While many teams were moving managers in an out, sometimes as many as three in one season, Hart lasted three full seasons. In his first year, his Louisville team finished fifth. The next year, they moved up to fourth, but that was not good enough and Hart was replaced. He resurfaced with Boston in 1889 and had a sensational year — 83–45. But it was only good enough for second place, and Hart was not invited back for the 1890 season. Frank Selee took over, beginning a long, successful National League career.

Year	Team	Record	Pct.	Standing
1885	Lou	53–59	.473	Fifth
1886	Lou	66–70	.485	Fourth
1889	Bos	83–45	.648	Second
3 years		**202–174**	**.537**	

John Hart

Born July 21, 1948; Cleveland Indians, September 12, 1989–November 3, 1989

John Hart was interim manager of the Cleveland Indians in 1989 and managed to win eight of the 19 games that bridged the tenures of Doc Edwards and John McNamara.

Year	Team	Record	Pct.	Standing
1989	Cleve	8–11	.421	Sixth

Charles Leo "Gabby" Hartnett

Born December 20, 1900, Woonsocket, Rhode Island; died December 20, 1972, Park Ridge, Illinois; Chicago Cubs, July 20, 1938–November 17, 1940

Gabby Hartnett was a Hall of Fame catcher for the Chicago Cubs who is best remembered for his "Homer in the Gloamin." The homer, hit into the left field bleachers as darkness set in at Wrigley Field, led to a 1938 pennant for the Cubs. But Hartnett was equally proud of a lesser known accomplishment. He was behind the plate, calling the pitches, in the 1934 All-Star game when the Giants' Carl Hubbell struck out Babe Ruth, Lou Gehrig, Jimmy Foxx, Al Simmons and Joe Cronin in succession. He was the player-manager for the Cubs in 1938, having replaced Charlie Grimm at mid-season. Chicago was 45–36 and had won seven in a row when owner Phil Wrigley dismissed Grimm, a popular Cub figure, and replaced him with the equally popular Hartnett. The Cubs went 44–27 the rest of the way, and Hartnett became the second manager in baseball history to take over a club with the season in progress and win a pennant. The first

Gabby Hartnett

was Grimm, who won with the 1932 Cubs after replacing Rogers Hornsby. Later, Harvey Kuenn did it with the Milwaukee Brewers. The Cubs slipped to fourth in 1939 and fifth in 1940, Hartnett's last year at the helm.

Year	Team	Record	Pct.	Standing
1938	Chi (N)	44–27	.620	First
1939	Chi	84–70	.545	Fourth
1940	Chi	75–59	.487	Fifth
3 years		**203–176**	**.536**	

WORLD SERIES

Year	Team	Record
1938	Chi (N)	0–4

Roy Thomas Hartsfield

Born October 25, 1925, Chattahoochee, Georgia; Toronto Blue Jays, October 20, 1976–September 30, 1979

Roy Hartsfield was an infielder for the Boston Red Sox for 265 games from 1950 to 1952. He stayed active in baseball as a coach and manager in the minor leagues and got his chance to manage at the major league level in 1977 with the expansion Toronto Blue Jays. It was his job to develop young talent so that some day the Blue Jays would be competitive. Eventually they were, but not while Hartsfield was around. They lost more than 100 games in all three of his years there.

Year	Team	Record	Pct.	Standing
1977	Tor	54–107	.335	Seventh
1978	Tor	59–102	.366	Seventh
1979	Tor	53–109	.327	Seventh
3 years		**166–318**	**.343**	

Winfield Scott Hastings

Born August 10, 1847, Hillsboro, Ohio; died August 14, 1907, Sawtelle, California; Rockford Forest Citys, 1871; Cleveland Forest Citys, 1872

Winfield Scott Hastings, named after Civil War general Winfield Scott, was not terribly successful in his field of battle, the ball field. Scott managed 45 games over two seasons in the National Association and his teams could win only 10 of them.

Year	Team	Record	Pct.	Standing
1871	Rockfd	4–21	.160	Ninth
1872	Cleve	6–14	.300	Seventh
2 years		**10–35**	**.222**	

John Van Buskirk Hatfield

Born July 20, 1847, New Jersey; died February 20, 1909, Long Island City, New York; New York Mutuals, 1872–1873

John Hatfield's career is the reverse of most managers — he played professional baseball after he managed, but not before. Hatfield managed the New York club in the National Association in 1872 and 1873. His only experience as a player came a year later when he got into one game for New York as a pitcher. He worked eight innings, giving up two runs on 11 hits and striking out 13. He did not get the decision.

Year	Team	Record	Pct.	Standing
1872	NY	24–14	.632	Third
1873	NY	11–17	.393	Fourth
2 years		**35–31**	**.530**	

Grady Edgebert Hatton

Born October 7, 1922, Beaumont, Texas; Houston Astros, December 12, 1965–June 18, 1968

Grady Hatton was a former major league infielder who was the third manager of the Houston Astros. Still in their infancy, the Astros had to depend on aging veterans and untested youngsters, and their record showed it. Under Hatton, they finished eighth and ninth and were mired in tenth place after 61 games of the 1968 season when he was relieved of his duties.

Year	Team	Record	Pct.	Standing
1966	Hous	72–90	.444	Eighth
1967	Hous	69–93	.426	Ninth
1968	Hous	23–38	.377	Tenth
3 years		**164–221**	**.426**	

Guy Jackson Hecker

Born April 3, 1856, Youngville, Pennsylvania; died December 3, 1938, Wooster, Ohio; Pittsburgh Alleghenys, 1890

Guy Hecker played first base and managed the Pittsburgh Pirates in 1890. The Pirates played 136 games and lost 113 of them, ending Hecker's chances for a second year at Pittsburgh or anywhere else. The right fielder on that team was Billy Sunday, who hit .257. Sunday later quit baseball and become one of the nation's leading evangelists.

Year	Team	Record	Pct.	Standing
1890	Pitt (N)	23–113	.169	Eighth

Donald Henry Heffner

Born February 11, 1911, Rouzerville, Pennsylvania; Cincinnati Reds, October 26, 1965–July 13, 1966

Don Heffner took over a Cincinnati Reds team that had gone through some traumatic experiences and were victimized by one of baseball's most surprising trades. The Cincinnati Reds won the National League championship in 1961 under manager Fred Hutchinson. They fell to third place in 1962 and to fifth in 1963. In 1964, the Reds finished second, but were aided by the collapse of the Philadelphia Phillies, who dropped from first place to third place in the last two weeks of the season by losing 11 of their last 12. Hutchinson, who was well-liked by players and fans, became ill with cancer and was forced to resign during the 1964 season. He died in November. Coach Dick Sisler took over. After the Reds retreated to fourth place in 1965, Sisler was replaced by Heffner, also a Reds coach. But in between the 1965 and 1966 seasons, the Reds traded their Hall of Fame outfielder, Frank Robinson, to Baltimore for Milt Pappas, Jack Baldschun and Dick Simpson. Reds management apparently thought that Robinson, who hit .296 with 33 home runs and 113 RBI, had seen his best days. For Baltimore in 1966, he won the Triple Crown and led the Orioles to the World Series. Meanwhile, for Cincinnati, Pappas was 12–11, Baldschun was 1–5 and Simpson hit four home runs and drove in 14 in limited duty. The Reds could not make up for the run production lost by the trade of Robinson — and Heffner was the victim. He was fired after 83 games and never managed again.

Year	Team	Record	Pct.	Standing
1966	Cin	37–46	.446	Eighth

Louis Wilbur Heilbroner

Born July 4, 1861, Fort Wayne, Indiana; died December 21, 1933, Fort Wayne; St. Louis Cardinals, August 18, 1900–September 30, 1900

Louis Heilbroner hardly had the qualifications to be a major league manager. He was the head of concessions at the St. Louis ballpark when the ball club's manager, Patsy Tebeau, quit in mid-season with the Cardinals at 45–55. The management needed a replacement in a hurry, and Heilbroner was a loyal employee. He was just a little over five feet tall and didn't know much about baseball. His players made him the butt of jokes. Cardinal players would sit on the bench and scoot in his direction, knocking Heilbroner, who preferred the end of the bench, onto the ground. On one occasion, a player picked him up and stuck him head first into a rain barrel. In the early 1900s, the dugout bench was on the field — in full view of the crowd.

Despite all the shenanigans, the Cardinals actually improved under Heilbroner, going 17–20 and moving from seventh to fifth place. At season's end, however, everyone agreed that Heilbroner was best suited for the hot dog wagon.

Year	Team	Record	Pct.	Standing
1900	StL (N)	17–20	.459	Seventh

Tommy Vann Helms

Born May 5, 1941, Charlotte, North Carolina; Cincinnati Reds, April 2, 1988–May 2, 1988; August 24, 1989–November 3, 1989

Tommy Helms was a coach with the Cincinnati Reds in 1988 when manager Pete Rose was suspended for 30 days for bumping umpire Dave Pallone during a game. In 1989 when Rose was forced to resign because of gambling allegations made against him, Helms took over for the rest of the season. Lou Piniella was hired to manage the Reds in 1990 and won the pennant and the World Series. Years later, Helms was philosophic about his last days with the Reds and Piniella's success, pointing out that Piniella did it with a team that Rose and Helms had developed. "That's baseball," he said.

Year	Team	Record	Pct.	Standing
1988	Cin	12–15	.444	Second
1989	Cin	16–21	.432	Fifth
2 years		**28–36**	**.437**	

Solomon Joseph Hemus

Born April 17, 1923, Phoenix, Arizona; St. Louis Cardinals, September 29, 1958–July 6, 1961

Solly Hemus was a major league infielder for 11 years who played for the St. Louis Cardinals and Philadelphia Phillies. He was playing for the Phillies in 1958 when the Cardinals were going through a transition. Fred Hutchinson was out as manager with 10 games left in the season. Stan Hack filled in the remainder of the way, and the Cardinals finished sixth. Hemus, who had a great relationship with Cardinal owner August Busch, is believed to have written a letter to Busch in 1958, expressing his desire to manage the Cardinals. On September 29, 1958, the Cardinals traded Gene Freese to the Phillies for Hemus, who was then named Cardinal manager. The Cardinals finished seventh under Hemus in 1959, then moved up to third place in 1960. After 75 games in 1961, the Cardinals were buried in sixth place and Hemus was fired.

Year	Team	Record	Pct.	Standing
1959	StL (N)	71–83	.461	Seventh
1960	StL	86–68	.583	Third
1961	StL	33–41	.446	Fifth
3 years		**190–192**	**.497**	

William C. Henderson

No biographical data available; Baltimore Monumentals, 1884

Bill Henderson managed the Baltimore franchise of the upstart Union League for 17 games in 1884. He won only five, putting an end to his short managerial career.

Year	Team	Record	Pct.	Standing
1884	Bal (U)	5–12	.294	Fourth

John Charles Hendricks

Born April 9, 1875, Joliet, Illinois; died May 19, 1943, Chicago, Illinois; St. Louis Cardinals, 1918; Cincinnati Reds, 1924–1929

Jack Hendricks got into 42 games as a reserve outfielder in the major leagues in 1902 and 1903. He was a successful minor league manager in Indianapolis and Denver when Branch Rickey tapped him to replace Miller Huggins as manager of the St. Louis Cardinals in 1918. The Cardinals had been an up-and-down club for several years and had undergone many management changes. They finished eighth in 1918, and Hendricks became another of the management changes when he was fired at season's end.

He hooked on as a coach with the Cincinnati Reds, one of the National League's most successful franchises, at that time under the direction of manager Pat Moran, the winning manager in the 1919 World Series marred by the Black Sox scandal. Moran took ill and died on March 7, 1924, about a month before the season started. Hendricks was named the new manager.

Like many managers, Hendricks did not have an illustrious playing career. But he was an intelligent man who had a knack for remembering small details about opposing teams and players, as well as how particular game situations had been successfully handled in the past — the little things that can make a difference between winning and losing. He spent six fairly successful years as manager of the Cincinnati Reds. His 1926 club engaged in a furious battle for the pennant, finishing second to Rogers Hornsby's Cardinals. Only seven games separated the first four teams. The Pittsburgh Pirates, featuring four future Hall of Famers in their starting lineup — KiKi Cuyler, Paul Waner, Max Carey and Pie Traynor — finished third. Joe McCarthy's Cubs, poised for a future era of greatness, came in fourth. Hendricks got the most out of a club led by Hall of Famer Edd Roush who hit .323. The first baseman was Wally Pipp, a former Yankee who had a headache one day and was replaced by Lou Gehrig, who went on to play 2,130 consecutive games. The third baseman was Charlie Dressen, later to become more famous as a manager than as a player. Hendricks' top pitchers were Carl Mays, who six years earlier had fatally beaned Ray Chapman, and Eppa Rixey, a dependable left hander who hung around long enough to become the National League's winningest left hander until Warren Spahn came on the scene. Hendricks had a winning record four out of his first five years at Cincinnati. When the Reds plunged to seventh place in 1929, he resigned.

With all of the veteran players, Hendricks did well in his first few years. But he had a tendency to use players who were past their primes rather than grooming replacements or trading for them. So while the club he inherited in 1924 was solid, the team he left behind was in need of major rebuilding.

Year	Team	Record	Pct.	Standing
1918	StL (N)	51–78	.395	Eighth
1924	Cin	83–70	.542	Fourth
1925	Cin	80–73	.523	Third

Year	Team	Record	Pct.	Standing
1926	Cin	87–67	.565	Second
1927	Cin	75–78	.490	Fifth
1928	Cin	78–74	.513	Fifth
1929	Cin	66–88	.429	Seventh
7 years		**520–528**	**.496**	

Edward S. Hengle

No biographical data available; Chicago Browns, 1884

In the free-wheeling early days of baseball, when loosely formed management groups scrambled to come up with franchises, sometimes the marriages were unusual. Such was the case of the Chicago-Pittsburgh club of the 1880s. Ed Hengle started the season as manager but was fired midway through the season and never managed again.

Year	Team	Record	Pct.	Standing
1884	Chi (U)	34–39	.466	Sixth

William Jennings Herman

Born July 7, 1909, New Albany, Indiana; died September 5, 1992, West Palm Beach, Florida; Pittsburgh Pirates, September 6, 1946–September 19, 1947; Boston Red Sox, October 3, 1964–September 8, 1966

Billy Herman was a Hall of Fame second baseman, mostly for the Chicago Cubs but also helping the Brooklyn Dodgers to a National League pennant late in his career. Herman played on better teams than he ever managed. He got his first major league managerial job with Pittsburgh in 1948 and was gone after one year and a 61–92 record. His successors for the next decade didn't do much better. He was hired to finish out the 1964 season with the Boston Red Sox. They won their last two games of the season under Herman but still finished eighth. In 1965, they finished ninth and were in tenth place in 1966 when Herman was replaced.

Year	Team	Record	Pct.	Standing
1947	Pitt	61–92	.399	Eighth
1964	Bos	2–0	1.000	Eighth
1965	Bos	62–100	.383	Ninth
1966	Bos	64–82	.438	Tenth
4 years		**189–274**	**.408**	

Charles Lincoln "Buck" Herzog

Born July 8, 1885, Baltimore, Maryland; died September 4, 1953, Baltimore, Maryland; Cincinnati Reds, January 3, 1914–August 1, 1916

Buck Herzog was a National League infielder-outfielder for 13 seasons. In three of those years, he was the third baseman and also the manager of the Cincinnati Reds. He could get the Reds no higher than seventh. In 1914, his first year, the Reds lost 19 straight games, a franchise all-time record for losses. In 1916, with the Reds headed for their second last place finish in three years, Herzog was traded with Wade Killifer to the New York Giants, where he went back to playing full-time. In exchange, the Reds got Christy Mathewson,

Ed Roush and Bill McKechnie, three future Hall of Famers (McKechnie's fame coming as a manager.)

Year	Team	Record	Pct.	Standing
1914	Cin	60–94	.380	Eighth
1915	Cin	71–83	.461	Seventh
1916	Cin	34–49	.410	Eighth
3 years		**165–226**	**.422**	

Dorrel Norman Elvert "Whitey" Herzog

Born November 9, 1931, New Athens, Illinois; Texas Rangers, October 4, 1972–September 7, 1973; California Angels, June 26–29, 1974; Kansas City Royals, July 24, 1975–October 2, 1979; St. Louis Cardinals, June 9, 1980–August 29, 1980; October 24, 1980–July 6, 1990

Whitey Herzog had six division champions, four second place finishes and three third place finishes in a brilliant 18-year managerial career. A utility outfielder in his playing days, he never forgot the value of using his bench frequently. It helped produce winners in both Kansas City and St. Louis.

Herzog began his managerial career with a one-year stint at Texas and a four-game sojourn at California. In 1975, he took over the Kansas City Royals in mid-season and guided them to a second-place finish. The Royals then won their division the next three years and finished second in 1979. Herzog then moved down the highway to St. Louis where his Cardinal teams won three division titles.

There wasn't much finesse to Herzog on or off the field. His managerial style was to field a team that would consistently outhustle the opponent. Herzog's squads rarely relied on power but almost always had speed, which helped on both offense and defense. Nine of his teams led the league in stolen bases while eight led the league in fielding percentage. The Royals and the Cardinals under Herzog were good at taking the extra base — and in keeping the opponent from taking the extra base. Those two elements alone often meant the difference in close games.

Herzog liked to use his entire bench, but he did so by late-inning replacement more than in platooning. One of the reasons managers platoon is to make sure they have enough left-handed batters against right-handed pitchers, and vice versa. Herzog solved that problem by loading his lineup with switch hitters — usually switch hitters with speed. His speedy switch hitters over the years included U.L. Washington and Willie Wilson at Kansas City and Garry Templeton, Ozzie Smith, Willie McGee, Terry Pendleton, Vince Coleman and Jose Oquendo at St. Louis.

Herzog didn't believe in having players become rusty sitting on the bench. He wanted to make sure all his players felt useful. His teams were almost always near the top of the league in pinch-hitting batting average.

His stint with the Cardinals started strangely. He was the third of four Cardinal managers in 1980. Ken Boyer started the year and lasted 51 games, giving way to Jack Krol, who filled in for one game. Then Herzog took over for 73 games, and Red Schoendienst finished out the last 37 games. Herzog went 38–35 and was hired to manage the Cardinals in 1981. He went on to become one of the most successful managers in St. Louis history.

His Cardinals advanced to the World Series in 1982 by sweeping the Atlanta Braves in the league championship series. They then downed the Milwaukee Brewers in the World

Series. In 1985, St. Louis beat Tom Lasorda's Dodgers, four games to two, in the league championship series and then lost in seven games to the Kansas City Royals in the World Series. In that Series, the Cardinals were up, three games to two, and had a 1–0 lead going into the ninth inning of Game Six. Kansas City scored two runs in the ninth to win the game, aided by a controversial "safe" call at first base by umpire Don Denkinger when hitter Jorge Orta appeared to be out. That started the game-winning rally. In 1987, the Cardinals beat the San Francisco Giants, four games to three, in the League Championship Series and then lost, four games to three, to the Minnesota Twins in the World Series.

Herzog once said if a manager gets good players and they play well, he's a genius. If a bad manager has good players, he'll be a genius for a while. Sometimes a genius manager will have bad players who will make him look dumb. So the best thing a manager can do is to try to get good players and then get them to play hard. And even if everything goes right, said Herzog, the manager's destiny is to be fired unless he owns the team or dies on the job.

As manager of a bad Texas Rangers team in 1973, Herzog said the club was just two players shy of being a contender—Babe Ruth and Walter Johnson. As manager of the Cardinals in 1980, he responded to a writer who said the Cardinals didn't have any chemistry, saying, "Yeah, and we're missing a little geography and arithmetic, too."

Year	Team	Record	Pct.	Standing
1973	Tex	47–91	.391	Sixth
1974	Cal	2–2	.500	Sixth
1975	KC	41–25	.621	Second
1976	KC	90–72	.556	First
1977	KC	102–60	.630	First
1978	KC	92–70	.568	First
1979	KC	85–77	.525	Second
1980	StL	38–35	.521	Fourth
1981	StL	30–20	.600	Second
1981	StL	29–23	.558	Second
1982	StL	92–70	.568	First
1983	StL	79–83	.488	Fourth
1984	StL	84–78	.519	Third
1985	StL	101–61	.620	First
1986	StL	79–82	.490	Third
1987	StL	95–67	.580	First
1988	StL	76–86	.460	Fifth
1989	StL	86–76	.580	Third
1990	StL	33–47	.410	Sixth
18 years		**1281–1055**	**.548**	

LEAGUE CHAMPIONSHIP SERIES

Year	Team	Record	Pct.
1976	KC	2–3	.400
1977	KC	2–3	.400
1978	KC	1–3	.250
1982	StL	3–0	1.000
1985	StL	4–2	.667
1987	StL	4–3	.571
6 years		**16–14**	**.533**

WORLD SERIES

Year	Team	Record	Pct.
1982	StL	4–3	.571
1985	StL	3–4	.429
1987	StL	3–4	.429
3 years		**10–11**	**.476**

Walter F. Hewett

Born in 1861, Washington, D.C.; died October 7, 1944, Washington; Washington Statesmen, 1888

Walter Hewett was one of the many men who got a chance to manage a team in the late 19th century. His chance ended abruptly when Washington won only 12 of 41 games under Hewett's direction.

Year	Team	Record	Pct.	Standing
1888	Wash	12–29	.293	Eighth

Nathaniel Woodhull Hicks

Born April 19, 1845, Hempstead, New York; died April 21, 1907, Hoboken, New Jersey; New York Mutuals, 1875

Nat Hicks was a catcher and outfielder for six seasons, mostly with New York in the National Association. That is where he got his one and only stint as a manager, taking the helm in 1875 for 68 games. He was unable to get his team any higher than seventh place.

Year	Team	Record	Pct.	Standing
1875	NY	30–38	.441	Seventh

Michael Franklin "Pinky" Higgins

Born May 27, 1909, Red Oak, Texas; died March 21, 1969, Dallas, Texas; Boston Red Sox, October 10, 1954–July 2, 1959; July 18, 1960–October 7, 1962

Pinky Higgins was an American League infielder for 14 years who finished with a .292 lifetime batting average and played on pennant winners with three different teams: the Athletics, the Tigers and the Red Sox. He is in the history books for a feat he accomplished June 19–21, 1938, when he got 12 straight hits. Walt Dropo later tied the record but no one has surpassed it.

He took over as manager of the Boston Red Sox in 1955 and had four successive winning seasons, finishing third twice and fourth twice. The Red Sox had good hitting with Ted Williams, Jackie Jensen, Jimmy Piersall, Frank Malzone and, later, Carl Yastrzemski. But they always seemed one pitcher short of being able to overtake the Yankees, White Sox or Indians. When Boston got off to a slow start in 1959, new general manager Bucky Harris replaced Higgins with Billy Jurges. The Red Sox finished fifth. In 1960, they slumped even further and Jurges was replaced by Higgins who finished out the year as the Red Sox finished seventh. Remarkably, Boston's record for Higgins in his two partial seasons was identical, 31–42. After two more losing seasons, Higgins was replaced again, never to return.

When he came to the Red Sox, he had the advantage of having managed many of their younger players in the minor leagues, so he got along well with them. But his tendency was to play the veterans. When the veterans got older, Boston began to slip in the standings because there wasn't enough talent waiting in the wings. One exception to that was the left-field position, where Ted Williams was succeeded by Yastrzemski.

Year	Team	Record	Pct.	Standing
1955	Bos	84–70	.545	Fourth
1956	Bos	84–70	.545	Fourth
1957	Bos	82–72	.532	Third
1958	Bos	79–75	.513	Third
1959	Bos	31–42	.425	Eighth
1960	Bos	31–42	.425	Seventh
1961	Bos	76–86	.469	Eighth
1962	Bos	76–84	.475	Eighth
8 years		**543–541**	**.501**	

Richard Higham

Born in 1851, England; died March 18, 1905, Chicago, Illinois; New York Mutuals, 1874

Dick Higham was a scrappy, good-hitting ballplayer who had a .307 lifetime batting average over eight seasons in the National Association and National League. But he was also one of the biggest trouble makers in the early days of baseball. In his only time as a manager, he led a mediocre New York team to a 29–11 record, carrying the club from near the bottom of the league to second place. The next year, he signed with Chicago but was expelled from the team for associating with gamblers and throwing games. He played for several teams over the next few years and was playing for Albany in 1879 when the team disbanded on May 9 amid allegations that games were fixed. Incredibly, despite his history, Higham became an umpire in 1881. He was banished from the game a year later when it was discovered he had written notes to gamblers, instructing them on who to bet on in games.

Year	Team	Record	Pct.	Standing
1874	NY	29–11	.725	Second

Benjamin Franklin Hilt

No biographical data available; Philadelphia Quakers, 1890

Not much is known about Ben Hilt except that he managed Philadelphia in the Players League in 1890 and just about broke even, losing just two more than he won in 36 games. He never got another opportunity to manage.

Year	Team	Record	Pct.	Standing
1890	Phil (P)	17-19	.472	Fifth

Avitus Bernard "Vedie" Himsl

Born April 2, 1917, Plevna, Montana; Chicago Cubs (rotating coach), 1961

Vedie Himsl is the answer to a trivia question: Who was the first man in Phil Wrigley's "rotating coach" system to be head coach of the Chicago Cubs. Wrigley, the owner of the

Vedie Himsl

Cubs, instituted the coaching plan in 1961 instead of having a field manager. Himsl shared duties that year with Elvin Tappe, Lou Klein and Harry Craft. After all the rotating was done, the Cubs finished seventh. Himsl having rotated to the top job three times during the season, compiled a record of 10–21. Wrigley tried it one more year, finished seventh again, and discarded the idea forever. Himsl was only there for one of the years. Looking back on the experience many years later, he said the situation provided players with excuses for poor performances but shouldn't have. "Attitude plays a big part in baseball," he said. "When you walk on the field, you've got a job to do no matter who's sitting on the bench in the dugout. The manager can't hit or field for you." After the 1961 season, Himsl remained with the Cubs as a minor league coach and scout until his retirement in 1976.

Year	Team	Record	Pct.	Standing
1961	Chi (N)	10-21	.323	Seventh

William Clyde Hitchcock

Born July 31, 1916, Inverness, Alabama; Detroit Tigers, August 3, 1960; Baltimore Orioles, October 10, 1961–November 19, 1963; Atlanta Braves, August 9, 1966–September 3, 1967

Billy Hitchcock is one of numerous managers who were average major league infielders during their playing days, coached and then managed in the big leagues. Hitchcock was a coach for the Detroit Tigers in 1960 when the Tigers traded their manager, Jimmy Dykes, to Cleveland for Indians manager Joe Gordon. It was a unique move but it didn't help either club much. Cleveland finished fourth and Detroit sixth. In the interim, while the managers traveled to be with their new clubs, Hitchcock managed the Tigers for one game and won it. In 1962, he was hired to manage the Baltimore Orioles, a team full of youngsters plus Robin Roberts and Johnny Temple. The Orioles finished seventh. Baltimore added veteran shortstop Luis Aparicio in 1963 and moved up to fourth place. They were on the verge of being one of the American League's premier teams for the next decade — but Hitchcock wouldn't be a part of it. He was replaced at the end of the 1963 season by Hank Bauer. The next stop for Hitchcock was with the Atlanta Braves, where he replaced Bobby Bragan for the last 51 games of the season. The Braves won 33 of them and finished fifth. The following year, they were five games under .500 with three games to play when Hitchcock was fired and replaced by coach Ken Silvestri.

Year	Team	Record	Pct.	Standing
1960	Det	1–0	1.000	Sixth
1962	Bal	77–85	.475	Seventh

Year	Team	Record	Pct.	Standing
1963	Bal	86–76	.531	Fourth
1966	Atl	33–18	.647	Fifth
1967	Atl	77–82	.484	Seventh
5 years		**274–261**	**.512**	

Clell Lavern "Butch" Hobson

Born August 17, 1951, Tuscaloosa, Alabama; Boston Red Sox, October 8, 1991–September 20, 1994

Butch Hobson was a major league third baseman for eight years, most of it with the Boston Red Sox. The Red Sox hired him to manage the club in 1992, but he could not get the club above the .500 mark in his three seasons at the helm.

Year	Team	Record	Pct.	Standing
1992	Bos	73–89	.458	Seventh
1993	Bos	80–82	.490	Fifth
1994	Bos	54–61	.460	Fourth
3 years		**207–232**	**.472**	

Gilbert Raymond Hodges

Born April 4, 1924, Princeton, Indiana; died April 2, 1972, West Palm Beach, Florida; Washington Senators, May 22, 1963–October 11, 1967; New York Mets, October 11, 1967–April 2, 1972

Gil Hodges was part of the "Boys of Summer" teams with the Brooklyn Dodgers in the 1950s and was one of the best first basemen of his era. He is one of eight players in baseball history to hit four home runs in one game. As a manager, he took over two teams that had achieved little success, the Washington Senators and the New York Mets. In five years with Washington, the Senators showed steady improvement but never had the talent to compete with most of the other teams in the American League. They finished tenth in Hodges' first year, then moved up to ninth, then eighth for each of the next two years and finally up to sixth in 1967. In 1968, Hodges took over a New York Mets team that had finished in last place five of the first six years of its existence, creeping up to ninth place only in 1966 when Leo Durocher's Cubs finished last. They set a club record with 73 wins in Hodges' first year but still finished ninth. Then came the miracle year, 1969, when the Mets caught fire in mid–August, caught the front-running Cubs in early September and won 100 games to capture their first National League championship. They then swept Atlanta in the National League Championship Series and won four out of five from the Baltimore Orioles in the World Series.

That Met team featured young right hander Tom Seaver, who won 25 games and lost only 7; left hander Jerry Koosman, who was 17–9; and Tug McGraw and Jim McAndrew, a tough lefty-righty bullpen combination. A lesser known pitcher on that squad would make a name for himself later in his career — future Hall of Famer Nolan Ryan. The starting lineup featured no superstars: Ed Kranepool at first; Ken Boswell at second; Bud Harrelson at short; Wayne Garrettt at third; Cleon Jones, Tommy Agee and Ron Swoboda in the outfield; and Jerry Grote behind the plate. Hodges found the right mix and got good years out of utility players Al Weis, Ed Charles and Art Shamsky to bring home a winner.

In his days with the Senators, Hodges had shown an ability to get the most out of teams that didn't have much collective talent. That was the quality the Mets were looking for when they fired Wes Westrum, Casey Stengel's successor, after the 1967 season. With both the Mets and the Senators, Hodges' style was to quietly impose a discipline system — how players were to act on and off the field — and he enforced it. He was mild-mannered and rarely raised his voice, but he was stern with his players in letting them know what he expected. He stressed fundamentals and taught the players that it was just as easy to win as it was to lose; the difference was all in how they executed. In 1969, the Mets were no longer a team that could be counted on to give the opponent two or three runs a game, as Cardinal manager Red Schoendienst once described them. They committed the fewest errors in the National League, led the league in fielding percentage, and were second in the league in earned run average. Hodges managed two more years, guiding the Mets to third place finishes both years. The following spring, he died of a heart attack two days before his 48th birthday.

Year	Team	Record	Pct.	Standing
1963	Wash	42–80	.344	Tenth
1964	Wash	62–100	.383	Ninth
1965	Wash	70–92	.432	Eighth
1966	Wash	71–88	.447	Eighth
1967	Wash	76–85	.472	Sixth
1968	NY (N)	73–89	.451	Ninth
1969	NY	100–62	.617	First
1970	NY	83–79	.512	Third
1971	NY	83–79	.512	Third
9 years		**660–754**	**.467**	

LEAGUE CHAMPIONSHIP SERIES

Year	Team	Record	Pct.
1969	NY (N)	3–0	1.000

WORLD SERIES

Year	Team	Record	Pct.
1969	NY (N)	4–1	.800

Frederick C. Hoey

Born in New York City, New York; died December 7, 1933, Paris, France; New York Giants, 1899

Fred Hoey replaced John Day as manager of the New York Giants midway through the 1899 season. The Giants were 30–40 and in ninth place with Day. They were 30–50 with Hoey in charge and finished tenth. He was not invited back and never managed again.

Year	Team	Record	Pct.	Standing
1899	NY (N)	30–50	.375	Tenth

Glenn Edward Hoffman

Born July 7, 1958, Orange, California; Los Angeles Dodgers, June 21, 1998–October 23, 1998

Glenn Hoffman was an infielder for the Boston Red Sox for five years in the early 1980s. In 1998, he took on the responsibility of managing the Los Angeles Dodgers, who were going through an unusual transition. After having had only two managers for more than 40 years — Walter Alson and Tom Lasorda — Hoffman took over for Bill Russell, Lasorda's successor, who lasted less than two years. Hoffman took over at mid-year 1998 and guided the Dodgers to a third place finish. Davey Johnson was hired to manage the team in 1999.

Year	Team	Record	Pct.	Standing
1998	LA	47–41	.530	Third

William Henry Holbert

Born March 14, 1855, Baltimore, Maryland; died March 20, 1935, Laurel, Maryland; Syracuse Stars, 1879

At the age of 21, Billy Holbert umpired in the National League's first year, 1876. He was umpiring in a game between Allegheny (Pittsburgh) and Louisville when the Louisville catcher was injured and unable to continue. Louisville had no other catchers. Holbert volunteered to fill in — and a new career was born. He was a catcher-outfielder who played professional baseball for 12 years, finishing with a lifetime batting average of .207. On July 29, 1879, he managed the Syracuse Stars to a 13–4 loss against Boston. Holbert quit after the game.

Year	Team	Record	Pct.	Standing
1879	Syrac	0–1	.000	Seventh

John Samuel "Holly" Hollingshead

Born January 17, 1853, Washington, D.C.; died October 6, 1926, Washington; Washington Nationals, 1884

Holly Hollingshead is one of the many 19th-century managers who had a brief stint as the top man in the dugout but disappeared quickly. Hollingshead's Washington ball club lost 51 of the 63 games in which he managed. Hometown boy all the way, Hollingshead was Born in Washington, played in Washington, managed in Washington, was fired and retired in Washington and died in Washington.

Year	Team	Record	Pct.	Standing
1884	Wash (AA)	12–51	.190	Thirteenth

Thomas Francis Holmes

Born March 29, 1917, Brooklyn, New York; Boston Braves, June 19, 1951–May 31, 1952

Tommy Holmes set the modern National League record for hitting streaks when he hit safely in 37 straight games in 1945, a record broken 33 years later by Pete Rose. Holmes, a popular figure in Boston, was called on to replace Billy Southworth as Braves manager in 1951. They were in fifth place when Holmes took over but moved up to a fourth place finish. In 1952, with the team nine games under .500 after the first 35 games, Holmes was replaced by Charlie Grimm.

Year	Team	Record	Pct.	Standing
1951	Bos (N)	48–47	.505	Fourth
1952	Bos	13–22	.371	Sixth
2 years		**61–69**	**.469**	

Rogers Hornsby

Born April 27, 1896, Winters, Texas; died January 5, 1963, Chicago, Illinois; St. Louis Cardinals, May 30, 1925–December 20, 1926; Boston Braves, May 23, 1928–November 8, 1928; Chicago Cubs, September 25, 1930–August 2, 1932; St. Louis Browns, July 26, 1933–July 21, 1937; 1952; Cincinnati Reds, August 5, 1952–September 17, 1953

Rogers Hornsby was a man cut out of the Ty Cobb mold — a great hitter with a proud, arrogant, overbearing personality that provided him few close friends in the baseball world. Hornsby played 23 years and hit over .400 three times. His .424 average in 1924 remains the best single-season batting average in modern baseball history. His lifetime batting average of .358 ranks second only to Ty Cobb's .367. Hornsby was a playing manager for 12 years, with the St. Louis Cardinals, Boston Braves, Chicago Cubs, and St. Louis Browns. In some cases, his stays were short, mostly because of the poor relationship he had with his players and team management.

Hornsby's greatest triumph as a manager came in 1926, his first full season at the helm, when the Cardinals won the World Series. Cardinal owner Sam Breadon had decided a month before the season ended that win or lose, Hornsby had to go. The two men had bitterly disagreed over a commitment Breadon had made earlier in the season to play a September exhibition game with the New Haven, Connecticut, minor league team. As the pennant race heated up, the Cardinals wanted to cancel the game. But New Haven's management had heavily advertised the contest, and the team's owner, George Weiss (later the general manager of the New York Yankees), pleaded with Breadon to play the game. Breadon felt an obligation to honor the contract. Hornsby accused him of being more interested in making a few bucks in an exhibition game than winning the pennant. After that exchange, Breadon decided that Hornsby must go. He was traded to the New York Giants for Frankie Frisch. Frisch's arrival in St. Louis was the start of a glorious era for the Cardinals. Meanwhile, Hornsby lasted one year in New York. He was then traded to Boston, where he managed the Braves for a year. But Braves management also tired of his tantrums.

He went to Chicago and took over a Cubs ball club that would win pennants in 1932, 1935 and 1938 — but not with Hornsby. He was fired after 97 games of the 1932 season and his Cubs in second place. He was replaced by "Jolly Cholly" — Charlie Grimm — an easy-going, fun-loving man whom the players respected. It was under Grimm, and not Hornsby, that the Cubs won three pennants.

After his dismissal from the Cubs, Hornsby was called on to try to rehabilitate struggling teams, but in his last seven years of managing, his teams finished no higher than sixth. He managed the lowly St. Louis Browns from 1933 to 1937 and then returned to the Browns briefly in 1952 — briefly because the players rebelled against his insensitive tactics and he was fired. He managed for a little over a year at Cincinnati and then retired.

Stories of his relationships with players are legendary. With the Browns in 1952, he told reporters there were only two players on his team that he would pay to see play, Clint Courtney and Jim Rivera. Players on that Browns team said Hornsby would send Courtney to the race track to place bets for him during games. In 1927, he told reporters the Giants would never win the pennant as long as Doc Farrell was at shortstop. He was eating dinner with Farrell at the time. In 1961, asked about Roger Maris beating Babe Ruth's home run record, Hornsby replied, "He couldn't carry my bat."

Year	Team	Record	Pct.	Standing
1925	StL (N)	64–51	.557	Fourth
1926	StL	89–65	.568	First
1928	Bos	39–83	.320	Seventh
1930	Chi (N)	4–0	1.000	Second
1931	Chi	84–70	.545	Third
1932	Chi	53–44	.546	Second
1933	StL (A)	20–34	.370	Eighth
1934	StL	67–85	.441	Sixth
1935	StL	65–87	.428	Seventh
1936	StL	57–95	.375	Seventh
1937	StL	25–50	.333	Eighth
1952	StL	22–28	.440	Seventh
1952	Cin	27–24	.529	Sixth
1953	Cin	64–82	.438	Sixth
13 years		**680–798**	**.460**	

WORLD SERIES

Year	Team	Record	Pct.
1926	StL (N)	4–3	.571

Ralph George Houk

Born August 9, 1919, Lawrence, Kansas; New York Yankees, October 20, 1960–October 22, 1963; May 7, 1966–October 1, 1973; Detroit Tigers, October 11, 1973–October 1, 1978; Boston Red Sox, October 27, 1980–September 30, 1984

Ralph Houk took over as manager of the New York Yankees in 1961 as Casey Stengel's 12-year reign came to an end. The Yankees had been the dominant team of the 1950s, winning the pennant every year except 1954 and 1959. In 1960, they were American League champions again but lost the World Series in seven games to the Pittsburgh Pirates. At age 70, Stengel was relieved of his duties. Houk, who had been one of Stengel's coaches, inherited a team that still had the most talent in the league. In his first season, Roger Maris hit 61 home runs, Mickey Mantle hit 54 and the Yankees won 109 games, two short of what was then the modern American League record. (The 2001 Mariners would win 116, tying the 1906 Cubs' major league mark.) They won the pennant in 1962 and 1963 also, making Houk the first manager to win championships in each of his first three years.

Houk made some changes from Stengel's managerial style almost immediately. Under Stengel, star left-handed pitcher Whitey Ford had some great years, but Stengel would sometimes juggle the pitching rotation so that Ford would get fewer turns in the rotation. Sometimes, too, he would hold Ford back a day or two from his normal routine so the pitcher could match up against the Yankees' toughest opponents, such as Chicago and Cleveland. Ford always did well but never won 20 games during Stengel's tenure. Under Houk, he had the most starts of his career and won 25 in 1961 and 24 in 1963. He led the league in innings pitched in both years, something he had never done before.

When Houk took over the Yankees, they had a powerhouse lineup. In addition to Mantle and Maris, New York had Yogi Berra, Bill Skowron, Hector Lopez and Elston Howard. Shortstop Tony Kubek and second baseman Bobby Richardson were great defensively and were good set-up men for the potent offense. Houk didn't need to use much strategy on offense, and that was a trait that carried through the rest of his managerial career. Houk's teams always bunted fewer times than other teams. In seven seasons, they were last in the league in bunting. His 1973 Yankee team set the all-time record for fewest sacrifice bunts, 27, and by that time Maris, Mantle, Berra and Skowron were long gone. Other indications that Houk's teams didn't rely on finesse: in his 20 years as a manager, none of his teams ever led the league in walks or stolen bases.

He inherited a dynasty at New York, kept it going as manager and then let it slip as general manager. He moved into the front office after the 1963 season and Berra, the popular catcher, took over as manager. The Yankees won the pennant in 1964, but when they lost the World Series to the St. Louis Cardinals, Berra was fired and replaced by Cardinal skipper Johnny Keane. As the great Yankee players grew older or retired, the front office did not restock the team with promising youngsters or make trades to fill in crucial gaps, as they once did. Under Keane, the Yankees slipped to sixth in 1965. When they lost 16 of their first 20 games in 1966, Houk came down from the front office to manage once again, but the talent wasn't there and New York finished tenth. He remained the manager through 1973. Except for a second-place finish in 1970, he could get them no higher than fourth. In nine years as manager of the Tigers and Red Sox, he had one third place finish with Boston.

Joe DeMaestri, a veteran infielder who played on the 1961 Yankees, said that with all the hoopla that Mantle and Maris received, Houk never got the credit he deserved for handling the pitching staff. Beyond Whitey Ford, the Yankees didn't have any big name pitchers. Houk, a former Yankee catcher, hired an old teammate, Johnny Sain, to be his pitching coach. Ralph Terry went 16–3, Bill Stafford was 14–9, and Rollie Sheldon and Jim Coates were each 11–5. In the bullpen, Luis Arroyo went 15–5 with 29 saves — sharing in 44 Yankee wins.

As manager of the Tigers, Houk was once asked what's the secret to winning a pennant. "Get 30 games over .500 and you can break even the rest of the way," he replied.

Year	Team	Record	Pct.	Standing
1961	NY (A)	109–53	.671	First
1962	NY	96–66	.593	First
1963	NY	104–57	.646	First
1966	NY	66–73	.475	Tenth
1967	NY	72–90	.444	Ninth
1968	NY	83–79	.512	Fifth
1969	NY	80–81	.497	Fifth
1970	NY	93–69	.574	Second
1971	NY	82–80	.506	Fourth
1972	NY	79–76	.510	Fourth
1973	NY	80–82	.494	Fourth
1974	Det	72–90	.444	Sixth
1975	Det	57–102	.358	Sixth
1976	Det	74–87	.460	Fifth
1977	Det	74–88	.457	Fourth
1978	Det	86–76	.531	Fifth
1981	Bos	30–26	.536	Fifth
1981	Bos	29–23	.558	Second
1982	Bos	89–73	.549	Third
1983	Bos	78–84	.481	Sixth
1984	Bos	86–76	.531	Fourth
20 years		**1619–1531**	**.514**	

WORLD SERIES

Year	Team	Record	Pct.
1961	NY (A)	4–1	.800
1962	NY	4–3	.571
1963	NY	0–4	.000
3 years		**8–8**	**.500**

Frank Oliver Howard

Born August 8, 1936, Columbus, Ohio; San Diego Padres, October 4, 1980–October 13, 1981; New York Mets, June 3, 1983–October 2, 1983

Frank Howard was a 6-foot, 7-inch outfielder-first baseman for 16 years in the major leagues, mostly with the Los Angeles Dodgers and Washington Senators. He was the largest player of his day and possessed tremendous power. He hit 382 home runs, including a memorable one in Wrigley Field in Chicago in which one hand slipped off the bat as he started his swing. He hit the ball one-handed and it landed in the left-field bleachers.

Howard got two opportunities to manage, both with sub-par teams. His first managerial stint came in 1981, a strike year, with the San Diego Padres. The season was split and San Diego finished sixth in both halves. Howard was not invited back. In 1983, he took over the New York Mets team after George Bamberger was fired. Again, his team finished sixth and again Howard was dismissed.

Year	Team	Record	Pct.	Standing
1981	SD	23–33	.411	Sixth
1981	SD	18–36	.333	Sixth
1983	NY (N)	52–64	.448	Sixth
2 years		**93–133**	**.412**	

Arthur Henry Howe, Jr.

Born December 15, 1946, Pittsburgh, Pennsylvania; Houston Astros, November 7, 1988–October 5, 1993; Oakland A's, November 16, 1995–present

Art Howe was a major league third baseman for 10 years, mostly with the Houston Astros, who hired him as manager in 1989. In three of his five years there, the Astros were .500 or better but could get no higher than third place. He took over the Oakland A's in 1996 and had the challenge of working with a young team that seemingly wasn't going anywhere. But the A's leaped from fourth in 1998 to second in 1999, Howe's fourth year with the club. He made a lot of adjustments, depending on the makeup of his ball club, rather than mold a team to fit any one particular style. For instance, his 1993 Astros had 193 steal attempts while his 1996 A's had only 93. His 1993 Astros team laid

Art Howe

down 107 sacrifice bunts; the 1996 A's executed 49. Howe nursed a young pitching staff in 1999 to win 87 games without an established star and then guided them to a division championship in 2000.

Year	Team	Record	Pct.	Standing
1989	Hous	86–76	.530	Third
1990	Hous	75–87	.460	Fourth
1991	Hous	65–97	.400	Sixth
1992	Hous	81–81	.500	Fourth
1993	Hous	85–77	.520	Third
1996	Oak	78–84	.480	Third
1997	Oak	65–97	.400	Fourth
1998	Oak	74–88	.450	Fourth
1999	Oak	87–75	.530	Second
2000	Oak	91–70	.565	First
2001	Oak	102–60	.630	Second
10 years		**889–892**	**.499**	

DIVISIONAL PLAYOFFS

Year	Team	Record	Pct.
2000	Oak	2–3	.400

Daniel Phillip Howley

Born October 16, 1885, East Weymouth, Massachusetts; died March 10, 1944, East Weymouth; St. Louis Browns, November 3, 1926–October 7, 1929; Cincinnati Reds, 1930–1932

Dan Howley is another example of a major league catcher who later became a manager. Howley got into 22 games as a backstop with the Philadelphia Phillies in 1913. His return to major league baseball was as manager of the St. Louis Browns. Howley is one of the few managers in Browns history who had reasonable success, enough to get him a job with the Cincinnati Reds — who turned out to be worse than the Browns. In four of his six years as a manager, Howley's teams won 60 games or fewer.

Year	Team	Record	Pct.	Standing
1927	StL (A)	59–94	.386	Seventh
1928	StL	82–72	.532	Third
1929	StL	79–73	.520	Fourth
1930	Cin	59–95	.383	Seventh
1931	Cin	58–96	.377	Eighth
1932	Cin	60–94	.390	Eighth
6 years		**397–524**	**.431**	

Richard Dalton Howser

Born May 14, 1937, Miami, Florida; died June 19, 1987, Kansas City, Missouri; New York Yankees, July 25, 1978; October 28, 1979–November 21, 1980; Kansas City Royals, August 31, 1981–July 18, 1986; October 1, 1986–February 23, 1987

Like Sparky Anderson, Dick Howser was a mediocre major league infielder who later became a top-notch major league manager. He became part of the George Steinbrenner managerial shuffle when he was called on to fill in after Steinbrenner fired Billy Martin, and before he hired Bob Lemon. Howser was interim skipper for one game, which the Yankees lost. Then in 1979, Steinbrenner fired Lemon in mid-season and brought back Billy Martin who lasted until the end of the season. He was fired again and Howser was named to replace him. In 1980, under Howser, New York won the Eastern Division championship but lost to Kansas City in the league championship series. The Yankees then hired Gene Michael as manager for the 1981 season (although Lemon would be back before the year was out.) Howser took over the Kansas City Royals in the second half of the strike-split season, guiding them to the second-half championship, but they were swept in the division playoff by the Oakland A's — who were managed by Billy Martin. Howser's Royals finally made it to the World Series in 1985 and defeated the St. Louis Cardinals in seven games.

In the middle of the 1986 season, Howser began having severe headaches and became disoriented while managing the American League All-Star team. He was diagnosed with brain cancer and was forced to resign. He died less than a year later.

Howser is not rated with baseball's great managers because he was blessed with great teams to manage. But he was a shrewd, smart manager who had the ability to think ahead. Baseball analyst Bill James points to the 1985 American League Championship Series pitting Howser's Royals against the Toronto Blue Jays, then managed by Bobby Cox. Toronto won two early games with the help of hits from Al Oliver, the Blue Jays' left-handed designated hitter, off of Dan Quisenberry, the Royals bullpen ace, who was right-handed. Howser needed Quisenberry as his closer but couldn't afford to let Oliver beat him. Down three games to two, Howser started right-hander Mark Gubicza in Game Six but switched to left-hander Bud Black in the sixth inning, even though Gubicza was cruising along with a 5–3 lead. With the left-hander, Cox pinch-hit for Oliver. When Quisenberry came in as the ninth-inning closer, Oliver was out of the game and the Royals won. In Game Seven, Howser started his ace, right-hander Bret Saberhagen, but used him for only three innings. Lefthander Charlie Liebrandt came in and worked the next five innings and the Royals built up a 6–2 lead. Cox once again pinch-hit for Oliver who was once again out of the game when Quisenberry was called on in the ninth inning to close it out. Howser's strategy with Quisenberry was a huge factor in Kansas City's making it to the World Series. Cox would have many glorious moments of his own in the next decade, as manager of the Atlanta Braves.

Year	Team	Record	Pct.	Standing
1978	NY (A)	0–1	.000	Third
1980	NY	103–59	.636	First
1981	KC	20–13	.606	First
1982	KC	90–72	.556	Second
1983	KC	79–83	.488	Second
1984	KC	91–71	.560	First
1986	KC	40–48	.450	Third
8 years		**507–425**	**.544**	

DIVISION PLAYOFF SERIES

Year	Team	Record	Pct.
1981	KC	0–3	.000

LEAGUE CHAMPIONSHIP SERIES

Year	Team	Record	Pct.
1985	KC	4–3	.571

WORLD SERIES

Year	Team	Record	Pct.
1985	KC	4–3	.571

George A. Huff

Born June 11, 1872, Champaign, Illinois; died October 1, 1936, Champaign; Boston Red Sox, 1907

The Boston Red Sox struggled to a 54–90 record in 1907 and had four managers during the season. George Huff was the second of the four, replacing Cy Young. But under Huff, the Red Sox won three of eight games before he was replaced. Boston was in fifth place when he took over, in sixth place when he left, and seventh at season's end. Huff never managed again.

Year	Team	Record	Pct.	Standing
1907	Bos (A)	3–5	.375	Sixth

Miller James Huggins

Born March 27, 1880, Cincinnati, Ohio; died September 25, 1929, New York City, New York; St. Louis Cardinals, November 12, 1912–October 25, 1917; New York Yankees, October 25, 1917–September 25, 1929

Miller Huggins was a second baseman for Cincinnati and St. Louis in a 13-year playing career and managed the Cardinals for five years. He achieved his greatest fame and success as manager of the New York Yankees from 1918 until his untimely death in 1929. He is best known for the many run-ins he had with his famous slugger Babe Ruth, who came to the Yankees in 1920. The Yankees won six pennants in eight years under Huggins as well as three World Series championships. The 1927 Yankee team is considered to be one of the greatest teams in baseball history.

Huggins was a scrappy second baseman who made up for his small size by trying to outsmart his opponents. He set a record in 1910 that still stands today: he reached base six consecutive times in a game without getting a hit, doing it with four walks and being hit by two pitches.

Huggins did not have an easy time as manager of the Cardinals. He took over for popular Roger Bresnahan in 1913. Bresnahan was physically big and was a Hall of Fame catcher in his playing days. Huggins, at 5-foot-4, was a stark contrast to his predecessor, and it was feared he would have immediate discipline problems. The club played poorly and finished last. In 1914, however, Huggins put together a team that rose all the way to third place, a fact largely overlooked because of the success of Boston's pennant-winning "Miracle Braves." Huggins gained the respect of his players and fans that year in a tie game against the Dodgers. In the

Miller Huggins

seventh inning, St. Louis got a runner as far as third base. Huggins, coaching at third, started yelling at the rookie Dodger pitcher Whitey Appleby that there was something wrong with the ball. "Let me see it," he shouted. Appleby absent-mindedly tossed the ball to Huggins, who stepped aside, letting the ball go by him. The eventual winning run scored from third. A little shady, maybe, but clearly within the rules. That was Miller Huggins.

He was also an excellent judge of talent and knew well the type of people he wanted working around him. He had a great scout in Bob Connery. In 1915, Connery brought up to the Cardinals a young infielder who Huggins thought had great potential. He worked him into the lineup and the kid stayed there. His name was Rogers Hornsby. Huggins, who had been the Cardinals' player-manager, relinquished his second base job to Hornsby, showing that his wisdom as a manager overshadowed his pride as a ballplayer. Huggins also worked with a shortstop named Charlie O'Leary who never developed like Hornsby but who had a great sense of the game and loyalty to Huggins. Years later, Huggins brought O'Leary to New York where he coached the Yankees during their glory years.

When Ruth joined the Yankees in 1920, Huggins had been there two years. The Yankees were developing into a powerhouse, but they also had a reputation for doing pretty much what they wanted to do, both on and off the field. Huggins achieved success not only through managerial strategies but by harnessing this great group of athletes and turning them into champions.

The statistics tell one story — how Huggins' teams led the American League in home runs 10 times, in strikeouts eight times, and in slugging percentage seven times. Those are statistics one would expect from teams that featured Ruth, Lou Gehrig, Bob Muesel, Tony Lazzerri and Earl Coombs. But the Yankees also had the lowest earned run average in the league six times and were always among the leaders in fielding. Huggins had created a well-disciplined team on the field. Off the field, he tangled constantly with Ruth. In 1925, Ruth stayed out all night three nights in a row. Huggins fined him $5,000 — ten times higher than any previous fine in baseball history. Ruth complained to Yankee owner Jacob Ruppert, who backed Huggins. He had succeeded in creating an atmosphere of discipline off the field by not backing down to the game's greatest player. In 1929, Huggins contracted blood poisoning and died at the age of 50.

Year	Team	Record	Pct.	Standing
1913	StL (N)	51–99	.340	Eighth
1914	StL	81–72	.529	Third
1915	StL	72–81	.471	Sixth
1916	StL	60–93	.392	Seventh
1917	StL	82–70	.539	Third
1918	NY (A)	60–63	.488	Fourth
1919	NY	80–59	.576	Third
1920	NY	95–59	.617	Third
1921	NY	98–55	.641	First
1922	NY	94–60	.610	First
1923	NY	98–54	.645	First
1924	NY	89–63	.586	Second
1925	NY	69–85	.448	Seventh
1926	NY	91–63	.591	First
1927	NY	110–44	.714	First
1928	NY	101–53	.556	First
1929	NY	82–61	.573	Second
17 years		**1413–1134**	**.555**	

WORLD SERIES

Year	Team	Record
1921	NY	3–5
1922	NY	0–4
1923	NY	4–2
1926	NY	3–4
1927	NY	4–0
1928	NY	4–0
6 years		**18–15**

George H. Hughson

Born August 1, 1834, Erie County, New York; died April 22, 1912; Buffalo Bisons, 1885

George Hughson was 50 years old when he was called on to manage the Buffalo ball club in 1885. Hughson was the second of three managers that year and could muster only 18 wins in 51 games. It was his only opportunity to manage.

Year	Team	Record	Pct.	Standing
1885	Buff (N)	18–33	.353	Seventh

Gordon William Hunter

Born June 4, 1928, Punxsutawney, Pennsylvania; Texas Rangers, June 23, 1977–October 1, 1978

In 1977, the Texas Rangers had a rocky year. Manager Frank Lucchesi had them at .500 near mid-season but had some celebrated altercations with his players, including one in which outfielder Lenny Randle punched him. The Rangers released Lucchesi and brought Eddie Stanky out of retirement to take over the rowdy club. Stanky managed one game, won it, and then quit. Coach Connie Ryan took over for six games, winning two of them, while the Ranger brass hunted for a new manager. They came up with Billy Hunter and the Rangers jelled under his direction. They were one game under .500 when he came on board but went 60–33 the rest of the way to finish a surprising second. In 1978, he directed them to an 87–75 second-place finish but did not return for the 1979 season.

Year	Team	Record	Pct.	Standing
1978	Tex	60–33	.645	Second
1979	Tex	87–75	.537	Second
2 years		**147–108**	**.576**	

Clinton Merrick Hurdle

Born July 30, 1957, South Gate, California; Colorado Rockies, April 26, 2002–present

Former major league outfielder Clint Hurdle took over for Buddy Bell early in the 2002 season. Under Bell, the Rockies' bats slumped through the first three weeks of the campaign, as the team fell to 6–16. Dissatisfied with this, and with the club's last-place finish in 2001, ownership fired Bell and promoted hitting coach Hurdle to get the offense going.

Timothy Carroll Hurst

Born June 30, 1865, Ashland, Pennsylvania; died June 4, 1915, Pottsville, Pennsylvania; St. Louis Browns/Cardinals, 1898

Tim Hurst was a famous umpire in the last part of the 19th century and first part of the 20th century. He is credited with eliminating a lot of the rough play that was associated with baseball in those days. A large man, Hurst often made his calls with a clenched fist, in effect daring players to challenge his decisions. He began umpiring in the minor leagues in 1888 and umpired in both the National and American leagues when he was fired for spiking Philadelphia second baseman Eddie Collins in an argument over a disputed call.

In 1898, he left umpiring for a year to manage the lowly St. Louis Browns, who had finished in last place, 63½ games out of first place the previous year. Under Hurst, the Browns again finished last and again were 63½ games out of first place. He returned to umpiring the following year.

Year	Team	Record	Pct.	Standing
1898	StL	39–111	.260	Twelfth

Frederick Charles Hutchinson

Born August 12, 1919, Seattle, Washington; died November 12, 1964, Bradenton, Florida; Detroit Tigers, July 5, 1952–September 29, 1954; St. Louis Cardinals, October 12, 1955–September 17, 1958; Cincinnati Reds, July 8, 1959–August 13, 1964

Fred Hutchinson was a pitcher for the Detroit Tigers for 11 years who then managed the Tigers, St. Louis Cardinals and Cincinnati Reds. As a manager, he had a reputation for getting along well with his players, and his teams often exceeded their expectations. His Detroit teams showed steady improvement, finishing eighth in 1952, sixth in 1953 and fifth in 1954. In 1956, the Cardinals hired him. They finished fourth that year but finished second in 1957. Hutchinson was named National League Manager of the Year. He stayed one more year in St. Louis and then headed for Cincinnati and had a pennant winner two years later. Hutchinson remained with the Reds until he became ill with cancer and was forced to resign during the 1964 season.

Hutchinson's success was due in part to the relationship he had with his players. He respected his players and empathized with those who got little playing time. Veteran player Hank Sauer, who joined the Cardinals in 1956, the same year Hutchinson became manager, said Hutchinson was one of the finest men he ever met and had a great managerial philosophy. Part of that philosophy involved paying attention to the guys on the bench because he believed if they were happy, the whole team would be more successful, said Sauer.

But Hutchinson was a tough disciplinarian who didn't put up with lazy play. He often tangled with young Frank Robinson and once benched him for three games because Hutchinson didn't like his attitude. This, even though he was clearly the team's best hitter.

Left-handed pitcher Jim O'Toole, who helped the Reds to their 1961 pennant, said Hutchinson was a nice man but a tough individual who was capable of winning a fight if it came to that. But he also had the respect of the players and instilled discipline on the Reds that helped them win. O'Toole said that when Hutchinson came to the mound and said something to the pitcher, the best response was, "Yes sir."

And Hutchinson didn't hesitate to go to the mound. "It's the pitcher's game for the first five innings. After that, it's mine," he once said. He recognized pitching talent when he saw it. When he managed a minor league club in Seattle, Jim Brosnan was pitching for the Los Angeles Angels and beat Hutchinson's team five times. Years later, when Hutchinson managed the Cardinals, he arranged a trade with the Cubs to get Brosnan. Then when he went to Cincinnati, he arranged a trade with the Cardinals to get Brosnan again. Brosnan was a top relief pitcher on the 1961 pennant winner.

Hutchinson was diagnosed with cancer in the winter of 1963 and had to retire after 109 games in the 1964 season. The Reds were in third place. Coach Dick Sisler took over. That was the year that Philadelphia lost 11 of its last 12 games in the final two weeks of the season, allowing the Cardinals to sneak into first place. Cincinnati finished second, one game out. Players, coaches, writers and many fans believed the Reds would have won had their feisty leader been healthy. He died November 12, 1964.

Year	Team	Record	Pct.	Standing
1952	Det	27–55	.329	Eighth
1953	Det	60–94	.390	Sixth
1954	Det	68–86	.442	Fifth
1956	StL	76–78	.494	Fourth
1957	StL	87–67	.565	Second
1958	StL	69–75	.479	Fifth
1959	Cin	39–35	.527	Fifth
1960	Cin	67–87	.435	Sixth
1961	Cin	93–61	.604	First
1962	Cin	98–64	.605	Third
1963	Cin	86–76	.531	Fourth
1964	Cin	60–49	.550	Third
12 years		**830–827**	**.501**	

WORLD SERIES

Year	Team	Record	Pct.
1961	Cin	1–4	.200

Arthur Albert Irwin

Born February 14, 1858, Toronto, Ontario, Canada; died July 16, 1921, Atlantic Ocean; Washington Senators, 1889, 1892, 1898–1899; Boston Reds, 1891; Philadelphia Athletics 1898–1899

Arthur Irwin managed three teams toward the end of the 19th century, including the Washington ball club in three different stints in 10 years, making him the Billy Martin of his day. In eight years of managing, he had one great year, 93–42 with Boston, two better than average years, finishing third and fourth with Philadelphia and five years in which his teams were at or near the bottom of the league. Irwin was 63 years old when died as a result of drowning in the Atlantic Ocean.

Year	Team	Record	Pct.	Standing
1889	Wash (N)	28–44	.389	Eighth
1891	Bos (AA)	93–42	.689	First
1892	Wash (N)	34–46	.425	Ninth

Year	Team	Record	Pct.	Standing
1894	Phil (N)	71–57	.555	Fourth
1895	Phil (N)	78–53	.595	Third
1896	NY (N)	38–53	.418	Ninth
1898	Wash	9–15	.375	Eleventh
1899	Wash	54–98	.355	Eleventh
8 years		**405–408**	**.498**	

Hugh Ambrose Jennings

Born April 2, 1869, Pittston, Pennsylvania; died February 1, 1928, Scranton, Pennsylvania; Detroit Tigers, November 1, 1906–December 18, 1920

Hughie Jennings was a winner from the time he entered professional baseball. He was a good-hitting, slick-fielding shortstop for the Baltimore club which won the league championship his first three years on the team, 1894–1896. One of his teammates, John McGraw, became a lifelong friend and colleague. Jennings became manager of the Detroit Tigers in 1907, and the Tigers won the American League championship in his first three years there, a record for success matched only by Ralph Houk with the New York Yankees from 1961 to 1963.

Jennings managed the Tigers until 1920 when Ty Cobb took over. He then coached for his old friend John McGraw with the New York Giants, who won the pennant four years in a row while Jennings was there.

His strategy as manager of the Tigers was dictated by the type of team he had. The Tigers could hit. He had two Hall of Fame outfielders in Cobb and Sam Crawford, each of whom consistently hit over .300. The Tigers led the league in hits seven times, in runs scored six times and in slugging percentage five times during Jennings' tenure. His teams were scrappy, in the mode of McGraw and the old Baltimore teams. "Hit or get hit," he would tell his players. (During his playing days Jennings often led the league in getting hit with pitches.) Jennings had a simple philosophy regarding discipline: "If you have to start fining them, it's time to get rid of them." He had to deal with

Hughie Jennings

Ty Cobb much like, years later, Miller Huggins had to deal with Babe Ruth. In both cases, their managerial success was due in large part, not to on-the-field strategy as much as it was dealing with the egos and antics of superstars who were depended upon to help the team.

Year	Team	Record	Pct.	Standing
1907	Det	92–58	.613	First
1908	Det	90–63	.588	First
1909	Det	98–54	.645	First
1910	Det	86–68	.558	Third
1911	Det	89–65	.578	Second
1912	Det	69–84	.451	Sixth
1913	Det	66–87	.431	Sixth
1914	Det	80–73	.523	Fourth
1915	Det	100–54	.649	Second
1916	Det	87–67	.565	Third
1917	Det	78–75	.510	Fourth
1918	Det	55–71	.437	Seventh
1919	Det	80–60	.571	Fourth
1920	Det	61–93	.396	Seventh
14 years		**1131–972**	**.538**	

WORLD SERIES

Year	Team	Record	Pct.
1907	Det	0–4	.000
1908	Det	1–4	.200
1909	Det	3–4	.429
3 years		**4–12**	**.250**

Darrell Dean Johnson

Born August 25, 1928, Horace, Nebraska; Boston Red Sox, 1974–July 16, 1976; Seattle Mariners, September 4, 1976–August 4, 1980; Texas Rangers, July 28, 1982–October 4, 1982

Darrell Johnson was manager of the Boston Red Sox for three years and led them in one of baseball's most exciting World Series. He also managed teams at Seattle and Texas that had less talent and achieved less success. He took over a Red Sox team that had finished second under Eddie Kasko the year before. It was an offensive powerhouse with future Hall of Famers Carlton Fisk and Carl Yastrzemski as well as Dwight Evans and Rico Petrocelli. Luis Tiant was the ace of the pitching staff, winning 22 games in 1974. The addition of two rookies, outfielders Fred Lynn and Jim Rice, completed the package in 1975. The Red Sox had five pitchers who won 13 games or more — none of them with an earned run average below 3.60. But the Red Sox won their division by five games and then dethroned the Oakland A's in the league championship series. The A's had won three straight world championships. In a classic World Series matchup, the Red Sox took on the Cincinnati Reds and lost in seven games. The sixth game was decided by Fisk's famous home run in the 12th inning. In 1976, the Red Sox got off to a slow start — too slow for team management, and Johnson was gone after 46 games. He managed four years at Seattle but could not get the Mariners higher than sixth place. After a partial year with the Texas Rangers, Johnson retired.

Year	Team	Record	Pct.	Standing
1974	Bos	84–78	.519	Third
1975	Bos	95–65	.594	First
1976	Bos	41–45	.477	Third
1977	Sea	64–98	.395	Sixth

Year	Team	Record	Pct.	Standing
1978	Sea	56–104	.350	Seventh
1979	Sea	67–95	.414	Sixth
1980	Sea	39–65	.375	Seventh
1982	Tex	26–40	.394	Sixth
8 years		**472–590**	**.444**	

LEAGUE CHAMPIONSHIP SERIES

Year	Team	Record	Pct.
1975	Bos	3–0	1.000

WORLD SERIES

Year	Team	Record	Pct.
1975	Bos	3–4	.429

David Allen Johnson

Born January 30, 1943, Orlando, Florida; New York Mets, October 2, 1983–May 29, 1990; Cincinnati Reds, May 25, 1993–October 25, 1995; Baltimore Orioles, October 25, 1995–November 6, 1997; Los Angeles Dodgers, October 23, 1998–October 6, 2000

Davey Johnson is one of the most successful modern major league managers. He averaged 97 wins a year for his first five seasons managing, all with the New York Mets. He was helped by the fact that his managerial career started at exactly the same time that Dwight Gooden began his major league pitching career. Gooden was 91–35 in his first five years with the Mets, an average of 18–7 each year. The Mets won the World Series championship in 1986, the series made famous by Boston first baseman Bill Buckner's misplay of Mookie Wilson's ground ball in a Mets come-from-behind victory. The Mets finished first or second in Johnson's first six years and were in second place, but with a mediocre 20–22 record, when he was fired in 1990. The Cincinnati Reds hired him midway through the 1993 season. After finishing fifth in 1993 and fifth again in the strike-shortened 1994 season, the Reds climbed to the top in 1995. But in a bizarre set of circumstances, Johnson was not rehired because Marge Schott, the Reds' maverick owner, had promised the managerial job to coach Ray Knight, who had once played for the Reds. By now, Johnson had a track record as a winner, and the Baltimore Orioles hired him. Baltimore finished second in 1996 and first in 1997, making the playoffs both years but not making it to the World Series. And once again, Johnson was fired after leading his team to a division championship. His relationship with owner Peter Angelos had been strained and reached the breaking point when Johnson ordered second baseman Roberto Alomar to pay a $10,500 fine to a charity that employed Johnson's wife. In 1999, the Los Angeles Dodgers hired him. In his first year, the Dodgers won only 77 games, the worst record of any team managed by Johnson. But he was back in 2000 to try to get back to his winning ways. The Dodgers rebounded to finish second but Johnson was let go at the end of the season.

Johnson was a conservative manager who didn't take uncalculated risks. He learned with his Mets teams to put the best nine players on the field every day, to leave the lineup untinkered with, and to develop both a solid corps of starting pitchers and a good closer, thereby eliminating the need to go to the bullpen frequently in the middle innings. Even in Cincinnati, after he had been managing 12 years, his style hadn't changed. He won the division championship in 1995 using only 18 pinch runners all season. Then at Baltimore in 1996, the conservative Johnson used pinch hitters just 85 times. Managing in the American League, where the designated hitter is used, required fewer opportunities for pinch hitters compared with the National League. Even so, the 85 pinch hitters used by Johnson's Orioles was the fewest in both the American and National Leagues.

Johnson has said he doesn't believe in a lot of technical talk in dealing with young ballplayers. "Paralysis by analysis," he calls it. He believes in telling young pitchers to use their best stuff and throw it in the strike zone, instead of spending time telling them how to pitch to every hitter they're going to face. He also believes in having a catcher who knows what the manager wants. Then the catcher calls the ball game and young pitchers aren't confused by everything they hear in pre-game meetings. Part of Johnson's success over the years was his development of young pitchers such as Gooden, Sid Fernandez and Rick Aguilera.

His 9–2 record in divisional playoffs is the highest among managers whose teams have been involved in 10 games or more. His teams have had a winning percentage of .600 or higher in six of his 13 years. His lifetime winning percentage is .567 — the percentage a team would have if it won 93 games a year on a 162-game schedule. All of these figures are higher than those of most managers who are in the Hall of Fame.

Year	Team	Record	Pct.	Standing
1984	NY (N)	90–72	.550	Second
1985	NY	98–64	.600	Second
1986	NY	108–54	.660	First
1987	NY	92–70	.560	Second
1988	NY	100–60	.620	First
1989	NY	87–75	.530	Second
1990	NY	20–22	.470	Second
1993	Cin	53–65	.440	Fifth
1994	Cin	66–48	.570	First
1995	Cin	85–59	.590	First
1996	Bal	88–74	.540	Second
1997	Bal	98–64	.600	First
1999	LA	77–85	.470	Third
2000	LA	86–76	.531	Second
14 years		**1148–878**	**.567**	

DIVISION PLAYOFFS

Year	Team	Record	Pct.
1995	Cin	3–0	1.000
1996	Bal	3–1	.750
1997	Bal	3–1	.750
3 years		**9–2**	**.818**

LEAGUE CHAMPIONSHIP SERIES

Year	Team	Record	Pct.
1986	NY (N)	4–2	.667
1988	NY	3–4	.429
1995	Cin	0–4	.000
1996	Bal	1–4	.200
1997	Bal	2–4	.333
5 years		**10–18**	**.357**

WORLD SERIES

Year	Team	Record	Pct.
1986	NY (N)	4–3	.571

Roy Cleveland Johnson

Born February 23, 1903, Pryor, Oklahoma; died September 11, 1973, Tacoma, Washington; Chicago Cubs, May 4, 1944

Roy Johnson was a major league outfielder for 10 years who then became a coach. In 1944, when the Chicago Cubs started the season by losing nine out of their first 10 games, owner Phil Wrigley fired Jimmy Wilson and hired Charlie Grimm, who had managed Cub pennant winners a decade earlier. In 1945, Grimm had the Cubs back in the World Series. But in 1944, in the interim between Wilson's dismissal and Grimm's arrival, Roy Johnson managed the club for one game — and lost it.

Year	Team	Record	Pct.	Standing
1944	Chi (N)	0–1	.000	Eighth

Timothy Evald Johnson

Born July 22, 1949, Grand Forks, North Dakota; Toronto Blue Jays, November 24, 1997–March 17, 1999

Tim Johnson had a nine-year major league playing career with the Milwaukee Brewers and Toronto Blue Jays and managed the Blue Jays for one year — in between the managerial tenures of Cito Gaston and Jim Fregosi. His won-loss record was excellent but his rapport with his players was poor. He was fired in spring training of 1999 after it was discovered that Johnson, who sometimes wore military fatigues on the practice field, had misrepresented his military record, including false stories about serving in combat in Vietnam, in an effort to motivate his players.

Year	Team	Record	Pct.	Standing
1998	Tor	88–74	.540	Third

Walter Perry Johnson

Born November 6, 1887, Humboldt, Kansas; died December 10, 1946, Washington, D.C.; Washington Senators, October 15, 1928–October 4, 1932; Cleveland Indians, June 11, 1933–August 4, 1935

Walter Johnson was one of baseball's greatest pitchers and one of its most beloved individuals. In a 21-year career with the Washington Senators, he won 416 games, second only to Cy Young on the all-time win list. He pitched nearly 6,000 innings and had a career earned run average of 2.17. He still holds the record for most shutouts in a career with 110. Johnson took over for Bucky Harris as manager of the Senators in 1929, and after one sub-par year (71–81), guided Washington to three straight 90-win seasons, finishing second and then third twice. He managed the Cleveland Indians for three years before retiring. When he was hired by the Indians, who had finished fourth three years in a row, he replaced popular manager Roger Peckinpaugh. The hiring was not warmly received by the fans or the press. Johnson was perceived to be a weak manager because he hadn't won the pennant in Washington though his predecessor, Bucky Harris, had.

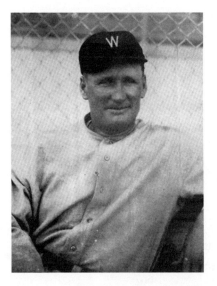

Walter Johnson

Johnson withstood two player rebellions in his three years at Cleveland from players who thought he ran too tight a ship. Johnson was particularly unsympathetic to players he thought were not tough enough. "I never had a sore arm in my life," he told his pitching staff. Cleveland finished fourth in 1933 and third in 1934. As they hovered in fifth place past the midway point of the 1935 season, and with attendance slipping, Johnson was fired, to be replaced by coach Steve O'Neill. Ever the gentleman, Johnson pointed out to management that the Indians were about to embark on a tough road trip in which they would probably lose many games. He said that would be a tough way for O'Neill to start and asked that he remain as manager until the club returned home — so the new man could get off to a good start. The club agreed and delayed the firing of Johnson.

Year	Team	Record	Pct.	Standing
1929	Wash	71–81	.467	Fifth
1930	Wash	94–60	.610	Second
1931	Wash	92–62	.597	Third
1932	Wash	93–61	.604	Third
1933	Cleve	49–51	.490	Fourth
1934	Cleve	85–69	.552	Third
1935	Cleve	46–48	.489	Fifth
7 years		**530–432**	**.551**	

Fielder Allison Jones

Born August 13, 1871, Shinglehouse, Pennsylvania; died March 13, 1934, Portland, Oregon; Chicago White Sox, 1904–1908; St. Louis Terriers, 1914–1915; St. Louis Browns, 1916–1918

Fielder Jones — and that was his real first name — managed the "Hitless Wonders." In 1906, the Chicago White Sox hit just seven home runs all year and had a team batting average of .230, lowest in the American League. Their leading hitter, Frank Isbell, mustered an average of only .279. But the White Sox had a team earned run average of 2.13, bolstered by 32 shutouts from pitchers such as Ed Walsh and Nick Altrock. Then they beat Frank Chance's Chicago Cubs in the World Series, a team that had won 116 games. It was Fielder Jones' finest hour. Over the course of his 10-year career, he would also finish second twice and third twice.

Jones believed his teams won because of their defense. "Leather is mightier than the wood," he told reporters. And he believed it: his teams played station-to-station baseball, manufacturing one- and two-run leads the defense would vigorously protect.

Jones played under Ned Hanlon with the old Baltimore club, so he knew how to play aggressive baseball. He often called Hanlon for advice when his team wasn't playing well. Jones' teams were adept at moving runners along with "productive outs." They led the league in sacrifice bunts five times and were near the top in all of his other seasons. He also learned from Hanlon not to be afraid to make a change if a change seemed necessary. In 1916 and 1917, Jones set the major league record two years in a row for use of relief pitchers.

Year	Team	Record	Pct.	Standing
1904	Chi (A)	67–47	.588	First
1905	Chi	92–60	.605	Second
1906	Chi	93–58	.616	First
1907	Chi	87–64	.567	Third
1908	Chi	88–64	.579	Third
1914	StL (F)	12–26	.316	Seventh
1915	StL	87–67	.565	Second
1916	StL (A)	79–75	.513	Fifth
1917	StL	57–97	.370	Seventh
1918	StL	23–24	.489	Fifth
10 years		**685–582**	**.541**	

WORLD SERIES

Year	Team	Record	Pct.
1906	Chi (A)	4–2	.667

Edwin David Joost

Born June 5, 1916, San Francisco, California; Philadelphia Athletics, November 4, 1953–November 18, 1954

When Connie Mack retired from managing the Philadelphia A's in 1951, he left behind a storied franchise but not a good ball club. Jimmy Dykes was Mack's unfortunate successor. Then along came Joost, for one year, in which the A's lost twice as many as they won. Joost never managed in the major leagues again.

Year	Team	Record	Pct.	Standing
1954	Phil (A)	51–103	.331	Eighth

Michael Jorgensen

Born August 16, 1948, Passaic, New Jersey; St. Louis Cardinals, September 16, 1995–October 23, 1995

Mike Jorgensen, who was born on the day that Babe Ruth died, had a 17-year major league career as a first baseman with 10 different teams: the New York Mets three different times, the Montreal Expos twice, the Atlanta Braves twice, and the Oakland A's, Texas Rangers and St. Louis Cardinals. In 1985, in his 17th and last season, he got into a World Series as a member of the Cardinals and then stayed on with the organization. Ten years later, he managed the Cardinals for 96 games, paving the way for the Tony LaRussa and Mark McGwire era to begin.

Year	Team	Record	Pct.	Standing
1995	StL (N)	42–54	.430	Fourth

William Michael Joyce

Born September 21, 1865, St. Louis, Missouri; died May 8, 1941, St. Louis; New York Giants, 1896–1898

Scrappy Bill Joyce played eight years of professional baseball, earning his nickname from his style of play. He finished with a lifetime batting average of .294. Joyce achieved some success as manager of the New York Giants for parts of three seasons before the McGraw era started. His best year was in 1898 when the Giants won 83 games and finished third.

Year	Team	Record	Pct.	Standing
1896	NY	28–14	.667	Seventh
1897	NY	83–48	.634	Third
1898	NY	68–60	.531	Seventh
3years		179–1		

William Frederick Jurges

Born May 8, 1908, Bronx, New York; Boston Red Sox, July 3, 1959–July 18, 1960

Billy Jurges, a terrific major league infielder in his playing days, was a coach for the Boston Red Sox in 1959 when he was called on to replace Pinky Higgins as manager. Under Jurges, the '59 Red Sox were 44–36 and moved from eighth place to fifth place. But in 1960, when Boston started out at 34–47, Jurges got the boot and Higgins came back.

Year	Team	Record	Pct.	Standing
1959	Bos	44–36	.550	Eighth
1960	Bos	34–47	.420	Eighth
2 years		**78–83**		

Edward Michael Kasko

Born June 27, 1932, Linden, New Jersey; Boston Red Sox, October 2, 1969–September 30, 1973

Eddie Kasko had a four-year managerial career that was a good one but also an example of how sometimes good isn't good enough. He became manager of the Boston Red Sox in 1970 and had a third-place finish. But the Red Sox were 21 games behind the division-winning Baltimore Orioles. In 1971, the Red Sox were third again, this time 16 games behind the Orioles. In 1972, Boston moved up to second place, just one game behind division-winning Detroit. After another second place finish in 1973, Kasko was out, never to manage again in the major leagues.

When Kasko took over as Red Sox manager, he announced that he was a player's manager. "I'll turn the game over to the players," he said. "I'll let them run on their own, hit their pitch, call their game. I'll never call a pitch from the dugout." He was replaced as manager by Darrell Johnson for the 1974 season.

Year	Team	Record	Pct.	Standing
1970	Bos	87–75	.537	Third
1971	Bos	85–77	.525	Third
1972	Bos	85–70	.548	Second
1973	Bos	89–73	.549	Second
4 years		**346–295**	**.540**	

John Joseph Keane

Born November 3, 1911, St. Louis Missouri; died January 7, 1967, Houston, Texas; St. Louis Cardinals, July 6, 1961–October 16, 1964; New York Yankees, October 20, 1964–May 7, 1966

Johnny Keane managed in the major leagues for six years and was involved in one of baseball's most hectic finishes. In 1964, his fourth year as manager of the St. Louis Cardinals, St. Louis appeared headed for a finish of third place or lower: Gene Mauch's Philadelphia Phillies were cruising toward the pennant. But the Phillies lost 11 of their last 12 games and finished third. The Cardinals snuck into first place and held on to nose out Cincinnati by one game. Then they beat the New York Yankees in the World Series, spelling the demise of rookie manager Yogi Berra. In a surprise move, the Yankees hired Keane but provided him with a team full of old-timers and untested youngsters. Keane's Yankees finished sixth his first year and were tenth—having lost 16 of their first 20 games—in his second year when he was fired and replaced by general manager Ralph Houk, who had hired him just two years before.

Year	Team	Record	Pct.	Standing
1961	StL	47–33	.588	Fifth
1962	StL	84–78	.519	Sixth
1963	StL	93–69	.574	Second
1964	StL	93–69	.574	First
1965	NY (A)	77–85	.475	Sixth
1966	NY	4–16	.200	Tenth
6 years		398–350	.532	

WORLD SERIES

Year	Team	Record	Pct.
1964	StL	4–3	.571

Joseph James Kelley

Born December 9, 1871, Cambridge, Massachusetts; died August 14, 1943, Baltimore, Maryland; Cincinnati Reds, 1902–February 2, 1906; Boston Braves, September 7, 1907–January 13, 1909

Joe Kelley was a Hall of Fame outfielder for the great Baltimore ball club of the 1890s. His manager was the influential Ned Hanlon and his teammates included Wee Willie Keeler and future managers Hughie Jennings and John McGraw. As manager of the Cincinnati Reds from 1902 to 1905, his ball clubs were always over the .500 mark, but he could get them no higher than third place. One of his young players was Miller Huggins, who went on to manage the St. Louis Cardinals and New York Yankees. He was replaced as Reds manager by Hanlon. Kelley finished out his managerial career with the Boston Doves (now the Braves) in 1908, his only losing season.

He was a colorful player who once went nine-for-nine in a doubleheader. When playing the outfield, he sometimes would hide a ball in the tall outfield grass and, when a ball was hit in the gap, he would retrieve the hidden ball and throw it in. He was caught in the act one day, when, playing left field, he threw in the dummy ball at the same time the center fielder threw in the live one. In 1903, as manager of the Reds, he released Branch Rickey because Rickey refused to play on Sundays. Rickey went on to become a successful manager and general manager in the major leagues; Kelley later became a scout for the New York Yankees. In 1915 and 1916, he didn't sign a single player—and was praised by Yankee management for the money he saved the team.

Year	Team	Record	Pct.	Standing
1902	Cin	33–26	.559	Fourth
1903	Cin	74–65	.532	Fourth

Year	Team	Record	Pct.	Standing
1904	Cin	88–65	.575	Third
1905	Cin	79–74	.516	Fifth
1908	Bos (N)	63–91	.409	Sixth
5 years		337–321	.512	

John O. Kelly

Born in 1856, New York City, New York; died March 27, 1926, Malba, New York; Louisville Colonels, 1887

John Kelly

Honest John Kelly got his nickname because of his superior skills and untarnished good name as an umpire. He left umpiring for a year to become manager of the Louisville franchise in the American Association in 1887. Though his team finished with a record 76–60, good enough for fourth place, he was fired, so he returned to umpiring. Later, he also became a famous boxing referee who worked several title fights.

Year	Team	Record	Pct.	Standing
1887	Lou (AA)	76–60	.559	Fourth

Michael Joseph "King" Kelly

Born December 31, 1857, Troy, New York; died November 8, 1894, Boston, Massachusetts; Boston Reds, 1890; Cincinnati Kelly's Killers, 1891

King Kelly was one of the most exciting players of the 19th century. He was an outstanding base stealer whose antics prompted the fan's cry—later a song—"Slide, Kelly, Slide." In 1890, he took part in a player revolt from the National League by agreeing to manage the Boston team in the Players League. Kelly managed the team and played almost every position as Boston won the championship. The next year he jumped to the American Association to manage a Cincinnati team that was more adept at partying than playing. Kelly was fired after 100 games, his team in seventh place. He died three years later at the age of 37.

Year	Team	Record	Pct.	Standing
1890	Bos (P)	81–48	.628	First
1891	Cin (AA)	43–57	.430	Seventh
2 years		124–105	.541	

Jay Thomas Kelly

Born August 15, 1950, Graceville, Minnesota; Minnesota Twins, September 12, 1986–October 12, 2001

In 1986, the Minnesota Twins decided to make a managerial change, something that had been fairly commonplace for the ball club. Ray Miller was the manager in 1985 and most of 1986; Billy Gardner in 1982, 1983 and 1984; John Goryl in 1981; Gene Mauch in 1980. All achieved roughly the same level of success—a spot in the American League cellar.

On September 12, 1986, Twins management chose as their new manager the 36-year-old Kelly, a coach who had 49 games' experience in the major leagues as a player (with the Twins) a decade earlier. With the hiring of Kelly, the Twins made a Dodger-like commitment throwing their support behind the man they wanted in charge, win or lose. As the 2001 baseball season began, the soft-spoken, cigar-smoking Kelly had the longest single-team tenure of any active manager. The Twins won their only World Series championships under Kelly, in 1987 and 1991. In 1987, Kelly's first full season, the Twins won it after finishing sixth the previous year; in 1991, the Twins won it after finishing seventh the year before. In both instances, Minnesota took the Series in seven games by winning all of their home games and losing all of their road games.

Kelly came to the Twins with good credentials as a minor league manager. He was the California League Manager of the Year in 1979 and 1980 and the Southern League Manager of the Year in 1981. In 1983, the Twins moved him up to be Minnesota's third base coach, and he was on the coaching staff when he was elevated to the manager's job.

Kelly's most successful years came when he was able to develop young players into role players and fit in veterans to plug key gaps. Young Frank Viola was a key to the Twins' championship in 1987, but it wouldn't have happened without grizzled veteran Bert Blyleven's having one more good year left. In 1991, Jack Morris, the winningest pitcher in the 1980s as a member of the Detroit Tigers, was the ace of the staff and voice of experience. Kelly is well known for staying calm and looking almost bored even during the most exciting of games. In the 1991 World Series, Morris shut out the Braves for nine innings in the seventh game, but the Twins were held scoreless also. All year long, the Twins had won big games with Kelly working his starters for as long as he thought they could go before he turned things over to the bullpen. And in Game Seven of the Series, Kelly would stay with a tired but steady Morris in the 10th. The Twins won, 1–0. Kelly said afterwards that Morris had really wanted to finish, adding, in characteristic nonchalance, "What the hell, it was just a ball game."

In the late 1990s, Twins management made the decision not to spend millions of dollars on salaries to try to compete financially with the New York Yankees, Cleveland Indians, Baltimore Orioles and other big spenders. The result was that the Twins could not compete well on the field, either. Kelly accepted the fate of the ball club, saying candidly, "We're providing entertainment." The Twins averaged 67 wins in 1997, 1998 and 1999.

Kelly's good teams always benefited from powerful lineups — with hitters such as Kirby Puckett, Kent Hrbek and Tom Brunansky — starting pitchers in whom he had confidence and stoppers in the bullpen. He lets his pitcher work with pitch calls decided on by the battery, not the bench. His teams are always at the bottom of the league in intentional walks and even in pitch-outs. Kelly's late 1990s teams were among the league leaders in pinch hitters used, indicating the number of times the Twins trailed in ball games and also Kelly's penchant for working young ballplayers into games. Managers facing the Twins had to worry about balls hit out of the park or into the outfield gaps — but they didn't have to worry about bunts. Under Kelly's stewardship, the Twins laid down a sacrifice bunt about once every eight games.

In 2001, the young Twins team, with the lowest payroll in all of baseball, challenged for the Central Division championship for much of the season before faltering in August and September. On October 12, Kelly surprised the baseball world by stepping down.

Year	Team	Record	Pct.	Standing
1986	Minn	12–11	.520	Sixth
1987	Minn	85–77	.520	First
1988	Minn	91–71	.560	Second
1989	Minn	80–82	.490	Fifth
1990	Minn	74–88	.450	Seventh
1991	Minn	95–67	.580	First
1992	Minn	90–72	.550	Second
1993	Minn	71–91	.430	Fifth
1994	Minn	53–60	.460	Fourth
1995	Minn	56–88	.380	Fifth
1996	Minn	78–84	.480	Fourth
1997	Minn	68–94	.410	Fourth
1998	Minn	70–92	.430	Fourth
1999	Minn	63–97	.390	Fifth
2000	Minn	69–93	.426	Fifth
2001	Minn	85–77	.525	Third
16 years		**1040–1244**	**.478**	

LEAGUE CHAMPIONSHIP SERIES

Year	Team	Record	Pct.
1987	Minn	4–1	.800
1991	Minn	4–1	.800
2 years		**8–2**	**.800**

WORLD SERIES

Year	Team	Record	Pct.
1987	Minn	4–3	.571
1988	Minn	4–3	.571
2 years		**8–6**	**.571**

Robert Daniel Kennedy

Born August 18, 1920, Chicago, Illinois; Chicago Cubs, February 20, 1963–June 11, 1965; Oakland Athletics, October 20, 1967–September 29, 1968

Bob Kennedy took over as manager of the Chicago Cubs following owner Phil Wrigley's disastrous two-year experiment with coaches rotating into and out of the manager's position. The Cubs responded for Kennedy by winning more games in a season than they had since 1946, and they also became the first Cubs team since '46 to finish above the .500 mark, with an 82–80 record. Kennedy's three-year tenure saw him develop young ballplayers who missed the individual attention they needed in previous years because of coaches shuffling in and out. Under Kennedy's direction, the Cubs formed a formidable infield: Ron Santo, there before Kennedy got there, was at third, Don Kessinger and Glenn Beckert, shortstop and at second, respectively, were rookies under Kennedy; and veteran Ernie Banks manned first. Also, Dick Ellsworth, a young left-handed pitcher, floundered for two years without direction under the college of coaches. In Kennedy's first year, Ellsworth won 22 of the club's 82, and lost only 10. When Kennedy left during the 1965 season, the nucleus of a good team was there. Leo Durocher came aboard in 1966 and within two years, with a couple of more trades, the Cubs were solid contenders. Kennedy also managed the Oakland A's for one year, long enough to witness to Catfish Hunter's perfect game in 1968.

Year	Team	Record	Pct.	Standing
1963	Chi (N)	82–80	.506	Seventh
1964	Chi	76–86	.469	Eighth
1965	Chi	24–32	.429	Ninth
1968	Oak	82–80	.506	Sixth
4 years		**264–278**	**.487**	

James C. Kennedy

Born in 1867, New York City, New York; died April 20, 1904, Brighton Beach, New York; Brooklyn Gladiators, 1890

Jim Kennedy was just 23 years old when he became manager of the Brooklyn franchise in the American Association. (The franchise, which began the season in Baltimore, as the Orioles, moved to Brooklyn after a 15–19 start. The Gladiators, as they were briefly known, saw even less success in their new environs, and returned to Baltimore at season's end.) Kennedy started the year but did not make it to the finish, his club losing nearly three out of every four games they played. It was his only opportunity to manage.

Year	Team	Record	Pct.	Standing
1890	Brklyn (AA)	26–73	.263	Eighth

Kevin Kennedy

Born May 26, 1954, Woodland Hills, California; Texas Rangers, October 26, 1992–October 12, 1994; Boston Red Sox, October 19, 1994–September 30, 1996

Kevin Kennedy had four fairly successful years as a major league manager and then retired to the broadcast booth for both ESPN and Fox Sports. His Texas Rangers team, though playing below .500, was in first place in the Western Division in the strike-shortened 1994 season. He moved on to manage the Boston Red Sox in 1995, where Boston won the Eastern Division championship but lost to the Cleveland Indians in the League Championship Series. After a third-place finish in 1996, Kennedy was also finished.

Year	Team	Record	Pct.	Standing
1993	Tex	86–76	.530	Second
1994	Tex	52–62	.450	First
1995	Bos	86–58	.590	First
1996	Bos	85–77	.520	Third
4 years		**309–273**	**.530**	

LEAGUE CHAMPIONSHIP SERIES

Year	Team	Record	Pct.
1995	Texas	2–4	.333

John Nelson Kerins

Born December 22, 1858, Indianapolis, Indiana; died December 15, 1919, Louisville, Kentucky; Louisville Colonels, 1888

Louisville was a powerful name in professional baseball prior to the 20th century, but in 1888, the going was tough. John Kerins' Louisville ball club was overmatched by the competition. Kerins managed 43 games but managed to win only 11 of them.

Year	Team	Record	Pct.	Standing
1888	Louis	11–32	.256	Eighth

Joseph Thomas Kerrigan

Born November 30, 1954; Boston Red Sox, August 16, 2001–March 5, 2002

Joe Kerrigan was the pitching coach of the Boston Red Sox, known for his meticulous record-keeping of the batting habits of opposing players. On August 16, 2001, he replaced Jimy Williams, who was fired as Red Sox manager. Kerrigan was in turn fired during spring training 2002, replaced by interim Mike Cubbage and then by Grady Little.

Year	Team	Record	Pct.	Standing
2001	Bos	17–26	.395	Second

Donald Eulon Kessinger

Born July 17, 1942, Forrest City, Arkansas; Chicago White Sox, October 19, 1978–August 2, 1979

Don Kessinger, an outstanding shortstop for a decade with the Chicago Cubs, finished his playing career in brief stints with the St. Louis Cardinals and Chicago White Sox. In 1978, White Sox manager Bob Lemon left in mid-season to manage the New York Yankees, who went on to the World Series under Lemon. Lemon's replacement in Chicago was Larry Doby. Under Doby, Chicago was 37–50, not good enough for him to stay on. Instead the White Sox hired the popular Kessinger. He lasted just a little longer than Doby, exiting with a 46–60 record.

Year	Team	Record	Pct.	Standing
1979	Chi (A)	46–60	.434	Fifth

William Lavier Killefer

Born October 10, 1887, Bloomingdale, Michigan; died July 2, 1960, Elsmere, Delaware; Chicago Cubs, 1921–1925; St. Louis Browns, June 17, 1930–September 20, 1933

Bill Killefer was manager of the Cubs in 1925, the first year the club ever finished in last place. In the next 75 years, Killefer had a lot of company as manager of a last-place Cubs team. He took over for Johnny Evers in 1921 with the team in seventh place and did not improve their standing. They finished over .500 in each of the next three seasons, climbing as high as fourth place. Then in 1925, the Cubs slipped into the cellar and Killefer was fired in mid-season, replaced by Rabbit Maranville. In 1930, Killefer was hired to manage the St. Louis Browns, a team with a talent pool shallower than the Cubs. He stayed four long, losing seasons.

Killefer, who played and managed in the era of Ty Cobb, believed speed was the key to success in baseball. "It's the most worthwhile talent a team can possess," he once said. "The proper way to build up a club is to depend upon youth and speed." His 1924 Cub team led the league in stolen bases — and had the best record of any Killefer-managed team.

Year	Team	Record	Pct.	Standing
1921	Chi (N)	22–33	.400	Seventh
1922	Chi	80–74	.519	Fifth

Year	Team	Record	Pct.	Standing
1923	Chi	83–71	.539	Fourth
1924	Chi	81–72	.529	Fifth
1925	Chi	33–42	.440	Seventh
1930	StL (A)	64–90	.416	Sixth
1931	StL	63–91	.409	Fifth
1932	StL	63–91	.409	Sixth
1933	StL	34–59	.366	Eighth
9 years		**523–623**	**.456**	

Bruce Edward Kimm

Born June 29, 1951, Cedar Rapids, Iowa; Chicago Cubs, July 5, 2002

Bruce Kimm, a former big league catcher, replaced Don Baylor as manager of the Cubs after Chicago slipped well below .500 before the All-Star break. Kimm, manager of the Iowa Cubs, was promoted and given the job for the remainder of the season.

Clyde Edward King

Born May 23, 1925, Goldsboro, North Carolina; San Francisco Giants, October 10, 1968–May 23, 1970; Atlanta Braves, June 21, 1974–August 30, 1975; New York Yankees, August 23, 1982–January 11, 1983

Clyde King won 32 games pitching in the major leagues for the Brooklyn Dodgers and Cincinnati Reds in the 1940s and 1950s, and he later began a long career as a coach, scout and manager.

In 1969, he replaced Herman Franks as manager of the San Francisco Giants and finished in second place with a team that had four future Hall of Famers: Willie Mays, Willie McCovey, Juan Marichal and Gaylord Perry. In 1970, with basically the same nucleus, the Giants got off to a 19–25 start and King was replaced by Charlie Fox. Four years later, King replaced Eddie Mathews as manager of the Atlanta Braves, finishing out the season with a 38–25 record. But the following season, the Braves were 59–76 after 135 games, and once again, King was sent packing. His last managerial stint came in 1982 as part of the George Steinbrenner merry-go-round with the New York Yankees. Gene Michael started the 1981 season as Yankee manager but was replaced by Bob Lemon. Lemon started the 1982 season as manager and was replaced by Michael, who was replaced by King. At the end of the season, King was replaced by Billy Martin.

Year	Team	Record	Pct.	Standing
1969	SF	90–72	.556	Second
1970	SF	19–25	.432	Fifth
1974	Atl	38–25	.603	Fourth
1975	Atl	59–76	.437	Fifth
1982	NY (A)	29–33	.468	Fifth
5 years		**235–231**	**.504**	

Malachi J. Kittridge

Born October 12, 1869, Clinton, Massachusetts; died June 23, 1928, Gary, Indiana; Washington Senators 1904

Malachi Kittridge didn't have much to work with when he took over the Washington Senators in 1904. The previous year, under Tom Loftus, the lowly Senators won only 43 games and finished last. Kittridge came on to try to turn the tide, but Washington lost 16 of its first 17 games. Kittridge was fired and never managed again, leaving him with a lifetime winning percentage of .059.

Year	Team	Record	Pct.	Standing
1904	Wash	1–16	.059	Eighth

Louis Frank Klein

Born October 22, 1918, New Orleans, Louisiana; died June 20, 1976, Metairie, Louisiana; Chicago Cubs, 1961–1962 (rotating coach), June 11, 1965–October 25, 1965

Lou Klein was involved in one of baseball's most unusual and least successful experiments. He was one of Phil Wrigley's rotating coaches with the Chicago Cubs during the 1961 and 1962 seasons. Wrigley decided that instead of having one manager, the Cubs would operate with eight coaches who would rotate from minor league positions up to the Cubs and then rotate back. The result was that the Cub players never had any clear direction because each coach had his own style. Catcher Dick Bertell recalls a time when he got 10 hits in a four-game series at Pittsburgh. At the start of the next series, the Cubs had a new coach — and he wanted to try someone else behind the plate. "Son of a gun. I hit myself out of the lineup," said Bertell. Klein was head coach for 12 games in 1961 and 30 in 1962. The Cubs finished seventh and ninth. He managed them for 106 games in 1965 with only slightly better results.

Year	Team	Record	Pct.	Standing
1961	Chi (N)	5–7	.417	Seventh
1962	Chi	12–18	.400	Ninth
1965	Chi	48–58	.453	Eighth
3 years		**65–83**	**.439**	

John Kling

Born February 25, 1875, Kansas City, Missouri; died January 31, 1947, Kansas City; Boston Braves, 1912

Johnny Kling preceded the 1914 "Miracle Braves" team by two years and performed no miracles. Boston won 52, lost 101, and Kling never managed again.

Year	Team	Record	Pct.	Standing
1912	Bos (N)	52–101	.340	Eighth

Franz Otto Knabe

Born June 12, 1884, Carrick, Pennsylvania; died May 17, 1961, Philadelphia, Pennsylvania; Baltimore Terrapins, 1914–April 21, 1916

Otto Knabe's one shot at managing came when the renegade Federal League was formed to compete with the American and National leagues. It lasted two years and so did Knabe as a manager. He was also the second baseman for his Baltimore ball club.

Year	Team	Record	Pct.	Standing
1914	Bal	84–70	.545	Third
1915	Bal	47–107	.305	Eighth
2 years		**131–177**	**.425**	

Alonzo P. Knight

Born June 16, 1853, Philadelphia, Pennsylvania; died April 23, 1932, Philadelphia; Philadelphia Athletics, 1895

Lon Knight lasted 35 games with the Philadelphia club in the old American Association, bowing out with a 16–19 record which turned out to be his lifetime managerial record.

Year	Team	Record	Pct.	Standing
1895	Phil (AA)	16–19	.457	Third

Charles Ray Knight

Born December 28, 1952, Albany, Georgia; Cincinnati Reds, October 21, 1995–July 25, 1997

Ray Knight was an All-Star third baseman for the Cincinnati Reds and later was the Most Valuable Player in the 1986 World Series with the New York Mets. He was a favorite of Reds owner Marge Schott; in fact, she promised him the opportunity to manage the Reds. After Davey Johnson led the Reds to the division playoffs in 1995, Schott delivered on her promise and handed over the manager's job to Knight.

He was an active, hands-on manager, constantly making moves during ball games. In 1996, his only full year as manager, the Reds led the National League in the number of different lineups used (147 in 162 games) and also led the league in intentional walks issued. Knight used 313 pinch hitters, an average of almost two a game, and went to the bullpen 425 times, an average of almost three times a game. For all of this maneuvering, the Reds played .500 ball and finished third in 1996. After 99 games of the 1997 season, and with the Reds 13 games under .500, Schott figured she had honored her promise. She fired Knight.

Year	Team	Record	Pct.	Standing
1996	Cin	81–81	.500	Third
1997	Cin	43–56	.430	Third
2 years		**124–137**	**.470**	

Robert Frank Knoop

Born October 18, 1938, Sioux City, Iowa; California Angels, May 15–May 16, 1994

Bobby Knoop was called on to fill in for the California Angels between the departure of Buck Rodgers and the hiring of Marcel Lachemann in 1994. He split his only two games as manager.

Year	Team	Record	Pct.	Standing
1994	Cal	1–1	.500	Second

John Thomas Krol

Born July 6, 1936, Chicago, Illinois; St. Louis Cardinals, April 25–29, 1978; June 9, 1980

Jack Krol was a St. Louis Cardinals coach who served as interim manager in 1978 and

1980, splitting the four games he was at the helm. In 1978, he filled in for three games between Vern Rapp and Ken Boyer. In 1980, he was one of four managers, replacing Boyer for one game and preceding Whitey Herzog and Red Schoendienst.

Year	Team	Record	Pct.	Standing
1978	StL	2–1	.667	Sixth
1980	StL	0–1	.000	Sixth
2 years		**2–2**	**.500**	

Karl Otto Kuehl

Born September 5, 1937, Monterey Park, California; Montreal Expos, October 1, 1975–September 3, 1976

Karl Kuehl took over the Montreal Expos after Gene Mauch's seven-year reign and had a lineup in which the leading hitter was Ellis Valentine at .279 and the leading RBI man was Larry Parrish with 61. Kuehl's top pitcher was aging Woody Fryman, who posted a 13–13 record. Kuehl was gone after 128 games, his team 42 games below .500.

Year	Team	Record	Pct.	Standing
1976	Mont	43–85	.336	Sixth

Harvey Edward Kuenn

Born December 4, 1930, Milwaukee, Wisconsin; died February 28, 1988, Peoria, Arizona; Milwaukee Brewers, September 28, 1975; June 2, 1982–October 3, 1983

Harvey Kuenn engineered one of the greatest mid-season turn-arounds in the history of baseball when he took over a fifth-place Milwaukee Brewers team in 1982 and led them to the American League championship. The Brewers were 62–47 in the 1981 split season under Buck Rodgers but were struggling at 23–24 in 1982 when Kuenn was hired to light a fire under them. The Brewers went 72–43 the rest of the way to beat out the Baltimore Orioles by one game. Milwaukee then beat California in the League Championship Series before losing a seven-game World Series to the St. Louis Cardinals.

Kuenn inherited a Brewers pitching staff that included starters Pete Vuckovich, 18–6; Mike Caldwell, 17–13; Moose Haas, 11–8; Bob McClure, 12–7; and Jim Slaton, 10–6. He had future Hall of Famer Rollie Fingers in the bullpen. He also had a tremendous lineup, which included the league's Most Valuable Player, Robin Yount, along with Paul Molitor, Cecil Cooper, Jim Gantner and Gorman Thomas, who led the American League in home runs with 39.

Kuenn didn't push many buttons. He had a set lineup and he let the players play. They became known as "Harvey's Wall Bangers." Yount hit .331; Cooper hit .313; Molitor hit .302; Gantner hit .295. Vuckovich and Caldwell each pitched more than 200 innings, and Haas threw 193. They threw as hard as they could for as long as they could, the hitters kept them in the game, and then Fingers would come in to shut the door.

The next year, the Brewers had another good year, 87–75, but finished fifth in Kuenn's last year as manager. He was ill with cancer and had part of one leg amputated. The popular skipper died of cancer five years later.

Year	Team	Record	Pct.	Standing
1975	Mil	1–0	1.000	Fifth
1981	Mil	72–43	.606	First
1982	Mil	87–75	.537	Fifth
3 years		**160–118**	**.576**	

LEAGUE CHAMPIONSHIP SERIES

Year	Team	Record	Pct.
1981	Mil	3–2	.600

WORLD SERIES

Year	Team	Record	Pct.
1981	Mil	3–4	.429

Joseph Anthony Kuhel

Born June 25, 1906, Kansas City, Kansas; died February 26, 1984, Kansas City, Missouri; Washington Senators, October 23, 1947–1949

Joe Kuhel had an 18-year career as a major league first baseman with the Washington Senators and Chicago White Sox. After his retirement as a player, Clark Griffith hired him to manage a Senators team drained of competitive talent. After two dismal seasons, Kuhel was replaced by another old Senator, Bucky Harris.

Year	Team	Record	Pct.	Standing
1948	Wash	56–97	.366	Seventh
1949	Wash	50–104	.325	Eighth
2 years		**106–201**	**.345**	

Marcel Ernest Lachemann

Born June 13, 1941, Los Angeles, California; California Angels, May 17, 1994–August 7, 1996

Marcel Lachemann and his brother, Rene, are the only two brothers to have managed in the major leagues at the same time. While Marcel was managing the California Angels in the American League, his brother was at the helm for the Florida Marlins in the National League. Marcel had been a pitcher who got into eight games in three years with the Oakland A's and posted a 4–1 record in his rookie year, 1969. As a manager, one statistic stands out and is a carryover from his days on the pitching mound: he called more pitchouts than any manager in the American League in 1996, and he didn't last the season. He was relieved of his duties in August. His best year as a manager was 1995 when the Angels finished second. But in 1996, they fell out of contention early and Lachemann was soon replaced.

Year	Team	Record	Pct.	Standing
1994	Cal	31–44	.410	Fourth
1995	Cal	78–67	.530	Second
1996	Cal	52–59	.460	Fourth
3 years		**161–170**	**.485**	

Rene George Lachemann

Born May 4, 1945, Los Angeles California; Seattle Mariners, May 6, 1981–June 25, 1983; Milwaukee Brewers, October 3, 1983–September 27, 1984; Florida Marlins, October 23, 1992–July 8, 1996

Rene Lachemann, brother of Marcel Lachemann, was a catcher who played parts of three years in the major leagues for the Kansas City Royals and Oakland A's. He managed three major league teams and was the first manager of the expansion Florida Marlins. Lachemann almost always had teams in need of development, for whom his role was not to win but to build a team that might someday be a winner. That's what happened in Florida, where the Marlins won the World Series championship a year after Lachemann was gone — with the help of some key free agent acquisitions and trades. Whereas his brother led the league in pitchouts with the California Angels, Rene Lachemann's Marlins had the fewest pitchouts in the National League. The difference was that Rene had Charles Johnson, a rifle-armed catcher, behind the plate, and runners were reluctant to take big lead-offs. Rene Lachemann's teams were among the league-leaders relievers used — less a matter of managerial strategy than an indication that the starting pitching was getting hit hard.

Year	Team	Record	Pct.	Standing
1981	Sea	15–18	.450	Sixth
1981	Sea	23–29	.440	Fifth
1982	Sea	76–86	.460	Fourth
1983	Sea	26–47	.350	Seventh
1984	Mil	67–94	.410	Seventh
1993	Fla	64–98	.390	Sixth
1994	Fla	51–64	.440	Third
1995	Fla	67–76	.460	Fourth
1996	Fla	40–47	.450	Third
8 years		**429–559**	**.430**	

Napoleon Lajoie

Born September 5, 1875, Woonsocket, Rhode Island; died February 7, 1959, Daytona Beach, Florida; Cleveland Naps, August 28, 1904–August 17, 1909

Nap Lajoie is the only man in major league baseball history to have a team named after him. He was so popular with the Cleveland fans that when he was named manager of the ball club in 1905, the Cleveland ownership changed the name of the team to the "Naps" in his honor. They remained the Naps until 1915 — six years after he was through managing, and they have been the Cleveland Indians ever since.

Lajoie was a great second baseman in his playing days, one whose services were much in demand. After rising to stardom with the Phillies, he jumped to the upstart American League in 1901, when Connie Mack and the crosstown A's offered more money. Throughout 1901, the Phillies fought through the courts, and by 1902 a judge had declared Lajoie ineligible to play for any team in Philadelphia but the Phillies. The shrewd Mack, acknowledging that his success was tied to the league's and recognizing Lajoie's potential drawing power, traded

Nap Lajoie

the young star to the Cleveland club, where Lajoie could play in all but the A's-Blues games slated for Philly. His .422 average — posted in the one full season spent with the A's — remains an American League record.

As a manager, Lajoie frequently exhibited a trait common to superstars — impatience with players who did not possess great talent. During a losing streak in 1909, Lajoie told the press, "You can't win in the major leagues unless you have players who know the game. We don't have time to teach and train youngsters up here. Our job is to win pennants, not run schools." Five days later, he was replaced as manager but continued as a player for several more years.

Year	Team	Record	Pct.	Standing
1905	Cleve	76–78	.494	Fifth
1906	Cleve	89–64	.582	Third
1907	Cleve	85–67	.559	Fourth
1908	Cleve	90–64	.587	Second
1909	Cleve	57–57	.500	Sixth
5 years		**397–330**	**.546**	

Frederick Lovett Lake

Born October 16, 1866, Nova Scotia, Canada; died November 24, 1931, Boston, Massachusetts; Boston Red Sox, 1908–1909; Boston Braves, January 31, 1910–February 13, 1911

Fred Lake managed for three topsy-turvy years, finishing fifth in a partial season and third in a full season with the Boston Red Sox and then eighth with the Boston Braves. After his eighth-place finish in 1910, Lake was fired and never managed again. He was something of an innovator. His 1909 club, the Red Sox team that finished third, set the major league record for use of relief pitchers. Lake went to the pen 94 times that year, an extraordinary number for that era. But the trend was beginning to catch on. The following year, managers went to the bullpen more than 100 times, a pattern that continued until 50 years later, when relief pitching became an integral part of the game and 100 appearances by a relief staff was routine.

Year	Team	Record	Pct.	Standing
1908	Bos (A)	22–17	.564	Fifth
1909	Bos	88–63	.583	Third
1910	Bos (N)	53–100	.346	Eighth
3 years		**163–180**	**.475**	

Gene William Lamont

Born December 25, 1946, Rockford, Illinois; Chicago White Sox, November 26, 1991–June 2, 1995; Pittsburgh Pirates, October 4, 1996–October 3, 2000

Soft-spoken, bespectacled Gene Lamont, who coached for Tony LaRussa with the Chicago White Sox, managed Chicago for three years and brought them home in first place in one of those years. The White Sox lost to the Toronto Blue Jays in the American League Championship Series in 1993 and were in first place in the Western Division in 1994 when a players' strike halted play. Despite his success, Lamont was not rehired. He took over a young Pittsburgh Pirate team in 1997 and guided them to a second-place finish.

In 1993, Lamont's White Sox were a blend of youth and experience — and some problem players. Veteran George Bell and slumping slugger Bo Jackson both sulked in the dugout during the league championship series because Lamont played percentages and used them sparingly. Both were gone the next season. Lamont was neither flashy nor he a risk taker. In Chicago and Pittsburgh, Lamont played conventional baseball. Statistics in hitting, pitching and fielding show nothing out of the ordinary. He was released by the Pirates after the 1999 season.

Year	Team	Record	Pct.	Standing
1992	Chi (A)	86–76	.530	Third
1993	Chi	94–68	.580	First
1994	Chi	67–46	.590	First
1997	Pitt	79–83	.480	Second
1998	Pitt	69–93	.420	Sixth
1999	Pitt	78–83	.480	Third
6 years		**473–449**	**.513**	

LEAGUE CHAMPIONSHIP SERIES

Year	Team	Record	Pct.
1993	Chi	2–4	.333

Harold Clifton Lanier

Born July 4, 1942, Denton, North Carolina; Houston Astros, November 5, 1985–October 3, 1988

Former major league infielder Hal Lanier became manager of the Houston Astros in 1986 and guided them to the Western Division championship, another example of a first-year manager winning a championship. The Astros lost the league championship series to the New York Mets. They slipped to third place in 1987 and to fifth in 1988, ending Lanier's managerial stay.

Year	Team	Record	Pct.	Standing
1986	Hous	96–66	.593	First
1987	Hous	76–86	.469	Third
1988	Hous	82–80	.506	Fifth
3 years		**254–232**	**.523**	

LEAGUE CHAMPIONSHIP SERIES

Year	Team	Record	Pct.
1986	Hous	2–4	.333

Henry E. Larkin

Born January 12, 1860, Reading, Pennsylvania; died January 31, 1942, Reading; Cleveland Infants, 1890

Henry "Ted" Larkin's only managerial stint was with Cleveland in the short-lived Players League in 1890 and, like so many managers of his day, he didn't last long. He was the second of three managers that year, and none could pull the team higher than seventh place.

Year	Team	Record	Pct.	Standing
1890	Cleve (P)	27–33	.450	Seventh

Anthony LaRussa

Born October 4, 1944, Tampa, Florida; Chicago White Sox, August 3, 1979–June 20, 1986; Oakland Athletics, July 8, 1986–October 23, 1995; St. Louis Cardinals, October 23, 1995–present

Tony LaRussa is the only manager in baseball history to have won division championships with three different teams: the Chicago White Sox in 1983, the Oakland A's in 1988, 1989, 1990 and 1992 and the St. Louis Cardinals in 1996, 2000, 2001 and 2002. During his good years in Oakland, he had baseball's best pair of power hitters in Mark McGwire and Jose Canseco. But the key to his success in the Bay area was in transforming a one-time reliever, Dave Stewart, into an outstanding starter and converting a starter who once threw a no-hitter, Dennis Eckersley, into the premier relief pitcher in baseball.

LaRussa's 1983 division champion White Sox caught fire during the second half of the season with starters LaMarr Hoyt, Floyd Bannister and Richard Dotson having career years and veteran hitters Carlton Fisk, Greg Luzinski and Harold Baines carrying the offensive load.

LaRussa is a master strategist who likes to make things happen with key personnel shifts during a game, allowing him to come up with the match-ups he wants in terms of who he wants his pitchers facing and who he wants his pinch hitters batting against. Consequently, he makes a lot of changes and uses his whole ball club. Oakland led the league in use of relief pitchers many of the years LaRussa was there, even the winning years. Part of the reason is that LaRussa had Eckersley to close out most of the victories. But Oakland went to the bullpen 397 times in 1991. It was up to 424 in 1993. The reason was not just the availability of Eckersley. It was also LaRussa's penchant for creating the situations he wanted. In addition to Eckersley, he almost always had a good left-hander in the bullpen to counterattack left-handed batters. LaRussa likes to keep the game moving on the base paths, too. His teams have led the league in executing the hit-and-run both at Oakland and at St. Louis.

He was the American League's Manager of the Year for 1983, 1988 and 1992. Going into the 2002 season, he had the most wins of any active manager in the major leagues.

Year	Team	Record	Pct.	Standing
1979	Chi (A)	27–27	.500	Fifth
1980	Chi	70–90	.430	Fifth
1981	Chi	31–22	.580	Third
1981	Chi	23–30	.430	Sixth
1982	Chi	87–75	.530	Third
1983	Chi	99–63	.610	First
1984	Chi	74–88	.450	Fifth
1985	Chi	85–77	.520	Third
1986	Chi	26–38	.400	Fifth
1986	Oak	45–34	.560	Third
1987	Oak	81–81	.500	Third
1988	Oak	104–58	.640	First
1989	Oak	99–63	.610	First
1990	Oak	103–59	.630	First
1991	Oak	84–78	.510	Fourth
1992	Oak	96–66	.590	First
1993	Oak	68–94	.410	Seventh
1994	Oak	51–63	.440	Second
1995	Oak	67–77	.460	Fourth

Year	Team	Record	Pct.	Standing
1996	StL	88–74	.540	First
1997	StL	73–89	.450	Fourth
1998	StL	83–79	.510	Third
1999	StL	75–86	.460	Fourth
2000	StL	95–67	.586	First
2001	StL	93–69	.574	Second
22 years		**1827–1647**	**.526**	

LEAGUE CHAMPIONSHIP SERIES

Year	Team	Record	Pct.
1983	Chi (A)	1–3	.250
1988	Oak	4–0	1.000
1989	Oak	4–1	.800
1990	Oak	4–0	1.000
1992	Oak	2–4	.333
2000	StL	1–4	.200
5 years		**16–12**	**.571**

WORLD SERIES

Year	Team	Record	Pct.
1988	Oak	1–4	.200
1989	Oak	4–0	1.000
1990	Oak	0–4	.000
3 years		**5–8**	**.384**

Thomas Charles Lasorda

Born September 22, 1927, Norristown, Pennsylvania; Los Angeles Dodgers, September 29, 1976–July 29, 1996

Tommy Lasorda won 1,599 games in 21 years as manager of the Los Angeles Dodgers. He is one of four men to manage one team for 20 years, along with John McGraw of the New York Giants, Connie Mack of the Philadelphia A's and Walter Alston of the Brooklyn and Los Angeles Dodgers.

Lasorda was 0–4 as a major league pitcher in the 1950s. He signed on as a scout for the Dodgers in 1961 and stayed with the organization as scout, coach, manager and, because of his loyalty and enthusiasm, one of the game's greatest goodwill ambassadors. Lasorda has always claimed to bleed "Dodger blue."

Lasorda took over for Alston at the end of the 1976 season. Under his direction, the Dodgers won the pennant in 1977 and 1978, making Lasorda only the second National League manager to have championship teams in his first two seasons. The other was Gabby Street with the St. Louis Cardinals in 1930 and 1931. Under Lasorda's guidance, the Dodgers would be division champions eight times, National League champions four times and World Series champions twice.

He liked a set lineup and hardly ever platooned. His infield of Steve Garvey at first, Davey Lopes at second, Bill Russell at shortstop and Ron Cey at third was a winning combination for many years. Lasorda liked to work and develop young players, a carryover from his days as a scout and minor league manager. The Dodgers had nine Rookies of the Year while Lasorda was managing: Fernando Valenzuela, Steve Sax, Rick

Sutcliffe, Mike Piazza, Raul Mondesi, Eric Karros, Steve Howe, Hideo Nomo and Todd Hollandsworth. But Lasorda also depended on veterans on his bench — someone who could come in and get a clutch hit at a key moment. Players such as Reggie Smith and Vic Davalillo filled that role over the years.

He had a tendency to rely more on his starting rotation than on his bullpen. Lasorda's teams led the league in complete games eight times and in shutouts six times. If his teams had a consistent weakness, it was defense, particularly in later years. Jose Offerman, a shortstop, led the National League in errors, and Steve Sax, a second baseman, developed a mental block about throwing the ball to first base — not a good thing for a second baseman. But Lasorda stuck with him.

Lasorda was often second-guessed, never more so than in the 1985 National League playoffs when the Dodgers carried a one-run lead into the ninth inning of the final game against the St. Louis Cardinals. The Cardinals put runners on second and third with slugger Jack Clark coming up and Andy Van Slyke on deck. Lasorda chose to pitch to Clark, rather than intentionally walk him. Clark homered, propelling the Cardinals into the World Series.

Lasorda was known for getting the most out of his players because of the great rapport he had with them. "Managing is like holding a dove in your hand," he once said. "If you hold it too tightly, you kill it. But if you hold it too loosely you lose it." His flamboyant personality also blended well with the star-studded crowds at Dodger Stadium. Heart problems forced him to resign in the middle of the 1996 season. He now works in the Dodger front office.

Year	Team	Record	Pct.	Standing
1976	LA	2–2	.500	Second
1977	LA	98–64	.605	First
1978	LA	95–67	.586	First
1979	LA	79–83	.488	Third
1980	LA	92–71	.564	Second
1981	LA	36–21	.632	First
1981	LA	27–26	.509	Fourth
1982	LA	88–74	.543	Second
1983	LA	91–71	.562	First
1984	LA	79–83	.488	Fourth
1985	LA	95–67	.586	First
1986	LA	73–89	.451	Fifth
1987	LA	73–89	.451	Fourth
1988	LA	94–67	.580	First
1989	LA	77–83	.481	Fourth
1990	LA	86–76	.530	Second
1991	LA	93–69	.574	Second
1992	LA	63–99	.388	Sixth
1993	LA	81–81	.500	Fourth
1994	LA	58–56	.508	Fourth
1995	LA	78–66	.541	First
1996	LA	41–35	.539	First
20 years		**1599–1439**	**.526**	

DIVISION CHAMPIONSHIP SERIES

Year	Team	Record	Pct.
1981	LA	3–2	.600
1995	LA	0–3	.000
Two years		**3–5**	**.375**

LEAGUE CHAMPIONSHIP SERIES

Year	Team	Record	Pct.
1977	LA	3–1	.750
1978	LA	3–1	.750
1981	LA	3–2	.600
1983	LA	1–3	.250
1985	LA	2–4	.333
1988	LA	4–3	.571
6 years		**16–14**	**.533**

WORLD SERIES

Year	Team	Record	Pct.
1977	LA	2–4	.333
1978	LA	2–4	.333
1981	LA	4–2	.666
1988	LA	4–1	.600
4 years		**12–11**	**.521**

George Warren Latham

Born September 6, 1852, Utica, New York; died May 26, 1914, Utica; New Haven Elm Citys, 1875; Philadelphia Athletics, 1882

George Latham, known as both "Juice" and "Jumbo" during his playing days, managed in two different leagues, seven years apart. He took over the New Haven ball club in the National Association in 1875 but could do no better than win four out of 22 games. In 1882, he fared better. His Philadelphia team in the American Association finished in second place.

Year	Team	Record	Pct.	Standing
1875	NHvn	4–14	.222	Eighth
1882	Phil	41–34	.547	Second
2 years		**45–48**	**.430**	

Walter Arlington Latham

Born March 15, 1859, West Lebanon, New York; died November 29, 1952, Garden City, New York; St. Louis Cardinals, 1896

Arlie Latham was a third baseman in the St. Louis organization known more for his practical jokes than his playing. Latham managed the ball club for two games in 1895 and lost them both. He lived to be 93 and stayed in baseball for most of that time. His last job was as a cop in the Yankee Stadium press box at the age of 83.

Year	Team	Record	Pct.	Standing
1896	StL	0–2	.000	Tenth

Harry Arthur "Cookie" Lavagetto

Born December 12, 1912, Oakland, California; died August 10, 1990, Orinda, California; Washington Senators/Minnesota Twins, May 6, 1957–June 6, 1961; June 13–23, 1961

Cookie Lavagetto is well known in baseball lore as the Brooklyn Dodger who broke up Bill Bevens' no-hitter in the ninth inning of a 1947 World Series game. Lavagetto was also the first manager of the Minnesota Twins, moving with them from Washington after the 1960 season. He had the misfortune of managing Washington Senators teams that had Roy Sievers and little else to brag about. Lavagetto replaced Chuck Dressen as Washington manager 21 games into the 1957 season. He had a starting rotation of Pedro Ramos, 12–16, Chuck Stobbs, 8–20, Camilio Pascuel, 8–17, and Russ Kemmerer, 7–11. Sievers led the league in home runs with 42 and runs batted in with 114. Jim Lemon, who finished with the second-highest total, had 50 fewer than Sievers. In 1960, the Senators snuck into fifth place, the first time they had ventured out of last place at season's end under Lavagetto's direction. After one more year, in Minnesota, Lavagetto was gone from managing.

Year	Team	Record	Pct.	Standing
1957	Wash	50–83	.376	Eighth
1958	Wash	61–93	.396	Eighth
1959	Wash	63–91	.409	Eighth
1960	Wash	73–81	.474	Fifth
1961	Minn	29–45	.392	Ninth
5 years		**276–393**	**.413**	

Robert H. Leadley

Born in 1851, Detroit, Michigan; only biographical data available; Detroit Wolverines, 1888; Cleveland Spiders, 1890–1891

Bob Leadley managed two teams for parts of three seasons from 1888 through 1891— a long tenure for most managers in those days. His first year was his best, winning 19 of 37 games to finish the season.

Year	Team	Record	Pct.	Standing
1888	Det (N)	19–18	.514	Fifth
1890	Cleve (N)	23–33	.411	Seventh
1891	Cleve	31–34	.477	Sixth
3 years		**73–85**	**.462**	

James Kenneth Lefebvre

Born January 7, 1943, Hawthorne, California; Seattle Mariners, November 7, 1988–October 10, 1991; Chicago Cubs, November 23, 1991–October 6, 1993

Jim Lefebvre was a switch-hitting infielder for the Los Angeles Dodgers for eight years. Both his Seattle Mariners and Chicago Cubs teams showed marked improvement after Lefebvre took over, but Lefebvre's performance was not good enough to satisfy team management. The Mariners climbed above .500 for one of the few times in their history in 1991, but in 1992, Lefebvre found himself in Chicago managing the Cubs. In 1993, the Cubs put on a late-season surge and finished six games above .500, something they had been able to do only twice in the previous 15 years. But Cubs management had decided in August that a change would be made. At season's end, Lefebvre was gone. He has coached with several major league teams since then.

Year	Team	Record	Pct.	Standing
1989	Sea	73–89	.450	Sixth
1990	Sea	77–85	.470	Fifth
1991	Sea	83–79	.510	Fifth
1992	Chi (N)	78–84	.480	Fourth
1993	Chi	84–78	.510	Fourth
5 years		395–415	.488	

Robert Granville Lemon

Born September 22, 1920, San Bernardino, California; died January 11, 2000, Long Beach, California; Kansas City Royals, June 9, 1970–October 3, 1972; Chicago White Sox, November 16, 1976–June 30, 1978; New York Yankees, July 26, 1978–June 18, 1979; September 6, 1981–April 25, 1982

Bob Lemon didn't pitch his first game until he was 26 years old, but he won 20 or more games seven times in his career and led the American League in wins three times. As a manager, he had a reputation for having patience with his developing players. All of Lemon's teams improved dramatically under his direction. In 1970, he took over a Royals team and moved them from sixth place to fourth place by the end of the season. In 1971, the Royals made a run at the championship but finished second with 91 wins. At Chicago, Lemon took over a team that had finished sixth, winning only 64 games in 1976. In 1977, Lemon's White Sox won 90 games and finished third with a starting rotation of Francisco Barrios, Chris Knapp, Ken Kravec and Steve Stone. Lemon's greatest miracle came the following year. He left the White Sox in mid-season to take over the New York Yankees, who were 10½ games behind the league-leading Boston Red Sox. Billy Martin had the Yankees playing at 10 games over .500 but was engaged in his annual power struggle with owner George Steinbrenner. Martin was fired, Lemon was hired and the Yankees went 48–20 the rest of the way to catch the Red Sox and then beat them in a one-game playoff highlighted by Bucky Dent's three-run homer. Lemon was called on again in 1981 to rescue the Yankees, and once again he directed them to the pennant.

Lemon was a hitter before he was a pitcher or manager, and the converted outfielder liked his batters to swing. His teams seldom sacrificed and twice led the major leagues in fewest bunts attempted.

Year	Team	Record	Pct.	Standing
1970	KC	46–62	.426	Fourth
1971	KC	85–76	.528	Second
1972	KC	76–78	.494	Fourth
1977	Chi (A)	90–72	.556	Third
1978	Chi	34–40	.459	Fifth
1978	NY (A)	48–20	.706	First
1979	NY	34–30	.531	Fourth
1981	NY	13–15	.464	Fourth (2nd half)
1982	NY	6–8	.429	Fourth
8 years		432–401	.519	

(In 1981, the season was divided into two segments. The Yankees finished first in the first segment. Lemon managed the club in the second segment, finishing fourth but winning the division playoff to advance to the League Championship Series.)

DIVISIONAL PLAYOFF SERIES

Year	Team	Record	Pct.
1981	NY	3–2	.600

LEAGUE CHAMPIONSHIP SERIES

Year	Team	Record	Pct.
1978	NY	3–1	.750
1981	NY	3–0	1.000
2 years		**6–1**	**.857**

WORLD SERIES

Year	Team	Record	Pct.
1978	NY	4–2	.666
1981	NY	2–4	.333
2 years		**6–6**	**.500**

James Robert Lemon

Born March 23, 1928, Covington, Virginia; Washington Senators, October 11, 1967–January 29, 1969

Jim Lemon was a slugging outfielder for the original Washington Senators but never played on a winning team there. The Senators moved to Minnesota and eventually won a pennant. Lemon managed the expansion Washington Senators for one season and didn't find winning any easier than he did as a player.

Year	Team	Record	Pct.	Standing
1968	Wash	65–96	.404	Tenth

William F. Lennon

Born in 1848, Brooklyn, New York; date and place of death unknown; Fort Wayne Kekiongas, 1871

Not much is recorded about the career of Bill Lennon. He played for three years and managed for part of one, winning five of 14 games at the helm of Fort Wayne in the National Association.

Year	Team	Record	Pct.	Standing
1871	FtW	5–9	.357	Eighth

Charles Levis

Born June 21, 1860, St. Louis, Missouri; died October 16, 1926, in St. Louis; Baltimore Monumentals, 1884

Charlie Levis managed the Baltimore club in the Union League and had the team going pretty well. But he departed before the end of the season, never to return to managing again.

Year	Team	Record	Pct.	Standing
1884	Bal (U)	53–35	.602	Fourth

Jim Leyland

Born December 15, 1944, Toledo, Ohio; Pittsburgh Pirates, November 20, 1985–July 29, 1996; Florida Marlins, October 4, 1996–October 1, 1998; Colorado Rockies, October 6, 1998–October 3, 1999

Jim Leyland managed the Pittsburgh Pirates for 11 years, won Eastern Division championships three years and finished second once. His teams were involved in classic league championship series, including one in which Atlanta's Sid Bream slid home with the winning run, keeping Leyland literally inches away from a World Series. In 1997, he accepted an offer to manage the Florida Marlins, a team heavily stocked with free agents and other high-priced players. The Marlins finished second in the Western Division but won the wild card berth in the playoffs and eventually got Leyland the World Series championship he had come so close to in Pittsburgh. But the team was dismantled because of payroll problems and Florida lost 108 games in 1998. It marked the second time in Leyland's career that a team had disintegrated because management wanted to unload and rebuild. In Pittsburgh, he lost the nucleus of his offense when Barry Bonds went to San Francisco and Bobby Bonilla went to the New York Mets. In Florida, Cy Young Award winner Kevin Brown, catcher Charles Johnson and outfielder Gary Sheffield all found new teams after the championship year.

Leyland had the reputation of being a clever manager, always trying to stay one step ahead and out-think the opposition. He sometimes tried to fool opposing managers by inserting a starting pitcher he hadn't really intended to use — just to have the opposing manager shake up his lineup to try to match the surprise starter. Then Leyland would pull the phantom starter early and replace him with a regular starter who threw with the opposite hand of the first man on the mound. He even employed this bit of trickery in a league championship game. He left Florida after the dismal 1998 season to manage the Colorado Rockies. The Rockies weren't much better than the Marlins, and after one season, Leyland, who had experienced life at the top and life at the bottom, decided that he had had enough.

Before becoming a manager, Leyland was a coach for Tony LaRussa with the Chicago White Sox. Gene Lamont was also a coach on that team.

Year	Team	Record	Pct.	Standing
1986	Pitt	64–98	.390	Sixth
1987	Pitt	80–82	.490	Fourth
1988	Pitt	85–75	.530	Second
1989	Pitt	74–88	.450	Fifth
1990	Pitt	95–67	.580	First
1991	Pitt	98–64	.600	First
1992	Pitt	96–66	.590	First
1993	Pitt	75–87	.460	Fifth
1994	Pitt	53–61	.460	Fourth
1995	Pitt	58–86	.400	Fifth
1996	Pitt	73–89	.450	Fifth
1997	Fla	92–70	.560	Second
1998	Fla	54–108	.330	Fifth
1999	Colo	72–90	.440	Fifth
14 years		**1069–1031**	**.509**	

LEAGUE CHAMPIONSHIP SERIES

Year	Team	Record	Pct.
1990	Pitt	2–4	.333
1991	Pitt	3–4	.429
1992	Pitt	3–4	.429
1997	Fla	4–2	.667
4 years		**12–14**	**.462**

WORLD SERIES

Year	Team	Record	Pct.
1997	Fla	4–3	.571

Nicholas Thomas Leyva

Born August 16, 1953, Ontario, California; Philadelphia Phillies, October 3, 1988–April 23, 1991

Nick Leyva managed the Philadelphia Phillies for two full seasons and the start of a third one but could not come up with a winning season and was relieved of his duties 13 games into the 1991 campaign.

Year	Team	Record	Pct.	Standing
1989	Phil	67–95	.414	Sixth
1990	Phil	77–85	.475	Fourth
1991	Phil	4–9	.308	Sixth
3 years		**148–189**	**.439**	

Robert Perry Lillis

Born June 2, 1930, Altadena, California; Houston Astros, August 10, 1982–October 7, 1985

Bob Lillis was a major league infielder for 10 years, spending about half of that time with the Houston Astros. He guided the Astros through four seasons when they were on the brink of contention. He was relieved of his position after the 1985 season and has never managed again.

Year	Team	Record	Pct.	Standing
1982	Hous	28–23	.549	Fifth
1983	Hous	85–77	.525	Third
1984	Hous	80–82	.494	Second
1985	Hous	83–79	.510	Third
4 years		**276–261**	**.514**	

John Joseph Lipon

Born November 10, 1922, Martin's Ferry, Ohio; Cleveland Indians, July 30, 1971–October 14, 1971

In 1971, the Cleveland Indians were on their way to losing 102 games. They started the season with Alvin Dark as manager but switched to Johnny Lipon with the Indians staggering at 42–61. Changing managers didn't help. Lipon's Indians went 18–41 the rest of the way, clinching last place. Ken Aspromonte replaced Lipon for the 1972 season.

Year	Team	Record	Pct.	Standing
1971	Cleve	18–41	.305	Sixth

William Grady Little

Born March 3, 1950, Abilene, Texas; Boston Red Sox, March 11, 2002–present

After 16 years of managing in the minor leagues, Grady Little got his chance in the majors when the Red Sox removed short-stint skipper Joe Kerrigan during spring training in 2002.

John Bernard "Hans" Lobert

Born October 18, 1881, Wilmington, Delaware; died September 14, 1968, Philadelphia, Pennsylvania;
Philadelphia Phillies, 1938, 1942

Hans Lobert had the unenviable task of managing a Philadelphia Phillies ball club that
was in financial straits and had trouble competing. Baseball historian Frederick Lieb said
the Phillie teams of 1939–1942 might be the worst teams in baseball history. All four lost
more than 100 games and only one had a winning percentage above .300. Lobert managed the Phillies for two games in 1938 and then was at the helm for all of the 1942 season in which the Phillies won 42 and lost 109. Shortly after that season, the National
League stepped in and arranged to find a buyer for the ball club, in an effort to make it
competitive again. But Lobert was long gone.

Year	Team	Record	Pct.	Standing
1938	Phil	0–2	.000	Eighth
1942	Phil	42–109	.278	Eighth
2 years		**42–111**	**.275**	

Carroll Walter "Whitey" Lockman

Born July 25, 1926, Lowell, North Carolina; Chicago Cubs, July 24, 1972–July 24, 1974

Whitey Lockman replaced his former boss, Leo Durocher, as manager of the Chicago
Cubs, a team that nearly won a division championship in 1969 and came close the next
three years as well. Lockman had been a first baseman on Durocher's great New York
Giant teams of the 1950s.

He took over a team in turmoil in 1972 with clubhouse bickering between Durocher and
the players getting almost as much press attention as the Cub games. Lockman steadied the
ship and helped bring in another second-place finish. But Lockman came at a time when Cub
management had made the decision to dismantle the nucleus of the '69 club. The starting
pitchers were the first to go — Ken Holtzman to Oakland after the 1971 season, Bill Hands to
Minnesota after the 1972 season and Ferguson Jenkins to Texas after the 1973 season. By 1974,
Lockman had a starting rotation of Bill Bonham, Steve Stone, Rick Reuschel and Burt Hooten.
The pitchers combined for a record of 39–53. By this time, three-fourths of the vaunted All-
Star infield was also gone. Ernie Banks had retired, Glenn Beckert had been shipped to San
Diego and Ron Santo to the crosstown Chicago White Sox. Even with all of the departures,
the Cubs finished just six games out of first place in 1973, though they finished fifth. In 1974,
with Jenkins gone, Chicago struggled to find a stopper. Lockman was let go after 93 games.

Looking back on his managerial career 30 years later, Lockman made no mention of
the trading of veteran ballplayers. He pointed out that Hooten and Reuschel were good
young pitchers and that Bill Madlock was establishing himself as a star third baseman.
The problem with the Cubs? "Maybe it was the manager," he said, steadfastly declining
to put any of the blame on owner Philip Wrigley.

Year	Team	Record	Pct.	Standing
1972	Chi (N)	39–26	.600	Second
1973	Chi	77–84	.478	Fifth
1974	Chi	41–52	.441	Fifth
3 years		**157–162**	**.492**	

Thomas Joseph Loftus

Born November 15, 1856, Jefferson City, Missouri; died April 16, 1910, Concord, Massachusetts; Milwaukee Cream Citys, 1884; Cleveland Blues, 1888; Cleveland Spiders, 1889; Cincinnati Reds, 1890–1891; Chicago Orphans, 1900–1901; Washington Senators, 1902–1903

Tom Loftus had a lifetime batting average of .182, settling precisely on that mark in each of the two partial seasons in which he played. But as a manager, he holds a record that will probably never be broken: he managed in four major leagues — the Union, the American Association, the National and the American.

None of his teams distinguished themselves with great records, but Loftus was a skilled teacher of the game and helped bring along players such as future Hall of Famers Jake Beckley and Ed Delahanty. He quit managing after having a disagreement with American League president Ban Johnson. After that, Loftus was recruited to help organize a new minor league, which became the 3–I League. He died of cancer at the age of 53.

Year	Team	Record	Pct.	Standing
1884	Mil	8–4	.667	Second
1888	Cleve	31–41	.431	Seventh
1889	Cleve	61–72	.459	Sixth
1890	Cin	77–55	.583	Fourth
1891	Cin	56–81	.409	Seventh
1900	Chi (N)	65–75	.464	Fifth
1901	Chi	53–86	.381	Sixth
1902	Wash (A)	61–75	.449	Sixth
1903	Wash	43–94	.314	Eighth
9 years		**455–583**	**.438**	

Edmund Walter Lopat

Born June 21, 1918, New York City, New York; died June 15, 1992, Darien, Connecticut; Kansas City Athletics, 1963–1964

Eddie Lopat was a steady, dependable winner for five consecutive New York Yankee championship teams from 1949 to 1953. He won 166 games in his 12-year career and had a 4–1 World Series record. He brought that knowledge of pitching with him when he was named to manage the Kansas City A's in 1963. Major league catcher Harry Chiti said he never met a man who knew more about pitching than Lopat. Chiti said Lopat had such a knowledge of the strengths and weaknesses of pitchers in the league that he could sit on the bench and call the pitches as the game went along. His problem with the A's was that they weren't the Yankees. When Lopat pitched, he was part of a mound corps that included Vic Raschi, Allie Reynolds and Whitey Ford. At Kansas City, as manager, his two best pitchers were Dave Wickersham and Orlando Peña. The pitching staff didn't get much offensive support. In 1963, Wayne Causey was the leading hitter at .294. Norm Siebern with 83 RBIs and Ed Charles with 79 were the only two hitters with more than 60 runs batted in. Lopat was fired midway into the 1964 season.

Year	Team	Record	Pct.	Standing
1963	KC	73–89	.451	Eighth
1964	KC	17–35	.327	Tenth
2 years		**90–124**	**.421**	

David Earl Lopes

Born May 3, 1948, Providence, Rhode Island; Milwaukee Brewers, November 3, 1999–April 18, 2002

Davey Lopes was the second baseman in the Los Angeles Dodgers' great infield of the 1970s and '80s which had Ron Cey at third, Bill Russell at short, Lopes at second and Steve Garvey at first. Lopes became manager of the Milwaukee Brewers in 2000. Two other members of that Dodger team became managers: Russell and catcher Mike Scioscia.

Year	Team	Record	Pct.	Standing
2000	Mil	73–89	.451	Third
2001	Mil	68–94	.420	Fourth
2002	Mil	3–12	.333	Sixth
3 years		**144–194**	**.425**	

Alfonzo Ramon Lopez

Born August 20, 1908, Tampa, Florida; Cleveland Indians, November 10, 1950–September 30, 1956; Chicago White Sox, October 25, 1956–November 5, 1965; July 12, 1968–May 2, 1969

Al Lopez was a great catcher and a great handler of pitchers in both his playing days and as a manager. He caught in 1,918 games which was a major league record until it was broken by Bob Boone and then by Carlton Fisk. Lopez was the only manager in the 1950s to break the New York Yankees' stranglehold on first place—and he did it twice, with two different teams—the Cleveland Indians in 1954 and the Chicago White Sox in 1959. He managed the Indians for six years, finishing first once and second five times. In 1957, he took over the White Sox. There, he finished first once and second twice in his first three years. In his first 15 years as a manager, Lopez had two pennant winners and 10 second-place finishes. His 1954 Cleveland Indians team won 111 games, an American League record that held for 44 years until the Yankees won 114 in 1998. His 1959 Chicago club won the first White Sox pennant in 40 years, and they haven't been in the World Series since then.

Lopez had good starting pitching to work with: Bob Feller, Mike Garcia and Herb Score in Cleveland; Billy Pierce and Dick Donovan with Chicago. Early Wynn pitched for him in both cities. But he also developed more than one stopper in his bullpens so his relief pitchers were not burned out when the stretch drive began. In Cleveland he had Don Mossi and Ray Narleski. In Chicago, he had Turk Lown and Gerry Staley. Lopez also had teams with speed and that played good defense. His style was not to rely on a three-run homer to bail him out. Rather, he relied on pitching, speed and defense to manufacture victories. In 17 years of managing, his teams never led the league in errors. They led the league in complete games six times, in earned run average six times, in fielding percentage five times and in stolen bases five times—thanks in large part to his speedy lead-off man in Chicago, Luis Aparicio.

Lopez had the philosophy that teams win with pitching and defense—that if you hold the other team to few runs, sooner or later they'll make the mistake that will provide you with the victory. Another Lopez theory: Don't bench good players because they're "in the doghouse" with you. Put the best players you have on the field every game.

Year	Team	Record	Pct.	Standing
1951	Cleve	93–61	.604	Second
1952	Cleve	93–61	.604	Second
1953	Cleve	92–62	.597	Second
1954	Cleve	111–43	.721	First
1955	Cleve	93–61	.604	Second
1956	Cleve	88–66	.571	Second
1957	Chi (A)	90–64	.584	Second
1958	Chi	82–72	.532	Second
1959	Chi	94–60	.610	First
1960	Chi	87–67	.565	Third
1961	Chi	86–76	.531	Fourth
1962	Chi	85–77	.525	Fifth
1963	Chi	94–68	.580	Second
1964	Chi	98–64	.605	Second
1965	Chi	95–67	.586	Second
1968	Chi	33–48	.407	Ninth
1969	Chi	8–9	.471	Fourth
17 years		**1422–1026**	**.581**	

WORLD SERIES

Year	Team	Record	Pct.
1954	Cleve	0–4	.000
1959	Chi	2–4	.333
2 years		**2–8**	**.200**

Harry Donald Lord

Born March 8, 1882, Porter, Maine; died August 9, 1948, Westbrook, Maine; Buffalo Blues, 1915

Harry Lord managed the Buffalo Blues franchise in the Federal League, which tried unsuccessfully to compete with the two established major leagues in 1915. He took over in mid-season and brought the club up from eighth place to sixth place, after which his managerial career was over.

Year	Team	Record	Pct.	Standing
1915	Buff	59–48	.551	Sixth

Robert Lincoln Lowe

Born July 10, 1868, Pittsburgh, Pennsylvania; died December 8, 1951, Detroit, Michigan; Detroit Tigers, 1904

Bobby Lowe, Detroit Tiger second baseman, took over for Ed Barrow during the 1904 season and could do no better than maintain Detroit's seventh-place standing. Barrow later managed the Boston Red Sox during Babe Ruth's pitching days and then was general manager of the New York Yankees during Ruth's hitting days. Lowe never managed again.

Year	Team	Record	Pct.	Standing
1904	Det	30–44	.405	Seventh

Henry V. Lucas

Born September 5, 1857, St. Louis, Missouri; died November 15, 1910, St. Louis; St. Louis Maroons, 1884–1885

Henry Lucas was a wealthy St. Louis businessman who decided to buck the reserve clause. Lucas encouraged players to jump the National League for the new Union League, where he lasted one year as manager of the St. Louis Maroons (though some historians believe he was manager in name only and that Arthur Irvin called the shots on the field). St. Louis won 94 and lost only 19. The next year the club was back in the National League and lost twice as many as it won, ending Lucas' managing career.

Year	Team	Record	Pct.	Standing
1884	StL (U)	94–19	.832	First
1885	StL (N)	36–72	.333	Eighth
2 years		**130–91**	**.588**	

John R. Lucas

No biographical data available; St. Louis Brown Stockings, 1877

John R. Lucas was the president of the first National League franchise in St. Louis, and he managed the club for part of one year. He had a falling out with league officials and dropped out of the National League for awhile. His nephew, Henry, managed the team in the Union League in 1884 and 1885.

Year	Team	Record	Pct.	Standing
1877	StL	14–12	.538	Third

Frank Joseph Lucchesi

Born April 24, 1926, San Francisco, California; Philadelphia Phillies, October 8, 1969–July 10, 1972; Texas Rangers, July 21, 1975–June 22, 1977; Chicago Cubs, September 8, 1987–October 1, 1987

Frank Lucchesi managed three major league teams and could not improve any of them beyond periodic mediocrity. He is remembered best as the victim of an assault on the field by one of his own players. In March of 1977, Lenny Randle, a second baseman for the Texas Rangers, approached manager Lucchesi during a team workout and complained about his lack of playing time in spring training. One thing led to another and Randle punched Lucchesi several times, knocking him to the ground. Lucchesi was hospitalized with a concussion, broken cheekbone and bruises. He returned to manage the ball club, but not for long. He was fired 62 games into the 1977 season. It would be 10 years before he ever managed again and that was as a fill-in for the Chicago Cubs.

Year	Team	Record	Pct.	Standing
1970	Phil	73–88	.453	Fifth
1971	Phil	67–95	.414	Sixth
1972	Phil	26–50	.342	Sixth
1975	Tex	35–32	.522	Third
1976	Tex	76–86	.469	Fifth
1977	Tex	31–31	.500	Fourth
1987	Chi (N)	8–17	.320	
7 years		**316–399**	**.435**	

Harry G. Lumley

Born September 29, 1880, Forest City, Pennsylvania; died May 22, 1938, Binghamton, New York; Brooklyn Superbas, 1909

Harry Lumley was a Brooklyn outfielder for seven years and was one of the most popular players with teammates and fans. When Charles Ebbets hired him to manage the team, it was with the assurance that Ebbets would find him some players to make the ball club competitive. Ebbets hired a scout, Larry Sutton, to find the players. Sutton stayed with the organization for nearly 50 years and became one of baseball's most well-respected scouts. And he did come up with a prospect — outfielder Zack Wheat — to help Lumley. But Wheat came up late in the season when Brooklyn already had a lock on last place. And at season's end, Ebbets decided Lumley, hired because he was so well liked, had to be replaced because he was not aggressive enough.

Year	Team	Record	Pct.	Standing
1909	Brklyn	55–98	.359	Sixth

Theodore Amar Lyons

Born December 28, 1900, Lake Charles, Louisiana; died July 25, 1986, Sulphur, Louisiana; Chicago White Sox, June 14, 1946–October 6, 1948

Ted Lyons was a Hall of Fame pitcher for the Chicago White Sox who played longer for one team without being on a pennant winner than any player in baseball history — including Ernie Banks. (Lyons played 21 years with the White Sox. Banks had a 19-year career with the Cubs.) Lyons took over as manager after Jimmy Dykes' 12-year reign and inherited a team where the cupboard was pretty bare. He took over a seventh-place team in 1946 and got them up to fifth place by the end of the season. The next year, 1947, the White Sox slipped back to seventh place. After a dismal 1948 season in which Chicago lost 101 games, Lyons was dismissed.

Year	Team	Record	Pct.	Standing
1946	Chi (A)	64–60	.516	Fifth
1947	Chi	70–84	.455	Seventh
1948	Chi	51–101	.336	Eighth
3 years		**185–245**	**.430**	

Connie Mack

Born December 22, 1862, East Brookfield, Massachusetts; died February 8, 1956, Germantown, Pennsylvania; Pittsburgh Pirates, September 3, 1894–September 21, 1896; Philadelphia Athletics, February 19, 1901–October 18, 1950

Early in his career Cornelius McGillicuddy changed his name to Connie Mack — so that it would fit in a baseball boxscore. He was an ordinary player with an extraordinary insight into how the game ought to be played. His first managerial job was with Pittsburgh. When he was fired from that position, Ban Johnson hired him to manage the Milwaukee minor league team in the Western League.

In 1901, Johnson formed a second major league, the American League, and hired Mack to manage the Philadelphia franchise, a spot he held for 50 years. When he retired after

Connie Mack

the 1950 season, at age 87, Mack had won 3,776 games — far more than any other manager. But he also lost 4,025 — far more than any other manager. Such are the statistics of a man who won nine pennants but also finished last 17 times. He had some incredible streaks: four pennants in five years between 1910 and 1914, seven straight last-place finishes from 1915 through 1921, three straight championships from 1929 to 1931, then nine last-place finishes in a 12-year span from 1935 to 1946. Almost always, the streaks were caused by Mack's unloading high priced players who helped him win championships.

Mack was a dignified man whose uniform was a business suit, straw boater and stiff-collared white shirt. He directed players with a rolled up scorecard. Mack most often used a set lineup and, particularly early in his career, liked to develop younger players. One of his prize pupils was Jimmie Foxx, whom Mack signed as a 17-year-old and nurtured into a superstar. He once bought an entire minor league team just so he could acquire Mickey Cochrane to be his catcher. When he could, he would sign aging veterans who could serve as examples to younger players and could also teach them. Ty Cobb is an example. When Cobb's playing days were over with the Detroit Tigers, Mack signed him. Cobb retired as a member of Mack's A's.

Mack preferred to get the most he could out of his starting lineup and did not make great use of his bench. He had some great pitchers over the years — Chief Bender, Rube Waddell, Eddie Plank and Lefty Grove, for example — and he liked to play for the big inning to win ball games. Mack was a pioneer in some aspects of the game (shifting his defense around to allow for a hitter's strengths or weaknesses for example), but virtually ignored other fundamental aspects of the game such as sacrifice bunts, intentional walks and use of pinch hitters.

Mack sometimes played hunches. In the 1930 World Series, Lefty Grove, the best starting pitcher in all of baseball, worked only in relief. Mack went with Howard Ehmke in Grove's spot in the rotation. Ehmke was a good pitcher — but he was no Lefty Grove. The A's won the World Series anyway.

When Mack formed the A's, he raided the existing Philadelphia team for players and won championships in 1902 and 1905. The Phillies sued. The state supreme court ruled that Mack either had to give the players back to the Phillies or trade them. Mack traded them.

Then he went out and got some more players. He won pennants in 1910, 1911, 1913 and 1914 with his "100,000 Infield" of Stuffy McInnis, Eddie Collins, Jack Barry and Frank Baker. Bender and Plank led the pitching staff.

After the "Miracle Braves" beat the A's in the 1914 World Series, Mack unloaded most of his best players and recruited a new crop of young players. It took him 15 years to win another pennant, but he did it with one of baseball's greatest teams. With a nucleus of

Foxx, Cochrane, Grove and Al Simmons, the A's won pennants in 1929, 1930 and 1931. The Great Depression hit Mack hard and he divested himself once again of his most expensive players. After this house-cleaning, the A's never were able to climb back up to the top during Mack's tenure — or for 20 years after that. Mack retired after the 1950 season, having spent 50 years as manager of the A's. He was two months shy of his 88th birthday.

Year	Team	Record	Pct.	Standing
1894	Pitt	12–10	.545	Seventh
1895	Pitt	71–61	.538	Seventh
1896	Pitt	66–63	.512	Sixth
1901	Phil (A)	74–62	.544	Fourth
1902	Phil	83–53	.610	First
1903	Phil	75–60	.556	Second
1904	Phil	81–70	.536	Fifth
1905	Phil	92–56	.622	First
1906	Phil	78–67	.538	Fourth
1907	Phil	88–57	.607	Second
1908	Phil	68–85	.444	Sixth
1909	Phil	95–58	.621	Second
1910	Phil	102–48	.680	First
1911	Phil	101–50	.669	First
1912	Phil	90–62	.592	Third
1913	Phil	96–57	.627	First
1914	Phil	99–53	.651	First
1915	Phil	43–109	.283	Eighth
1916	Phil	36–117	.235	Eighth
1917	Phil	55–98	.359	Eighth
1918	Phil	52–76	.406	Eighth
1919	Phil	36–104	.257	Eighth
1920	Phil	48–106	.312	Eighth
1921	Phil	53–100	.346	Eighth
1922	Phil	65–89	.422	Seventh
1923	Phil	69–83	.454	Sixth
1924	Phil	71–81	.467	Fifth
1925	Phil	88–64	.579	Second
1926	Phil	83–67	.553	Third
1927	Phil	91–63	.591	Second
1928	Phil	98–55	.641	Second
1929	Phil	104–46	.693	First
1930	Phil	102–52	.662	First
1931	Phil	107–45	.704	First
1932	Phil	94–60	.610	Second
1933	Phil	79–72	.523	Third
1934	Phil	68–82	.453	Fifth
1935	Phil	58–91	.389	Eighth
1936	Phil	53–100	.346	Eighth
1937	Phil	54–97	.358	Seventh
1938	Phil	53–99	.349	Eighth
1939	Phil	55–97	.362	Seventh
1940	Phil	54–100	.351	Eighth
1941	Phil	64–90	.416	Eighth
1942	Phil	55–99	.357	Eighth
1943	Phil	49–105	.318	Eighth

Year	Team	Record	Pct.	Standing
1944	Phil	72–82	.468	Fifth
1945	Phil	52–98	.347	Eighth
1946	Phil	49–105	.318	Eighth
1947	Phil	78–76	.506	Fifth
1948	Phil	84–70	.545	Fourth
1949	Phil	81–73	.526	Fifth
1950	Phil	52–102	.338	Eighth
53 years		**3776–4025**	**.484**	

WORLD SERIES

Year	Team	Record	Pct.
1905	Phil (A)	1–4	.200
1910	Phil	4–1	.800
1911	Phil	4–2	.667
1913	Phil	4–1	.800
1914	Phil	0–4	.000
1929	Phil	4–1	.800
1930	Phil	4–2	.667
1931	Phil	3–4	.429
8 years		**24–19**	**.559**

Dennis Joseph Mack

Born in 1851, Easton, Pennsylvania; died April 10, 1888, Wilkes-Barre, Pennsylvania; Louisville Eclipse, 1882

Dennis Mack's birth name was Dennis Joseph McGee, but he adopted the shortened version of his last name and was known as that throughout his career. Mack managed Louisville in the American Association in the 1882 season, his only time as a manager.

Six years later he died at the age of 37.

Year	Team	Record	Pct.	Standing
1882	Louis	42–38	.525	Third

Earle Thaddeus Mack

Born February 1, 1890, Spencer, Massachusetts; died February 4, 1967, Upper Darby Township, Pennsylvania; Philadelphia Athletics, 1937, 1939

If ever there was a man born with a baseball pedigree, it was Earle Mack. His father, Connie Mack, owned and managed the Philadelphia Athletics for a half-century. Earle Mack played briefly for his father, getting into a few games in 1910, 1911 and 1914. He also coached for his father for 25 years. In two different seasons, Connie Mack fell ill and Earle Mack replaced him as field manager. Connie Mack didn't leave his son much to work with, and the A's finished in seventh place in both of those seasons.

Year	Team	Record	Pct.	Standing
1937	Phil (A)	15–17	.469	Seventh
1939	Phil	30–60	.333	Seventh
2 years		**45–77**	**.369**	

James F. Macullar

Born January 16, 1855, Boston, Massachusetts; died April 8, 1924, Baltimore, Maryland; Syracuse Stars, 1879

Jimmy "Little Mac" Macullar played ball for six years and managed for part of one. He was one of several men who took on the task of managing Syracuse in the National League in 1879. He managed for 26 games, won only five of them, and never managed again.

Year	Team	Record	Pct.	Standing
1879	Syra	5–21	.192	Seventh

Joseph Maddon

Born September 19, 1948, Hazeton, Pennsylvania; California/Anaheim Angels, August 22, 1996–September 13, 1996; September 3, 1999–November 3, 1999

Joe Maddon served two stints as interim manager of the Anaheim Angels. He finished the 1996 season with an 8–14 record. In 1999, he was called on to take over for Terry Collins, who quit, saying the ball club had been underachievers under his direction. The Angels were 51–82 when Collins resigned. Under Maddon, they were 19–10 the rest of the way. The Angels then hired Mike Scioscia as manager for the 2000 season.

Year	Team	Record	Pct.	Standing
1996	Ana	8–14	.360	Fourth
1999	Ana	19–10	.655	Fifth
2 years		**27–24**	**.529**	

Lee Christopher Magee

Born June 4, 1889, Cincinnati, Ohio; died March 14, 1966, Cincinnati; Brooklyn Tiptops, January 2, 1915–January 14, 1916

Lee Magee's only chance at managing in the big leagues came with the renegade Federal League in 1915. Magee had the Brooklyn franchise but could get the club no higher than seventh place before he was fired.

Year	Team	Record	Pct.	Standing
1915	Brklyn (F)	53–64	.453	Seventh

Ferguson G. Malone

Born in 1842, Ireland; died January 18, 1905, Seattle, Washington; Philadelphia Philadelphias, 1873, 1884; Chicago White Stockings, 1874

Back in the days when baseball was trying to come up with a league to match the National League, Fergy Malone did his part by managing the Philadelphia club in the Union League — but not for long. His team lost 30 of its first 41 games, ending Malone's managerial career.

Year	Team	Record	Pct.	Standing
1873	Phil Phils	8–2	.800	Second
1874	Chi	18–18	.500	Fifth
1884	Phil	11–30	.268	Sixth
3 years		**47–66**	**.416**	

James H. Manning

Born January 31, 1862, Fall River, Massachusetts; died October 22, 1929, Edinburg, Texas; Washington Senators, 1901

Jimmy Manning was a pioneer manager — directing the Washington Senators in the first year of the American League. He stayed the full year — a new concept for the new millennium. (Nineteenth century managers rarely made it through the year.) But he was gone after that one year and his team's sixth-place finish.

Year	Team	Record	Pct.	Standing
1901	Wash	61–73	.455	Sixth

John E. Manning

Born December 20, 1853, Braintree, Massachusetts; died August 15, 1929, Boston, Massachusetts; Cincinnati Red Stockings, 1877

Jack Manning pitched in professional baseball for four years and had consecutive years of 15–2 and 18–5 with Boston after starting his career with a 4–16 mark with Baltimore. Though his rookie won-loss record was awful, Manning hit .346. He stuck around for 12 years. In one of them, he managed the storied Cincinnati Red Stockings club in 1877, the second year of the National League but could only win seven of 19 games. During that time, he hit .437 but it wasn't enough bring home many wins for his club.

Year	Team	Record	Pct.	Standing
1877	Cin	7–12	.368	Sixth

Charles Manuel

Born January 4, 1944; Cleveland Indians, November 1, 1999–July 11, 2002

Charlie Manuel took on the challenge of keeping Cleveland on top of the American League Central Division when he took over for the highly successful Mike Hargrove in 2000. But the White Sox got hot at about the same time the Indians experienced injuries and pitching lapses. While Cleveland finished second, just five games out, the White Sox were the dominant team in the division all year.

After seeing the Indians to a 39–47 start in 2002, and with his stars rumored to be trade bait, Manuel sensed a new era was coming — one spent rebuilding. He asked for some indication that he was still part of the long-range plans, and when he didn't get it, he stepped down.

Year	Team	Record	Pct.	Standing
2000	Cleve	90–72	.556	Second
2001	Cleve	91–71	.562	First
2002	Cleve	39–47	.453	Third
3 years		**210–190**	**.525**	

Jerry Manuel

Born December 23, 1953, Hahira, Georgia; Chicago White Sox, December 4, 1997–present

Jerry Manuel was a major league infielder for five years and played on the Montreal

Expo team that made it to the National League Championship Series in 1981. In his first two years as manager of the Chicago White Sox, Chicago finished second — a distant second to the powerhouse Cleveland Indians. In 2000, the White Sox got off to a fast start and never looked back, winning their first division title since 1993. They were then swept by Seattle in the divisional playoffs.

Year	Team	Record	Pct.	Standing
1998	Chi (A)	80–82	.490	Second
1999	Chi	75–86	.466	Second
2000	Chi	95–67	.586	First
2001	Chi	83–79	.512	Third
4 years		**333–314**	**.515**	

DIVISIONAL PLAYOFFS

Year	Team	Record
2000	Chi	0–3

Walter James Vincent "Rabbit" Maranville

Born November 11, 1891, Springfield, Massachusetts; died January 5, 1954, New York City, New York; Chicago Cubs, July 7, 1925–September 2, 1925

Rabbit Maranville had a 22-year major league career in which he was an exact contemporary of Babe Ruth; both played from 1914 through 1935. Maranville was a member of the 1914 "Miracle Braves," who came from nowhere to win the National League pennant. In 1925, Maranville's only year with the Chicago Cubs, he was the second of three managers and had the reputation of a jokester rather than a manager. The Cubs finished eighth, Maranville went on his way and played 10 more seasons but never managed in the major leagues again.

Year	Team	Record	Pct.	Standing
1925	Chi (N)	23–30	.434	Eighth

Martin Whitford Marion

Born December 1, 1917, Richburg, South Carolina; St. Louis Cardinals, November 29, 1950–November 28, 1951; St. Louis Browns, June 10, 1952–November 11, 1953; Chicago White Sox, September 14, 1954–October 25, 1956

Marty Marion was an All-Star shortstop for the St. Louis Cardinals for 11 seasons. His first two managerial jobs were in St. Louis, one year with the Cardinals and two years with the hapless St. Louis Browns. In 1954, he replaced Paul Richards as manager of the Chicago White Sox with nine games left in the season. The White Sox won only three of them. The following year, Marion's first full year with Chicago, the White Sox might have won the pennant had pitcher Dick Donovan not been sidelined three weeks with appendicitis. Chicago was in first place and Donovan was cruising along with a 13–4 record when he was stricken. When he came back, he did not return to his old form. He was 2–5 the rest of the way and Chicago finished third. After another third-place finish in 1956, White Sox management dumped Marion in favor of Al Lopez, the highly successful Cleveland manager who wanted out of Cleveland. So Marion, who averaged 88 wins in his two full seasons, was fired and never managed again.

Marion was not afraid to shuffle the deck to try to make things happen. In 1956, the White Sox hit a stretch where they were not playing well and there was no obvious reason for the bad spell. Marion decided to shake up his lineup. He moved Minnie Minoso, his leading RBI man, into the leadoff spot. Minoso went on a 23-game hitting streak and the White Sox started winning. He once sent Bobby Adams, a bench-warmer hitting .095 up to pinch-hit for future Hall of Famer Nellie Fox. That demonstrated another Marion managerial trait. He once said, "I don't care if you're hitting .350. If I don't think you can hit a particular pitcher, I'm going to take you out." To do otherwise, he said, would be to pay too much attention to a player's individual statistics — a batter's chance to win the batting title, for example. A manager's job is to try to win each ball game, not to pad players' numbers, said Marion.

Year	Team	Record	Pct.	Standing
1951	StL (N)	81–73	.526	Third
1952	StL (A)	42–62	.404	Seventh
1953	StL	54–100	.351	Eighth
1954	Chi (A)	3–6	.333	Third
1955	Chi	91–63	.591	Third
1956	Chi	85–69	.552	Third
6 years		**356–373**	**.488**	

Rufus James Marshall

Born May 25, 1932, Danville, Illinois; Chicago Cubs, July 24, 1974–November 25, 1976; Oakland Athletics, February 15, 1979–October 2, 1979

Jim Marshall is one of many former players Chicago Cub owner Philip Wrigley hired to manage the team. Marshall took over not long after the Leo Durocher reign and after the club had unloaded most of its talented players from the 1969 team and those of the early 1970s. Under Marshall, the "rebuilding Cubs" finished sixth, fifth and fourth. In 1979, he managed the Oakland A's, his last managerial job.

Year	Team	Record	Pct.	Standing
1974	Chi (N)	25–44	.362	Sixth
1975	Chi	75–87	.463	Fifth
1976	Chi	75–87	.463	Fourth
1979	Oak	54–108	.333	Seventh
4 years		**229–326**	**.413**	

Alfred Manuel "Billy" Martin

Born May 16, 1928, Berkeley, California; died December 25, 1989, Johnson City, New York; Minnesota Twins, October 11, 1968–October 13, 1969; Detroit Tigers, October 2, 1970–September 2, 1973; Texas Rangers, September 7, 1973–July 21, 1975; New York Yankees, August 2, 1975–July 24, 1978; June 18, 1979–October 28, 1979; Oakland Athletics, February 20, 1980–October 20, 1981; New York Yankees, January 11, 1983–December 16, 1983; April 28, 1985–October 27, 1985; October 19, 1987–June 23, 1988

Billy Martin was a hot-headed, two-fisted ballplayer and manager who had unprecedented success in improving five different teams that he managed. But his fights with ballplayers and fans and his rebellious attitude led to his departure at almost every stop along the way.

Martin was an infielder for the New York Yankees whom Casey Stengel liked more for his spirit than his bat. Martin got two hits in the same inning in his major league debut, made a game-saving catch to help the Yankees win the 1952 World Series and became a celebrated drinking pal of Mickey Mantle during the Yankees glory years. But he was thought to be a troublemaker — and he wasn't a superstar like Mantle and some of the other players he was thought to be influencing. So Martin was traded in 1957 and played for six other teams in the next five years. As a member of the Cincinnati Reds in 1960, he charged the mound at Wrigley Field and punched Jim Brewer, breaking the Cub pitcher's nose.

He began his remarkable managerial career in 1969, taking over a Minnesota Twins team that had finished seventh in 1968. In Martin's first year, the Twins won 97 games on their way to the Western Division championship. But his brash attitude was too much for the conservative Griffith family who chose to replace Martin with the more traditional Bill Rigney in 1970. In 1971, the Detroit Tigers hired Martin to try to improve on their fourth place, 79–83 performance of the previous year. Under Martin, they won 91 games in 1971, finishing second behind Baltimore. In 1972, Martin's Tigers won the division championship. In September of 1973, the Rangers hired him away from the Tigers, in the hope he would rejuvenate the franchise in Texas. Martin was 9–14, but the Rangers overall were 57–105, buried in last place. The following year, Martin's Rangers won 84 games and finished second, behind Oakland. It was the only time that he managed a team that did not win a championship under his direction — and the Rangers might have, had Martin stayed. But midway in the 1975 season, George Steinbrenner hired him to manage the New York Yankees. The fabled Yankees had not been in a World Series in 11 years. Under manager Bill Virdon, they were having a so-so year, 53–51 after 104 games. And attendance at Yankee Stadium was down. Steinbrenner needed someone to light a fire under the ball club and to bring customers back into the ballpark. In Martin, he found someone who did both. Thus began a love-hate relationship in which Martin was hired and fired five times.

The Yankees won American League championships in 1976, 1977, and 1978, but Martin didn't last through the 1978 season. He was replaced by Bob Lemon after his first skirmish with Steinbrenner. Midway through the 1979 season, Steinbrenner lost confidence in Lemon and hired Martin back. But he was not rehired for the 1980 season. The baton was passed instead to Dick Howser, who won the division championship. Martin hooked on with Oakland in 1981, the split-season, and won the right to play in the divisional playoff. The A's won that but were eliminated in the league championship series. Playing what came to be known as "Billy Ball," the A's entertained fans and frustrated opponents that year by manufacturing runs. Bunts, hit and runs, speed and defense were the main ingredients. In 1982, the Yankees limped home in fifth place with three managers — Lemon, Gene Michael and Clyde King. Once again, Steinbrenner turned to Martin, who moved them up to third place in 1983, winning 91 games. He had two more stints with the Yankees, in 1985 when he led them to a second-place finish and in 1988 when they went 40–28 under his direction.

Martin once said that the only thing he ever demanded of a ballplayer was hustle. "If the player doesn't hustle, it shows the club up — and then I show the player up," he said. A celebrated example of this occurred in a nationally televised game between the Yankees and the Red Sox when Martin pulled slugger Reggie Jackson from his right field position because he didn't think he was hustling. The two exchanged heated words in the dugout.

Martin thought his greatest strength was in evaluating the talent of his players and being able to use them to the best advantage of the teams he managed. He considered himself a professor of player personnel, saying he could have managed Hitler or Mussolini if he had to. And he preached the virtue of resilience to his players, exhorting them not to brood over what happened yesterday. "When you're a professional, you always come back tomorrow," he said.

He died on Christmas Day in 1989 in a traffic accident near his home.

Year	Team	Record	Pct.	Standing
1969	Minn	97–65	.599	First
1971	Det	91–71	.562	Second
1972	Det	86–70	.551	First
1973	Det	76–67	.531	Third
1973	Tex	9–14	.391	Sixth
1974	Tex	84–76	.525	Second
1975	Tex	44–51	.463	Fourth
1975	NY (A)	30–26	.536	Third
1976	NY	97–62	.610	First
1977	NY	100–62	.617	First
1978	NY	52–42	.553	Third
1980	Oak	83–79	.512	Second
1981	Oak	37–23	.617	First
1981	Oak	27–22	.551	Second
1982	Oak	68–94	.420	Fifth
1983	NY (A)	91–71	.562	Third
1985	NY	91–54	.620	Second
1988	NY	40–28	.580	Fifth
16 years		**1258–1018**	**.553**	

DIVISIONAL PLAYOFF SERIES

Year	Team	Record	Pct.
1981	Oak	3–0	1.000

LEAGUE CHAMPIONSHIP SERIES

Year	Team	Record	Pct.
1969	Minn	0–3	.000
1972	Det	2–3	.400
1976	NY (A)	3–2	.600
1977	NY	3–2	.600
1981	Oak	0–3	.000
5 years		**8–13**	**.381**

WORLD SERIES

Year	Team	Record	Pct.
1976	NY	0–4	.000
1977	NY	4–2	.600
2 years		**4–6**	**.400**

John Albert "Buck" Martinez

Born November 7, 1948, Redding, California; Toronto Blue Jays, November 2, 2000–June 4, 2002

Buck Martinez, a major league catcher for 15 years with Kansas City, Milwaukee and

Toronto, was a broadcaster for ESPN when the Toronto Blue Jays lured him back on the playing field to be their manager for the 2001 baseball season.

Year	Team	Record	Pct.	Standing
2001	Tor	80–82	.494	Third

Orlando Olivo "Marty" Martinez

Born August 23, 1941, Havana, Cuba; Seattle Mariners, May 8, 1986

Marty Martinez was a major league infielder for seven years who filled in for one game as manager of the Seattle Mariners in 1986. The Mariners lost. He has not had an opportunity to manage again.

Year	Team	Record	Pct.	Standing
1986	Sea	0–1	.000	Sixth

Samuel Leech Maskrey

Born February 16, 1856, Mercer, Pennsylvania; died April 1, 1922, Mercer; Louisville Colonels 1882–1883

In an era when many managers did not last much longer than two months, Leech Maskrey hung on for parts of two years with the Louisville franchise in the American Association. It was his entire career as a manager.

Year	Team	Record	Pct.	Standing
1882	Louis (AA)	12–13	.480	Third
1883	Louis	24–16	.600	Fifth
2 years		**36–29**	**.554**	

Charles E. Mason

Born June 25, 1853, New Orleans, Louisiana; died October 21, 1936, Philadelphia, Pennsylvania; Philadelphia Athletics, 1882, 1884, 1885

Charlie Mason managed the Philadelphia ball club in the American Association in parts of three different seasons, a period in which the ball club had seven managers. Mason was the most successful of the seven, coming up with winning records in two of his three partial seasons.

Year	Team	Record	Pct.	Standing
1882	Phil (AA)	21–15	.583	Third
1884	Phil	28–23	.549	Seventh
1885	Phil	17–21	.447	Fourth
3 years		**66–59**		

Edwin Lee Mathews

Born October 13, 1931, Texarkana, Texas; died March 24, 2001, Los Angeles, California; Atlanta Braves, August 7, 1972–June 21, 1974

Eddie Mathews played for the Braves in three different cities: Boston, Milwaukee and Atlanta. The Hall of Fame third baseman hit 512 home runs, most by a third baseman until that mark was surpassed by Mike Schmidt 20 years after Mathews retired. He was the Braves manager in 1974 when his old teammate Henry Aaron hit his 715th career home run, surpassing Babe Ruth's all-time mark. There weren't many other highlights in his three year managerial career, which included only one full season at the helm.

Year	Team	Record	Pct.	Standing
1972	Atl	23–27	.460	Fourth
1973	Atl	76–85	.472	Fifth
1974	Atl	50–49	.505	Fourth
3 years		**149–161**	**.481**	

Christopher Mathewson

Born August 12, 1880, Factoryville, Pennsylvania; died October 7, 1925, Saranac Lake, New York; Cincinnati Reds, July 20, 1916–August 27, 1918

Christy Mathewson was one of baseball's greatest pitchers, winning 373 games. Only Walter Johnson and Cy Young won more. He once said his best pitch was "the one they ain't hittin' today."

He took over as manager of the Cincinnati Reds in 1916 and moved them from eighth to seventh place by the end of the season. They continued to improve and finished fourth in both 1917 and 1918. Mathewson was replaced during the 1918 season. The club he left behind won the pennant in 1919 and beat the Chicago White Sox in the World Series — the series tainted by the "Black Sox" scandal that led to the banishment of eight Chicago players from baseball for allegedly conspiring with gamblers to throw the World Series.

Mathewson believed that ball games often came down to one crucial point, one decision to be made when the game was obviously on the line. In those situations, he believed, most of the pressure was on the pitcher, so it was up to the manager to have the right pitcher in at the right time.

"You can learn a little from winning. You learn a lot from losing," said Mathewson.

Year	Team	Record	Pct.	Standing
1916	Cin	25–43	.368	Seventh
1917	Cin	78–76	.506	Fourth
1918	Cin	61–57	.517	Fourth
3 years		**164–176**	**.482**	

Robert James Mattick

Born December 5, 1915, Sioux City, Iowa; Toronto Blue Jays, October 18, 1979–October 15, 1981

Bobby Mattick managed the Toronto Blue Jays through two unproductive years in which the Blue Jays finished seventh twice. It was his only chance at managing in the major leagues.

Year	Team	Record	Pct.	Standing
1980	Tor	67–95	.414	Seventh
1981	Tor	16–42	.276	Seventh
1981	Tor	21–27	.438	Seventh
2 years		**104–164**	**.388**	

Gene William Mauch

Born November 18, 1925, Salina, Kansas; Philadelphia Phillies, April 14, 1960–June 15, 1968; Montreal Expos, September 5, 1968–October 1, 1975; Minnesota Twins, November 24, 1975–August 24, 1980; California Angels, May 28, 1981–October 22, 1982; October 16, 1984–March 11, 1988

When Gene Mauch was managing the Philadelphia Phillies, he was interviewed in Chicago by Cubs broadcaster Jack Brickhouse. "Do you think there will ever come a day when baseball teams will have coaches in the pressbox like football teams do?" asked Brickhouse. Mauch scoffed at the idea: "What would they do? Would they phone down to the dugout and say, 'we need to hit a double.' I don't think so."

Gene Mauch was a no-nonsense, demanding type of manager who was well-respected by his peers but not always by his players. He believed the worst thing that can befall a manager is to realize he wants to win more than his players do. Mauch endured the longest tenure of any major league manager who never made it to a World Series — 26 years. And some of his managerial moves have been second-guessed almost 40 years after they occurred. His 1964 Phillies team had a 6½ game lead with 12 games to play. The Phillies had been in first place most of the year with an outstanding pitching staff led by Jim Bunning, Chris Short and Dennis Bennett. But as the Phillies entered the last two weeks of the season, Mauch lost confidence in Bennett and tried to win by starting just Bunning and Short. The Phillies lost 10 straight and 11 of their last 12. The Cardinals won the pennant.

In 1982, Mauch's Angels won the American League West title and took the first two games of the best-of-five league championship series against Milwaukee. The Brewers won the next three to eliminate the Angels. In 1985, the Angels and Kansas City Royals were neck-and-neck in September. In a crucial series, Kansas City took three out of four from the Angels, who finished second, one game behind Kansas City. Then in 1986, the Angels won the division and were up three games to one in the best-of-seven league championship series against Boston. The Red Sox won the next three to win the pennant.

"Losing streaks are funny," Mauch once said. "If you lose at the beginning, you got off to a bad start. If you lose in the middle of a season, you're in a slump. If you lose at the end, you're choking." His 1961 Phillies team lost 23 straight games, still the major league record.

Mauch believed in pushing runs across the plate any way he could. While some managers of his day, like Earl Weaver, considered the sacrifice bunt a wasted out, Mauch lived by it. In his 26 years as a manager, Mauch's teams led the league in sacrifice bunts 15 times and were always near the top of the league in that statistic.

Phillies players give Mauch credit for turning an awful team into a pennant contender but say he cracked the whip too much. Relief pitcher Johnny Klippstein said Mauch didn't want his players to talk about anything but baseball, on or off the field. He was the type of manager who would pace in the dugout and frequently ask his bench players questions about the game to see if they were paying attention. He tried to be innovative. In 1961, he told his starting pitchers he would buy a new suit for whoever could sit the opposition down in order during the last three innings of a game. In 1963, he experimented with "pitching practice" in addition to batting practice.

Mauch believed the keys to day-to-day managing are percentages and knowledge — knowledge about your own players and their capabilities as well as those of your opponents. That kind of knowledge puts you in a position to play the percentages. It was this theory that made him a believer in platooning players, because some players always seemed to do better against certain teams. But Mauch did not believe in platooning up the middle. He wanted his catcher, shortstop, second baseman and center fielder to play as a unit.

He was a master at thinking ahead during a ball game. He once had a pitcher lay down a squeeze bunt only to see the runner on third thrown out easily at the plate. Mauch blamed himself because, prior to the squeeze play, he had his eighth-place hitter sacrifice a runner from second to third. "I telegraphed that I was going to put on the squeeze," he said.

After his managing days were over, at the age of 69, he accepted a coaching job with the Kansas City Royals and manager Bob Boone, who was one of his former players. He ranks among the all-time leaders in number of games managed as well as in wins and losses.

Year	Team	Record	Pct.	Standing
1960	Phil	58–94	.382	Eighth
1961	Phil	47–107	.305	Eighth
1962	Phil	81–80	.503	Seventh
1963	Phil	87–75	.537	Fourth
1964	Phil	92–70	.568	Second
1965	Phil	85–76	.528	Sixth
1966	Phil	87–75	.537	Fourth
1967	Phil	82–80	.506	Fifth
1968	Phil	26–27	.491	Fourth
1969	Mon	52–110	.321	Sixth
1970	Mon	73–89	.451	Sixth
1971	Mon	71–90	.441	Fifth
1972	Mon	70–86	.449	Fifth
1973	Mon	79–83	.488	Fourth
1974	Mon	79–82	.491	Fourth
1975	Mon	75–87	.463	Fifth
1976	Minn	85–77	.525	Third
1977	Minn	84–77	.522	Fourth
1978	Minn	73–89	.451	Fourth
1979	Minn	82–80	.506	Fourth
1980	Minn	54–71	.432	Sixth
1981	Cal	9–4	.692	Fourth
1981	Cal	20–30	.400	Seventh
1982	Cal	93–69	.574	First
1985	Cal	90–72	.556	Second
1986	Cal	92–70	.568	First
1987	Cal	75–87	.463	Sixth
26 years		**1902–2037**	**.483**	

LEAGUE CHAMPIONSHIP SERIES

Year	Team	Record	Pct.
1982	Cal	2–3	.400
1986	Cal	3–4	.429
2 years		**5–8**	**.385**

James Robert McAleer

Born July 10, 1864, Youngstown, Ohio; died April 29, 1931, Youngstown; Cleveland, 1901; St. Louis Browns, 1902–1909; Washington Senators, 1910–1911

Jimmy McAleer was the first manager to use a pinch hitter as part of his everyday game plan. Other managers had begun using relief pitchers and sometimes pinch-hit for a pitcher who was going to be leaving the game anyway. But McAleer recognized the value of putting extra punch in the lineup by freely using pinch hitters. One of his players, Dode Criss, pinch-hit an average of 50 times a year between 1908 and 1911.

McAleer had plenty of opportunities to test his pinch-hitting theory. In 11 years of managing, his teams finished eighth once, seventh four times and sixth three times.

Year	Team	Record	Pct.	Standing
1901	Cleve	55–82	.401	Seventh
1902	StL (A)	78–58	.574	Second
1903	StL	65–74	.468	Sixth
1904	StL	65–87	.428	Sixth
1905	StL	54–99	.353	Eighth
1906	StL	76–73	.510	Fifth
1907	StL	69–83	.454	Sixth
1908	StL	83–69	.546	Fourth
1909	StL	61–89	.407	Seventh
1910	Wash	66–85	.437	Seventh
1911	Wash	64–90	.416	Seventh
11 years		**736–889**	**.453**	

George Florian McBride

Born November 20, 1880, Milwaukee, Wisconsin; died July 2, 1973, Milwaukee; Washington Senators, 1921

George McBride was a major league shortstop for 16 years, the last 13 years with the Washington Senators. In 1921, the year after he retired, owner Clark Griffith hired McBride to manage the Senators. He lasted one year, even though he posted a respectable 80–73 record. Each of the next two Senator managers also lasted one year until Bucky Harris took over in 1924 and led Washington through its only period of glory.

Year	Team	Record	Pct.	Standing
1921	Wash	80–73	.523	Fourth

James Dickson McBride

Born in 1845, Philadelphia, Pennsylvania; died October 10, 1916, Philadelphia; Philadelphia Athletics, 1871–1875

Dick McBride was one of the most successful early managers, primarily because he was one of the most successful early pitchers. Playing and managing for Philadelphia between 1871 and 1875, McBride pitched 18 of his team's 21 wins, the next year all 30 of his team's wins, the next year 24 of Philly's 28 wins, then all 33 of its wins and then 44 of the team's 49 wins.

His career ended abruptly. In 1875, he had been removed as Philadelphia's main starter for a while to give a youngster a chance. Late in the season, McBride was brought back to pitch and was hit hard by Boston. The game was stopped, and after a quick meeting, McBride was not only removed from the game but was also stripped of his title of captain. That went to a youngster named Adrian "Cap" Anson, who was on his way to a Hall of Fame career.

McBride has kept his place in baseball history as one of the early stars of the game.

Year	Team	Record	Pct.	Standing
1871	Phil (Athl)	21–7	.750	First
1872	Phil	30–14	.682	Fourth
1873	Phil	28–23	.549	Fifth
1874	Phil	33–23	.589	Third
1875	Phil	49–18	.731	Second
5 years		**161–85**	**.654**	

Jack McCallister

Born January 19, 1879, Marietta, Ohio; died October 18, 1946, Marietta; Cleveland Indians, 1927

Jack McCallister managed the Cleveland Indians for one year, 1927 — the year the Yankees' legendary Murderers' Row dominated the American League. McCallister's Indians finished sixth and he never managed again.

Year	Team	Record	Pct.	Standing
1927	Cleve	66–87	.431	Sixth

Joseph Vincent McCarthy

Born April 21, 1887, Philadelphia, Pennsylvania; died January 13, 1978, Buffalo, New York; Chicago Cubs, October 12, 1925–September 25, 1930; New York Yankees, October 10, 1930–May 24, 1946; Boston Red Sox, September 29, 1947–July 22, 1950

Joe McCarthy has the highest winning percentage of any manager in both regular season play and in World Series play. In 24 years of major league managing, his teams finished first nine times and second seven times. McCarthy is best known for his 16 years with the New York Yankees, but he was also successful in managing the Chicago Cubs at the start of his career and the Boston Red Sox at the end of it.

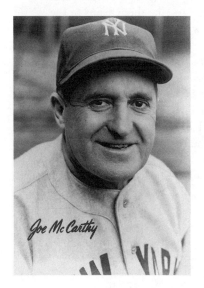

Joe McCarthy

All of McCarthy's teams scored a lot of runs. In fact, nine of the top 14 scoring teams in baseball history were McCarthy ball clubs — six Yankee teams, plus the 1950 Boston Red Sox and the 1929 and 1930 Chicago Cubs. He was a big-inning manager who built his teams on power hitting, executing fundamentals and developing a good, young pitching staff. His teams didn't bunt very often, didn't steal bases and didn't hit and run. Jimmy Dykes called McCarthy the "Push-Button Manager." One of the reasons he was able push the buttons is that he had the players to do it, but that relates to another great McCarthy strength, foresight. He had the ability to look ahead, anticipate when he was going to need personnel changes and make them.

McCarthy preferred a set lineup to platooning. Ballplayers made the lineup if they played ball his way. If they didn't, they were gone. Not many managers would have released Grover Cleveland Alexander, but

McCarthy did in 1926 with the Cubs. The aging Alexander didn't fit with what McCarthy wanted to do with the ball club. Alexander went to St. Louis and helped the Cardinals win a pennant. Meanwhile, McCarthy nurtured a young Cub pitching staff and was able to take problem players or other teams' trouble-makers — KiKi Cuyler, Rogers Hornsby and Hack Wilson, for example — and be successful. McCarthy won the pennant with the Cubs in 1929.

With the Yankees, McCarthy had a string of four consecutive World Series championships from 1936 to 1939, and they won again from 1941 to 1943. Babe Ruth was gone by the time this run started, and Lou Gehrig retired with a tragic fatal illness in 1939. The Yankees were winning with players like Bill Dickey, Joe DiMaggio and George Selkirk, and with pitchers such as Lefty Gomez and Red Ruffing. But a turning point for the Yankees was McCarthy's pioneering use of the relief specialist. Bucky Harris had won pennants with the Senators a decade earlier using Firpo Marberry in that role, but the idea hadn't caught on. McCarthy put Pat Malone and Johnny Murphy in the bullpen and decided that pitchers like Ruffing would start.

McCarthy's belief in the value of good hitters was so strong that some of his players could get by with less than sparkling fielding. In 1936, the Yankees won 102 games, even though their shortstop and second baseman each led the American League in errors. Second baseman Tony Lazzeri had 25 errors, shortstop Frankie Crosetti 43. But they hit .287 and .288, respectively, and drove in a combined 187 runs.

He became the first manager to win a pennant without having major league playing experience when he won with the Cubs in 1929. When he won three years later with the Yankees, he was the first manager, with or without experience playing, to win pennants in both leagues.

He won nine league championships overall — eight with the Yankees and one with the Cubs — and had World Series champions in seven of those nine years. He remained with the Yankees through the 1946 season, then resigned because of poor health. He returned in 1948 to manage the Boston Red Sox from 1948 to 1950 before calling it a career.

McCarthy came close to becoming the first manager to take three teams to the World Series. In 1948, his Red Sox finished in a tie for first with the Cleveland Indians but lost a one-game playoff.

McCarthy is credited with helping Cub slugger Hack Wilson attain stardom. Wilson was an average ballplayer with a serious drinking problem. Under McCarthy in 1930, Wilson hit .356 with 56 home runs and 190 RBIs. The 56 home runs stood as the National League record for more than 60 years until Mark McGwire and Sammy Sosa both surpassed it in 1998. Wilson still holds the single-season RBI record. In 1931, with McCarthy gone, Wilson hit .261 with 13 HRs and 61 RBIs — the biggest one-season drop in those statistics in baseball history.

In McCarthy's 24 years, his teams were never out of the first division.

Year	Team	Record	Pct.	Standing
1926	Chi (N)	82–72	.532	Fourth
1927	Chi	85–68	.556	Fourth
1928	Chi	91–63	.591	Third
1929	Chi	98–54	.645	First
1930	Chi	86–64	.573	Second
1931	NY (A)	94–59	.614	Second
1932	NY	107–57	.695	First

Year	Team	Record	Pct.	Standing
1933	NY	91–59	.607	Second
1934	NY	94–60	.610	Second
1935	NY	89–60	.597	Second
1936	NY	102–51	.667	First
1937	NY	102–52	.662	First
1938	NY	99–53	.651	First
1939	NY	106–45	.702	First
1940	NY	88–66	.571	Third
1941	NY	101–53	.656	First
1942	NY	103–51	.669	First
1943	NY	98–56	.636	First
1944	NY	83–71	.539	First
1945	NY	81–71	.533	Fourth
1946	NY	22–13	.629	Second
1948	Bos	96–59	.619	Second
1949	Bos	96–58	.623	Second
1950	Bos	32–30	.516	Fourth
24 years		**2126–1335**	**.614**	

WORLD SERIES

Year	Team	Record	Pct.
1929	Chi (N)	1–4	.200
1932	NY	4–0	1.000
1936	NY	4–2	.667
1937	NY	4–1	.800
1938	NY	4–0	1.000
1939	NY	4–0	1.000
1941	NY	4–1	.800
1942	NY	1–4	.200
1943	NY	4–1	.800
9 years		**30–13**	**.700**

Thomas Michael Francis McCarthy

Born July 24, 1864, Boston, Massachusetts; died August 5, 1922, Boston; St. Louis Browns, 1890

Tommy McCarthy was one of the stars of 19th century baseball and was elected to the Hall of Fame in 1946. He was known for his hustle and his desire to outsmart his opponents. As a fielder, he developed a skill of juggling a ball in his glove before finally catching it — or dropping it, a ploy to try to fool baserunners. His antics led to the adoption of the infield fly rule.

As a manager, he was able to win only half his games and he didn't last long — gone after 26 games of the 1890 season.

Year	Team	Record	Pct.	Standing
1890	StL (N)	13–13	.500	Fourth

Lloyd McClendon

Born January 11, 1956, Gary, Indiana; Pittsburgh Pirates, October 23, 2000–present

Lloyd McClendon was a power-hitting outfielder who played two partial seasons for

Cincinnati before blossoming with the Chicago Cubs in their division-winning year of 1989. After spending several years as a coach, he was hired to manage the Pittsburgh Pirates in 2001.

Year	Team	Record	Pct.	Standing
2001	Pitt	62–100	.383	Sixth

John James McCloskey

Born April 4, 1862; Louisville, Kentucky; died November 17, 1940, Louisville, Kentucky; Louisville Colonels, 1895–1896; St. Louis Cardinals, 1906–1908

Honest John McCloskey was one of the legends of early baseball. He was a batboy for Louisville in 1876, the National League's first season, and worked in baseball all of his life. He is credited with organizing 10 minor leagues and owning or being a part of teams in 47 towns during his career. He managed Louisville for a couple of years but the highlight of his career was managing the St. Louis Cardinals. McCloskey toiled for three years, each of which saw the Cardinals lose more than 100 games. He was replaced by Roger Bresnahan after the 1908 season, in which St. Louis lost 105 games. The managerial stint was not a success but McCloskey is still revered as a pioneer in major league baseball.

Year	Team	Record	Pct.	Standing
1895	Lou	35–96	.267	Twelfth
1896	Lou	9–34	.209	Twelfth
1906	StL	52–98	.347	Seventh
1907	StL	52–101	.340	Eighth
1908	StL	49–105	.318	Eighth
5 years		**197–434**	**.312**	

James McCormick

Born in 1856, Glasgow, Scotland; died March 10, 1918, Paterson, New Jersey; Cleveland Blues, 1879–1880

The first Scotsman to manage a major league team had a two-year tenure with Cleveland in a career that lasted 170 games.

Year	Team	Record	Pct.	Standing
1879	Cleve	27–59	.355	Sixth
1880	Cleve	47–37	.560	Third
2 years		**74–96**	**.446**	

Fred Melvin McGaha

Born September 26, 1926, Bastrop, Louisiana; Cleveland Indians, October 2, 1961–October 1, 1962; Kansas City Athletics, June 11, 1964–May 15, 1965

Mel McGaha took over the Cleveland Indians a year after general manager Frank Lane engineered the trading of Indians manager Joe Gordon to Detroit for Tiger manager Jimmy Dykes. Including the time Mel Harder served as interim manager, McGaha was the fourth Cleveland skipper in less than two years. He brought them to an 80–82 finish, largely on the strength of Dick Donovan's arm. Donovan was 20–10. But McGaha's performance wasn't good enough for Cleveland management. In 1963, Birdie Tebbetts replaced McGaha, who later managed a weak Kansas City team for parts of two years.

Year	Team	Record	Pct.	Standing
1962	Cleve	80–82	.494	Sixth
1964	KC	40–70	.364	Tenth
1965	KC	5–21	.192	Tenth
3 years		**125–173**	**.419**	

Michael Henry McGeary

Born in 1851, Philadelphia, Pennsylvania; Philadelphia Philadelphias, 1875; Providence Grays, 1880; Cleveland Blues, 1881

Cleveland was an early National League franchise when Mike McGeary was in charge of the club. In his last year as manager, he lost 12 more than he won and finished seventh. He had been more successful in two previous managerial stints.

Year	Team	Record	Pct.	Standing
1875	Phil	34–27	.557	Fifth
1880	Prov	8–7	.533	Second
1881	Cleve	36–48	.429	Seventh
3 years		**46–41**	**.529**	

John Joseph McGraw

Born April 7, 1873, Truxton, New York; died February 25, 1934, New Rochelle, New York; Baltimore Orioles, 1899, 1901–1902; New York Giants, July 8, 1902–June 3, 1932

"There is only one manager," Connie Mack once said, "and that is John McGraw." McGraw was a scrappy ballplayer who did not have great skills but had great desire and an outstanding knowledge of the game. McGraw never had soaring batting averages but he had exceptional on-base percentages. He knew what it took to win ball games and, as a manager, one of his greatest skills was teaching that know-how to young ballplayers.

McGraw managed the New York Giants for 32 years. There are numerous examples of how he took youngsters under his wing, nurtured them and then inserted them in his lineup when they were ready. The greatest example is Mel Ott, who sat on the bench as a 17-year-old, played occasionally the next few years, and then took over in right field when Ross Youngs came down with what turned out to be a fatal illness. Ott hit 511 home runs in his Hall of Fame career. Youngs is also in the Hall of Fame.

Frankie Frisch, another Hall of Famer, credited McGraw with giving him a chance to play. McGraw worked with Frisch countless hours to make him a better infielder, hitting him ground balls and teaching him the proper plays to make.

John J. McGraw

McGraw was both a teacher and a disciplinarian. His players knew their roles. He taught young players what he wanted them to do. He acquired older ballplayers and told them what role they would play. "Learn to know every man under you," he once said. "Get under his skin; know his faults. Then cater to him — with kindness or roughness as the case may be." He enforced curfews, disallowed fraternization with opposing ballplayers, and sometimes he checked his players' dinner bills to make sure they were eating properly.

He was among the earliest to use pinch hitters frequently, and he was the first to develop pinch-running as a role-playing duty for a ballplayer. McGraw wasn't the first to use relief pitchers, but he was the first to use them continuously and successfully. His teams led the league in complete games only twice, yet his teams won nine pennants.

McGraw was a stickler for smart, fundamentally sound baseball. His teams played good defense and his pitchers were expected to have good control. Control was more important than speed, as far as McGraw was concerned, because there is no defense against a walk. In 33 years of managing, no McGraw team ever led the league in walks allowed. That is more than coincidence. McGraw did not depend on power to win games, yet for most of his career he was loath to bunt; He wanted his players to swing the bats to move runners around. The Giants generally were at the top of the league in use of the hit-and-run, and McGraw's teams led the National League in runs scored 14 times.

Not all of McGraw's hunches worked out. On September 23, 1908, he played rookie Fred Merkle for the injured Fred Toney. In the ninth, Merkle, on first base, stopped short of second when what would have been the winning run crossed the plate and the crowd stormed the field. But Merkle, playing his first full game, would be called out when wily Cub second baseman Johnny Evers called for the ball — or, at least, a ball — and stepped on second. The run was nullified and the Giants would go on to lose the game. They would end the season tied with the Cubs and then lose the pennant when the game was replayed. The play, coming late and seeming to cost so much, ensured "Merkle's Boner" a place in baseball lore. McGraw took some heat for having Merkle in the game at that crucial point, but it typifies McGraw's style of using and grooming youngsters. He had an outfielder named Earl Webb for part of one year but didn't think he fit in. Six years later, playing for the Boston Red Sox, Webb hit 67 doubles — still the major league record and later finished his career batting average of .306.

McGraw played for the great Baltimore teams of the 1890s with Wee Willie Keeler and Hughie Jennings. He hit .300 or better for nine straight years and had an on-base percentage of over .400. He was named manager of the Baltimore Orioles in the newly formed American League in 1901 but crossed to the National League's New York Giants the following year.

American League president Ban Johnson had lured McGraw into the Junior Circuit, but the feisty McGraw became upset with Johnson for always backing umpires in their disputes with players and managers. In 1904, McGraw's Giants won the National League pennant but did not play in the World Series because McGraw — some say Giants owner John Brush — refused to acknowledge a team champion from Johnson's league. It would be 90 years before another World Series was cancelled.

The Giants won again in 1905 and McGraw, for his part, consented to play in the World Series. They beat the Philadelphia A's, the first of three world championships McGraw would win. The Giants won 10 pennants under McGraw, including four in a row from 1921 to 1924 — a record that held up until Casey Stengel's Yankees won five in a row, 1949–1953.

While McGraw's aggressive tactics never changed, players' attitudes did, and he became less and less effective as a manager. When he turned over the reins to his first baseman, Bill Terry, in 1932, it broke a long period in which the two men had not spoken to one another.

McGraw's teams won 2,840 games. Only Connie Mack won more. Perhaps one McGraw statement, more than any other, sums up his attitude: "I see no point in *philosophical* wins."

Year	Team	Record	Pct.	Standing
1899	Balt	86–62	.581	Fourth
1901	Balt	68–65	.511	Fifth
1902	Balt	28–34	.452	Seventh
1902	NY (N)	25–38	.397	Eighth
1903	NY	84–55	.604	Second
1904	NY	106–47	.693	First
1905	NY	105–48	.686	First
1906	NY	96–56	.632	Second
1907	NY	82–71	.536	Fourth
1908	NY	98–56	.636	Second
1909	NY	92–61	.601	Third
1910	NY	91–63	.591	Second
1911	NY	99–54	.647	First
1912	NY	103–48	.682	First
1913	NY	101–51	.664	First
1914	NY	84–70	.545	Second
1915	NY	69–83	.454	Eighth
1916	NY	86–66	.566	Fourth
1917	NY	98–56	.636	First
1918	NY	71–53	.573	Second
1919	NY	87–53	.621	Second
1920	NY	86–68	.558	Second
1921	NY	94–59	.614	First
1922	NY	93–61	.604	First
1923	NY	95–58	.621	First
1924	NY	93–60	.608	First
1925	NY	86–66	.566	Second
1926	NY	74–77	.490	Fifth
1927	NY	92–62	.597	Third
1928	NY	93–61	.604	Second
1929	NY	84–67	.556	Third
1930	NY	87–67	.565	Third
1931	NY	85–67	.572	Second
1932	NY	17–23	.425	Eighth
33 years		**2840–1984**	**.589**	

WORLD SERIES

Year	Team	Record	Pct.
1905	NY	4–1	.800
1911	NY	2–4	.333
1912	NY	3–4	.429
1913	NY	1–4	.200
1917	NY	2–4	.333
1921	NY	5–3	.625

Year	Team	Record	Pct.
1922	NY	4–0	1.000
1923	NY	2–4	.333
1924	NY	3–4	.429
9 years		**26–28**	**.481**

James Thomas "Deacon" McGuire

Born November 2, 1865, Youngstown, Ohio; died October 31, 1936, Albion, Michigan; Washington Senators, 1898; Boston Red Sox, 1907–1908; Cleveland Naps, 1909–1911

Deacon McGuire was a coach for the Cleveland ball club in 1909 when Napoleon Lajoie got tired of managing and asked to be returned to full-time player status. McGuire was named to replace him. The move worked well for Lajoie, considerably less well for McGuire. The Naps finished sixth in 1909. In 1910, Lajoie hit .384 but an aging Cy Young went 7–10 and Addie Joss, stricken with what would prove a fatal illness, was 5–5 as the Naps finished fifth. Cleveland newspapers began to call the team "the Molly McGuires." Seventeen games into the next season, McGuire resigned. Prior to managing Cleveland, he had managerial stints at Washington and Boston.

Year	Team	Record	Pct.	Standing
1898	Wash (N)	19–49	.279	Eleventh
1907	Bos (A)	45–61	.425	Seventh
1908	Bos	53–62	.461	Sixth
1909	Cleve	14–25	.359	Sixth
1910	Cleve	71–81	.467	Fifth
1911	Cleve	6–11	.353	Fifth
6 years		**208–289**	**.419**	

William Henry McGunnigle

Born January 1, 1855, East Stoughton, Massachusetts; died March 9, 1899, Brockton, Massachusetts; Buffalo Bisons, 1880; Brooklyn Gladiators, 1888–1890; Pittsburgh Burghers, 1891; Louisville Colonels, 1892

Bill McGunnigle's managerial career was not long, but he was well traveled. McGunnigle managed five teams in six years — teams that seemed to be at one extreme or the other. He had two first-place teams and a second-place team, as well as two that finished eighth and one that wound up twelfth. He had his first managerial job at age 25, his last at age 41. He died two years later.

Year	Team	Record	Pct.	Standing
1880	Buff	4–13	.235	Eighth
1888	Bklyn (AA)	88–52	.629	Second
1889	Bklyn	93–44	.679	First
1890	Bklyn (N)	86–43	.667	First
1891	Pitt	24–33	.421	Eighth
1892	Lou	29–59	.330	Twelfth
6 years		**324–244**	**.570**	

John Phalen "Stuffy" McInnis

Born September 19, 1890, Gloucester, Massachusetts; died February 16, 1960, Ipswich, Massachusetts; Philadelphia Phillies, October 20, 1926–November 7, 1927

The Philadelphia Phillies were so bad in the late 1920s that they tried to hire managers who would be crowd pleasers. Former players Jack Coombs and Bill Donovan each had a shot at it, and in 1927, Stuffy McInnis, the first baseman in Connie Mack's old "100,000 Infield" got the call. The Phillies lost 103 and finished eighth.

Year	Team	Record	Pct.	Standing
1927	Phil	51–103	.331	Eighth

William Boyd McKechnie

Born August 7, 1886, Wilkinsburg, Pennsylvania; died October 29, 1965, Bradenton, Florida; Newark Pepper, 1915; Pittsburgh Pirates, 1922–1926; St. Louis Cardinals, November 7, 1927–November 21, 1928; July 23, 1929–October 6, 1929; Boston Bees, October 6, 1929–October 15, 1937; Cincinnati Reds, October 15, 1937–September 30, 1946

Bill McKechnie is one of three major league managers to win pennants with three different teams. McKechnie won at Pittsburgh in 1925, St. Louis in 1928 and Cincinnati in 1939 and 1940. (The other managers with trifectas are Billy Martin with the Twins, Tigers and Yankees and Dick Williams with Boston, Oakland and San Diego.)

McKechnie's 1925 Pirate club — with the Waner brothers, Pie Traynor and KiKi Cuyler — won the World Series. In 1926, former Pirate manager Fred Clarke bought an interest in the club and began sitting in the dugout. His presence caused divided loyalties and resulted in McKechnie's firing at the end of the season. McKechnie went to St. Louis and won a pennant in 1928. Strangely, the Cardinals also experienced some internal bickering, and the affable McKechnie was fired once again just a year after he produced a winner. He spent several years with woeful Boston Braves teams before being hired by Cincinnati in 1938. The Reds had finished eighth in 1937. Under McKechnie, they moved up to fourth in 1938 and won pennants in 1939 and 1940.

McKechnie was a polite, mild-mannered man who didn't believe in screaming at ballplayers. Quiet and methodical, he was one of the few managers of his era who platooned players frequently and was always looking for any kind of edge he could get on the opposition. "If you take care of the percentages, the percentages will take care of you," he said. He liked his teams to bunt and to hit-and-run (his 1939 and 1940, pennant-winning Reds both led the National League in sacrifice bunts), but more than anything else, he wanted his teams to play good defense.

McKechnie liked to play for one run on offense and then win the game with good defense and good pitching. He often converted shortstops to second basemen or third basemen and then stuck them in the lineup along with the regular shortstop. This gave him three infielders with good range and good arms. He was willing to do with less power in his lineup if he could have a good defensive player in the lineup instead. He believed in having strong starting pitchers, and he did not depend on his bullpen. Nine of his teams led the league in complete games.

Bill McKechnie

After he retired as a manager, he signed on as pitching coach for Lou Boudreau's Cleveland Indians. McKechnie worked with veteran Bob Feller, an outfielder-turned-pitcher named Bob Lemon and an aging rookie by the name of Satchel Paige to help win a World Series title for the Indians.

Year	Team	Record	Pct.	Standing
1915	Nwk (F)	54–45	.545	Sixth
1922	Pitt	53–36	.596	Fifth
1923	Pitt	87–67	.565	Third
1924	Pitt	90–63	.588	Third
1925	Pitt	95–58	.621	First
1926	Pitt	84–69	.549	Third
1928	StL (N)	95–59	.617	First
1929	StL	33–29	.532	Fourth
1930	Bos (N)	70–84	.455	Sixth
1931	Bos	64–90	.416	Seventh
1932	Bos	77–77	.500	Fifth
1933	Bos	83–71	.539	Fourth
1934	Bos	78–73	.517	Fourth
1935	Bos	38–115	.248	Eighth
1936	Bos	71–83	.461	Sixth
1937	Bos	79–73	.520	Fifth
1938	Cin	82–68	.547	Fourth
1939	Cin	97–57	.630	First
1940	Cin	100–53	.654	First
1941	Cin	88–66	.571	Third
1942	Cin	76–76	.500	Fourth
1943	Cin	87–67	.565	Second
1944	Cin	89–65	.578	Third
1945	Cin	61–93	.396	Seventh
1946	Cin	67–87	.435	Sixth
25 years		**1898–1724**	**.524**	

WORLD SERIES

Year	Team	Record	Pct.
1925	Pitt	4–3	.571
1928	StL	0–4	.000
1939	Cin	0–4	.000
1940	Cin	4–3	.571
4 years		**8–14**	**.364**

John Aloysius McKeon

Born November 23, 1930, South Amboy, New Jersey; Kansas City Royals, October 3, 1972–July 24, 1975; Oakland Athletics, November 5, 1976–June 10, 1977; May 23, 1978–October 1978; San Diego Padres, May 28, 1988–July 11, 1990; Cincinnati Reds, July 25, 1997–October 2, 2000

Jack McKeon was a cigar-smoking strategist who demanded the best from his players but had patience with them as they developed. He was a catcher in his playing days, retiring after he was charged with two passed balls in the same inning in a minor league game. His unusual managerial career totaled 11 seasons in a span of 27 years, with gaps of seven and 10 years between managing jobs.

McKeon's philosophy and his attitude toward his players can be summed up in four words (and these are his words): "Get off your duff." He wanted his players to hustle and to be thinking, always, about game situations. He managed four major league teams and achieved reasonable success wherever he was, with the exception of Oakland, where he was hired, fired and rehired by meddling owner Charlie Finley.

McKeon said Finley used to call the dugout during games and order him to have his batters choke up more on the bat. One time, according to McKeon, Finley came in the dressing room after a game and told the coaches they weren't demonstrative enough. He then got into a crouch and demonstrated how he wanted them to coach at first base and third base. In his three years at Kansas City, the Royals finished second, fifth and were in second when McKeon was fired. In three years at San Diego, his Padres finished second, third and fifth — but they won the pennant in 1984 when McKeon was their general manager.

In 1997, he returned to managing, after having been away from it for seven years, when the Reds hired him. He finished fourth in his first full season. In his second, Cincinnati finished second, but their fate wasn't decided until the last game of the season. He was released after the 2000 season and replaced by Bob Boone.

Year	Team	Record	Pct.	Standing
1973	KC	88–74	.540	Second
1974	KC	77–85	.470	Fifth
1975	KC	50–46	.520	Second
1977	Oak	26–27	.490	Seventh
1978	Oak	45–78	.360	Sixth
1988	SD	67–48	.580	Third
1989	SD	89–73	.540	Second
1990	SD	37–43	.460	Fifth
1997	Cin	33–30	.520	Third
1998	Cin	77–85	.470	Fourth
1999	Cin	96–67	.580	Second
2000	Cin.	86–77	.525	Second
12 years		**770–733**	**.512**	

Alexander J. McKinnon

Born August 14, 1956, Boston, Massachusetts; died July 24, 1887, Charleston, Massachusetts; St. Louis Maroons, 1885

Alex McKinnon was a first baseman–outfielder for four seasons and was enlisted to manage the National League's St. Louis team for a short time in 1885.

The Redbirds lost 32 of 38 games with McKinnon at the helm.

Year	Team	Record	Pct.	Standing
1885	StL (NL)	6–32	.158	Eighth

Henry Dennis McKnight

Born in 1847, Pittsburgh, Pennsylvania; died May 5, 1900, Pittsburgh; Pittsburgh Alleghenys, 1884

Denny McKnight was a hometown boy when he was hired to manage the Pittsburgh franchise in the American Association in 1884. His team had won 12, lost 17 and tied one — good for twelfth place — by the time he was replaced.

Year	Team	Record	Pct.	Standing
1884	Pitt	12–17	.414	Twelfth

George McManus

Born in October 1846; died October 2, 1918, New York, New York; St. Louis Brown Stockings, 1877

George McManus was one of baseball's earliest managers, guiding the fortunes of the St. Louis franchise that preceded the Cardinals in 1877, the second year of the National League. His team was 14–20 when he was replaced, never to return to managing.

Year	Team	Record	Pct.	Standing
1877	StL	14–20	.412	Fourth

Martin Joseph McManus

Born March 14, 1900, Chicago, Illinois; died February 18, 1966, St. Louis, Missouri; Boston Red Sox, September 10, 1931–October 2, 1933

Marty McManus was a veteran American League infielder who became player-manager of the Boston Red Sox midway through the 1932 season. McManus took over a team that had finished in last place eight of the 10 previous seasons. He could not bring them out of the cellar. In 1933, he guided them to a seventh-place finish and then decided he had enough. In 1934, he was a full-time infielder for the crosstown Boston Braves.

Year	Team	Record	Pct.	Standing
1932	Bos (A)	32–65	.330	Eighth
1933	Bos	63–86	.423	Seventh
2 years		**95–151**	**.386**	

Roy David McMillan

Born July 17, 1930, Bonham, Texas; died November 3, 1997, Bonham, Texas; Milwaukee Brewers, 1972; New York Mets, August 6, 1975–October 1976

Roy McMillan was a light-hitting, great-fielding shortstop for the Cincinnati Reds in the 1950s in an infield that had three All-Stars: McMillan, Johnny Temple at second base and Ted Kluszewski at first base. He was a coach with Milwaukee in 1972 when he was called on to be interim skipper and split the two games he managed. In 1975, he took over for Yogi Berra with the New York Mets and brought them home one game under .500 for his tenure. It was not good enough, and McMillan was replaced by Joe Frazier for the 1976 season.

Year	Team	Record	Pct.	Standing
1972	Mil	1–1	.500	Sixth
1975	NY (N)	26–27	.491	Third
2 years		**27–28**	**.491**	

John Francis McNamara

Born June 4, 1932, Sacramento, California; Oakland A's, September 19, 1969–October 2, 1970; San Diego Padres, February 2, 1974–May 28, 1977; Cincinnati Reds, November 28, 1978–July 21, 1982; California

Angels, November 2, 1982–October 9, 1984; Boston Red Sox, November 18, 1984–July 13, 1988;
Cleveland Indians, November 3, 1989–July 6, 1991; California Angels, August 6, 1996–November 4,
1996

John McNamara was one of the most well-traveled managers of the 20th century, piloting seven teams, including the California Angels twice. He had division championship teams at Cincinnati in 1979 and at Boston in 1986 and 1988. His 1986 Red Sox lost the World Series to the New York Mets. The Series featured a Game Six in which the Mets rallied to win, helped by first baseman Bill Buckner's famous error with two outs in the ninth and the Red Sox leading.

McNamara is one of the few managers in baseball history to have managed in four decades. The fact that his teams were under .500 more often than not and that his team lost in his only World Series appearance in 19 years prevents his name from being mentioned with some of the great managers who had similarly long tenures.

McNamara went pretty much by the book. His teams led the league in sacrifice bunts four times — three times with San Diego and once with California; and two of his San Diego teams set National League records for most intentional walks issued in a season.

Year	Team	Record	Pct.	Standing
1969	Oak	8–5	.610	Second
1970	Oak	89–73	.540	Second
1974	SD	60–102	.370	Sixth
1975	SD	71–91	.430	Fourth
1976	SD	73–89	.450	Fifth
1977	SD	20–28	.410	Fifth
1979	Cin	90–71	.550	First
1980	Cin	89–73	.540	Second
1981	Cin	35–21	.620	Second
1981	Cin	31–21	.590	Second
1982	Cin	34–58	.360	Sixth
1983	Cal	70–92	.430	Fifth
1984	Cal	81–81	.500	Second
1985	Bos	81–81	.500	Fifth
1986	Bos	95–66	.590	First
1987	Bos	78–84	.480	Fifth
1988	Bos	43–42	.501	First
1990	Cleve	77–85	.470	Fourth
1991	Cleve	25–52	.320	Seventh
1996	Cal	10–18	.350	Fourth
19 years		**1160–1233**	**.484**	

LEAGUE CHAMPIONSHIP SERIES

Year	Team	Record	Pct.
1979	Cin	0–3	.000
1986	Bos	4–3	.571
1988	Bos	0–4	.000
3 years		**4–10**	**.286**

WORLD SERIES

Year	Team	Record	Pct.
1986	Bos	3–4	.429

John Alexander "Bid" McPhee

Born November 1, 1859, Massena, New York; died January 3, 1943, San Francisco, California; Cincinnati Reds, 1901–1902

Bid McPhee managed the Cincinnati Reds in 1901 and 1902 but could get them no higher than seventh place. He was relieved of his duties after 64 games in his second season. He never managed again.

Year	Team	Record	Pct.	Standing
1901	Cin	52–87	.374	Eighth
1902	Cin	27–37	.422	Seventh
2 years		**79–124**	**.389**	

Harold Abraham McRae

Born July 11, 1946, Avon Park, Florida; Kansas City Royals, May 24, 1991–September 16, 1994; Tampa Bay Devil Rays, April 19, 2001–present

Hal McRae, a major league outfielder and designated hitter for 16 years, played 12 years for the Kansas City Royals and was a favorite player of the fans. In 1991, Royals management followed a recent tradition, elevating a popular player to the manager's role. Other recent Royal examples have been Bob Boone and John Wathan. McRae was the third of three managers in 1991, and the Royals finished eight games above .500 for him but wound up in sixth place. They moved up to fifth in 1992 but were 18 games below .500. They finished third in both 1993 and the strike-shortened 1994 season but were far behind the front-running Cleveland Indians in both years. McRae was relieved of his job after the 1994 season. He replaced Larry Rothschild as manager of Tampa Bay early in the 2001 season.

Year	Team	Record	Pct.	Standing
1991	KC	66–58	.530	Sixth
1992	KC	72–90	.440	Fifth
1993	KC	84–78	.510	Third
1994	KC	64–51	.550	Third
2001	TB	58–90	.392	Fifth
5 years		**344–367**	**.484**	

Calvin Alexander McVey

Born August 30, 1850, Montrose Lee County, Iowa; died August 20, 1926, San Francisco, California; Lord Baltimores, 1873; Cincinnati Reds, 1878–1879

The National League was just two years old when Cal McVey took over as manager of the Cincinnati Reds, having come to it from the National Association, where he managed the Lord Baltimores. He had two decent seasons but was managing in an era when the burn-out rate was high because of all the off-the-field duties required of managers. He lasted only 125 games but finished with a winning percentage of .581.

Year	Team	Record	Pct.	Standing
1873	Bal–LBs	20–13	.606	Third
1878	Cin	37–23	.617	Second
1879	Cin	35–29	.547	Fifth
3 years		**91–64**	**.587**	

Sabbath Anthony "Sam" Mele

Born January 21, 1923; Astoria, New York; Minnesota Twins, June 6–13, 1961; June 23, 1961–June 9, 1967

Sam Mele, an American League outfielder in his playing days, took over in 1961 as manager of the newly transplanted Senators, now called the Minnesota Twins. The Twins were in ninth place when Mele took over for Cookie Lavagetto, trailing even the expansion Los Angeles Angels. Under Mele, the club went 41–45 and finished seventh. In 1962, Mele's first full season, Minnesota won 91 games and finished second behind the New York Yankees. In 1963, they won 91 again, finishing third behind New York and Chicago but better established as a pennant contender. They fell back to seventh in 1964 but rebounded to win the pennant in 1965 — the first Twins league championship and first for the franchise in 32 years.

Harmon Killebrew said part of Mele's success was attributable to his keeping everyone on the ball club happy, including those who weren't playing regularly. Johnny Klippstein said Mele reminded him of Walter Alston, quiet and thorough. Mele also used veterans like Jim Kaat, Killebrew and Camilo Pascuel to teach formative youngsters like Bob Allison, Earl Battey and Don Mincher. When the Twins acquired Mudcat Grant from Cleveland, they had the missing piece to the puzzle. Quiet Sam and his Twins won the championship in 1965 with Grant winning 21 games. In 1967, with the Twins at 25–25, Mele stepped down, retiring with a winning percentage of .548.

Year	Team	Record	Pct.	Standing
1961	Minn	41–45	.477	Seventh
1962	Minn	91–71	.562	Second
1963	Minn	91–70	.565	Third
1964	Minn	79–83	.488	Sixth
1965	Minn	102–60	.630	First
1966	Minn	89–73	.549	Second
1967	Minn	25–25	.500	Sixth
7 years		**518–427**	**.548**	

WORLD SERIES

Year	Team	Record	Pct.
1965	Minn	3–4	.429

Oscar Donald Melillo

Born August 4, 1899, Chicago, Illinois; died November 14, 1963, Chicago; St. Louis Browns, 1938

Oscar "Ski" Melillo was a major league infielder for 12 years with the St. Louis Browns and Boston Red Sox, hitting .260 for his career. In 1938, he became part of Browns manager Gabby Street's coaching staff and replaced Street for the last nine games of the season. The Browns were 53–90 when he took over, 55–97 when the season ended.

Year	Team	Record	Pct.	Standing
1938	StL (A)	2–7	.222	Seventh

Carl Harrison "Stump" Merrill

Born February 25, 1944; New York Yankees, June 6, 1990–October 16, 1991

Stump Merrill joined George Steinbrenner's manager merry-go-round in 1990 and made it through the 1991 season before he was fired. The Yankees didn't play well during his tenure, hastening his demise.

Year	Team	Record	Pct.	Standing
1990	NY (A)	49–64	.430	Seventh
1991	NY	71–91	.430	Fifth
2 years		**120–155**	**.430**	

Charles Metro

Born April 28, 1919, Nanty-Glo, Pennsylvania; Chicago Cubs (head coach), June 4, 1962–November 8, 1962; Kansas City Athletics, October 8, 1969–June 9, 1970

Charlie Metro was one of the Chicago Cubs "rotating coaches" in 1962 and rotated up to head coach for much of the 1962 season. By that time, Cub players were frustrated and disheartened by having had a new head man about every two weeks for the past two seasons. They finished 43–69 under Metro, in ninth place behind even the expansion Houston Colt .45s team. Metro didn't manage again until 1970 when he was hired by the Kansas City A's. He was released after 54 games, never to manage again.

Year	Team	Record	Pct.	Standing
1962	Chi (N)	43–69	.384	Ninth
1970	KC	19–35	.352	Sixth
2 years		**62–104**	**.373**	

William Adam Meyer

Born January 14, 1892, Knoxville, Tennessee; died March 31, 1957, Knoxville; Pittsburgh Pirates, May 4, 1948–October 1, 1952

Billy Meyer is remembered in Pittsburgh Pirate history as the manager who pulled off a miracle — getting the Pirates to finish fourth in his first season, 1948. Pittsburgh had fallen on tough times after the end of World War II, finishing seventh in 1946 and eighth in 1947 despite having superb power hitters in an aging Hank Greenberg and a young Ralph Kiner. The Pirates' problem was that they didn't have much else. Meyer and the Pirate front office made some deals for both veterans and youngsters who could provide balance in the lineup and flexibility for the manager to make some moves during ball games. Newcomer Bob Chesnes, a pitcher recruited from the Pacific Coast League, went 14–6. Veteran Rip Sewell responded with a 13–3 record. Shortstop Stan Rojek and second baseman Danny Murtaugh each hit .290 and gave the Pirates a slick double play combination. The magic lasted one year. The Pirates slipped back to sixth in 1949, eighth in 1950, seventh in 1951 and eighth again in a disastrous 1952 in which they won only 42 and lost 112. By this time, general manager Branch Rickey had decided to rebuild the Pirates with young, untested players. He did it without Meyer, who was fired after the 1952 season.

Year	Team	Record	Pct.	Standing
1948	Pitt	83–71	.539	Fourth
1949	Pitt	71–83	.461	Sixth
1950	Pitt	57–96	.373	Eighth
1951	Pitt	64–90	.416	Seventh
1952	Pitt	42–112	.273	Eighth
5 years		**317–452**	**.412**	

Gene Richard Michael

Born June 2, 1938, Kent, Ohio; New York Yankees, November 21, 1980–September 6, 1981; April 25, 1982–August 23, 1982; Chicago Cubs, June 12, 1986–September 8, 1987

Gene Michael was a light-hitting utility infielder for 10 years, seven of them with the New York Yankees. Yankee owner George Steinbrenner took a liking to him and hired him first to manage in between the managerial stints of Billy Martin and then to work in the Yankee front office. Michael managed the Chicago Cubs for parts of two seasons.

Year	Team	Record	Pct.	Standing
1981	NY (A)	34–22	.600	First
1981	NY	14–12	.530	Sixth
1986	Chi (N)	46–56	.450	Fifth
1987	Chi	66–66	.500	Sixth
3 years		**160–156**	**.506**	

Jesse Clyde Milan

Born March 25, 1887, Linden, Tennessee; died March 3, 1953, Orlando, Florida; Washington Senators, 1922

Clark Griffith had been owner and manager of the Washington Senators and wanted to relieve himself of managerial duties. But it took him awhile to settle on a successor. Griffith hired four managers in four years — George McBride, Clyde Milan, Donie Bush and Bucky Harris, who eventually led the Senators to the top. For Milan's part, the Senators got out of the gate slowly and continued that pace for the entire season, finishing sixth. Milan never managed again.

Year	Team	Record	Pct.	Standing
1922	Wash	69–85	.448	Sixth

George C. Miller

Born February 19, 1853, Newport, Kentucky; died July 25, 1929, Cincinnati, Ohio; St. Louis Cardinals, 1894

George "Calliope" Miller, a catcher, managed the St. Louis ball club for one year and brought them home in ninth place — which was an improvement, but not enough of one for Miller to return as manager the next year.

Year	Team	Record	Pct.	Standing
1894	StL	56–76	.324	Ninth

Joseph Wick Miller

Born July 24, 1850, Germany; died August 30, 1891, White Bear Lake, Minnesota; Washington Nationals, 1872

At age 22, German-born Joe Miller managed the Washington team in the National Association for 11 games and was unable to bring his team to victory in any of them.

Year	Team	Record	Pct.	Standing
1872	Wash (Ntls)	0–11	.000	Eleventh

Ray Miller

Born April 30, 1945, Takoma Park, Maryland; Minnesota Twins, June 21, 1985–September 12, 1986; Baltimore Orioles, November 11, 1997–October 6, 1999

Ray Miller was a pitching coach for Earl Weaver who helped the Baltimore Orioles to huge success. Always considered a great handler of pitchers, he was never able to transfer that effectiveness into his managing. He managed a promising Minnesota Twins team for part of 1985 and all of 1986, finishing fourth and sixth. Tom Kelly took the job in 1987 and won a World Series championship in his first year. Miller's next managerial chance came with the Baltimore Orioles in 1998 and 1999. The Orioles had one of baseball's highest payrolls and Miller was expected to produce a winner. Baltimore finished fourth twice and Miller was fired.

Year	Team	Record	Pct.	Standing
1985	Minn	50–50	.500	Fourth
1986	Minn	59–80	.420	Sixth
1998	Bal	79–83	.480	Fourth
1999	Bal	78–84	.480	Fourth
4 years		266–297	.472	

Colonel Buster Mills

Born September 16, 1908, Ranger, Texas; died December 1, 1991, Arlington, Texas; Cincinnati Reds, September 17–29, 1953

Buster Mills had an eight-game stint as manager of the Cincinnati Reds in 1953, filling in the rest of the season after the firing of Rogers Hornsby. Birdie Tebbetts was hired to manage the club in 1954.

Year	Team	Record	Pct.	Standing
1953	Cin	4–4	.500	Sixth

Everett Mills

Born January 20, 1845, Newark, New Jersey; died June 22, 1908, Newark; Baltimore Lord Baltimores, 1872

Everett Mills got his shot at managing a professional baseball team in 1872, four years before the National League was formed. Mills was the leader of the Baltimore ball club for 14 games, winning eight of them. He never managed again.

Year	Team	Record	Pct.	Standing
1872	Bal	8–6	.571	Second

Frederick Francis Mitchell

Born June 5, 1878, Cambridge, Massachusetts; died October 13, 1970, Newton, Massachusetts; Chicago Cubs, March 17, 1917–1920; Boston Braves 1921–1923

During his playing days, Fred Mitchell was a mediocre pitcher for the Chicago Cubs, but he played under a great manager, Frank Selee, who helped build the dominating Cub teams of the era. Mitchell became manager of the Cubs in 1918. He has a claim to fame as a Cubs manager that no Cub skipper since 1945 has: Mitchell managed a Cub pennant winner in 1918. His teams also finished fifth twice and third once before he moved on to Boston, where he fell on harder times.

In their World Series appearance, the Cubs lost to the Red Sox, four games to two, with Babe Ruth earning two wins for Boston and posting a 1.06 earned run average.

Mitchell was a bit of an innovator and is credited with devising the "Cy Williams shift" to try to control the Phillies power hitter. Mitchell moved three of his infielders over to the right side of the infield, a maneuver Lou Boudreau used 30 years later against Ted Williams. Mitchell would not have needed the shift had he not traded Cy Williams to the Phillies in 1918.

Year	Team	Record	Pct.	Standing
1917	Chi (N)	74–80	.481	Fifth
1918	Chi	84–45	.651	First
1919	Chi	75–65	.536	Third
1920	Chi	75–79	.487	Fifth
1921	Bos (N)	79–74	.516	Fourth
1922	Bos	53–100	.346	Eighth
1923	Bos	54–100	.351	Eighth
7 years		**494–543**	**.476**	

WORLD SERIES

Year	Team	Record
1918	Chi (N)	2–4

John Joseph Mizerock

Born December 8, 1960, Punxsutawny, Pennsylvania; Kansas City Royals, April 30, 2002–May 15, 2002

Serving as interim manager after the 2002 firing of Tony Muser, John Mizerock led the Kansas City Royals to a 5–8 record before handing the club over to the permanent replacement, Tony Peña.

Year	Team	Record	Pct.	Standing
2002	KC	5–8	.385	Fourth

Jackie Spencer Moore

Born February 19, 1939, Jay, Florida; Oakland Athletics, May 24, 1984–June 26, 1986

Jackie Moore managed the Oakland A's for parts of three seasons in the early 1980s and could not get them over .500. He took over in the 1984 season when they were mired in fifth place and got them up to fourth by the end of the season. They were fourth again in 1985. But they had slipped to sixth in 1986 when Moore was replaced by Tony LaRussa.

Year	Team	Record	Pct.	Standing
1984	Oak	57–61	.483	Fifth
1985	Oak	77–85	.475	Fourth
1986	Oak	29–44	.397	Sixth
3 years		**163–190**	**.462**	

Terry Bluford Moore

Born May 27, 1912, Vernon, Alabama; died March 19, 1995, Collinsville, Illinois; Philadelphia Phillies, June 15, 1954–October 14, 1954

Terry Moore was a fleet-footed outfielder on the great St. Louis Cardinal teams of the 1940s. He was hired to replace Steve O'Neill as manager of the Philadelphia Phillies at exactly the halfway point of the 1954 season. The Phillies went 35–42 under Moore and finished fourth. Philadelphia then hired Mayo Smith for the 1955 season.

Year	Team	Record	Pct.	Standing
1954	Phil	35–42	.455	Fourth

Patrick Joseph Moran

Born February 7, 1876, Fitchburg, Massachusetts; died March 7, 1924, Orlando, Florida; Philadelphia Phillies, October 20, 1914–October 1, 1918; Cincinnati Reds, January 30, 1919–March 7, 1924

Pat Moran has the distinction of twice winning a pennant in his first year of managing a team — with the 1915 Philadelphia Phillies and the 1919 Cincinnati Reds. His managing the latter club spells a distinction more dubious: He was the manager of the team that won the World Series thrown by the Chicago "Black Sox." Moran, to his dying day, contended the Reds would have won it anyway.

Called "Whiskey Face" by some opponents because he was known to have a drink now and then, Moran, a catcher in his playing days, was a stickler for detail. With the Phillies in 1915, he made the players walk two miles from the hotel to the practice field every day and then walk back to the hotel. Sometimes he held two-a-day practices with twice as many two-mile walks. He also instituted the practice by which catchers flash series of signs to the pitcher instead of a single sign. One of the signs in the set was the "indicator," letting the pitcher know which one of the next signs was the real one. Also, Moran's spring trainings were devoted to practicing hour after hour on all the plays that make up the average game — pickoffs, cutoffs, fielding bunts, backing up teammates on defense. During ball games, he assigned a pitcher on the bench to study the opposing pitcher and report to others on what he was throwing. Catchers on the bench were expected to try to steal the signs of the opponent. Moran's goal was to have everyone on the team play a role in every game.

His greatest talent, and the one that gave him such great success at both Philadelphia and Cincinnati, was in working with a pitching staff. Moran would stand behind the catcher when a pitcher was warming up before a game and he would yell game situations to the pitcher. For example, he would say something like "runners on first and third, Hornsby up — what are you going to throw?" The Phillies finished first in 1915, second in 1916 and 1917 and then slipped to sixth in 1918. Moran was fired, despite his three great years prior to 1918. When Christy Mathewson, Cincinnati manager, was late getting back from his military service in 1919, Moran was named manager of the Reds. In five years with the Reds, he finished first once, second twice, third and sixth. In his typical no-nonsense style, Moran said the key to success in any business is hard work — and the same was true with baseball. Moran took ill after the 1923 season and died on March 7, 1924, as the Reds were preparing for spring training. Though the cause of death was listed as Bright's Disease, many observers thought his heavy drinking caught up with him. He was 48.

Year	Team	Record	Pct.	Standing
1915	Phil (N)	90–62	.592	First
1916	Phil	91–62	.595	Second
1917	Phil	87–65	.572	Second
1918	Phil	55–68	.447	Sixth
1919	Cin	96–44	.686	First
1920	Cin	82–71	.536	Third
1921	Cin	70–83	.458	Sixth
1922	Cin	86–68	.568	Second
1923	Cin	91–63	.591	Second
9 years		**748–586**	**.561**	

WORLD SERIES

Year	Team	Record	Pct.
1915	Phil	1–4	.200
1919	Cin	5–3	.625
2 years		**6–7**	.462

Joseph Michael Morgan

Born November 19, 1930, Walpole, Massachusetts; Boston Red Sox, July 13, 1988–October 8, 1991

Joe Morgan bears the same name as the Hall of Fame second baseman but not the same statistics. Joseph Michael Morgan played for five teams in four years as a major league third baseman and outfielder. He got into only 88 games. As manager of the Boston Red Sox, he finished first twice and second and third once each. But the Red Sox never made it to the World Series and Morgan was replaced after the 1991 season.

Year	Team	Record	Pct.	Standing
1988	Bos	46–31	.590	First
1989	Bos	83–79	.510	Third
1990	Bos	88–74	.540	First
1991	Bos	84–78	.510	Second
4 years		**301–262**	**.535**	

LEAGUE CHAMPIONSHIP SERIES

Year	Team	Record	Pct.
1988	Bos	0–4	.000
1990	Bos	0–4	.000
2 years		**0–8**	.000

George Joseph Moriarty

Born July 7, 1884, Chicago, Illinois; died April 8, 1964, Tampa, Florida; Detroit Tigers, November 3, 1926–October 17, 1928

George Moriarty was a major league third baseman for 13 years who later had a distinguished career as a major league umpire. In between those two careers, Moriarty managed the Detroit Tigers for two years, finishing fourth and sixth.

Year	Team	Record	Pct.	Standing
1927	Det	82–71	.536	Fourth
1928	Det	68–86	.444	Sixth
2 years		**150–157**	**.489**	

John Francis Morrill

Born February 19, 1855, Boston, Massachusetts; died April 2, 1932, Boston; Boston Braves, 1882–1888; Washington Senators, 1889

Honest John Morrill had a fairly long run as a 19th-century manager. In the early days of baseball, managers were called on to handle many aspects of ball clubs. Some field managers were also expected to sell tickets or even concessions. Some argue that their on-field performances suffered, leading to short, unsuccessful tenures. Morrill, despite these challenges, spent seven successful years managing his hometown Boston team. Then he ended his career at Washington in the midst of a horrendous year that saw his club lose three out of every four games before he was fired.

Year	Team	Record	Pct.	Standing
1882	Bos (N)	45–39	.536	Third
1883	Bos	32–9	.780	Second
1884	Bos	73–38	.658	Second
1885	Bos	46–66	.411	Fifth
1886	Bos	56–61	.479	Fifth
1887	Bos	61–60	.504	Fifth
1888	Bos	70–64	.522	Fourth
1889	Wash	13–39	.250	Eighth
8 years		**396–376**	**.513**	

Robert Morrow

Born September 27, 1838, England; died February 6, 1898; Providence Grays, 1881

Englishman Bob Morrow had a short but relatively successful stint as manager of Providence in the early days of the National League, winning 30 of 50 games before he bowed out.

Year	Team	Record	Pct.	Standing
1881	Prov	30–20	.600	Third

Jacob Charles Morse

Born June 7, 1860, Concord, New Hampshire; died April 12, 1937, Brookline, Massachusetts; Boston Reds, 1884

As professional baseball was developing, several leagues started and folded. One of those was the Union League. Jake Morse managed the Boston entry in the Union League for part of one season and left with a .622 winning percentage.

Year	Team	Record	Pct.	Standing
1884	Bos (U)	46–28	.622	Fifth

Charles Hazen Morton

Born October 12, 1854, Kingsville, Ohio; died December 13, 1921, Akron, Ohio; Toledo Blue Stockings, 1884; Toledo Maumees, 1890; Detroit Wolverines, 1885

Charlie Morton had a managerial career of 301 games, an extremely high number for managers in the 19th century. Numbers like that usually were linked to player-managers such as Cap Anson who were regarded as stars. Morton managed Toledo of the American Association in two different years. Sandwiched in between was a year in which he piloted the National League Detroit Wolverines.

Year	Team	Record	Pct.	Standing
1884	Tol (AA)	46–58	.442	Eighth
1885	Det (N)	18–39	.316	Seventh
1889	Tol	68–64	.515	Fourth
3 years		**132–161**	**.451**	

Felix I. Moses

Born in Richmond, Virginia; Richmond Virginians, 1884

Felix Moses was a hometown boy who was called on to manage the Richmond club in the American Association. The ball club won on 12 of 42 games after which Moses went back home and never managed again.

Year	Team	Record	Pct.	Standing
1884	Rich	12–30	.286	Tenth

John Lester Moss

Born May 14, 1925, Tulsa, Oklahoma; Chicago White Sox, July 23–25, 1968; Detroit Tigers, October 1, 1978–June 12, 1979

Les Moss was a major league catcher who got a brief chance to manage the Chicago White Sox in 1968, serving for two games after Eddie Stanky was fired and before Al Lopez arrived for his second tenure as manager of the White Sox. Chicago lost both games Moss managed, on their way to a ninth-place finish under all three managers. In 1979, the Detroit Tigers hired Moss but fired him after only 53 games with the team hovering around the .500 mark. He was succeeded by Sparky Anderson.

Year	Team	Record	Pct.	Standing
1968	Chi (A)	0–2	.000	Ninth
1979	Det	27–26	.509	Fifth
2 years		**27–28**	**.491**	

Timothy Hayes Murnane

Born June 4, 1852, Naugatuck, Connecticut; died February 13, 1917, Boston, Massachusetts; Boston Reds, 1884

Tim Murnane had a long and distinguished career involving baseball, but hardly any of it was in managing. He played baseball for several years and managed the Boston team in the Union League briefly in 1884. But Murnane is best known as one of the great sportswriters of the 19th century and one of the first to write a baseball column.

As a manager, he had some quirks. He disliked bunting and didn't think foul balls should be counted as strikes. In 1900, he advocated having a designated hitter for the pitcher. Seventy-two years later, the American League adopted the idea.

Year	Team	Record	Pct.	Standing
1884	Bos (U)	8–17	.320	Fifth

William Jeremiah Murray

Born April 13, 1864, Peabody, Massachusetts; died March 25, 1937, Youngstown, Ohio; Philadelphia Phillies, 1907–1909

Billy Murray believed in encouraging his ballplayers rather than criticizing them. Murray was a good-hearted Irishman who was managing at Providence when the Phillies hired him to replace Hugh Duffy in 1907. Murray's goal was to develop the young players, blend them in with the veterans and keep everyone happy. In a game in 1907, pitcher Harry Coveleskie failed to hold a runner on first base. The runner stole second easily and later scored. After the game, Murray had a meeting with Coveleskie and his four infielders. He talked about the stolen base and asked each of the infielders if they knew that there had been a man on first. They all answered that they had. He then asked if any of them had told Coveleskie that there was a man on first. They all said they hadn't. "Gentlemen," said Murray, "from now on there will be no secrets on this team." That incident portrays Murray's style of managing for the three years he guided the Phillies.

Year	Team	Record	Pct.	Standing
1907	Phil (N)	83–64	.565	Third
1908	Phil	83–71	.539	Fourth
1909	Phil	74–79	.484	Fifth
3 years		**240–214**	**.529**	

Daniel Edward Murtaugh

Born October 8, 1917, Chester, Pennsylvania; died December 2, 1976, Chester; Pittsburgh Pirates, August 3, 1957–October 1, 1964; July 18, 1967–October 1, 1967; October 9, 1969–November 23, 1971; September 6, 1973–October 2, 1976

Danny Murtaugh managed the Pittsburgh Pirates in four different stints, leading them to four league championship series appearances and winning two World Series appearances. Murtaugh, a major league infielder for nine years, took over a Pirate team in 1957 that had been at or near the bottom of the National League for the entire decade. He led them in their last 51 games of the year, moving the Pirates up to seventh place by season's end. The next year, they finished second. Two years after that, they were in the World Series, winning it in the seventh game on Bill Mazeroski's ninth-inning home run.

Murtaugh's teams were generally strong up the middle, had good starting pitchers and at least one top relief pitcher. On his 1960 pennant winner, Vernon Law and Bob Friend were the aces of the pitching

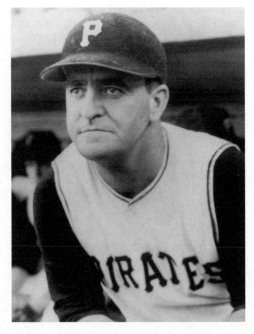

Danny Murtaugh

staff and Elroy Face was the best relief pitcher in the National League. Dick Groat and Bill Mazeroski formed one of the best double play combinations of all time at shortstop and second base, and fleet-footed Bill Virdon was in center field. The Pirates led the National League in double plays executed for six consecutive years, 1959–1964. His 1971 pennant winner had 19-game winner Doc Ellis and 15-game winner Steve Blass leading the pitching staff with Dave Giusti contributing a league-leading 30 saves out of the bullpen. Catcher Manny Sanguillen, shortstop Gene Alley, second baseman Dave Cash and center fielder Al Oliver made the Pirates strong up the middle once again. Both the 1960 and 1971 pennant winners had Roberto Clemente in right field, as did every Pirate team in between, helping Pittsburgh lead the National League in batting four times and in hits five times.

Murtaugh had the strength up the middle, and he had Clemente and Willie Stargell for many years as well. But Murtaugh's biggest strength was his patience with players who didn't have the natural ability of Clemente or Stargell. Murtaugh once said, "I had to learn never to expect a man to do something that he was not capable of doing." The key to good managing, he said, was to analyze a player's capabilities and never ask him to exceed them.

Murtaugh also played the percentages and went by the book, a style that some of his players complained was too predictable.

Groat and Face both said many years after they retired that Murtaugh knew baseball and knew how to handle players, crediting him with giving them and other players confidence in their abilities. The turn-around of the Pirates started when their confidence began to build.

He died three months after the end of the 1976 season.

Year	Team	Record	Pct.	Standing
1957	Pitt	26–25	.510	Seventh
1958	Pitt	84–70	.545	Second
1959	Pitt	78–76	.506	Fourth
1960	Pitt	95–59	.617	First
1961	Pitt	75–79	.486	Sixth
1962	Pitt	93–68	.578	Fourth
1963	Pitt	74–88	.457	Eighth
1964	Pitt	80–82	.494	Sixth
1967	Pitt	39–39	.500	Sixth
1970	Pitt	89–73	.541	First
1971	Pitt	97–65	.599	First
1973	Pitt	13–13	.500	Second
1974	Pitt	88–74	.543	First
1975	Pitt	92–69	.571	First
1976	Pitt	92–70	.568	Second
15 years		**1115–950**	**.540**	

League Championship Series

Year	Team	Record	Pct.
1970	Pitt	0–3	.000
1971	Pitt	3–1	.750
1974	Pitt	1–3	.250
1975	Pitt	0–3	.000
4 years		**4–10**	**.286**

WORLD SERIES

Year	Team	Record	Pct.
1960	Pitt	4–3	.571
1971	Pitt	4–3	.571
2 years		**8–6**	**.571**

Anthony Joseph Muser

Born August 1, 1947, Van Nuys, California; Kansas City Royals, July 9, 1997–April 29, 2002

Tony Muser was a major league first baseman for nine years and was a coach for the Milwaukee Brewers for several years. His name came up frequently as a potential manager and was a candidate for several jobs before getting his chance in 1997 with the Kansas City Royals. He was fired early in the 2002 season when his club stumbled to an 8–15 start.

Year	Team	Record	Pct.	Standing
1997	KC	31–48	.390	Fifth
1998	KC	72–89	.440	Third
1999	KC	64–97	.390	Fourth
2000	KC	77–85	.475	Fourth
2001	KC	65–97	.401	Fifth
2002	KC	8–15	.348	Fourth
6 years		**317–431**	**.424**	

James J. Mutrie

Born June 13, 1851, Chelsea, Massachusetts; died January 24, 1938, New York, New York; New York Metropolitans, 1883–1891

Jim Mutrie managed the New York entries in both the American Association and the National League for nine years and was one of the most successful managers of the early days of baseball. He had only one losing season, and his lifetime percentage of .611 is second only to Joe McCarthy. Mutrie's 1885 team had a record of 85–27, a .759 winning percentage — and finished second. That team had two future Hall of Fame pitchers: Mickey Welch, who was 44–11, and Tim Keefe, who was 32–13. Cap Anson's Chicago Cubs won the championship that year with an 87–25 record. Mutrie's 1884 pennant winner also had a winning percentage that topped the .700 mark.

Mutrie was listed as the manager but he was chiefly responsible for the team's finances. His catcher, Buck Ewing, was the ball club's chief strategist. Mutrie is said to have nicknamed his players "my big fellows," which eventually led to their permanent monicker — the Giants.

Year	Team	Record	Pct.	Standing
1883	NY (AA)	54–42	.563	Fourth
1884	NY	75–32	.701	First
1885	NY (N)	85–27	.759	Second
1886	NY	75–44	.630	Third
1887	NY	68–55	.553	Fourth
1888	NY	84–47	.641	First
1889	NY	83–43	.659	First
1890	NY	63–68	.481	Sixth
1891	NY	71–61	.538	Third
9 years		**658–419**	**.611**	

George Edward Myatt

Born June 14, 1914, Denver, Colorado; Philadelphia Phillies, June 15–18, 1968; August 7, 1969–October 8, 1969

George Myatt served two short stints as manager of the Philadelphia Phillies. Had he retired after the first one, he would have had a perfect record. In 1968, he filled in between Gene Mauch and Bob Skinner and was victorious in both games he managed. When Skinner was fired in 1969, Myatt filled in for the rest of the season and was not as successful as he had been the previous year, winning only 19 of 54 games.

Year	Team	Record	Pct.	Standing
1968	Phil	2–0	1.000	Eighth
1969	Phil	19–35	.352	Fifth
2 years		**21–35**	**.375**	

Henry C. Myers

Born in May 1858, Philadelphia, Pennsylvania; died April 18, 1895, Philadelphia; Baltimore Orioles, 1882

Henry Myers, a native of Philadelphia, ventured over to nearby Baltimore in 1882 to manage the ball club there. He was only 24 years old. His career did not last long. The ball club lost 54 of 73 games, after which Myers returned to his home in Philadelphia, where he died in 1895 at the age of 36.

Year	Team	Record	Pct.	Standing
1882	Bal	19–54	.260	Sixth

Jerry Narron

Born January 15, 1956, Goldsboro, North Carolina; Texas Rangers, May 3, 2001–present

Jerry Narron, who played sparingly for several teams in a nine-year major league career, was a third base coach for the Texas Rangers when manager Johnny Oates resigned in May 2001 after the Rangers, loaded with free agent talent and hungry for a championship, got off to a dismal 11–17 start.

Year	Team	Record	Pct.	Standing
2001	Tex	62–72	.463	Fourth

William Mitchell Nash

Born June 24, 1865, Richmond, Virginia; died November 16, 1929, East Orange, New Jersey; Philadelphia Phillies, 1896

Early histories of the Philadelphia Phillies indicate Bill Shettsline managed the club in 1896 and that Billy Nash was the team captain. Official records list Nash as the manager. The confusion arises because managers in those days were often business managers. Team captains were responsible for directing play on the field. Nash was team captain. *The Baseball Encyclopedia* also identifies him as team manager. One fact that is indisputable is that the Phillies finished eighth.

Year	Team	Record	Pct.	Standing
1896	Phil (N)	62–68	.477	Eighth

John Henry Neun

Born October 28, 1900, Baltimore, Maryland; died March 28, 1990, Baltimore; New York Yankees, September 12, 1946–October 1, 1946; Cincinnati Reds, November 5, 1946–August 6, 1948

Coach Johnny Neun bridged the gap between the departure of Joe McCarthy and the naming of Bill Dickey as manager of the New York Yankees in 1946. Neun won eight and lost six and kept the Yankees in their third-place position. In 1947, he was hired to manage the Cincinnati Reds, a post he held for one season and part of another. As a player, he once executed an unassisted triple play — quite a feat for a first baseman.

Year	Team	Record	Pct.	Standing
1946	NY (A)	8–6	.571	Third
1947	Cin	73–81	.474	Fifth
1948	Cin	44–56	.440	Seventh
3 years		**125–143**	**.466**	

Jeffrey Lynn Newman

Born September 11, 1948, Fort Worth, Texas; Oakland Athletics, June 26, 1986–July 8, 1986

Jeff Newman caught for nine years, seven of them with the Oakland A's, retiring in 1984. Two years later, he filled in for 10 games as A's manager after Jackie Moore was fired. Tony LaRussa took over at the start of the 1987 season, leaving Newman with a 2–8 record as manager.

Year	Team	Record	Pct.	Standing
1986	Oak	2–8	.200	Sixth

Charles Augustus "Kid" Nichols

Born September 14, 1896, Madison, Wisconsin; died April 11, 1953, Kansas City, Missouri; St. Louis Cardinals, December 20, 1903–1905

Kid Nichols was one of the great pitchers of the 19th century and was elected to the Hall of Fame in 1949. He was less successful as a manager. He took over the St. Louis Cardinals in 1904, a gentleman in an era of rowdy ballplayers. He elevated the Cardinals to a fifth-place finish in his first year but was gone after 48 games in his second season, his Cardinals entrenched in sixth place.

Year	Team	Record	Pct.	Standing
1904	StL (N)	75–79	.487	Fifth
1905	StL	19–29	.396	Sixth
2 years		**94–108**	**.465**	

Hugh N. Nicol

Born January 1, 1858, Campsie, Scotland; died June 27, 1921, Lafayette, Indiana; St. Louis Cardinals, 1897

Hugh Nicol was one of three managers for the St. Louis Cardinals in 1897 as they tried to improve on their eleventh place finish of the year before. Instead, they finished twelfth.

Nicol was the second of the three managers that season and one of five managers the Cardinals employed in a two-year span.

Year	Team	Record	Pct.	Standing
1897	StL (N)	9–29	.237	Twelfth

Russell Eugene Nixon

Born February 19, 1935, Cleveland, Ohio; Cincinnati Reds, July 21, 1982–October 4, 1983; Atlanta Braves, May 23, 1988–June 22, 1990

Russ Nixon was a major league catcher for 12 years. His managerial career covered five seasons, two full and three partial seasons — with two teams, the Cincinnati Reds and Atlanta Braves. His teams finished in sixth place every year and never got to the .500 mark.

Year	Team	Record	Pct.	Standing
1982	Cin	27–43	.386	Sixth
1983	Cin	74–88	.457	Sixth
1988	Atl	42–79	.340	Sixth
1989	Atl	63–97	.390	Sixth
1990	Atl	25–40	.380	Sixth
5 years		**231–347**	**.400**	

Henry Willis Patrick Norman

Born July 16, 1910, St. Louis, Missouri; died April 21, 1962, Milwaukee, Wisconsin; Detroit Tigers, June 10, 1958–May 3, 1959

Bill Norman was hired early in the 1958 season as manager of the Detroit Tigers and brought them to a fifth place finish. In 1959, the Tigers got off to a horrible start, losing 15 of their first 17 games before losing their manager as well. Norman was fired.

Year	Team	Record	Pct.	Standing
1958	Det	56–49	.533	Fifth
1959	Det	2–15	.118	Eighth
2 years		**58–64**	**.475**	

Ennis Telflair "Rebel" Oakes

Born December 17, 1886, Homer, Louisiana; died February 29, 1948, Shreveport, Louisiana; Pittsburgh Rebels, 1914–1915

Rebel Oakes was an outfielder for the St. Louis Cardinals and Cincinnati Reds when, true to his nickname, he bolted from the National League for the Federal League where he managed the Pittsburgh entry, known variously as the PittsFeds, Stogies and, more often, the Rebels. He was the league's youngest skipper. The Federal League lasted two years — which was also the duration of Oakes' managerial career.

Year	Team	Record	Pct.	Standing
1914	Pitt (F)	58–74	.439	Seventh
1915	Pitt	86–67	.562	Third
2 years		**144–141**	**.505**	

Johnny Lane Oates

Born January 21, 1946, Sylvan, Texas; Baltimore Orioles, September 23, 1991–September 26, 1994; Texas Rangers, October 19, 1994–May 3, 2001

Johnny Oates, a major league catcher for 11 years, was a successful manager with two American League teams. He took over as manager of the Baltimore Orioles in 1991 and moved them from sixth to third to second place in four years. He won division titles in three out of his first five years with the Texas Rangers but was unable to break the stranglehold of the New York Yankees on the American League championship.

Oates believed in putting the best lineup on the field for every game and leaving it there. He hardly ever platooned and his teams were at the bottom of the league in use of pinch hitters. He also believed in letting his starting pitchers go longer than most managers did. His teams seldom used the pitchout as a defensive strategy — odd considering Oates was a former catcher. Twice in the 1990s, Oates' teams pitched out fewer than 10 times, the Orioles with just three in 1994, and the Rangers with six in 1996.

Texas finished first in the Western Division in 1996, 1998 and 1999. In 2000, they slipped to fourth place, 20 games below .500. In the off-season, Texas spent millions of dollars on free agents, landing Alex Rodriguez from Seattle in a $252 million, 10-year deal, the largest contract in baseball history. They also picked up Ken Caminiti and Andres Galarraga, two National League sluggers. The Rangers got off to an 11-17 start, mostly because their pitchers were allowing 6.2 runs a game. But Oates felt responsible for the team's lack of motivation and resigned on May 3. Coach Jerry Narron took over.

Year	Team	Record	Pct.	Standing
1991	Bal	54–71	.432	Sixth
1992	Bal	89–73	.549	Third
1993	Bal	85–77	.525	Third
1994	Bal	63–49	.562	Second
1995	Tex	74–70	.514	Third
1996	Tex	90–72	.556	First
1997	Tex	77–85	.475	Third
1998	Tex	88–74	.543	First
1999	Tex	95–67	.586	First
2000	Tex	71–91	.438	Fourth
2001	Tex	11–17	.308	Fourth
11 years		**868–819**	**.515**	

LEAGUE CHAMPIONSHIP SERIES

Year	Team	Record	Pct.
1996	Tex	1–3	.250
1998	Tex	0–3	.000
1999	Tex	0–3	.000
3 years		**1–9**	**.100**

John Joseph O'Connor

Born March 3, 1867, St. Louis, Missouri; died November 14, 1937, St. Louis; St. Louis Browns, 1910

Jack O'Connor spent 21 years as an outfielder for several teams in a career that began in 1887. His last major league stop was in St. Louis with the Browns; and he was named their manager in 1910. The Browns were at the beginning of losing a tradition that lasted half a century. O'Connor's Browns won only 47 games, bringing an end to his managerial career.

Year	Team	Record	Pct.	Standing
1910	StL (A)	47–107	.305	Eighth

Henry Francis O'Day

Born July 8, 1863, Chicago, Illinois; died July 2, 1935, Chicago; Cincinnati Reds, 1912; Chicago Cubs, 1914

Hank O'Day was a pitcher in the late 1800s who once won 21 games in a season. He began a distinguished career as a National League umpire in 1895 and remained in that job through the end of the 1913 season. Then owner Garry Hermann tabbed him to manage the Cincinnati Reds. The Reds got off to a good start but faded as the season went along and finished fourth. O'Day returned to umpiring the next season but in 1914 was hired to manage the Chicago Cubs. He lasted one year there, too, and once again returned to umpiring.

O'Day was an extremely quiet man who did not like to talk unless it was absolutely necessary. He would have had at least one great story to tell: he was the home plate umpire in 1908 when Fred Merkle failed to touch second base on what appeared to be a game-winning hit for the New York Giants. Merkle, a rookie, was on first base when a single drove in a run from third base — almost. Merkle, who had started to run for second, stopped as the winning run scored and the crowd poured onto the field. Cub second baseman Johnny Evers called for the ball and touched second base for the force out, nullifying the run. The game ended in a tie, was replayed later, and the Cubs won. Nothing quite that exciting or bizarre occurred during his two years as a manager.

Year	Team	Record	Pct.	Standing
1912	Cin	75–78	.490	Fourth
1914	Chi (N)	78–76	.506	Fourth
2 years		**153–154**	**.499**	

Robert Arthur O'Farrell

Born October 19, 1896, Waukegan, Illinois; died February 20, 1988, Waukegan; St. Louis Cardinals, December 28, 1926–November 7, 1927; Cincinnati Reds, November 10, 1932–July 28, 1934

Bob O'Farrell was the catcher on the St. Louis Cardinals 1926 pennant winner and was the National League's Most Valuable Player that season. Cardinal owner Sam Breadon, upset with manager Rogers Hornsby's moodiness, sarcasm and bad attitude, fired him even though the Cardinals were the World Series champions. He offered the job to Bill Killifer, one of Hornsby's coaches, who turned it down out of loyalty to Hornsby. So Breadon turned to his star catcher, O'Farrell. The Cardinals played well under O'Farrell, but O'Farrell didn't play well while he was managing. A sore arm limited him to 59 games and other injuries severely hampered the Cardinals. They finished the season 1½ games behind the Pirates, and that was enough to get O'Farrell fired. At Cincinnati, O'Farrell, who had not managed for seven years, was thought complacent, too happily a loser to suit new general manager Larry McPhail, who wanted to light a fire under the Reds. O'Farrell was dismissed in July and was replaced by Chuck Dressen.

Year	Team	Record	Pct.	Standing
1927	StL (N)	92–61	.601	Second
1934	Cin	26–58	.310	Eighth
2 years		**118–119**	**.498**	

Daniel O'Leary

Born October 22, 1856, Detroit, Michigan; died June 24, 1922, Chicago, Illinois; Cincinnati Outlaw Reds, 1884

Dan O'Leary got his one chance at managing in 1884 when the Union League was competing for players and attention with the American Association and the National League. O'Leary managed Cincinnati for 52 games before calling it a career.

Year	Team	Record	Pct.	Standing
1884	Cin (U)	33–29	.532	Third

Stephen Francis O'Neill

Born July 6, 1891, Minooka, Pennsylvania; died January 26, 1962, Cleveland, Ohio; Cleveland Indians, August 4, 1935–October 20, 1937; Detroit Tigers, December 11, 1942–November 16, 1948; Boston Red Sox, July 22, 1950–November 27, 1951; Philadelphia Phillies, June 28, 1952–June 15, 1954

Steve O'Neill managed four major league teams over a 14-year career in which he won a World Series with the Detroit Tigers in 1945 and finished in the first division nine times. His career started in Cleveland in 1935 where he developed the reputation of a nice guy, too nice a guy for Indian management tastes. O'Neill was fired after the 1937 season and was replaced by Ossie Vitt, whose hard-nosed tactics resulted in a player rebellion. O'Neill's Tigers beat the Chicago Cubs in the 1945 World Series even though Detroit scored in a total of only four innings in the first four games.

O'Neill built his teams around solid, consistent pitching. His Cleveland teams had steady Mel Harder, temperamental Johnny Allen and young Bob Feller. His 1945 pennant winner at Detroit had Virgil Trucks and Hal Newhouser. O'Neill's teams led the league in complete games in seven of his 14 years of managing. His ball clubs led the league in shutouts and in fewest walks six times. His teams never led the league in home runs.

One of the most remarkable statistics of O'Neill's career — he never had a losing season.

Year	Team	Record	Pct.	Standing
1935	Cleve	36–23	.610	Third
1936	Cleve	80–74	.519	Fifth
1937	Cleve	83–71	.539	Fourth
1943	Det	78–76	.506	Fifth
1944	Det	88–66	.571	Second
1945	Det	88–65	.575	First
1946	Det	92–62	.597	Second
1947	Det	85–69	.552	Second
1948	Det	78–76	.506	Fifth
1950	Bos (A)	62–30	.674	Third
1951	Bos	87–67	.565	Third

Year	Team	Record	Pct.	Standing
1952	Phil (N)	59–32	.648	Fourth
1953	Phil	83–71	.539	Third
1954	Phil	40–37	.519	Fourth
14 years		**1039–819**	**.559**	

WORLD SERIES

Year	Team	Record	Pct.
1945	Det	4–3	.571

John James Onslow

Born October 13, 1888, Scottsdale, Pennsylvania; died December 22, 1960, Concord, Massachusetts; Chicago White Sox, October 1, 1948–October 10, 1950

Jack Onslow took over a Chicago White Sox team that had lost 101 games the year before under Ted Lyons and had a 20-game loser in Bill Wight. For Onslow, Wight won 15, lost 13, and the ball club experienced a 12-game improvement, finishing sixth. When they began the 1950 season by losing 22 of their first 30 games, Onslow was fired.

Year	Team	Record	Pct.	Standing
1949	Chi (A)	63–91	.409	Sixth
1950	Chi	8–22	.267	Eighth
2 years		**71–113**	**.386**	

James Henry O'Rourke

Born August 24, 1852, Bridgeport, Connecticut; died January 8, 1919, Bridgeport; Buffalo Bisons, 1881–1884; Washington Senators, 1885

Orator Jim O'Rourke, so nicknamed because of his penchant for long, drawn out sentences, was one of the early successful managers in the National League. His lifetime statistics, showing him 12 games below .500, are deceiving. He had four straight winning seasons at Buffalo and then, eight years later, one horrible season at Washington which brought an end to his managerial career.

As a player, O'Rourke has a distinction that can never be duplicated. On April 22, 1876, playing for the Boston Red Stockings, he hit a single in a game against Philadelphia. It was the first hit in major league history.

Jim O'Rourke

Year	Team	Record	Pct.	Standing
1881	Buff	45–38	.542	Third
1882	Buff	45–39	.536	Third
1883	Buff	52–45	.536	Fifth
1884	Buff	64–47	.577	Third
1893	Wash	40–89	.310	12th
5 years		**246–258**	**.488**	

David L. Orr

Born September 29, 1859, New York, New York; died June 3, 1915, Brooklyn, New York; New York Metropolitans, 1887

Dave Orr, a native New Yorker, didn't have to go far to manage the New York ball club in the American Association in 1887. He also had a short return trip, being summoned into retirement after 66 games at the helm.

Year	Team	Record	Pct.	Standing
1887	NY (AA)	28–36	.438	Seventh

Melvin Thomas Ott

Born March 2, 1909, Gretna, Louisiana; died November 21, 1958, New Orleans, Louisiana; New York Giants, February 6, 1942–July 16, 1948

Mel Ott, one of the greatest hitters in New York Giants history, managed the Giants from 1942 to 1948. He was a kind, polite man who was well liked by team members, fans, and even opposing players — but it wound up hurting his reputation as a manager. Leo Durocher, then managing the Dodgers, was referring to Ott when he said, "Nice guys finish last." Ott finished last twice as Giants manager and was never able to elevate them higher than fourth place during his seven years at the helm. A quirk of fate: When Ott was fired in 1948, he was replaced by Durocher. Ott's teams never quite had the pitching to match that of the pennant contenders, but, like their manager, his Giants could hit. In 1947, they set the National League home-run record by clouting 221 — yet the Giants finished fourth. Ott will be best remembered in New York Giants history as the schoolboy that John McGraw took under his wing at the age of 16 and groomed to one day be a Giant starter. Twenty-two years later, he retired as the National League's all-time home run leader. Ott died on November 21, 1958, from injuries he received in a head-on auto accident in Louisiana.

Year	Team	Record	Pct.	Standing
1942	NY (N)	85–67	.559	Third
1943	NY	55–98	.359	Eighth
1944	NY	67–87	.435	Fifth
1945	NY	78–74	.513	Fifth
1946	NY	61–93	.396	Eighth
1947	NY	81–73	.526	Fourth
1948	NY	37–38	.493	Fourth
7 years		464–530	.467	

Paul Francis Owens

Born February 7, 1924, Salamanca, New York; Philadelphia Phillies, July 10, 1972–November 1, 1972; July 18, 1983–September 30, 1984

The Philadelphia Phillies went through a stretch in the 1970s and 1980s when they had some good teams and had a revolving door of managers. During the period, Paul Owens served as both general manager and field manager of the Phillies. He first filled in during 1972, taking over for Frank Lucchesi on a Phillies team made famous by Steve Carlton, who won 27 games for a team that won only 59. Danny Ozark took over in 1973.

By 1976 the Phillies were Eastern Division champions. Ozark was gone after the 1979 season, and Dallas Green, who also worked in the Phillies front office, took over in 1980 and led the Phillies to the World Series. He left after the 1981 campaign to become general manager of the Chicago Cubs. Pat Corrales managed the Philadelphia club in 1982 and part of 1983 before resigning to become manager of the Cleveland Indians. Owens once again stepped in, managing the Phillies for the rest of 1983, and guiding them to the World Series. After a .500 season in 1984, he never managed again.

Year	Team	Record	Pct.	Standing
1972	Phil	33–47	.413	Sixth
1983	Phil	47–30	.610	First
1984	Phil	81–81	.500	Fourth
3 years		161–158	.505	

LEAGUE CHAMPIONSHIP SERIES

Year	Team	Record	Pct.
1983	Phil	3–1	.750

WORLD SERIES

Year	Team	Record	Pct.
1983	Phil	1–4	.200

Daniel Leonard Ozark

Born November 23, 1923, Buffalo, New York; Philadelphia Phillies, November 1, 1972–September 1, 1979; San Francisco Giants, August 5, 1984–October 30, 1984;

Danny Ozark's Phillie teams won three consecutive Eastern Division championships in his seven years as Philadelphia manager. They were eliminated in the league championship series every time.

Those teams had a veteran pitching staff led by Hall of Famer Steve Carlton, ex–Boston Red Sox star Jim Lonborg, and former Twins and White Sox 20-game winner Jim Kaat. Bullpen ace Tug McGraw was the sidelines cheerleader as he had been for the 1969 and 1973 Mets. And they had Mike Schmidt, the dominant slugger of his era.

With pitching depth and hitters like Schmidt, Ozark was never a manager to play for one run. He let his hitters swing away and relied on his pitching staff to keep the Phillies in a position to win, which they did more often than not. Ozark's only failing, so the statistics and absence of hardware suggest, was his inability to get the Phillies into the World Series. In 1980, under Dallas Green, Ozark's successor, the Phillies played in their first World Series in 30 years. Ozark ended his managerial career filling in as interim skipper of the San Francisco Giants in 1984.

Year	Team	Record	Pct.	Standing
1973	Phil	71–91	.438	Sixth
1974	Phil	80–82	.494	Third
1975	Phil	86–76	.531	Second
1976	Phil	101–61	.623	First
1977	Phil	101–61	.623	First
1978	Phil	90–72	.556	First
1979	Phil	65–67	.492	Fifth
1984	SF	24–32	.429	Sixth
8 years		618–542	.533	

LEAGUE CHAMPIONSHIP SERIES

Year	Team	Record	Pct.
1976	Phil	0–3	.000
1977	Phil	1–3	.250
1978	Phil	1–3	.250
3 years		**2–9**	**.182**

Charles Henry Pabor

Born September 24, 1846, New York, New York; died April 13, 1913, New Haven, Connecticut; Cleveland Forest Citys, 1871; Brooklyn Atlantics, 1875; New Haven Elm Citys, 1875

Charlie Pabor was a pitcher-outfielder for five professional seasons and did some managing during that time. At Cleveland in 1871, his team lost almost twice as many as it won. Pabor did not manage again until 1875 when two amazing things happened. The first was that his Brooklyn team in the National Association won only two of 42 games under Pabor. The second was that despite that dismal record that sent him packing from Brooklyn, New Haven hired him the same year. He lost five out of six at the helm for New Haven and never managed again.

Year	Team	Record	Pct.	Standing
1871	Cleve	10–19	.345	Seventh
1875	Brklyn	2–40	.086	Twelfth
1875	NHvn	1–5	.167	Eighth
3 years		**13–64**	**.169**	

Francis James "Salty" Parker

Born July 8, 1913, East St. Louis, Illinois; died July 27, 1992, Houston, Texas; New York Mets, September 19–30, 1967; Houston Astros, August 25, 1972

Salty Parker was a veteran National League coach who was called on to manage twice for brief stints, 11 games for the New York Mets in 1967 and, five years later, one game for the Houston Astros.

Year	Team	Record	Pct.	Standing
1967	NY (N)	4–7	.364	Tenth
1972	Hous	1–0	1.000	Second
2 years		**5–7**	**.417**	

William Robert Parks

Born June 4, 1849, Easton, Pennsylvania; died October 10, 1911, Easton; Washington Washingtons, 1875

Bill Parks had a short playing career and a shorter managerial career. He played parts of two seasons and managed for a small part of one, in 1875. He directed the Washington club in the National Association to one win in eight games, ending his career as a manager.

Year	Team	Record	Pct.	Standing
1875	Wash	1–7	.125	Tenth

Larry Alton Parrish

Born November 10, 1953, Winter Haven, Florida; Detroit Tigers, September 1, 1998–October 14, 1999

Larry Parrish was an 11-year outfielder and third baseman for the Montreal Expos and Texas Rangers. In 1998, he took over a Detroit Tiger team that had struggled since Sparky Anderson's retirement three years earlier. Parrish managed the Tigers for the last 25 games of the 1998 season, winning one more than he lost. In 1999, Detroit was back to its old ways, losing 92 games. Parrish was fired at the end of the 1999 season.

Year	Team	Record	Pct.	Standing
1998	Det	13–12	.520	Fifth
1999	Det	69–92	.429	Third
2 years		**82–104**	**.441**	

Richard J. Pearce

Born February 29, 1836, Brooklyn, New York; died October 12, 1908, Wareham, Massachusetts; New York Mutuals, 1872; St. Louis Brown Stockings, 1875

As a player for seven years, Dickey Pearce played every position but catcher, spending most of his time as an infielder with several National Association teams. He had some success during stints as manager of two of those teams, New York in 1872 and St. Louis in 1875, but never got the opportunity to manage again.

Year	Team	Record	Pct.	Standing
1872	NY	10–6	.625	Third
1875	StL Brown	39–29	.574	Fourth
2 years		**49–35**	**.583**	

Roger Thorpe Peckinpaugh

Born February 5, 1891, Wooster, Ohio; died November 17, 1977, Cleveland, Ohio; New York Yankees, September 12, 1914–October 1, 1914; Cleveland Indians, December 10, 1927–June 9, 1933; November 12, 1940–November 15, 1941

Roger Peckinpaugh was a major league shortstop for 17 years. In 1914, at the age of 23, he filled in as player-manager of the New York Yankees for 17 games when Frank Chance quit and picked "Peck" to replace him. He got his chance at a full-time managing job 14 years later when the Cleveland Indians hired him. After suffering through a first season in which the Indians finished seventh, 30 games below .500, Peckinpaugh was able to right the ship enough to get the Indians up to fourth place, if no higher. Peckinpaugh was a pleasant man who got along well with all of the players. Ultimately, it was decided that he was too nice a guy, however, and it cost him his job at the end of the 1933 season. Eight years later, in 1941, he was rehired by Indians owner Alva Bradley — precisely because Peckinpaugh was a nice guy. Peckinpaugh was picked to try to smooth relations in the clubhouse after the ill-fated player revolt against manager Oscar Vitt in 1940. Peckinpaugh posted another fourth-place finish and was replaced by Lou Boudreau the following year.

Year	Team	Record	Pct.	Standing
1914	NY (A)	9–8	.529	Seventh
1928	Cleve	62–92	.403	Seventh

Year	Team	Record	Pct.	Standing
1929	Cleve	81–71	.533	Third
1930	Cleve	81–73	.526	Fourth
1931	Cleve	78–76	.506	Fourth
1932	Cleve	87–65	.572	Fourth
1933	Cleve	26–25	.510	Fourth
1941	Cleve	75–79	.487	Fourth
8 years		**499–489**	**.505**	

Antonio Francisco (Padilla) Peña

Born June 4, 1957, Monte Cristi, Dominican Republic; Kansas City Royals, May 15, 2002–present

When Kansas City stumbled out of the gate in 2002, manager Tony Muser was fired and replaced by interim John Mizerock. Sixteen days later, the Royals named Houston Astros bench coach Tony Peña the permanent replacement.

Atanasio Rigal "Tony" Perez

Born May 14, 1942, Camaguey, Cuba; Cincinnati Reds, October 30, 1992–May 25, 1993; Florida Marlins, May 28, 2001–February 11, 2002

Tony Perez, the Hall of Fame first baseman for the Cincinnati Reds, got a chance to manage the Reds in 1993. Lou Piniella had completed a successful run as Reds manager, leading the club to a World Series championship three years earlier. Controversial owner Marge Schott named Perez to the post but inexplicably fired him 44 games into the 1993 season. Perez was mystified, feeling that he had not been given an adequate opportunity to show what he could do with the team.

He was named interim manager of the Florida Marlins when John Boles was fired on May 28, 2001.

Year	Team	Record	Pct.	Standing
1993	Cin	20–24	.455	Fifth
2001	Fla	54–60	.474	Fourth
2 years		**74–84**	**.468**	

Ralph Foster "Cy" Perkins

Born February 27, 1896, Gloucester, Massachusetts; died October 2, 1963, Philadelphia, Pennsylvania; Detroit Tigers, May 25, 1937

Cy Perkins was a major league catcher for 17 years, 15 with the Philadelphia Athletics, then ending his career with single seasons with both the New York Yankees and Detroit Tigers. While playing for the A's, Perkins helped develop catcher Mickey Cochrane who eventually took over Perkins' place in the starting lineup. With Detroit, Perkins was reunited with Cochrane, who had become not only a Hall of Fame caliber catcher but was now managing the Tigers. When Perkins retired as a player, Cochrane hired him as a coach. On May 25, 1937, player-manager Cochrane was severely beaned, leaving him unconscious for 10 days and ending his playing career. Cochrane remained as manager of the Tigers for another year, but during his recuperation time in 1937, Perkins filled in for 15 games, his only managerial experience. He later coached for the Philadelphia Phillies and is credited with developing two young pitchers, Robin Roberts and Curt Simmons.

Year	Team	Record	Pct.	Standing
1937	Det	6–9	.400	Second

John Michael Pesky

Born September 27, 1919, Portland, Oregon; Boston Red Sox, October 7, 1962–October 3, 1964; October 1–3, 1980

Johnny Pesky, a former major league infielder, spent two full seasons as Boston Red Sox manager in which Boston finished seventh and eighth. The longtime Red Sox coach had one more shot at managing when he filled in for four games in 1980.

Year	Team	Record	Pct.	Standing
1963	Bos	76–85	.472	Seventh
1964	Bos	70–90	.438	Eighth
1980	Bos	1–3	.250	Fourth
3 years		147–178	.452	

Nathaniel Frederick Pfeffer

Born March 17, 1860, Louisville, Kentucky; died April 10, 1932, Chicago, Illinois; Louisville Colonels, 1892

Fred Pfeffer took over for Jack Chapman in mid-season 1892 with the Louisville ball club struggling and in eleventh place. Pfeffer was able to help move them to ninth place by the end of the season and never got the chance to improve on that finish. He never managed again.

Year	Team	Record	Pct.	Standing
1892	Lou	9–14	.426	Tenth
1892	Lou	33–42	.440	Ninth

Lewis G. Phelan

No biographical data available; St. Louis Cardinals, 1895

In 1895, the St. Louis Cardinals were owned by Chris Von Der Ahe, a saloon owner who was as interested in selling beer at the ballpark as in winning games. Lew Phelan was the third of four managers engaged by Von Der Ahe that year, Von Der Ahe himself being the fourth. The Cardinals won 39 games and finished in eleventh place.

Year	Team	Record	Pct.	Standing
1895	StL	8–21	.276	Eleventh

Harold Ross "Lefty" Phillips

Born May 16, 1919, Los Angeles, California; died June 10, 1972, Fullerton, California; California Angels, May 27, 1969–October 7, 1971

Lefty Phillips was hired to manage the California Angels at a tumultuous time in their history. Fred Haney, the expansion team's only general manager, had been fired and, a few months later, Bill Rigney, the team's only manager, was also fired. New general manager Dick Walsh had an insensitive dictatorial style that was evident when, in firing Rigney, he did it by messenger who provided him with a plane ticket home. Players disliked Walsh, and their unhappiness made for a tense clubhouse. This was the environment Phillips found himself in when he took over in 1969. Coupled with all of that was the fact that the Angels weren't very good. The team he inherited finished last in the American League in team batting average, runs scored, home runs, RBIs, hits and total bases. At one point in the dismal season, Phillips said, "Our phenoms aren't phenominating." They picked up hard-hitting outfielder Alex Johnson in the off-season and he won the batting title in 1970. But the tempermental Johnson created more clubhouse dissention because of his failure to hustle on the field and his taunting of teammates. Outfielder Ken Berry and pitcher Clyde Wright had to be restrained from exchanging blows with Johnson, and infielder Chico Ruiz became so angry with him that he pulled a gun on him. The team seemed to be out of control and Phillips was fired at the end of the 1971 season.

It ended a distinguished career in which he had a positive influence on two future Hall of Fame managers. Phillips was a pitching coach for Walter Alston with his great Brooklyn Dodger teams of the 1950s and, as a minor league manager, was a mentor to Sparky Anderson, who was to one day be manager of the Cincinnati Reds. Phillips suffered from asthma and had asthma attacks dealing with the storms in the Angels clubhouse. On June 10, 1972, less than a year after he was fired by the Angels, Phillips had a fatal asthma attack. He was 53.

Year	Team	Record	Pct.	Standing
1969	Cal	60–63	.488	Third
1970	Cal	86–76	.531	Third
1971	Cal	76–86	.469	Fourth
3 years		**222–225**	**.497**	

Horace B. Phillips

Born May 14, 1853, Salem, Ohio; date of death unknown; Troy Trojans, 1879; Columbus Buckeyes, 1883; Pittsburgh Alleghenys, 1884–889

Horace Phillips managed for eight years in the American Association and the National League in the early days of baseball. In 1879, the 26-year-old Phillips managed the Troy, New York, team which won only 12 of its first 58 games. Phillips was fired. He didn't manage again for four years. He then managed seven more years and had one second-place and one third-place finish. Otherwise he didn't get any of his teams higher than sixth.

Year	Team	Record	Pct.	Standing
1879	Troy	12–46	.207	Eighth
1883	Col	32–65	.330	Sixth
1884	Pitt (AA)	10–30	.250	Twelfth
1885	Pitt	56–55	.505	Third
1886	Pitt	80–57	.584	Second
1887	Pitt (N)	55–69	.444	Sixth
1888	Pitt	66–68	.493	Sixth
1889	Pitt	28–43	.394	Seventh
8 years		**339–433**	**.439**	

William Corcoran Phillips

Born November 9, 1868, Allenport, Pennsylvania; died October 25, 1941, Charleroi, Pennsylvania; Indianapolis Hoosiers, 1914; Newark Pepper, 1915

Bill Phillips managed in the upstart Federal League and didn't do too badly. But when the league folded after two years, the men who managed in it were destined not to be offered jobs managing in the two established major leagues — and such was the case for Phillips.

Year	Team	Record	Pct.	Standing
1914	Ind	88–65	.575	First
1915	Nwk	26–27	.491	Sixth
2 years		**114–92**	**.553**	

Lipman Emanuel Pike

Born May 25, 1845, New York, New York; died October 10, 1893, Brooklyn, New York; Troy Haymakers, 1871; Hartford Dark Blues, 1874; Cincinnati Reds, 1877

Lip Pike was the second manager in Cincinnati's National League history, following Charlie Gould. But he only lasted 14 games at the start of the Reds' second season, losing 11 of them.

Year	Team	Record	Pct.	Standing
1871	Troy	1–3	.250	Sixth
1874	Htfd	16–37	.320	Seventh
1877	Cin	3–11	.214	Sixth
3 years		**91–64**	**.587**	

Louis Victor Piniella

Born August 28, 1943, Tampa, Florida; New York Yankees, October 27, 1985–October 19, 1987; June 23, 1988–October 7, 1988; Cincinnati Reds, November 3, 1989–October 18, 1992; Seattle Mariners, November 9, 1992–present

Lou Piniella was a major league outfielder for 18 years who developed a reputation for being a good hitter who hustled and was a tough competitor. He finished with a lifetime batting average of .291. George Steinbrenner hired him to manage the New York Yankees in 1986. He guided the Yankees to a second-place finish. They fell to fourth in 1987 and the following year, with the team staggering at 45–49 and in fifth place, Piniella was fired. Marge Schott hired him to manage the Cincinnati Reds in 1990, and the Reds shocked the baseball world by winning the National League pennant and then sweeping the heavily favored Oakland A's in the World Series. Piniella lasted two more years in Cincinnati before moving on to Seattle, bringing the Mariners their first playoff appearance in 1995. They beat the Yankees in the divisional playoffs but lost to the Cleveland Indians in the league championship series. In 2000, the Mariners were back in the playoffs, sweeping the Chicago White Sox in the divisional playoffs before losing to the Yankees in the league championship series.

Piniella learned a lot about managing from Yogi Berra, his manager in 1984. Piniella adopted Berra's philosophy of recognizing that pitchers have limits, that if you want them to be strong next week, next month and next year, you can't overuse them today. In his autobiography, Piniella says a manager must look at an entire season, not at just a game or a series, and make his decisions accordingly. Piniella believes in using his entire bench and in hiring coaches who work hard with players to improve their skills. With Cincinnati in 1990, he used Berra's pitching philosophy to lead the Reds to the championship. Jose Rijo was the ace of the staff, but the Reds won because of Piniella's adept use of a bullpen trio known as the "Nasty Boys," Randy Myers, Rob Dibble and Norm Charlton. As for using his entire bench — in Seattle in 1994 and 1995, Piniella led the American League in the use of pinch hitters despite having the most potent starting lineup in the American League, featuring Ken Griffey Jr., Jay Buhner and Edgar Martinez. He also had Randy Johnson, one of baseball's best pitchers, for several years in Seattle. What he didn't have in Seattle that he had in Cincinnati was a bullpen he could depend on. For instance, in 1997, Bobby Ayala posted a 10–5 record and a 3.82 earned run average. In 1998, Ayala slumped to 1–10 and had a 7.29 earned run average. Despite the pounding the pitcher consistently took, Piniella continually called on Ayala, who happens to be his son-in-law. In 1999, Ayala was sent to the Chicago Cubs. Piniella also tried to resurrect the career of Charlton, one of his bullpen aces at Cincinnati. He brought him to Seattle in 1993 where he had 18 saves and a 2.34 earned run average. He was back with the Mariners in 1995, 1996 and 1997 and had one good year, 1996, when he had 20 saves. In the other two years, his earned average topped 7.00.

After his 2001 Mariners tied the major league record for wins (116), Piniella was named American League Manager of the Year.

Year	Team	Record	Pct.	Standing
1986	NY (A)	90–72	.556	Second
1987	NY	89–73	.549	Fourth
1988	NY	45–48	.484	Fifth
1990	Cin	91–71	.562	First
1991	Cin	74–88	.457	Fifth
1992	Cin	90–72	.556	Second
1993	Sea	82–80	.506	Fourth
1994	Sea	49–63	.438	Third
1995	Sea	79–66	.545	First
1996	Sea	85–76	.528	Second
1997	Sea	91–72	.558	First
1998	Sea	76–85	.472	Third
1999	Sea	79–83	.488	Third
2000	Sea	91–71	.562	Second
2001	Sea	116–46	.716	First
14 years		**1226–1066**	**.535**	

DIVISIONAL PLAYOFFS

Year	Team	Record	Pct.
1995	Sea	3–2	.600
1997	Sea	1–3	.250
2000	Sea	3–0	1.000
2 years		**7–5**	**.583**

LEAGUE CHAMPIONSHIP SERIES

Year	Team	Record	Pct.
1995	Sea	2–4	.333
2000	Sea	2–4	.333
2 years		**4–8**	**.333**

William Francis Plummer

Born March 21, 1947, Anderson, California; Seattle Mariners, October 29, 1991–October 13, 1992

Bill Plummer was a major league catcher for 10 years who finished his career with the Seattle Mariners. In 1992, he managed the Mariners for a year but could get them no higher than seventh place. He was replaced by Lou Piniella in 1993.

Year	Team	Record	Pct.	Standing
1992	Sea	64–98	.395	Seventh

Edward Joseph Popowski

Born August 20, 1913, Sayreville, New Jersey; Boston Red Sox, September, 23, 1969–October 2, 1969

Eddie Popowski took over for Dick Williams as manager of the Boston Red Sox with nine games left in the 1969 season. Popowski would not manage again until 1973, when the Red Sox had him fill in for a single game, which the Red Sox won.

Year	Team	Record	Pct.	Standing
1969	Bos	5–4	.556	Third
1973	Bos	1–0	1.000	Second
2 years		**6–4**	**.600**	

Matthew Sheldon Porter

No biographical data available; Kansas City Cowboys, 1884

Matt Porter had a short career with Kansas City in the Union League in 1884.

Year	Team	Record	Pct.	Standing
1884	KC (U)	3–13	.188	Eighth

Patrick Thomas Powers

Born June 27, 1860, Trenton, New Jersey; died August 29, 1925, Belmar, New Jersey; Rochester Broncos, 1890; New York Giants, 1892

Pat Powers managed two different teams in two different leagues but had no particular claims to fame.

Year	Team	Record	Pct.	Standing
1890	Roch (AA)	63–63	.500	Fifth
1892	1) NY (N)	71–80	.470	Tenth
1892	2) NY (N)	40–37	.519	Sixth
2 years		**134–143**	**.484**	

Albert G. Pratt

Born November 19, 1847, Pittsburgh, Pennsylvania; died November 21, 1937, Pittsburgh; Pittsburgh Pirates, 1882–1883

Uncle Al Pratt became Pittsburgh's first manager. His club managed to break even in his first year, but when Pittsburgh got off to a 12–20 start in 1883, Pratt was relieved of his duties and never managed again.

Year	Team	Record	Pct.	Standing
1882	Pitt (AA)	39–39	.500	Fourth
1883	Pitt	12–20	.375	Seventh
2 years		**51–59**	**.464**	

Thomas J. Pratt

Born in 1844, Worcester, Massachusetts; died September 28, 1908, Philadelphia, Pennsylvania; Philadelphia Keystones, 1884

In 1884, Tom Pratt took over a struggling Philadelphia team that was in sixth place. He managed for the last 26 games. Philadelphia won only 10. The ball club finished last. Pratt was finished as manager.

Year	Team	Record	Pct.	Standing
1884	Phil (U)	10–16	.385	Eighth

James L. Price

Born 1847, New York, New York; died October 6, 1931, Chicago, Illinois; New York Giants, 1884

In 1884, Jim Price managed the New York ball club that eventually would be the National League's Giants. His ball club played well, finishing 14 games above .500, but finished fourth in Price's only year as a manager.

Year	Team	Record	Pct.	Standing
1884	NY (N)	56–42	.571	Fourth

James Thompson Prothro

Born July 16, 1893, Memphis, Tennessee; died October 14, 1971, Memphis; Philadelphia Phillies, November 2, 1938–October 1941

Philadelphia Phillies owner Gerry Nugent was heavily in debt at about the time Doc Prothro, former major league player, minor league manager, and a dentist in the off-season, was brought in to manage the Phillies. Prothro had been part of the Bucky Harris pennant winner with Washington in the 1920s, and Nugent was hoping Prothro could make some magic with the hapless Phillies. But while Prothro tried to manage on the field, Nugent continually sold his best players to help pay off debts. The result was the worst three-year run for any manager in baseball history: Prothro lost more than 100 games all three years.

Year	Team	Record	Pct.	Standing
1939	Phil (N)	45–106	.298	Eighth
1940	Phil	50–103	.327	Eighth
1941	Phil	43–111	.279	Eighth
3 years		**138–320**	**.301**	

Luis Bienvenido (Toribio) Pujols

Born November 18, 1955, Santiago Rodriquez, Dominican Republic; Detroit Tigers, April 8, 2002

When the Detroit Tigers started their 2002 season with six straight losses, manager Phil Garner was replaced with bench coach Luis Pujols. Pujols promptly appointed former manager and baseball guru Felipe Alou his bench coach, establishing a dugout brain trust in the style of the Yankees famous duo Joe Torre (manager) and Don Zimmer (former manager, bench coach).

William Aloysius Purcell

Born March 16, 1884, Paterson, New Jersey; date of death unknown; Philadelphia Phillies, 1883

William "Blondie" Purcell is better remembered for the color of his hair than his record as a manager. Blondie's Philadelphia ball club won only 13 of 81 games under his direction in 1883. He replaced Bob Ferguson, who was 4–13 when he was fired. The two combined for a 17–81 record.

Year	Team	Record	Pct.	Standing
1883	Phil (N)	13–68	.160	Eighth

Melvin Douglas Queen

Born March 26, 1942, Johnson City, New York; Toronto Blue Jays, September 25–30, 1997

Mel Queen, the son of a major league pitcher, was a major league pitcher himself for nine years with the Cincinnati Reds and California Angels, winning 20 games over that span. In 1997, Queen filled in at the end of the season after Cito Gaston was let go — and the Blue Jays won four out of five. Queen never managed again — so he has the most wins without a loss of any manager in major league baseball history.

Year	Team	Record	Pct.	Standing
1997	Tor	4–1	.800	Fifth

Frank Ralph Quilici

Born May 11, 1939, Chicago, Illinois; Minnesota Twins, July 6, 1972–November 24, 1975

Frank Quilici was a utility infielder for five years with the Minnesota Twins who played on the Twins' 1965 American League championship team. He retired as a player in 1970 and was hired two years later, at age 32, to replace Bill Rigney as manager of the ball club. Rod Carew won the batting title in 1972, but with just a .318 average, and he didn't hit any home runs — the only time in baseball history that a batting champion was homerless. The two top pitchers, Bert Blyleven and Dick Woodson, each had .500 records at 17–17 and 14–14, respectively. The Twins were close to .500 under Quilici at 41–43, and they hovered at or near the .500 mark for the next two years, finishing third both times. The Twins slipped to fourth in 1975, after which Quilici was replaced by Gene Mauch.

Year	Team	Record	Pct.	Standing
1972	Minn	41–43	.488	Third
1973	Minn	81–81	.500	Third
1974	Minn	82–80	.506	Third
1975	Minn	76–83	.478	Fourth
4 years		**280–287**	**.497**	

Joseph J. Quinn

Born December 25, 1864, Sydney, Australia; died November 12, 1940, St. Louis, Missouri; St. Louis Cardinals, 1895; Cleveland Spiders, 1899

Joe Quinn was the first Australian major leaguer, a popular outfielder who played 17 seasons. A foreign-born ballplayer (novel enough) was known to be an undertaker during the off-season, and the baseball-going public thought him colorful. Sportswriters in the 1890s didn't hesitate to point out that he got some practice for his sideline because of the teams he was called on to manage. In two years, one at St. Louis and one at Cleveland, his teams lost more than five times as many as they won.

Year	Team	Record	Pct.	Standing
1895	StL	13–27	.325	Eleventh
1899	Cleve	12–104	.103	Twelfth
2 years		**25–131**	**.160**	

Douglas Lee Rader

Born July 30, 1944, Chicago, Illinois; Texas Rangers, November 1, 1982–May 17, 1985; Chicago White Sox, June 20–22, 1986; California Angels, November 14, 1988–August 25, 1991

Doug Rader was a good-hitting, great-fielding major league third baseman who won Gold Glove awards five years in a row with the Houston Astros. He was also a practical joker and a flake, once defecating in a birthday cake in the Houston clubhouse. As a rookie manager with Texas in 1983, he talked publicly about how the division-leading Chicago White Sox "won ugly." The White Sox picked it up as a rallying cry. They showed replays of previous victories on their scoreboard as an announcer described each one as "another ugly win" for the White Sox. The Rangers finished third, more than 20 games behind the Sox. Rader managed the White Sox for two games in 1986, between the tenures of Tony LaRussa and Jim Fregosi. He had his most successful year in 1989, the first of his three years at the helm of the California Angels.

Year	Team	Record	Pct.	Standing
1983	Tex	77–85	.475	Third
1984	Tex	69–92	.429	Seventh
1985	Tex	9–23	.281	Seventh
1986	Chi (A)	1–1	.500	Fifth
1989	Cal	91–71	.562	Third
1990	Cal	80–82	.494	Fourth
1991	Cal	61–63	.492	Seventh
7 years		**388–417**	**.482**	

Vernon Fred Rapp

Born May 11, 1928, St. Louis, Missouri; St. Louis Cardinals, October 7, 1976–April 25, 1978; Cincinnati Reds, October 4, 1983–August 16, 1984

Vern Rapp was a successful minor-league manager — was, in fact, Manager of the Year with the Denver Bears in 1976 — when he was hired to manage the St. Louis Cardinals. He had problems almost from the start, not because of strategy but because of approach. He alienated players with strict rules, including no long hair, sideburns or mustaches. Even before mid-season, players such as veteran pitcher John Denny and outfielder Bake McBride began asking to be traded. Relief pitcher Al Hrabosky, one of the league's stars, was known as the "Mad Hungarian" and was known for his Fu Manchu mustache. Rapp ordered him to shave it. Veteran catcher Ted Simmons said Rapp was not only strict but had a negative attitude. Simmons said that when a relief pitcher was brought into a game, Rapp would hand him the ball and say something like "don't walk anybody." He was fired

15 games into his second season. He resurfaced in 1984, managing Cincinnati for 120 games before being fired from that job, his last one as a major league manager.

Year	Team	Record	Pct.	Standing
1977	StL	83–79	.512	Third
1978	StL	5–10	.333	Sixth
1984	Cin	51–69	.425	Fifth
3 years		**139–158**	**.468**	

Alfred James Reach

Born May 25, 1840, London, England; died January 14, 1928, Atlantic City, New Jersey; Philadelphia Phillies, 1890

Al Reach played five years of professional baseball but didn't get a chance to manage until 15 years after his playing days were over. In 1890, at the age of 50, he managed Philadelphia's National League ball club for 11 games, winning four of them.

Year	Team	Record	Pct.	Standing
1890	Phil (N)	4–7	.364	Third

William J. Reccius

Born in 1847, Frankfurt-on-Main, Germany; died January 25, 1911, Louisville, Kentucky; Louisville Colonels, 1882–1883

Bill Reccius, a native of Germany, was living in Louisville at the time Louisville was looking for a baseball manager. He came on board as the second of three managers in 1882 and then was the first of two managers in 1883, posting winning records in both partial seasons.

Year	Team	Record	Pct.	Standing
1882	Lou (AA)	24–18	.571	Third
1883	Lou	12–10	.545	Fifth
2 years		**36–28**	**.563**	

Philip Raymond Regan

Born April 6, 1937, Ostego, Michigan; Baltimore Orioles, October 17, 1994–October 20, 1995

Phil Regan was one of baseball's outstanding relief pitchers in the 1960s and early 1970s with the Detroit Tigers, Los Angeles Dodgers and Chicago Cubs. With the Dodgers in 1966, he was 14–1 with 29 saves, playing a part in 43 of the team's 95 wins. He was a member of the Chicago Cubs 1969 team that led the National League for most of the season before giving way to the "Miracle Mets."

After retiring as a player, he served as a pitching coach for several teams and was named manager of the Baltimore Orioles in 1995. The Orioles finished two games below .500, not a bad record but one that represented an under-achievement for a team with a high payroll and an owner with higher expectations.

Year	Team	Record	Pct.	Standing
1995	Bal	71–73	.493	Third

Delbert W. Rice

Born October 27, 1922, Portsmouth, Ohio; January 26, 1983, Buena Park, California; California Angels, October 7, 1971–October 11, 1972

In 1972, California Angels owner Gene Autry was in need of a healer. For the past two years, the Angels had been beset with problems: changes for the first time in general manager and field manager, player dissention that led to an incident with a gun in the clubhouse — and a team that won 10 fewer games in 1971 than it had in 1970. Autry turned to Del Rice to lead the club from turmoil and hired Harry Dalton, the successful Baltimore Oriole executive, to be general manager. Under Rice, the Angels won 75 games, one less than they had the year before under Lefty Phillips. Dalton fired Rice, who had a good pitching staff but a lineup that produced only 78 home runs and averaged less than three runs a game.

Rice, a 17-year major league catcher, is credited with helping shape the career of Nolan Ryan, who came to the Angels in a deal with the Mets. Years later, Ryan said that Rice had given him the chance he needed to succeed by putting him in the regular rotation and keeping him there. Ryan contended that the Mets pitching staff in those days was aligned to fit the needs of Tom Seaver and no one else. Ryan assessed Rice's fate by calling him "a good manager with a bad team."

Year	Team	Record	Pct.	Standing
1972	Cal	75–80	.484	Fifth

Paul Rapier Richards

Born November 21, 1908, Waxahachie, Texas; died May 5, 1986, Waxahachie; Chicago White Sox, October 10, 1950–September 14, 1954; Baltimore Orioles, September 14, 1954–September 1, 1961; Chicago White Sox, December 17, 1975–November 17, 1976

Paul Richards was an innovative manager who turned the Chicago White Sox into a consistent winner and then moved on to help the Baltimore Orioles before going to the front office of the Houston Colt .45s expansion club.

He took over a Chicago White Sox team that won 60 and lost 94 games in 1950. In each of his first two years, the White Sox won 81. His third year they won 89. In his fourth and final season, they won 91. Richards felt that he had the White Sox moving in the right direction. He resigned to try to do the same thing as manager of the Orioles. In 1954, Baltimore won 54 and lost 100. Under Richards in 1955, they bettered the mark, just barely, winning 57. They improved year by year and in 1960 won 89 games and finished second behind the New York Yankees.

Among his innovations: He was the first modern day manager to make a defensive double switch, moving his pitcher to an infielder's position to make room for a reliever who might pitch to a batter or two. Then the reliever would be removed and Richards would bring back the starting pitcher. With the White Sox, he did it with pitchers Harry Dorish (who played third base for one batter), Billy Pierce (who played first base for one batter) and Sandy Consuegra (who also played third base for one batter). When Consuegra was moved to third base, he put on his jacket but an umpire made him remove it. At Baltimore, Richards, who was a catcher in his playing days, created an oversized catcher's mitt to help his catcher Gus Triandos handle the knuckleball of Hoyt Wilhelm.

Another Richards ploy: in traditional sacrifice bunt situations, he wanted the batter to try to bunt the ball hard to the right side between the pitcher and first baseman, causing both to be out of position to cover first base. He tried it twice with George Kell at Baltimore and it worked both times. Not all of his experiments worked. In 1976, when Bill Veeck coaxed him back to manage the White Sox at the age of 67, Richards took Goose Gossage out of the bullpen and made him a starter. Gossage, one of the best relief pitchers of all time, was 9–17 as a starter.

Richards liked to build teams around speed, defense and pitching. When he came to the White Sox, Chicago traded Gus Zernial, who set the White Sox home run record with 29 the year before, in a three-way deal in which Minnie Minoso came to Chicago. In Minoso, Richards had a solid hitter who could steal bases, take the extra base on a ball hit in the gap, and, defensively, track down balls hit in the gap.

Richards also believed in working with young ballplayers and teaching them how to win by executing fundamentals. The White Sox led the American League in sacrifice bunts in three of Richards' four years in Chicago. Another Richards theory: Have a lead-off hitter who draws a lot of walks and second-place hitter who knows how to hit to right field.

Richards' former players remember him as someone who was always thinking three innings ahead and who might have been baseball's smartest manager. But some remember his lack of patience for players who failed to execute. For them, he is remembered as one of baseball's meanest managers.

Year	Team	Record	Pct.	Standing
1951	Chi (A)	81–73	.526	Fourth
1952	Chi	81–73	.526	Fourth
1953	Chi	89–65	.578	Third
1954	Chi	91–54	.628	Third
1955	Bal	57–97	.370	Seventh
1956	Bal	69–85	.448	Sixth
1957	Bal	76–76	.500	Fifth
1958	Bal	74–79	.484	Sixth
1959	Bal	74–80	.481	Sixth
1960	Bal	89–65	.578	Second
1961	Bal	78–57	.578	Third
1976	Chi (A)	64–97	.398	Sixth
12 years		**923–901**	**.506**	

Daniel Richardson

Born January 25, 1863, Elmira, New York; died September 12, 1926, New York, New York; Washington Senators, 1892

Danny Richardson was the second of two managers for Washington in 1892 when it was a National League franchise. The ball club won only 11 of 37 games under Richardson, who did not return the following season.

Year	Team	Record	Pct.	Standing
1892	Wash (N)	11–26	.297	Tenth

Wesley Branch Rickey

Born December 20, 1881, Lucasville, Ohio; died December 9, 1965, Columbia, Missouri; St. Louis Browns, September 17, 1913–1915; St. Louis Cardinals, February 8, 1919–May 30, 1925

Branch Rickey is remembered as the baseball executive who broke the color line by bringing Jackie Robinson to the major leagues. But before he was in the front office, he was a major league catcher and a manager for 10 years. As manager of the St. Louis Cardinals in 1919, Rickey helped start what came to be known as the farm system, and the Cardinals' chain fed many great players into the major leagues. He had the same skill as a manager that he had as a general manager: the ability to evaluate a young player's strengths and weaknesses and judge when he would be ready for major league competition.

But the Cardinals did not produce for him. The best he could do in seven years at the helm was two third-place finishes. In 1925, with the Cardinals in last place, owner Sam Breadon was faced with dwindling attendance. He removed Rickey and replaced him with star infielder Rogers Hornsby. Rickey pleaded with Breadon not to make the change, saying it would ruin him. Breadon disagreed, saying it would be the best thing that happened to Rickey's career. Breadon was right. Rickey was a front office genius for several teams for half a century, and some of his actions had a dramatic impact on the game. There was the Jackie Robinson breakthrough. The farm system he devised for St. Louis in 1919 helped develop the future Cardinal teams that won five pennants in nine years between 1926 and 1934. In 1942, he moved on to the Dodgers and used the farm system there, plus his integration of the game, to make Brooklyn hugely successful. At one time, Rickey alone had 800 players under contract with his major league team and his farm system. He ended his career as general manager of the Pittsburgh Pirates.

Year	Team	Record	Pct.	Standing
1913	StL (A)	5–6	.455	Eighth
1914	StL	71–82	.464	Fifth
1915	StL	63–91	.409	Sixth
1920	StL (N)	75–79	.487	Fifth
1921	StL	87–66	.569	Third
1922	StL	85–69	.552	Third
1923	StL	79–74	.516	Fifth
1924	StL	65–89	.422	Sixth
1925	StL	13–25	.342	Eighth
10 years		**597–664**	**.473**	

Gregory Riddoch

Born July 17, 1945, Greeley, Colorado; San Diego Padres, July 11, 1990–September 23, 1992

Greg Riddoch never played major league baseball but had been part of the San Diego Padres organization when he took over as manager of the Padres in mid-season 1990. That club finished in fifth place. In 1991, his only full season as manager, he guided the Padres to a third-place finish. They were headed in that direction in 1992 when Riddoch was relieved of his duties and replaced by Jim Riggleman.

Year	Team	Record	Pct.	Standing
1990	SD	38–44	.463	Fifth
1991	SD	84–78	.519	Third
1992	SD	78–72	.520	Third
3 years		**200–194**	**.508**	

James Riggleman

Born November 9, 1952, Fort Dix, New Jersey; San Diego Padres, September 23, 1992–October 21, 1994; Chicago Cubs, October 21, 1994–October 3, 1999

Jim Riggleman never played a day in the major leagues but was a respected coach when the San Diego Padres tabbed him as their new manager in the middle of the 1992 season. Riggleman spent parts of three seasons with San Diego before moving on to the Chicago Cubs, where he stayed five years, serving the longest tenure of any Cub manager since Leo Durocher (1966–1972). In Riggleman's tenure, Sammy Sosa set club records with 66 and 63 homers in 1998 and 1999, respectively, and rookie Kerry Wood struck out 20 Houston Astros in 1998. That year was Riggleman's best. The Cubs finished in second place in the Central Division and won a one-game playoff with the San Francisco Giants to win the National League wildcard berth. The Cubs then lost four in a row to Atlanta in the division playoffs. In 1999, Wood hurt his arm in spring training and was out for the season. Kevin Tapani and Steve Trachsel, who had been mainstays of the 1998 pitching staff, each had the worst years of their careers. The Cubs finished last in the Central Division and Riggleman was fired at the end of the season.

Riggleman was a low key, even-tempered manager, but his style was to be active, making many moves as the games went along. His teams at both San Diego and Chicago led the National League in the number of intentional walks issued—clearly the call of the manager. Riggleman's teams twice led the league in pinch hitters used and were always near the top of the league in that category. In the dugout, he didn't pace, like some managers do, but his eyes were always focused on the field and his hands were often moving, giving one signal or another to his players or coaches. One thing Riggleman didn't have in Chicago was speed, even on the bench. In 1995, the Cubs used only nine pinch runners the entire season.

Year	Team	Record	Pct.	Standing
1992	SD	4–8	.333	Third
1993	SD	61–101	.377	Seventh
1994	SD	47–70	.402	Third
1995	Chi (N)	73–71	.507	Third
1996	Chi	76–86	.469	Fourth
1997	Chi	68–94	.420	Fifth
1998	Chi	90–73	.552	Second
1999	Chi	67–95	.414	Sixth
8 years		**486–598**	**.448**	

DIVISIONAL PLAYOFFS

Year	Team	Record	Pct.
1998	Chi (N)	0–4	.000

William Joseph Rigney

Born January 29, 1918, Alameda, California; died February 20, 2001, Oakland, California; New York/San Francisco Giants, September 24, 1955–June 18, 1960; California Angels, December 12, 1960–May 27, 1969; Minnesota Twins, October 22, 1969–July 6, 1972; San Francisco Giants, November 20, 1975–October 7, 1976

Bill Rigney, one-time infielder for the New York Giants under manager Leo Durocher, later replaced Durocher as Giants manager in 1956. Johnny Antonelli won 20 games and

Willie Mays and Bill White provided some offensive punch for that club, but not enough to offset an otherwise weak lineup. The Giants finished sixth in both 1956 and again in 1957. They moved up to third in 1958, the team's first year in San Francisco, with the help of rookie slugger Orlando Cepeda. In 1959, they added another rookie slugger, Willie McCovey. It appeared Rigney had a team that was on the verge of contending. The Giants finished third again in 1959 and were in second place in May of 1960 when owner Horace Stoneham decided to make a change. He fired Rigney and replaced him with Alvin Dark.

The next year, Rigney was hired to manage the Los Angeles Angels expansion team in the American League, a position he held for eight years. Durocher was a leading candidate for that job but was rejected because of his reputation for not working well with young, unproven players. That was one of Rigney's strengths, as evidenced by the success of Cepeda and McCovey, as well as third baseman Jim Davenport and outfielder Felipe Alou. Both Davenport and Alou later became major league managers.

The Angels won 70 games in their first year and shocked the baseball world with an 86–76 second year, finishing in third place. Again, Rigney was in a familiar element, developing young ballplayers, including eccentric pitcher Bo Belinsky, who started out 5–0 including a no-hitter, and Dean Chance, who would one day also throw a no hitter and become a Cy Young Award winner. But the Angels never came close to achieving that kind of success again and Rigney was fired in 1969. He moved on to manage the Minnesota Twins in 1970 and had his one and only division championship team. The Twins were swept by the Baltimore Orioles in the league championship series. He managed the Twins for three years and then went back to the Giants for one season before retiring.

Rigney always credited Durocher for his style of managing, which involved throwing out The Book when it was found insufficient to the task. "You don't play it the same all the time," he once said. Even with the power hitters he had with the Giants, Rigney tended to be a manager who played for one run. He liked to hit-and-run, to bunt, to do whatever it took to get runners in scoring position. In 1961 and 1962, Rigney's Angels led the American League — and set major league records both years — in number of relief pitchers used during the season.

Year	Team	Record	Pct.	Standing
1956	NY (N)	67–87	.435	Sixth
1957	NY	69–85	.448	Sixth
1958	SF	80–74	.519	Third
1959	SF	83–71	.539	Third
1960	SF	33–25	.569	Second
1961	LA (A)	70–91	.435	Eighth
1962	LA	86–76	.531	Third
1963	LA	70–91	.435	Ninth
1964	LA	82–80	.506	Fifth
1965	Cal	75–87	.463	Seventh
1966	Cal	80–82	.492	Sixth
1967	Cal	84–77	.522	Fifth
1968	Cal	67–94	.414	Eighth
1969	Cal	11–28	.282	Sixth
1970	Min	98–64	.605	First
1971	Min	74–86	.463	Fifth
1972	Min	36–34	.514	Third
1976	SF	74–88	.457	Fourth
18 years		**1239–1321**	**.484**	

Year	Team	Record	Pct.
1970	Min	0–3	.000

Calvin Edwin Ripken, Sr.

Born December 17, 1935, Aberdeen, Maryland; died March 25, 1999, Aberdeen; Baltimore Orioles, September 30, 1985; October 6, 1986–April 12, 1988

Cal Ripken, Sr., was a longtime coach of the Baltimore Orioles who managed them for one game in 1985 — and won — and then got the chance to manage full-time in 1987. The Orioles finished sixth. When they started the 1988 season by losing their first six games, Ripken was fired. He was replaced by Frank Robinson. Under Robinson, the Orioles lost their next 15 games. Ripken's managerial career was brief and uneventful, but he did get the chance to manage his sons, Cal Jr. and Billy.

Year	Team	Record	Pct.	Standing
1985	Bal	1–0	1.000	Fourth
1987	Bal	67–95	.414	Sixth
1988	Bal	0–6	.000	Seventh
3 years		**68–101**	**.402**	

Matthew Stanley Robison

Born March 30, 1859, Pittsburgh, Pennsylvania; died March 24, 1911, St. Louis, Missouri; St. Louis Cardinals, 1905

Matt Robison was president of the St. Louis Cardinals, owned by his brother, when he took over as manager of the club for a short period in 1905. The Cardinals finished sixth and Robison returned to the sidelines at the end of the season.

Year	Team	Record	Pct.	Standing
1905	StL	22–35	.386	Sixth

Frank Robinson

Frank Robinson

Born August 31, 1935, Beaumont, Texas; Cleveland Indians, October 3, 1974–June 19, 1977; San Francisco Giants, January 14, 1981–August 5, 1984; Baltimore Orioles, April 12, 1988–May 24, 1991; Montreal Expos, February 14, 2002–present

Frank Robinson was one of baseball's greatest hitters and went on to become the first black manager in both the American and National leagues. Robinson, a star player for the Cincinnati Reds, was National League Rookie of the Year in 1956 and the league's Most Valuable Player in 1961. Before the 1966 season, he was traded to the Baltimore Orioles, where he won the Triple Crown and was the American League's Most Valuable Player. In 1989, he was named Manager of the Year in the American

League for the remarkable turnaround he engineered with the Baltimore Orioles, who won 33 more games than they had the previous year.

Robinson, who hit 586 home runs in his career — only Henry Aaron, Babe Ruth and Willie Mays hit more — was known for his intensity as both a player and a manager. American League umpire John "Red" Flaherty, who saw a lot of players in his 20-plus years, said he never saw a player work harder than Robinson. And Robinson expected the same kind of desire and attitude from his players.

At Cleveland, where he began the 1975 season as player-manager, Robinson homered in his first at-bat — raising public expectations for a new era of competitiveness in Cleveland. The Indians finished one game below .500, slight improvement over the 1974 finish of eight games under. The Indians finished at 81–78 in 1976, their first season above .500 since 1968. When the Indians got off to a slow start in 1977, Robinson was fired.

He was hired by the San Francisco Giants in 1981 and finished third, but after three seasons of steadily moving back in the standings, Robinson was relieved of his duties there. In 1988, he was hired to manage the Orioles, who had lost their first six games of the season under Cal Ripken, Sr. They lost their next 15 games under Robinson for an 0–21 record — the worst start of a season in baseball history. The Orioles only won 54 games that year. But in 1989, they won 87 and finished second. He would not manage again until 2002, when he took over in Montreal for the Expos' final season.

Robinson stressed fundamentals and had little patience with players who didn't execute the basic plays. In his autobiography, he talks of his frustration in Cleveland when he tried to set up a kangaroo court, in which players would serve as judge and jury and fine each other for not executing properly. The system had worked well when he played in Baltimore, he said, but at Cleveland, players were fining each other for dating ugly girls and things of that nature. It was obvious, he said, that the players were not concentrating on baseball, something for which Robinson had little tolerance.

He was an admirer of Earl Weaver, for whom he played, because he said Weaver was the best at getting the most out of his entire 25-man roster. Where he differed from Weaver was in day-to-day strategy. Robinson believed in moving runners around the bases with bunts, hit-and-runs, hitting to the opposite field and taking the extra base, whereas Weaver always believed that if you play for one run, that's all you'll get.

Robinson's legacy as a manager is the same as it was as a player: he was someone who constantly demonstrated an intense desire to win. He went on to work in the office of the commissioner and to a job that made him baseball's disciplinarian. He levied fines to ballplayers, coaches and managers who had gotten out of line on the field. After Major League Baseball assumed ownership of the Montreal Expos in 2002, with contraction the aim, Robinson was appointed the franchise's manager.

Year	Team	Record	Pct.	Standing
1975	Cleve	79–80	.490	Fourth
1976	Cleve	81–78	.512	Fourth
1977	Cleve	26–31	.450	Fifth
1981	SF	27–32	.450	Fifth
1981	SF	29–23	.550	Third
1982	SF	87–75	.530	Third
1983	SF	79–83	.480	Fifth
1984	SF	42–64	.390	Sixth
1988	Bal	54–101	.340	Seventh
1989	Bal	87–75	.530	Second

Year	Team	Record	Pct.	Standing
1990	Bal	76–85	.470	Fifth
1991	Bal	13–24	.350	Sixth
11 years		**680–751**	**.475**	

Wilbert Robinson

Born June 2, 1864, Hudson, Massachusetts; died August 8, 1934, Atlanta, Georgia; Baltimore Orioles, July 16, 1902; Brooklyn Dodgers, 1914–October 23, 1931

Wilbert Robinson was a beloved manager of the Brooklyn Dodgers for 18 seasons. For many years, the team was known as the Robins in his honor. He had the ability to get the most out of his players with his patience, his knowledge of the game, as well as his ability to teach it, and his humor. He is credited with hastening the development of future Hall of Fame pitcher Rube Marquard by working with him early in his career, establishing a regular rotation for him to pitch and helping him learn new pitches and build confidence. Later, Robinson brought Dazzy Vance along the same way.

Robinson was a catcher for the great Baltimore clubs of the 1890s and once went 7-for-7 with 11 RBIs in one game. At Baltimore, he developed a friendship with John McGraw, and they even went into business together, co-owning a bowling alley. To save money, they bought used pins and shaved them down, thus creating what came to be known as duckpin bowling. When McGraw publicly accused his coach, Robinson, of missing a sign and thereby costing the Giants the 1912 World Series, the two men had a falling out and a bitter rivalry ensued.

Wilbert Robinson

At Brooklyn, Robinson presided over some of the game's zaniest characters and may have been the first manager to institute a kangaroo court. He called it the "Bonehead Club" and fined players for making stupid plays. He fined himself twice, once for turning in the wrong lineup card at the start of a game and once when he changed first basemen at the last minute because he couldn't spell the name of the player he wanted to start. He may be best known for a stunt in which he agreed to try to catch a baseball dropped from an airplane. As a gag, a grapefruit was dropped instead, and when Robinson caught it, it splattered all over his chest. When he felt the mass of liquid on him, he thought he was bleeding to death before discovering the truth.

Most of Robinson's teams finished in the second division. But he did manage to win two pennants, in 1916 and 1920, in each case beating out McGraw. Robinson had the longest managerial tenure for the Dodgers until Walter Alston came along in the 1950s and stayed on board for 23 years. In Robinson's last year as manager, the Dodgers went 79–73, pushing Robinson's lifetime totals to two games over .500.

Year	Team	Record	Pct.	Standing
1902	Bal (A)	22–54	.289	Eighth
1914	Brklyn	75–79	.487	Fifth
1915	Brklyn	80–72	.526	Third
1916	Brklyn	94–60	.610	First
1917	Brklyn	70–81	.464	Seventh
1918	Brklyn	57–69	.452	Fifth
1919	Brklyn	69–71	.493	Fifth
1920	Brklyn	93–61	.604	First
1921	Brklyn	77–75	.507	Fifth
1922	Brklyn	76–78	.494	Sixth
1923	Brklyn	76–78	.494	Sixth
1924	Brklyn	92–62	.597	Second
1925	Brklyn	68–85	.444	Sixth
1926	Brklyn	71–82	.464	Sixth
1927	Brklyn	65–88	.425	Sixth
1928	Brklyn	77–76	.503	Sixth
1929	Brklyn	70–83	.458	Sixth
1930	Brklyn	86–68	.558	Fourth
1931	Brklyn	79–73	.520	Fourth
19 years		**1397–1395**	**.500**	

WORLD SERIES

Year	Team	Record	Pct.
1916	Brklyn	1–4	.200
1920	Brklyn	2–5	.286
2 years		**3–9**	**.250**

Robert Leroy "Buck" Rodgers

Born August 16, 1938, Delaware, Ohio; Milwaukee Brewers, March 6, 1980–June 6, 1980; September 6, 1980–June 2, 1982; Montreal Expos, November 14, 1984–June 2, 1991; California Angels, August 26, 1991–May 17, 1994

Buck Rodgers was an American League catcher for nine years who managed teams in both leagues for a combined total of 13 years. In the 1981 season, split because of a strike, his Milwaukee Brewers finished first in the second half of the season but lost the divisional playoff to the New York Yankees.

The Brewers got off to a disappointing 23–24 start in 1982 and Rodgers was fired. Harvey Kuenn took over and Milwaukee surged to the division championship and the World Series. Rodgers didn't manage again until 1985 when he was hired by the Montreal Expos. It was at Montreal that he achieved his greatest success as a manager, winning the Manager of the Year Award in 1987 as the Expos finished third. In 1991, he managed both the Expos and the California Angels. In 1992, which would have been his first full season with California, Rodgers was seriously injured when a bus carrying the team went out of control and ran into a grove of trees. He returned and managed the Angels for two more years.

Year	Team	Record	Pct.	Standing
1980	Mil	26–21	.550	Third
1980	Mil	13–10	.560	Third
1981	Mil	31–25	.550	Third
1981	Mil	31–22	.580	First
1982	Mil	23–24	.480	Fifth
1985	Mon	84–77	.522	Third
1986	Mon	78–83	.484	Fourth
1987	Mon	91–71	.562	Third
1988	Mon	81–81	.500	Third
1989	Mon	81–81	.500	Third
1990	Mon	85–77	.525	Third
1991	Mon	20–29	.408	Sixth
1991	Cal	20–18	.526	Seventh
1992	Cal	33–40	.452	Fifth
1993	Cal	71–91	.438	Fifth
1994	Cal	16–24	.400	Fourth
13 years		**784–774**	**.503**	

DIVISIONAL PLAYOFF

Year	Team	Record	Pct.
1981	Mil	2–3	.400

James F. Rogers

Born April 9, 1872, Hartford, Connecticut; died January 21, 1900, Bridgeport, Connecticut; Louisville Colonels, 1897

Jim Rogers was manager of Louisville for a short time in 1897 when he was 25 years old. His team was able to win only 17 of 43 games and Rogers was out. Three years later, he died at the age of 28.

Year	Team	Record	Pct.	Standing
1897	Lou	17–26	.395	Ninth

Octavio Rivas "Cookie" Rojas

Born March 6, 1939, Havana, Cuba; California Angels, March 11, 1988–September 23, 1988

Cookie Rojas was a major league second baseman for 16 years, mostly with the Philadelphia Phillies and Kansas City Royals. At Philadelphia, he teamed with shortstop Bobby Wine to form a double play combination known as "The Days of Wine and Rojas."

His opportunity to manage in the major leagues came with the California Angels in 1988. The Angels finished in fourth place, four games below .500. Rojas never managed again.

Year	Team	Record	Pct.	Standing
1988	Cal	75–79	.487	Fourth

Robert Abial "Red" Rolfe

Born October 17, 1908, Penacook, New Hampshire; died July 8, 1969, Gilford, New Hampshire; Detroit Tigers, February 17, 1949–July 5, 1952

Red Rolfe was a New York Yankee infielder for 10 years and had a .289 lifetime batting average. The Yankees made it to the World Series six times in his career. In 1949, he took over for Steve O'Neill as manager of the Detroit Tigers. Detroit had finished fifth in 1948 with a 78–76 record. In Rolfe's first year, his starting pitching staff of Hal Newhouser, Virgil Trucks, Art Houtemann and Fred Hutchinson had 67 of Detroit's 87 wins. In 1950, the Tigers almost ended Casey Stengel's pennant streak at one, but the Yankees held on to win the pennant by three games over Rolfe's Tigers. Trucks, Houtemann and Hutchinson combined for 51 wins and Dizzy Trout won 13. But the Tigers fell to fifth in 1951 and in 1952, they were in the cellar after 52 games and Rolfe, so close to the pennant two years earlier, was fired.

Rolfe had a good eye for young talent. Under the direction of Rolfe and his coaching staff, Houtemann went from a 2–16 record in 1948 to 15–10 in 1949 and 19–12 in 1950. Then something happened beyond Rolfe's control: Houtemann was drafted into the armed services. He missed the 1951 season. When he came back in 1952, he struggled to an 8–20 season as he worked to regain his form. Rolfe's top hitters, George Kell, Vic Wertz and Walter "Hoot" Evers, all of whom had career years in 1950, did well in 1951 but not nearly as well as they had the year before. The once solid pitching staff faltered as well. Houtemann was in the Army, Hutchinson, nearing the end of his career, was 10–10. Newhouser, trying to overcome a sore arm, was 6–6. When the Tigers won only 23 of their first 72 games in 1952, Rolfe was fired and Hutchinson took over as manager.

Year	Team	Record	Pct.	Standing
1949	Det	87–67	.565	Fourth
1950	Det	95–59	.617	Second
1951	Det	73–81	.474	Fifth
1952	Det	23–49	.319	Eighth
4 years		**278–256**	**.521**	

Peter Edward Rose

Born April 14, 1931, Cincinnati, Ohio; Cincinnati Reds, August 16, 1984–August 24, 1989

Pete Rose once said that the trouble with baseball is that "they only remember your last at-bat." For Rose, his last at-bat in baseball occurred when commissioner A. Bartlett Giamatti banned him for life in 1989 for his alleged gambling on baseball games, an allegation Rose always denied. But he agreed not to challenge the ruling in court. In 1990, he was convicted of income tax evasion and served time in federal prison. In 1991, the Baseball Hall of Fame induction committee voted to deny induction to anyone banned from baseball.

All of these actions came after a 22-year playing career in which Rose surpassed Ty Cobb's record for total hits, accumulating 4,256, and was first in number of games played, 3,562, and at-bats, 14,053. He was the National League Rookie of the Year in 1963, tied the National League record for longest hitting streak, 44 games, in 1978, won three batting titles and had a lifetime batting average .303. Rose was named player-manager of the Reds in 1984. He retired as a player two years later but continued to manage until his suspension.

Rose's problems off the field overshadow his record as a manager which shows that the Reds finished second in each of his four full seasons (1985–1988). They were in fifth place in the trouble-filled 1989 season when Rose and his team had to work through the distraction of the investigation of his alleged gambling. He was known as a player's manager who was respected for his knowledge of the game and the attitude that earned him the nickname "Charlie Hustle" during his playing days. Rose had sluggers like Eric Davis in his lineup but his style was to play for one run. His 1987 Reds team set a major league record for number of relief pitchers used during a season (392), a mark that has been surpassed several times since then. In 1990, the Reds won the pennant under Rose's successor, Lou Piniella, and then swept the Oakland A's in the World Series.

Year	Team	Record	Pct.	Standing
1984	Cin	19–22	.463	Fifth
1985	Cin	89–72	.553	Second
1986	Cin	86–76	.531	Second
1987	Cin	84–78	.519	Second
1988	Cin	75–59	.560	Second
1989	Cin	59–66	.472	Fifth
6 years		**412–373**	**.525**	

James John Roseman

Born in 1856, New York, New York; died July 4, 1938, Brooklyn, New York; St. Louis Browns, 1890

Jim "Chief" Roseman was the second of three managers to lead St. Louis in the American Association in 1890. Roseman took over with the team in fourth place, compiled a 32–19 record to move them up to second, and then was replaced, never to manage again. St. Louis regressed after Roseman left, finishing fourth.

Year	Team	Record	Pct.	Standing
1890	StL (AA)	32–19	.627	Second

Lawrence Lee Rothschild

Born March 12, 1954, Chicago, Illinois; Tampa Bay Devil Rays, November 7, 1997–April 19, 2001

Larry Rothschild was a right-handed pitcher who appeared in seven games for the Detroit Tigers in 1981 and 1982 without a decision. He remained in baseball, coaching and managing at the minor league level and got his shot at major league managing in 1998 with the expansion Tampa Bay Devil Rays. They finished fifth in their division each of his first two years, but increased their win total by six games in his second season. He was fired 14 games into the 2001 season and replaced by Hal McRae.

Year	Team	Record	Pct.	Standing
1998	TBay	63–99	.389	Fifth
1999	TBay	69–93	.426	Fifth
2000	TBay	69–92	.426	Fifth
2001	TBay	4–10	.286	Fifth
4 years		**205–294**	**.410**	

David Eli Rowe

Born February 1856, Jacksonville, Illinois; died October 12, 1918; Kansas City Cowboys, 1886, 1888

Dave Rowe and his brother Jack, 10 months apart in age, both played ball and managed in the American Association in the late 1800s. Dave Rowe had two stints managing

Kansas City but could not inspire his team to even a .300 winning percentage. His brother had about the same fate at Buffalo.

Year	Team	Record	Pct.	Standing
1886	KC (AA)	30–91	.248	Seventh
1888	KC	14–35	.286	Eighth
2 years		**44–126**	**.259**	

John Charles Rowe

Born December 18, 1856, Harrisburg, Pennsylvania; died April 25, 1911, St. Louis Missouri; Buffalo Bisons, 1890

Jack Rowe, younger brother of Dave, was a ballplayer who had one brief stint as a manager. He led the Buffalo ball club in the Players League in 1890, a team that won only 36 of 132 games it played. He never managed again.

Year	Team	Record	Pct.	Standing
1890	Buff (P)	36–96	.273	Eighth

Clarence Henry "Pants" Rowland

Born February 12, 1879, Platteville, Wisconsin; died May 17, 1969, Chicago, Illinois; Chicago White Sox, December 17, 1914–December 31, 1918

Pants Rowland has the distinction of being the last Chicago White Sox manager to win a World Series, achieving that distinction in 1917. Rowland managed the White Sox for four years, relinquishing the job to Kid Gleason in 1919. Rowland left after the White Sox plunged from World Series champions to a sixth-place finish in 1918. After Rowland was gone, they rebounded to win the pennant again in 1919, after which eight players were accused of being involved, in one way or another, with conspiring with gamblers to fix the World Series. By that time, Rowland was on to other ventures. He never managed again but was a longtime scout and executive with the Chicago Cubs who had a knack for spotting good pitching prospects in sandlot games.

His 1917 pennant winner had strong pitching from Red Faber and Eddie Cicotte and the hitting of Joe Jackson and Eddie Collins. Faber was the star of the World Series, pitching in four games and winning three of them. Rowland's 1918 roster was depleted after several players joined the war effort, including Jackson.

\Year	Team	Record	Pct.	Standing
1915	Chi (A)	93–61	.603	Third
1916	Chi	89–65	.578	Second
1917	Chi	100–54	.649	First
1918	Chi	57–67	.460	Sixth
4 years		**339–247**	**.578**	

WORLD SERIES

Year	Team	Record	Pct.
1917	Chi (A)	4–2	.600

Jeron "Jerry" Kennis Royster

Born October 18, 1952, Sacramento, California; Milwaukee Brewers, April 18, 2002–present

Former infielder Jerry Royster was named manager of the free-falling Milwaukee

Brewers after the club got off to the worst start, 3–12, in franchise history. Royster, close friend and bench coach of outgoing manager Davey Lopes, was first the interim and then the permanent replacement.

Herold Dominic "Muddy" Ruel

Born February 20, 1896, St Louis, Missouri; died November 13, 1963, Palo Alto, California; St. Louis Browns, September 30, 1946–November 21, 1947

Muddy Ruel was a major league catcher for 19 years who was behind the plate on the Washington Senator World Series teams of 1924 and 1925. His only opportunity to manage came with a team that had far less talent — the 1947 St. Louis Browns. The Browns won only 59 games and finished in last place.

Year	Team	Record	Pct.	Standing
1947	StL (A)	59–95	.383	Eighth

James Edward "Pete" Runnels

Born January 28, 1928, Lufkin, Texas; died May 20, 1991, Pasadena, Texas; Boston Red Sox, September 8–30, 1966

Pete Runnels was a hard-hitting infielder who later coached for the Boston Red Sox. In 1966, he was called on to finish the season after manager Billy Herman was fired. Under Runnels the Red Sox were 8–8, moving up from tenth to ninth place. Boston opted to hire a new manager, Dick Williams, in 1967. The Red Sox won the pennant under Williams. Runnels never managed again.

Year	Team	Record	Pct.	Standing
1966	Bos	8–8	.500	Ninth

Tom Runnells

Born April 17, 1955; Montreal Expos, June 2, 1991–May 22, 1992

Tom Runnells managed the Montreal Expos for parts of two seasons but could not raise them above the .500 level. He was released during the 1992 season and replaced by Felipe Alou. He has not managed in the major leagues again.

Year	Team	Record	Pct.	Standing
1991	Mon	51–61	.455	Sixth
1992	Mon	17–20	.459	Second
2 years		**68–81**	**.456**	

William Ellis Russell

Born October 21, 1948, Pittsburgh, Kansas; Los Angeles Dodgers, July 30, 1996–June 21, 1998

Bill Russell was the shortstop on a great Los Angeles Dodger infield that included Ron Cey at third base, Davey Lopes at second base and Steve Garvey at first base. He then became a coach and manager in the Dodger organization. In August of 1996, when illness forced the sudden retirement of Tom Lasorda, Russell was tabbed to replace the legendary manager. The Dodgers didn't do badly statistically under Russell, but he lacked the charisma of Lasorda. His quiet, methodical nature was a sharp contrast to the flamboyant Lasorda. When the Dodgers stumbled to a 36–38 record at the start of the 1998 season, Russell was fired.

Year	Team	Record	Pct.	Standing
1996	LA	49–37	.570	Second
1997	LA	88–74	.543	Second
1998	LA	36–38	.486	Third
3 years		**173–149**	**.537**	

Cornelius Joseph Ryan

Born February 27, 1920, New Orleans, Louisiana; Atlanta Braves, August 31, 1975; Texas Rangers, June 24–28, 1977

Veteran major league coach Connie Ryan was called on twice to serve as an interim manager, once in each league. He served a 26 game stint with the Atlanta Braves in 1975, finishing the season for the fired Clyde King. Two years later, he filled in for six games with the Texas Rangers during an unusual period. The Rangers had fired Frank Lucchesi and named Eddie Stanky as his replacement. Stanky managed one game, won it and then quit. Ryan then filled in until a replacement for Stanky could be found. Billy Hunter was hired, ending Ryan's managing career.

Year	Team	Record	Pct.	Standing
1975	Atl	8–18	.308	Fifth
1977	Tex	2–4	.333	Fourth
2 years		**10–22**	**.313**	

Edwin Milby Sawyer

Born September 10, 1910, Westerly, Rhode Island; Philadelphia Phillies, July 27, 1948–June 27, 1952; July 22, 1958–April 14, 1960

Eddie Sawyer, who never played major league baseball, had the ability to develop young ballplayers and used it to lead the 1950 Philadelphia Phillies "Whiz Kids" to the World Series. The Phillies' average age that year was 26. The lineup was filled with youngsters in whom Sawyer had shown confidence since he took over the ball club for Ben Chapman in 1948. Chapman was an intense individual who spoke his mind and was purposely intimidating. Sawyer, who once taught college biology, was a thoughtful, sensitive man who had been a successful minor league coach. Under his direction, centerfielder Richie Ashburn and second baseman Granny Hamner became key players and young pitchers Curt Simmons and Robin Roberts were on the verge of stardom. Sawyer mixed the youngsters with veterans such as outfielder Del Ennis, catcher Andy Semnick and first baseman Dick Sisler to make a pennant contender out of a second division team. His greatest accomplishment, however, was taking Jim Konstanty, who had a mediocre 7–5 record in three partial seasons, and turning him into the most dominant relief pitcher in baseball. In 1950, Konstanty appeared in 74 games, a major league record at the time, finished 62 of them, also a record, compiled a won-loss mark of 16–7 and under today's rules would have been credited with at least 22 saves. The Phillies won the pennant.

Ennis described Sawyer's offense as being this simple: "Ashburn would lead off and get on base and we'd drive him in."

Sawyer took a calculated risk in the World Series. Simmons had been drafted into the Army and Roberts had pitched the pennant-clincher on the last day of the season. Sawyer chose to open the Series against the New York Yankees with Konstanty, who had not started a major league game since 1946. He pitched well for eight innings but lost to Vic Raschi, 1–0. The Yankees and Allie Reynolds beat Roberts, 2–1, in 10 innings in Game Two. The Yankees won the third game, 3–2, the third straight game decided by one run. In Game Four, with the championship at stake, Sawyer was reluctant to go with Konstanty again, thinking he would be needed in the bullpen. He didn't want to chance starting Roberts on two days' rest after the right-hander had worked 10 innings in Game Two. And Ken Heintzelman, the Game Three starter, had worked into the eighth inning. So Sawyer went with spot starter Bob Miller and the Yankees immediately touched him up for two runs before he could get out of the first inning. Sawyer was forced to bring in Konstanty in the first inning and he worked the next 6⅔ in a 5–2 series-ending loss. So Sawyer's decision to start Konstanty in the first game forced him to rearrange his staff for the rest of the Series.

The Phillies fell to fifth place in 1951. In 1952, the ball club slumped to sixth place and Sawyer was fired. Six years later, he was brought back to replace Mayo Smith but didn't have the talent or the prospects that he enjoyed during his first tenure. The Phillies finished last in 1959. In 1960, Philadelphia lost on Opening Day. Sawyer resigned — and retired.

Year	Team	Record	Pct.	Standing
1948	Phil	23–41	.359	Sixth
1949	Phil	81–73	.526	Third
1950	Phil	91–63	.591	First
1951	Phil	73–81	.474	Fifth
1952	Phil	28–35	.444	Sixth
1958	Phil	30–41	.423	Eighth
1959	Phil	64–90	.416	Eighth
1960	Phil	0–1	.000	Eighth
8 years		**390–425**	**.479**	

WORLD SERIES

Year	Team	Record	Pct.
1950	Phil	0–4	.000

Michael B. Scanlon

Born in 1847, Cork, Ireland; died January 18, 1929, Washington D.C.; Washington Nationals, 1884; Washington Senators, 1886

Irishman Mike Scanlon managed the Washington franchise in two different years in two different leagues without much success. After guiding the Union League team to a seventh-place finish in 1884, he managed the National League team in 1886 but was relieved of his duties when the ball club lost 66 of its first 79 games.

Year	Team	Record	Pct.	Standing
1884	Wash (U)	47–66	.416	Seventh
1886	Wash (N)	13–66	.165	Eighth
2 years		**60–132**	**.313**	

Robert Schaefer

Born May 22, 1944, Putnam, Connecticut; Kansas City Royals, May 22, 1991

Bob Schaefer served as interim manager for the Kansas City Royals, filling the gap between John Wathan and Hal McRae. The Royals won Schaefer's only game as manager.

Year	Team	Record	Pct.	Standing
1991	KC	1–0	1.000	Sixth

Raymond William Schalk

Born August 12, 1892, Harvey, Illinois; died May 19, 1970, Chicago, Illinois; Chicago White Sox, November 11, 1926–July 4, 1928

Ray "Cracker" Schalk was one of the tragic figures of the 1919 "Black Sox" scandal in which eight of his teammates were accused of conspiring with gamblers to fix the World Series. Schalk, the team's fiery catcher, looked on helplessly as pitching ace Eddie Cicotte, one of the conspirators, pitched poorly and several of his teammates made errors, lacked hustle and didn't swing the bat effectively. Always the competitor, Schalk insisted to his dying day that the White Sox still would have won the Series had pitcher Red Faber not missed it because of injury.

The ball club fell on hard times after eight of its stars were suspended. In 1927, management called on Schalk, a fan favorite, to take over the team. He lasted two years but could bring the White Sox in no higher than fifth place.

Year	Team	Record	Pct.	Standing
1927	Chi (A)	70–83	.453	Fifth
1928	Chi	32–42	.432	Sixth
2 years		**102–125**	**.449**	

Robert Boden Scheffing

Born August 11, 1915, Overland, Missouri; died October 26, 1985, Phoenix, Arizona; Chicago Cubs, October 11, 1956–September 28, 1959; Detroit Tigers, November 21, 1960–June 17, 1963

Bob Scheffing was another of the former Chicago Cub players that owner Phil Wrigley promoted to manager, following Phil Cavarretta and Stan Hack in succession. Scheffing didn't have much to work with on the Cubs except a young pitching staff that needed developing. His first Cub team won only 62 games and lost 92. But 28 of the 62 wins came from rookies Dick Drott (15 wins) and Moe Drabowsky (13 wins). In 1958, another young pitcher, Glen Hobbie, joined the staff. He won 10 games and the Cubs improved to 72–82. In 1959, aided by the righty-lefty bullpen combination of Don Elston and Bill Henry, the Cubs won 74 games and seemed poised to make a run for the first division in 1960. Hobbie, who won 16 games, said he recalled saying good-bye to Scheffing after the last game of the season at Wrigley Field and they both talked of their high hopes for 1960. As Hobbie was driving to his home in southern Illinois, he heard on the car radio that Scheffing had been fired. He was stunned as were many other Cub players who thought Scheffing was leading them in the right direction after two consecutive fifth-place finishes. The Cubs reversed themselves and won only 60 games in 1960 under Charlie Grimm and Lou Boudreau, finishing seventh.

In 1961, Scheffing was hired to manage the Detroit Tigers. There he made a strategic move with a veteran pitcher that kept the Tigers in the pennant race most of the season against a Yankee team that is still rated as one of the greatest of all time. The Tigers had finished sixth in 1960, the year that Jimmy Dykes and Joe Gordon switched managerial roles at Detroit and Cleveland. In 1961, under the steady leadership of Scheffing, the Tigers made a 30-game improvement, winning 101 games and losing only 61. Don Mossi, a former star relief pitcher, had his finest year as a starter under Scheffing's guidance in 1961. The Tigers won 85 in 1962 but dropped to fourth place. In 1963, Detroit nose-dived and was in ninth place at 24–36 when Scheffing was fired. He became general manager of the New York Mets and helped put together a young pitching staff that fared a little better than his Cub rookies of the 1950s. Tom Seaver, Jerry Koosman and Nolan Ryan pitched the Mets to the 1969 pennant and World Series — with the help of a Scheffing acquisition, right-handed pitcher Don Cardwell, who at one time pitched for the Cubs.

Year	Team	Record	Pct.	Standing
1957	Chi (N)	62–92	.403	Seventh
1958	Chi	72–82	.468	Fifth
1959	Chi	74–80	.481	Fifth
1961	Det	101–61	.623	Second
1962	Det	85–76	.528	Fourth
1963	Det	24–36	.400	Ninth
6 years		**418–427**	**.495**	

Harry Lawrence Schlafly

Born September 20, 1878, Port Washington, Ohio; died June 27, 1919, Beach City, Ohio; Buffalo Buffeds, 1914–1915

Larry Schlafly managed the Buffalo ball club in the upstart Federal League in 1914 and 1915. He was fired mid-way through the 1915 season. When that league folded after the 1915 season, it also marked the end of Schlafly's managerial career.

Year	Team	Record	Pct.	Standing
1914	Buff (F)	80–71	.530	Fourth
1915	Buff	14–29	.326	Eighth
2 years		94–100	.485	

Gustavas Heinrich Schmelz

Born September 26, 1850, Columbus, Ohio; died October 14, 1925, Columbus, Ohio; Columbus Buckeyes, 1884, 1890–1891; St. Louis Maroons, 1886; Cincinnati Reds, 1887–1889; Cleveland Spiders, 1890; Washington Senators, 1894–1897

Gus Schmelz is one of the few managers prior to 1900 who stayed around long enough to manage in more than 1,000 games. He did it in two stints with Columbus, and one each with St. Louis, Cincinnati, Cleveland and Washington. He was a native of Columbus, Ohio, but his German name made him popular with the German populations in both Columbus and Cincinnati when he managed there. Despite his relatively long tenure, he is best remembered in baseball history books for his bushy red beard.

Year	Team	Record	Pct.	Standing
1884	Col (AA)	69–39	.639	Second
1886	StL (U)	43–79	.352	Sixth
1887	Cin	81–54	.600	Second

Year	Team	Record	Pct.	Standing
1888	Cin	80–54	.597	Fourth
1889	Cin	76–63	.547	Fourth
1890	Cleve (N)	21–55	.276	Seventh
1890	Col	37–13	.740	Fifth
1891	Col	61–76	.445	Sixth
1894	Wash	45–87	.341	Eleventh
1895	Wash	43–85	.336	Tenth
1896	Wash	58–73	.443	Ninth
1897	Wash	9–25	.265	Eleventh
11 years		**623–703**	**.470**	

Alfred Fred "Red" Schoendienst

Born February 2, 1923, Germantown, Illinois; St. Louis Cardinals, October 20, 1964–October 7, 1976; August 29, 1980–October 24, 1980; July 6, 1990–August 1, 1990

Red Schoendienst played most of his career as the second baseman for the St. Louis Cardinals although he also was on Milwaukee Brave pennant winners in 1957 and 1958. Early in his career, he played on the Cardinals' 1946 pennant winner. He was named manager of the Cardinals in 1965 after Johnny Keane quit to manage the New York Yankees. Keane's Cardinals had won the 1964 World Series, so Schoendienst had a tough act to follow. The Cardinals had won the pennant in '64 when the Philadelphia Phillies lost 11 of their last 12 games to blow a 6½ game lead in the final two weeks. In 1965 and 1966, Schoendienst's first two years, the Los Angeles Dodgers, behind the one-two pitching punch of Sandy Koufax and Don Drysdale, won back to back pennants. In the next two years, Schoendienst was able to blend a lineup made up of veterans acquired from other teams, such as Orlando Cepeda and Roger Maris, and veteran Cardinal players such as Lou Brock, Dal Maxvill, Julian Javier and Mike Shannon to put together a winner. The Cardinal pitching staff that year had two future Hall of Famers, Bob Gibson and Steve Carlton, but Dick Hughes led the team in wins with 16. The Cards repeated in 1968 with Gibson registering one of the best years in modern baseball history—22 wins, 1.12 earned run average, 28 complete games in 34 starts, 13 shutouts and 268 strikeouts. Nelson Briles won 19 as St. Louis finished nine games ahead of second-place San Francisco. The

Red Schoendienst

popular Schoendienst never came close to that kind of success again although he remained at the helm for 12 years. Schoendienst had two rules he wanted his players to follow: "Run everything out and be in by 12."

In 1977, he was replaced by veteran minor league manager Vern Rapp, who was the direct opposite of the soft-spoken Schoendienst. Rapp ran the Cardinals like it was a military operation, setting clubhouse rules, banning facial hair and generally setting an authoritative tone that was not well received by the players. Rapp was fired 15 games into his second season. Cardinal owner August Busch, trying to restore order, named Ken Boyer as manager. Boyer was a former Cardinal third baseman and, like Schoendienst, was a fan favorite. But the Cardinals did not play well and in 1980, Schoendienst was called on to finish out a season in which St. Louis had already had three managers: Boyer, coach Jack Krol for one game, and Whitey Herzog for much of the season. It was an audition for Herzog, who was hired to manage the Cardinals for the 1981 season and led them to the first of several pennants. Schoendienst was called on one more time in 1990, finishing out that season on an interim basis. Overall, he is one of the few men to manage the same team in four decades and ended his career one game shy of 2,000 as a manager (including four tie games).

Schoendienst's managerial career might not have occurred at all — or surely would have been delayed — if Busch had followed through on his first choice for manager in 1965, Leo Durocher. But word leaked out that Busch had talked with Durocher and the reaction was not good. Busch opted for the safer choice, Schoendienst, launching his managerial career.

Year	Team	Record	Pct.	Standing
1965	StL	80–81	.497	Seventh
1966	StL	83–79	.512	Sixth
1967	StL	101–60	.627	First
1968	StL	97–65	.599	First
1969	StL	87–75	.537	Fourth
1970	StL	76–86	.469	Fourth
1971	StL	90–72	.556	Second
1972	StL	75–81	.481	Fourth
1973	StL	81–81	.500	Second
1974	StL	86–75	.534	Second
1975	StL	82–80	.506	Third
1976	StL	72–90	.444	Fifth
1980	StL	18–19	.486	Fifth
1990	StL	13–11	.540	Sixth
14 years		**1041–955**	**.523**	

WORLD SERIES

Year	Team	Record	Pct.
1967	StL	4–3	.571
1968	StL	3–4	.429
2 years		7–7	**.500**

Joseph Charles Schultz, Jr.

Born August 29, 1918, Chicago, Illinois; Seattle Pilots, October 11, 1968–November 20, 1969; Detroit Tigers, September 9, 1973–October 11, 1973

Joe Schultz managed the Seattle Pilots in the their only year of existence. The Pilots lasted a year in Seattle, 1969, after which the franchise was moved to Milwaukee. Schultz did not go with them. He did manage to win his first game as Pilots manager when Gary Bell shut out the White Sox. But the Pilots won only 63 more games after that. Schultz managed the Detroit Tigers briefly in 1973.

Year	Team	Record	Pct.	Standing
1969	Sea	64–90	.395	Sixth
1973	Det	9–10	.474	Third
2 years		**73–100**	**.422**	

Michael Scioscia

Born November 27, 1958, Darby, Pennsylvania; Anaheim Angels, November 19, 1999–present

Mike Scioscia was a 13-year catcher for Tommy Lasorda's Los Angeles Dodgers and became the third member of that team to become a major league manager, along with Davey Lopes and Bill Russell. In his first year at the helm, Scioscia guided the Anaheim Angels to a respectable 82–80 finish, a third-place finish in the four-team Western Division of the American League.

Year	Team	Record	Pct.	Standing
2000	Ana	82–80	.506	Third
2001	Ana	75–87	.463	Third

Frank Gibson Selee

Born October 26, 1859, Amherst, New Hampshire; died July 5, 1909, Denver, Colorado; Boston Beaneaters, 1890–1901; Chicago Cubs, 1902–1905

Frank Selee was one of the great managers of the early days of baseball. His Boston Beaneater team won five pennants in 12 years. Later, he helped set the stage for the Chicago Cubs dynasty of the early 1900s. In 16 years of managing, his teams never finished lower than fifth.

Selee was a little man who was partially bald and had a flowing mustache. Like Connie Mack, Selee wore a suit and tie as he managed his players from the sidelines. He was a master strategist on both offense and defense. He was one of the first to use the hit-and-run and his teams practiced and executed the 3-6-3 double play on defense. Selee was also one of the first managers to use signals and to shift his defense around, depending on who was batting and how his hurler intended to pitch to him. His greatest legacy as a manager, however, was his ability to judge talent, to develop young ballplayers and find the position they were best suited to play. When the mighty Beaneaters slipped to fourth place in 1900 and to fifth in 1901, Selee was relieved of his duties. He signed on to manage the Chicago Cubs. As the Cubs prepared for the 1902 season, Selee took a young catcher, Frank Chance, and made him his first baseman; a third baseman, Joe Tinker, and moved him to shortstop; and a shortstop, Johnny Evers, and moved him to second base. In so doing, he not only established the backdrop for one of baseball's most famous poems, but he solidified his defense. In coming years, he signed pitchers Mordecai "Three Finger" Brown and Ed Ruelbach. The Cubs were ready to make their move. They won 68 games in 1902, 82 in 1903 and 93 in 1904. In 1905, Selee fell ill with tuberculosis. At about the same time, the Cubs underwent several front office changes. Selee was replaced as manager with Chance, Selee's first baseman, and finished in third place. Between 1906 and 1910, the Cubs won four pennants with the team that Selee had developed and nurtured. He died in 1909 at the age of 49. Tinker, Evers and Chance were elected to the Hall of Fame in 1946. Selee was voted in by the Veterans Committee in 1999, 109 years after he began his managerial career and 90 years after his death.

His won-loss percentage of .598 is the fourth highest in baseball history.

Year	Team	Record	Pct.	Standing
1890	Bos (N)	76–57	.571	Fifth
1891	Bos	87–51	.630	First
1892	Bos	102–48	.680	First
1893	Bos	86–43	.667	First
1894	Bos	83–49	.629	Third
1895	Bos	71–60	.542	Fifth
1896	Bos	74–57	.565	Fourth
1897	Bos	93–39	.705	First
1898	Bos	102–47	.685	First
1899	Bos	95–57	.625	Second
1900	Bos	66–72	.478	Fourth
1901	Bos	69–69	.500	Fifth
1902	Chi (N)	68–69	.496	Fifth
1903	Chi	82–56	.594	Third
1904	Chi	93–60	.608	Second
1905	Chi	52–38	.578	Fourth
16 years		**1299–872**	**.598**	

James Luther "Luke" Sewell

Born January 5, 1901, Titus, Alabama; died May 14, 1987, Marion, Ohio; St. Louis Browns, June 5, 1941–August 31, 1946; Cincinnati Reds, September 26, 1949–July 28, 1952

Luke Sewell was a catcher for four American League teams for 20 years and was the brother of Joe Sewell, the toughest man to strike out in major league history. Sewell managed for 10 years and has two distinctions: he had a winning record in six seasons as manager of the St. Louis Browns and his 1944 Browns team won the American League pennant. Sewell later managed the Cincinnati Reds, and it was his tenure there that brought his overall managerial record below the .500 mark. The Browns won the 1944 American League championship by one game over the second place Detroit Tigers. Nels Potter was the ace of the staff, winning 19 games. Shortstop Vern Stephens, who would later be a star with the Boston Red Sox, hit 20 home runs and drove in 109 runs. The Browns hit only 72 home runs but Sewell, the old catcher, got the most out of his war-time pitching staff. Browns pitchers led the league in strikeouts with 581, they combined for second lowest earned run average in the league, 3.17, and were second in shutouts and second in saves. Sewell's starting staff consisted of Nelson Potter, Jack Kramer, George Caster and Sig Jakucki and won the pennant by sweeping the New York Yankees in a four-game series at the end of the season. Sewell also recruited a pitcher, Denny Galehouse, and an outfielder, Chet Laubs, who could only play on weekends because they had weekday jobs considered essential to the war effort. The Browns led the league in 4-F players—4-F being the military classification for men deemed physically unfit to be in military service. Sewell took this group of baseball misfits and won the pennant with them. The Browns lost to the St. Louis Cardinals, four games to two, in a World Series in which every game was played in the same ballpark, Sportsman's Park in St. Louis.

Year	Team	Record	Pct.	Standing
1941	StL (A)	55–55	.500	Sixth
1942	StL	82–69	.543	Third
1943	StL	72–80	.474	Sixth
1944	StL	89–65	.578	First
1945	StL	81–70	.536	Third
1946	StL	53–71	.427	Seventh
1949	Cin	1–2	.333	Seventh
1950	Cin	66–87	.431	Sixth
1951	Cin	68–86	.442	Sixth
1952	Cin	39–59	.398	Seventh
10 years		**606–644**	**.485**	

World Series

Year	Team	Record	Pct.
1944	StL (A)	2–4	.333

Daniel W. Shannon

Born March 23, 1865, Bridgeport, Connecticut; died October 25, 1913, Bridgeport; Louisville Colonels, 1889; Washington Senators, 1891

Dan Shannon managed two American Association teams, Louisville and Washington, for portions of two seasons. His ball clubs lost over three times as many games as they won, bringing Shannon's managerial career to an abrupt conclusion.

Year	Team	Record	Pct.	Standing
1889	Lou	9–43	.173	Eighth
1891	Wash	12–25	.324	Eighth
2 years		**21–68**	**.236**	

William A. Sharsig

Born in 1855, Philadelphia, Pennsylvania; died February 1, 1902, Philadelphia; Philadelphia Athletics, 1884–1891

Bill Sharsig had an unusual career as a 19th-century manager for at least two reasons. First, he managed for parts of eight consecutive seasons, a long tenure for a manager in those days — and all with the same team, Philadelphia of the American Association. In five of those years, including four years in a row, he replaced managers in mid-season. Through it all, Sharsig had only two seasons in which his team finished below the .500 mark.

Year	Team	Record	Pct.	Standing
1884	Phil (AA)	33–23	.589	Seventh
1885	Phil	22–17	.564	Fourth
1886	Phil	22–17	.564	Fourth
1887	Phil	42–44	.488	Fifth
1888	Phil	81–52	.609	Third
1889	Phil	75–58	.564	Third
1890	Phil	54–78	.409	Seventh
1891	Phil	15–17	.469	Fourth
8 years		**344–306**		

James Robert Shawkey

Born December 4, 1890, Brookville, Pennsylvania; died December 31, 1980, Syracuse, New York; New York Yankees, October 23, 1929–October 10, 1930

Bob Shawkey took over as manager of the New York Yankees under the worst of circumstances. Miller Huggins, who led the Yankees in their dynasty years, had died of blood poisoning on September 25, 1929, at the age of 50. Coach Art Fletcher served as interim manager for the few remaining games but declined the offer to manage the Yankees on a full-time basis. Col. Jake Ruppert, the Yankees owner, then sought out both Donie Bush and Eddie Collins to see if either one of them was interested. They weren't. The 39-year-old Shawkey, a former pitcher who played much of his career under Huggins, accepted the job. The Yankees played well but were no match for Connie Mack's powerhouse Philadelphia A's as New York finished third. When Joe McCarthy was fired as manager of the Chicago Cubs in September of 1930, Ruppert met privately with him and offered him the Yankee job. McCarthy accepted. Shawkey had expected to be rehired and was shocked at his dismissal, calling it "a dirty deal." He never managed again.

Year	Team	Record	Pct.	Standing
1930	NY (A)	86–68	.558	Third

Thomas Clancy Sheehan

Born March 31, 1894, Grand Ridge, Illinois; died December 1, 1982, Chillicothe, Ohio; San Francisco Giants, June 18, 1960–November 1, 1960

Affable San Francisco Giant scout Tom Sheehan was the oldest man in baseball history to be a first-year manager. Giants owner Horace Stoneham turned to his old friend after firing veteran manager Bill Rigney. Sheehan was 66 years old. As a pitcher 44 years earlier, he had a 1–16 record with Connie Mack's Philadelphia A's. The Giants were in second place with a 33–25 record when Rigney was dismissed. Under Sheehan, they went 46–50 and finished in fifth place. After the season, Stoneham hired Alvin Dark to replace Sheehan.

Year	Team	Record	Pct.	Standing
1960	SF	46–50	.479	Fifth

Lawrence William Shepard

Born April 3, 1919, Lakewood, Ohio; Pittsburgh Pirates, October 13, 1967–September 26, 1969

Pittsburgh Pirate coach Larry Shepard was hired to manage the Pirates after the Pirates had underachieved in 1967, finishing with a .500 record and in sixth place. Harry Walker had started the '67 season as manager and was replaced almost exactly halfway through the season by Danny Murtaugh, the former Pirate manager who accepted the job only on an interim basis. Both men broke even, Walker at 42–42, Murtaugh at 39–39 for the year. Under Shepard, the Pirates fared just about as well in 1968, finishing with an 80–82 record, but in sixth place. The following year, they moved up to third place. But Shepard was released at season's end and Murtaugh was brought back for yet another stint as Pirates manager. Pittsburgh won the Eastern Division championship under Murtaugh, but the 1970s were dominated by Sparky Anderson's Cincinnati Reds. Anderson's pitching coach was Larry Shepard.

Year	Team	Record	Pct.	Standing
1968	Pitt	80–82	.494	Sixth
1969	Pitt	84–73	.535	Third
2 years		**164–155**	**.514**	

Norman Burt Sherry

Born July 16, 1931, New York, New York; California Angels, July 23, 1976–July 11, 1977

Norm Sherry is another of numerous former major league catchers who went on to become a big league manager. Sherry was a catcher for five years in the National League and at one time was a battery mate of his brother, Larry, with the Los Angeles Dodgers. He got his opportunity to manage in 1976 and 1977 when California Angels owner Gene Autry was struggling to bring stability to the managerial position. Bill Rigney had been the franchise's first manager and served from 1961 to 1969. Since that time, the Angels had gone through four managers: Lefty Phillips, Del Rice, Bobby Winkles and Dick Williams. In 1977, Sherry's first full season, Autry and general manager Harry Dalton spent millions of dollars in the free agent market and came up with veteran outfielders Joe Rudi and Don Baylor and second baseman Bobby Grich. The Angels had a pitching staff led by Nolan Ryan and Frank Tanana but had a shaky bullpen that had come up with only nine saves the year before. When Grich suffered a herniated disc lifting an air conditioner in his apartment, Rudi was sidelined after a pitch break his right hand and Baylor fought through a slump that lasted about half a season, the Angels struggled. Sherry was fired and replaced by Dave Garcia, the Angels' fifth manager in 5½ years.

Year	Team	Record	Pct.	Standing
1976	Cal	37–29	.561	Fourth
1977	Cal	39–42	.481	Fifth
2 years		**76–71**	**.517**	

William Joseph Shettsline

Born October 25, 1863, Philadelphia, Pennsylvania; died February 22, 1963, Philadelphia; Philadelphia Phillies, 1898–1902

Bill Shettsline had a turbulent but successful stint as manager of the Philadelphia Phillies. He was named manager of the club in 1898 after many players revolted against the hardline tactics of manager George Stallings and informed management that they refused to play for him any longer. Stallings went on to manage the Detroit Tigers, New York Yankees and Boston Braves. Shettsline was able to calm the storm and move the Phillies from their eighth-place position to a sixth-place finish in 1898. The following year, his first full season, the Phillies won 94 games and finished third. Their .618 percentage was the best in club history. After another third-place finish in 1899, more trouble brewed, this time from big-money baseball people who were trying to form a new major league. Ban Johnson and Charles Comiskey worked during 1900 to form what became the American League. When new franchises were developed, they freely raided players from the National League, and Shettsline and the Phillies were hard hit. The

Phillies finished second in 1901, the first year of the American League. But by 1902, the club had lost Nap Lajoie, the best all-around player of his day, Ed Delahanty, the game's greatest slugger, as well as several frontline pitchers. Philadelphia plunged to seventh place and Shettsline exited much like he had entered, with a team in disarray.

Year	Team	Record	Pct.	Standing
1898	Phil (N)	59–44	.573	Sixth
1899	Phil	94–58	.618	Third
1900	Phil	75–63	.543	Third
1901	Phil	83–57	.593	Second
1902	Phil	56–81	.409	Seventh
5 years		**367–303**	**.548**	

Burton Edwin Shotton

Born October 18, 1884, Brownhelm, Ohio; died July 29, 1962, Lake Wales, Florida; Philadelphia Phillies, November 7, 1927–February 23, 1934; Cincinnati Reds, 1934; Brooklyn Dodgers, April 18, 1947–April 21, 1948; July 16, 1948–November 28, 1950

Burt Shotton gained fame as the manager of the Brooklyn Dodgers in the late 1940s, but that would have never happened if not for a relationship that developed 30 years earlier. Shotton was an outfielder and leadoff hitter for the St. Louis Browns from 1909 through 1917, then played a year with the Washington Senators and finished his career with the St. Louis Cardinals from 1919 to 1923. His manager on the Cardinals was Branch Rickey, who for religious reasons refused to work on Sundays, so he had his prize outfielder, Shotton, run the team. Shotton got his first full-time managing experience with the Philadelphia Phillies from 1928 to 1933, a time period in which Phillie management did little to improve a team that was not competitive. He served as interim manager for one game for the Cincinnati Reds in 1934. In 1947, his old friend Rickey called him to help out in a tough situation. Rickey had brought Jackie Robinson to the major leagues, breaking the segregation barrier. But Brooklyn manager Leo Durocher was suspended for a year by commissioner Happy Chandler for Durocher's alleged association with gamblers. Rickey asked Shotton to come out of retirement and manage the Dodgers. Shotton, 62 years old at the time, agreed. Standing in the dugout each game in a suit, bow tie, and usually a straw hat, Shotton guided a young ball club that developed into the famed "Boys of Summer" of the 1950s — Robinson, Roy Campanella, Gil Hodges, Duke Snider and the veteran PeeWee Reese at shortstop. The Dodgers won 93 games and won the National League pennant. They lost the World Series to the New York Yankees in seven games, a series highlighted by Yankee pitcher Bill Bevens' near no-hitter, broken up by Cookie Lavagetto in the ninth inning, and by Al Gionfriddo's great catch at the center-field fence on a drive hit by Joe DiMaggio. Shotton played a hunch in sending up Lavagetto in the ninth inning against Bevens. Lavagetto had only 18 hits all season and was released after the World Series, never to play in the major leagues again. Yet Shotton sent him up to pinch hit for Eddie Stanky, and Lavagetto lashed the game-winning double that broke up the no-hitter.

Durocher came back in 1948 but shocked the baseball world by leaving in mid-season to become manager of the arch-rival New York Giants. Once again, Rickey called his friend Shotton and once again Shotton returned to the Dodger dugout. Under his direction the club moved from fifth place, where they were perched when Durocher quit, to a third-place finish. In 1949, the Dodgers won the pennant again and again lost to the Yankees in the World Series. In 1950, the Dodgers were eliminated on the last day of the season when Dick Sisler hit a 10th-inning home run to give the championship to the Philadelphia Phillies. Shotton then retired.

He was a soft-spoken man who knew baseball and had learned a lot of the tricks of the trade from his mentor, Rickey. When Shotton was managing the Phillies, team management unloaded some top players in order to get some cash. Rickey was one of the prime purchasers. When he was managing the Dodgers, he had a calming effect on the young, inexperienced ballplayers. Players recalled that he would hold meetings before each game to go over the opposition's lineup. At the end of those sessions, he would divert into telling old baseball stories that were like fireside chats for his young, eager troops.

Year	Team	Record	Pct.	Standing
1928	Phil (N)	43–109	.283	Eighth
1929	Phil	71–82	.464	Fifth
1930	Phil	52–102	.338	Eighth
1931	Phil	66–88	.429	Sixth
1932	Phil	78–76	.506	Fifth
1933	Phil	60–92	.395	Seventh
1934	Cin	1–0	1.000	Eighth
1947	Brklyn	93–60	.608	First
1948	Brklyn	47–32	.595	Third
1949	Brklyn	97–57	.630	First
1950	Brklyn	89–65	.578	Second
11 years		**697–763**		

WORLD SERIES

Year	Team	Record	Pct.
1947	Brklyn	3–4	.429
1949	Brklyn	1–4	.200
2 years		**4–8**	**.333**

William Nathaniel "Bucky" Showalter

Born May 23, 1957, DeFuniak, Florida; New York Yankees, October 29, 1991–October 31, 1995; Arizona Diamondbacks, November 15, 1995–October 1, 2000

Bucky Showalter managed the New York Yankees for four seasons and had a first-place finish, two second-place finishes and a fourth-place finish to show for it. Unfortunately for him, the first-place finish was in the strike-shortened 1994 season, so he didn't have the chance to get to the World Series. Also unfortunate for him was that George Steinbrenner did not rehire him after his second-place showing in 1995, even though the Yankees made it to the divisional playoffs before losing to the Seattle Mariners. Showalter was then hired as manager of the expansion Arizona Diamondbacks, more than a year before they played their first game. They finished fifth in their first year. In 1999, bolstered with the acquisition of ace left-hander Randy Johnson, the Diamondbacks won the National League West but lost to San Diego in the divisional playoffs.

With the Yankees, Showalter tended to not take chances, to go with a set lineup and to make few substitutions. One situation in which he deviated from his norm is when he used starter Jack McDowell in relief in the 1995 league championship series against

Cleveland. McDowell, who had started the day before, made his first major league relief appearance but eventually lost the game.

Year	Team	Record	Pct.	Standing
1992	NY (A)	76–86	.469	Fourth
1993	NY	88–74	.543	Second
1994	NY	70–43	.619	First
1995	NY	79–65	.549	Second
1998	Ariz	65–97	.401	Fifth
1999	Ariz	100–62	.617	First
6 years		**478–427**	**.528**	

DIVISIONAL PLAYOFFS

Year	Team	Record	Pct.
1995	NY (A)	2–3	.400

Kenneth Joseph Silvestri

Born May 3, 1916, Chicago, Illinois; died March 31, 1992, Tallahassee, Florida; Atlanta Braves, September 30, 1967–October 7, 1967

Ken Silvestri, a backup catcher who appeared in 102 games over an eight-year period, was a coach for the Atlanta Braves when he was called on to finish the 1967 season after Billy Hitchcock had been fired as manager. The Braves lost three games under his direction. Lum Harris took over as manager in 1968.

Year	Team	Record	Pct.	Standing
1967	Atl	0–3	.000	Seventh

Joseph S. Simmons

Born June 13, 1845, New York, New York; date of death unknown; Keokuk Westerns, 1875; Wilmington Quicksteps, 1884

Joe Simmons had a rough ride as manager of the Keokuk and Wilmington teams. His ball club lost 25 of the 28 games he managed, giving him a winning percentage of .097 as a manager.

Year	Team	Record	Pct.	Standing
1875	Keokuk	1–12	.077	Thirteenth
1884	Wil	2–16	.111	Twelfth
2 years		**3–28**	**.097**	

Lewis Simmons

Born August 27, 1838, New Castle, Pennsylvania; died September 2, 1911, Jamestown, Pennsylvania; Philadelphia Athletics, 1882, 1883, 1886

Lew Simmons had an unusual career. He started the 1882 season as manager of the Philadelphia ball club in the American Association but was replaced with his team in third place, sporting a 20–19 record. He was rehired at the start of the 1883 season and won the championship as Philadelphia won more than twice as many as they lost. But

Simmons was replaced as manager for the 1884 season. In 1886, he was hired by Philadelphia for the third time but was fired in mid-season. He never managed again.

Year	Team	Record	Pct.	Standing
1882	Phil (AA)	20–19	.533	Third
1883	Phil	66–32	.673	First
1886	Phil	41–55	.427	Sixth
3 years		**127–106**	**.545**	

Richard Allan Sisler

Born November 2, 1920, St. Louis, Missouri; Cincinnati Reds, August 13, 1964–October 4, 1965

Dick Sisler, son of Hall of Famer George Sisler, was a major league first baseman who hit the game-winning home run against Brooklyn to propel the Philadelphia Phillie "Whiz Kids" into the 1950 World Series. Sisler was a coach with Cincinnati in 1964 when he was called on to manage the team for Fred Hutchinson, who was very ill and who died of cancer later that year. Under Sisler, the Reds went 32–21 and finished second in the year of the great Phillie fold. Philadelphia lost 11 of its last 12 games, giving both the Reds and the Cardinals the chance to overtake them. St. Louis won the pennant, finishing one game ahead of the Reds. One of the games that started the Phillies' slide was against Sisler's Reds. Rookie Chico Ruiz stole home for the only run of the game. In 1965, Sisler managed for the full season, but the Reds fell to fourth. Don Heffner replaced Sisler as manager in 1967.

Year	Team	Record	Pct.	Standing
1964	Cin	32–21	.604	Second
1965	Cin	89–73	.549	Fourth
2 years		**121–94**	**.563**	

George Harold Sisler

Born March 24, 1893, Manchester, Ohio; died March 26, 1973, St. Louis, Missouri; St. Louis Browns, 1924–October 11, 1926

George Sisler was one of baseball's greatest hitters. In 15 seasons, most of them with the St. Louis Browns, he had a lifetime batting average of .340 and hit over .400 in a season twice. He served as player-manager in three of those years but was fired after a seventh-place finish in 1926.

Year	Team	Record	Pct.	Standing
1924	StL (A)	74–78	.487	Fourth
1925	StL	82–71	.536	Third
1926	StL	62–92	.403	Seventh
3 years		**218–241**	**.475**	

Francis Michael Skaff

Born September 30, 1913, LaCrosse, Wisconsin; died April 12, 1988, Towson, Missouri; Detroit Tigers, May 16, 1966–August 5, 1966

Frank Skaff was the third of three managers for the Detroit Tigers in 1966. Chuck

Dressen began the season but was replaced by Bob Swift after 26 games. At mid-season, Swift was replaced by Skaff, who guided the Tigers to a 40–39 record the rest of the way, maintaining the third-place position he inherited. In 1967, Mayo Smith took over as manager.

Year	Team	Record	Pct.	Standing
1966	Det	40–39	.506	Third

Joel Patrick Skinner

Born February 21, 1961, LaJulia, California; Cleveland Indians, July 11, 2002–present

With all things seeming to indicate that the post–Municipal Stadium boom years of Cleveland baseball were coming to an end, Charlie Manuel asked ownership for a show of good faith — word that he was their manager for the future. When he didn't get the assurance he sought, Manual stepped down and was replaced by Joel Skinner, his third-base coach, on an interim basis.

Robert Ralph Skinner

Born October 3, 1931, La Jolla, California; Philadelphia Phillies, June 16, 1968–August 7, 1969; San Diego Padres, May 29, 1977

Bob Skinner took over the reins of the Philadelphia Phillies in 1968, ending Gene Mauch's long tenure in Philadelphia. Skinner, an outfielder who played most of his career with the Pittsburgh Pirates, saw the Phillies' fortunes fall in the second half of the season, as the club skidded from fifth place to eighth place after Mauch's dismissal. In 1969, things weren't much better when Skinner was relieved of his duties after 108 games. Eight years later, he was called on to manage the San Diego Padres on an interim basis for one game.

Year	Team	Record	Pct.	Standing
1968	Phil	48–59	.449	Eighth
1969	Phil	44–64	.407	Fifth
1977	SD	1–0	1.000	Fifth
3 years		**93–123**	**.431**	

John Terrence Slattery

Born January 6, 1877, Boston, Massachusetts; died July 17, 1949, Boston; Boston Braves, November 2, 1927–May 23, 1928

Jack Slattery can lay claim to being one of the first catchers in the American League. He appeared in one game for the Boston Red Sox in 1901, the league's first year. He then played in 102 games over the next six years before retiring as a player. In 1928, his hometown Boston Braves had hit on tough times. Mired in the second division, Slattery was hired to replace Dave Bancroft as manager. But when the Braves won only 11 of their first 31 games, Slattery was dismissed and was replaced by Rogers Hornsby who didn't fare much better. The Braves finished seventh. Slattery's managerial career was also finished.

Year	Team	Record	Pct.	Standing
1928	Bos (N)	11–20	.355	Seventh

Edward Mayo Smith

Born January 17, 1915, New London, Missouri; died November 24, 1977, Boynton Beach, Florida; Philadelphia Phillies, October 15, 1954–July 22, 1958; Cincinnati Reds, September 29, 1958–July 8, 1959; Detroit Tigers, October 3, 1966–October 2, 1970

Mayo Smith managed in the major leagues for nine years but is remembered primarily for one of them, the 1968 season in which his Detroit Tigers won the American League pennant and then beat the St. Louis Cardinals in the World Series. Smith, who played one year in the major leagues as an outfielder for the Philadelphia Phillies in 1945, was hired to manage the Phillies ten years later. The Phillies had won the pennant in 1950 but hadn't come close since then. They won 59 games for Jimmy Dykes in 1953 and 75 for Steve O'Neill and Terry Moore in 1954. In Smith's first year, buoyed by batting championship Richie Ashburn's .338 average and Robin Roberts' league-high 23 wins, the Phillies climbed to .500 at 77–77. They won 73 games in 1956 and were back at .500 in 1957 as Jack Sanford won 19 games and earned Rookie of the Year honors. But in 1958, when the Phillies continued their every-other-year swoon, Smith was fired and replaced by Eddie Sawyer at about mid-season. Cincinnati hired him to manage the Reds in 1959 but released him after 80 games in favor of Fred Hutchinson. Smith's record at Philadelphia was good, considering he was not well respected by his players. Several, including Del Ennis, Ed Bouchee, and Frankie Baumholtz criticized him for not communicating well with his players and, in particular, for not giving young players words of encouragement. Some Cincinnati players, including young hurler Jim O'Toole, had the same criticism of Smith in his short stay with the Reds.

Smith's next opportunity came with the Tigers in 1967, and he guided them to 91 wins and a second-place finish in a season in which four teams had a chance to win the pennant going into the last weekend of the season. The 1968 season was Smith's finest. Denny McLain became the last pitcher in the major leagues to win 30 games—he won 31—and the Tigers won their first pennant since 1945. They had a powerful lineup that included future Hall of Famer Al Kaline in right field, Willie Horton in left field, Norm Cash at first base and Bill Freehan behind the plate. If the Tigers had a weakness offensively, it was at shortstop, where Ray Oyler hit .135 and Tom Matchick hit .203. Kaline was hit by a pitch in mid-season and was sidelined for several weeks. Smith went with an outfield of Horton in left, Mickey Stanley in center and Jim Northrup in right. Northrup hit 21 home runs and drove in 90 runs as Kaline's replacement. So when Kaline returned to the lineup, Smith had to do some juggling. He moved Stanley, a great fielder, to shortstop, to keep him in the lineup and still get Kaline back in. Stanley finished the season at short and played all seven games of the World Series at his new position. Stanley had 11 home runs and 59 runs batted in for the year. Oyler and Matchick combined for four home runs and 26 RBIs. Another strategic Smith move paid off in the World Series. McLain had won 31 games during the regular season. Mickey Lolich, a portly left-hander, was a 17-game winner. McLain was not scheduled to start the first game of the World Series because it would have given him less rest than Lolich. Smith could have started McLain on short rest to put him in line to start three games, if necessary. Instead, he went with Lolich. Lolich was 3–0 with a 1.67 earned run average in the Series. He also hit the only home run of his career. McLain struggled and was 1–2 in the World Series, giving up 18 hits in 16⅔ innings. Smith managed the Tigers for two more years before retiring.

Year	Team	Record	Pct.	Standing
1955	Phil	77–77	.500	Sixth
1956	Phil	71–83	.461	Fifth
1957	Phil	77–77	.500	Fifth
1958	Phil	39–44	.470	Eighth
1959	Cin	35–45	.438	Fifth
1967	Det	91–71	.562	Second
1968	Det	103–59	.636	First
1969	Det	90–72	.556	Second
1970	Det	79–83	.488	Fourth
9 years		**662–611**	**.520**	

WORLD SERIES

Year	Team	Record	Pct.
1968	Det	4–3	.571

George Henry "Heinie" Smith

Born October 24, 1871, Pittsburgh, Pennsylvania; died June 25, 1939, Buffalo, New York; Boston Braves, 1902

Heinie Smith had a brief exposure to managing, and it wasn't a pleasant one. Under his direction, the New York Giants lost 22 of 27 games in 1902, putting an end to Smith's managerial career.

Year	Team	Record	Pct.	Standing
1902	NY (N)	5–22	.156	Eighth

Harry T. Smith

Born October 31, 1874, Yorkshire, England; died February 17, 1933, Salem, New Jersey; Boston Braves, April, 26, 1909–June 1909

Harry Smith, a utility catcher in his playing days, had the unenviable task of picking up the pieces when Boston started the 1909 season at 23–55 under Frank Bowerman. When Bowerman was fired, Smith led the ball club the rest of the way and compiled almost the identical record. Smith's troops were 22–53.

Year	Team	Record	Pct.	Standing
1909	Bos (N)	22–53	.293	Eighth

William J. Smith

Date of birth unknown; died August 9, 1886, Baltimore, Maryland; Baltimore Marylands, 1873

In Bill Smith's only year in professional baseball, he did a little bit of everything. He played infield and outfield for the Baltimore Marylands and managed the team for five games. One thing he didn't do was win a game as manager.

Year	Team	Record	Pct.	Standing
1873	Bal	0–5	.000	Ninth

Charles N. "Pop" Snyder

Born October 6, 1854, Washington, D.C.; died October 29, 1924, Washington; Cincinnati Red Stockings, 1882–1884; Washington Senators, 1891

Pop Snyder was a catcher for 15 years with seven different teams between 1876 and 1891. He wasn't much of a hitter but was considered one of baseball's best catchers of the 19th century. He played in 90 percent of his team's games over his career and developed hand signals from behind the plate to communicate with his pitcher and with fielders. He was player-manager for Cincinnati for three seasons and played in eight games for Washington while managing that club seven years later. He had much greater success in Cincinnati, where he was playing more regularly than in Washington, with whom he spent most of his time in the dugout managing. Snyder was lauded in his day for his knowledge of the game and for teaching and stressing fundamentals. When his playing and managing days were over, Snyder umpired for several years.

Year	Team	Record	Pct.	Standing
1882	Cin	55–25	.688	First
1883	Cin	61–37	.622	Third
1884	Cin	25–16	.610	Fourth
1891	Wash	23–46	.333	Eighth
4 years		**164–124**	**.569**	

James R. Snyder

Born August 15, 1932, Dearborn, Michigan; Seattle Mariners, June 6, 1988–November 7, 1988

Jim Snyder had a brief major league playing career — 41 games over three seasons as a utility infielder for the Minnesota Twins between 1961 and 1964. His only venture into major league managing came in 1988 when he completed the season that Dick Williams had started as Mariners manager. Seattle finished seventh.

Year	Team	Record	Pct.	Standing
1988	Sea	45–60	.429	Seventh

Allen Sutton Sothoron

Born April 29, 1893, Laura, Ohio; died June 17, 1939, St. Louis, Missouri; St. Louis Browns, September 21–25, 1933

Al Sothoron filled in as manager of the St. Louis Browns in 1933, sandwiched between Bill Killefer and Rogers Hornsby. He managed for four games and the Browns lost three of them.

Year	Team	Record	Pct.	Standing
1933	StL (A)	1–3	.250	Eighth

William Harrison Southworth

Born March 9, 1893, Harvard, Nebraska; died November 15, 1969, Columbus, Ohio; St. Louis Cardinals, November 21, 1928–July 23, 1929; June 13, 1940–November 6, 1945; Boston Braves, November 6, 1945–August 15, 1949; October 1, 1949–June 19, 1951

Billy Southworth was a manager who lived and died on fundamentals. He believed in using his entire roster and therefore platooned frequently. No manager in baseball history bunted more than Southworth. His St. Louis Cardinals teams led the National League in bunting for four consecutive years, 1941–1944, and again in 1947 and 1948 with the Boston Braves. Southworth believed in encouraging players and did not second-guess them. He was the most successful manager of the 1940s, and unlike other great managers such as Connie Mack, John McGraw, and Casey Stengel, Southworth won championships with two different teams, never changing his style. Whereas some modern managers such as Earl Weaver don't believe in sacrifice bunts because they represent an out every time, Southworth believed in pushing a run across early in a game to put the pressure on the opponent. His teams bunted, they hit behind runners, they executed the hit-and-run. And they won. His St. Louis Cardinals won 106 games in 1942 and 105 each in 1943 and 1944. In 1946, Southworth moved to the Boston Braves. Within two years, the Braves were in the World Series with a pitching staff remembered best for its top two starting pitchers, Warren Spahn and Johnny Sain (they of "Spahn and Sain and pray for rain"). The team led the league in sacrifice bunts.

Southworth got his first chance at managing in 1929 when Cardinals owner Sam Breadon fired Bill McKechnie, who had led the Cardinals to the pennant in 1928 but failed to bring home the World Series. A disappointed Breadon named Southworth, a veteran outfielder, to manage the team. When the Cardinals faltered early in 1929, Breadon made a quick adjustment and brought back McKechnie. Southworth managed in the minor leagues for several years and was at the Cardinals' top farm club in Rochester when he was named once again as Cardinal manager in 1940. This time Southworth was the beneficiary of the impatience of Cardinal management. Ray Blades had managed St. Louis to a second-place finish in 1939 with 92 wins. In 1940, the Cardinals were sluggish at the start of the season and Blades got a quick dismissal after 39 games and a 15–24 record. Under Southworth, the Cardinals rebounded, won 84 games, and finished third. In 1941, Southworth's first full season, St. Louis moved up to second place. In that year, Southworth started working a youngster into his lineup who he thought had great potential — Stan Musial. By 1942, Musial was a regular and on his way to 3,630 career hits and seven batting titles. And the Cardinals were the dominant team in the National League.

The "Spahn and Sain and pray for rain" phrase came about as the result of Southworth's decision in the 1948 stretch drive to pitch Spahn and Sain with two days' rest. Sain started nine games in September and won eight of them. The Braves lost the World Series to the Cleveland Indians in six games.

Southworth had one drawback as a manager. He was a heavy drinker and it sometimes affected his relationship with his players. When he became manager of the Braves, he arranged trades for three Cardinal players whom Brave players thought were his drinking buddies. Southworth's drinking problems increased after his son, who was a pilot, was killed in a plane crash. In 1949, Southworth was on the verge of a nervous breakdown when Braves owner Lou Perini persuaded him to take some time off. Johnny Cooney filled in as manager. Southworth returned to manage again in 1950 and 1951 but was replaced at mid-season in 1951. In his 13 seasons as a major league manager, Southworth's teams finished first four times, second twice and third once.

Year	Team	Record	Pct.	Standing
1929	StL (N)	43–45	.489	Fourth
1940	StL	69–40	.633	Seventh

Year	Team	Record	Pct.	Standing
1941	StL	97–56	.634	Second
1942	StL	106–48	.688	First
1943	StL	105–49	.682	First
1944	StL	105–49	.682	First
1945	StL	95–59	.617	Second
1946	StL	81–72	.529	Fourth
1947	Bos (N)	86–68	.558	Third
1948	Bos	91–62	.595	First
1949	Bos	55–54	.505	Fourth
1950	Bos	83–79	.539	Fourth
1951	Bos	28–31	.475	Fifth
13 years		**1044–704**	**.597**	

WORLD SERIES

Year	Team	Record	Pct.
1942	StL (N)	4–1	.800
1943	StL	1–4	.200
1944	StL	4–2	.600
1948	Bos	2–4	.333
4 years		**11–11**	**.500**

Albert Goodwill Spalding

Albert Spalding

Born September 2, 1850, Byron, Illinois; died September 9, 1915, Point Loma, California; Chicago White Stockings, 1876–1877

In 1876, Albert Spalding won 47 games on the mound and engineered 5 more from the dugout, becoming the first player-manager in the National League. His Chicago White Stockings, forerunner to the Cubs, sprinted to a first-place finish in the National League's first year, 1876. Despite his potential as a pitcher, Spalding won only one more game in the next two years as he became more and more interested in the business side of baseball. He was a staunch proponent of clean living and actively campaigned against gambling and other potential problems in baseball. In 1888, Spalding organized the first world tour of baseball, taking two teams on a tour of 14 countries. Before he left on the tour, he had started the sporting goods company that bears his name today. In 1901, baseball executives asked him to intervene in a dispute between the National League and a group that was forming to compete with it. Spalding met with Ban Johnson, Charles Comiskey and National League officials and worked out an agreement. The result was the formation of the American League. Spalding was a success in most of his ventures, including his brief stint as a manager. The White Stockings won the championship in the National League's first year.

Year	Team	Record	Pct.	Standing
1876	Chi (N)	52–14	.788	First
1877	Chi	26–33	.441	Fifth
2 years		**78–47**	**.624**	

Tristram E. Speaker

Born April 4, 1888, Hubbard, Texas; died December 8, 1958, Lake Whitney, Texas; Cleveland Indians, June 12, 1919–October 1, 1926

Tris Speaker was one of the greatest hitters in baseball history. He had 3,515 career hits and hit more doubles than anyone in baseball history — 793. His 223 triples are sixth highest. Speaker was a brash ballplayer. When he was traded from the Boston Red Sox to the Cleveland Indians in 1915, Boston got $50,000 as part of the deal. Speaker refused to report unless he got $10,000 of the money. He got it. Speaker became the Indians player-manager in 1919. The next year, he led the Indians to their first American League pennant, helped greatly by his .388 batting average.

As Cleveland manager, Speaker was known for his fiery spirit, his imaginative dealings with some of his ballplayers and his platooning. When the Indians acquired Ray Caldwell, a big right-handed pitcher who had serious drinking problems when he was with the Yankees and Red Sox, Speaker made him sign a contract that allowed him to get drunk after ball games he pitched in but he could not drink any other time during the season. Caldwell won 20 games in his first year under that contract. Speaker's Indians did well in the last half of the 1919 season but were no match for the Chicago White Sox. As the 1920 season approached, Speaker began fiddling with his roster. Jack Graney had been a regular in the Cleveland outfield for several years. In 1920, he appeared in only 62 games because Speaker replaced him with Charlie Jamieson. Then he platooned

Jamieson, a left-handed batter, with Doc Evans, a right-handed batter. Evans hit .349 in 55 games. Jamieson hit .319 in 108 games. He also platooned Elmer Smith and Joe Wood in right field and Doc Johnston and George Burns at first base. The Indians won the American League championship and then defeated Wilbert Robinson's Brooklyn Dodgers in the World Series. Speaker never won another pennant, but finished second three times and third once, in addition to his championship, in eight years as Cleveland manager. Not long after he retired as manager, Speaker and Tiger great Ty Cobb were accused of conspiring to fix a ball game in which both had participated in 1919. The allegation was made by Dutch Leonard, a pitcher Speaker had released and Cobb had declined to sign when he managed the Tigers. Commissioner Kenesaw Mountain Landis, who several years earlier had banned eight Chicago White Sox

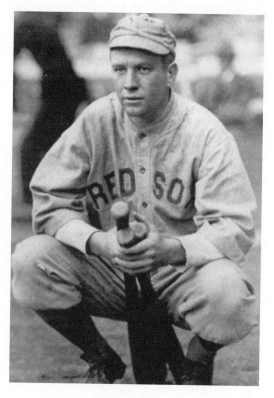

Tris Speaker

players for similar offenses in the 1919 World Series, exonerated both Cobb and Speaker for lack of evidence to substantiate the allegation.

Year	Team	Record	Pct.	Standing
1919	Cleve	39–21	.650	Second
1920	Cleve	98–56	.636	First
1921	Cleve	94–60	.610	Second
1922	Cleve	78–76	.506	Fourth
1923	Cleve	82–71	.536	Third
1924	Cleve	67–86	.438	Sixth
1925	Cleve	70–84	.455	Sixth
1926	Cleve	88–66	.571	Second
8 years		**616–520**	**.542**	

WORLD SERIES

Year	Team	Record	Pct.
1920	Cleve	5–2	.714

Harrison L. Spence

Born February 2, 1856, Virginia; died May 17, 1908, Chicago, Illinois; Indianapolis Hoosiers, 1888

Harry Spence managed the Indianapolis entry in the National League in 1888 but could win only 50 of 135 games. Indianapolis ended the season in seventh place. Spence's managerial career was also at an end.

Year	Team	Record	Pct.	Standing
1888	Ind (N)	50–85	.370	Seventh

Charles Sylvester "Chick" Stahl

Born January 10, 1873, Fort Wayne, Indiana; died March 28, 1907, West Baden, Indiana; Boston Red Sox, 1906–March 28, 1907

Chick Stahl managed the Boston Red Sox for the last 18 games of the 1906 baseball season. The ball club won only five, finishing in last place. On March 28, 1907, about two weeks before the start of the next season, Stahl committed suicide by drinking carbolic acid during spring training.

Year	Team	Record	Pct.	Standing
1906	Bos (A)	5–13	.278	Eighth

Garland "Jake" Stahl

Born April 13, 1879, Elkhart, Indiana; died September 18, 1922, Los Angeles, California; Washington Senators, 1905–1906; Boston Red Sox, 1912–July 15, 1913

Jake Stahl, younger brother of Chick Stahl, managed one of baseball's best teams in the early part of the 20th century. His 1912 Boston Red Sox club won 105 games behind the pitching of Joe Wood, who was 34–5, and two 20-game winners, Hugh Bedient and Buck O'Brien. Tris Speaker, the centerfielder, hit .383 and led the American League in home runs with 10. Stahl was the first baseman. In 1913, the Red Sox slipped and Stahl was replaced as manager by catcher Bill Carrigan as the Red Sox finished fourth. Had Stahl been able stay on for another year, he would have had the benefit of a burly left-hander named Babe Ruth. By 1915, Ruth was one of the dominant pitchers in the American League, and the Red Sox won the pennant under Carrigan. Stahl, who managed Washington for two years early in his career, never managed again.

Year	Team	Record	Pct.	Standing
1905	Wash	64–87	.424	Seventh
1906	Wash	55–95	.367	Seventh
1912	Bos (A)	105–47	.691	First
1913	Bos	39–41	.488	Fourth
4 years		**263–270**	**.493**	

WORLD SERIES

Year	Team	Record	Pct.
1912	Bos	4–3	.571

George Tweedy Stallings

Born November 17, 1867, Augusta, Georgia; died May 13, 1929, Haddock, Georgia; Philadelphia Phillies, 1897–June 18, 1898; Detroit Tigers, 1901; New York Yankees, 1909–September 23, 1910; Boston Braves, 1913–December 18, 1920

George Stallings was one of the most colorful managers of his era, an era that included John McGraw, Wilbert Robinson, Charles Comiskey and Connie Mack. Stallings was tough, foul-mouthed and sarcastic — not well liked by many of the players on the teams he managed but respected by most of them. He is best known for being the manager of the 1914 "Miracle Braves," a team that was in last place on July 4 but roared through August and September to win the National League pennant by 10½ games and then swept Mack's A's in the World Series. Mack was so demoralized by the drubbing that he unloaded many of his top players. It took him almost 15 years to build another winner.

Stallings was a player-manager for the Philadelphia Phillies in 1897 and 1898, but managed more than he played. The son of a Confederate general and educated at a military institute, he ran his ball clubs as if he was a drill sergeant and his ballplayers were recruits. Even in his early years, Stallings approached the game as all-out war, wherein no maneuver was unfit so long as it afforded him some advantage. In 1898, a Cincinnati coach got his spikes caught in a wire in the ground by the coaching box. When he began pulling the wire up, he discovered that it led into the Phillie clubhouse. A Philadelphia reserve catcher was in the clubhouse, looking out a window onto the field, trying to steal the opposing catcher's signals. He would then tap on the wire, in Morse code fashion, to let the third base coach know what pitch was coming. Even when Phillie hitters knew what pitch was coming, they didn't hit it often enough. Philadelphia finished tenth and seventh in Stallings' two years. In 1898, his heavy-handed tactics led to a player revolt and Stallings was fired. In 1901, he resurfaced as the first manager of the Detroit Tigers but he lasted there only one year. His next stop was with the New York Highlanders, forerunner of the Yankees, in 1909 and 1910. The Highlanders had finished last in 1908. Under Stallings, they moved up to fifth in 1909 and to second in 1910, though he was fired with 11 games left in the season. First baseman

Hal Chase, a controversial figure in his own right because of his suspected gambling on ball games, undermined Stallings with team president Frank Farrell, convincing him to get rid of Stallings and to name him as manager. Farrell did, and the Yankees finished seventh in Chase's one full year as manager.

Three years later, Stallings was named manager of the Boston Braves, where he stayed eight years and then retired. He described his 1914 Braves team as "one .300 hitter, the worst outfield that ever flirted with sudden death, three pitchers, and a good working combination around second base." The .300 hitter was outfielder Joe Connolly, who hit .306. The three pitchers were Dick Rudolph, Bill James and Lefty Tyler, none of them household names then or now but who won 69 games between them. The middle infield combination was rookie Rabbit Maranville at shortstop and veteran second baseman Johnny Evers, who had played on the Chicago Cubs championship teams. Maranville, Evers and first baseman Butch Schmidt led the league in executing double plays and were by some accounts more proficient than the Tinker-to-Evers-to-Chance combination made famous by the Franklin Adams poem nearly a decade earlier.

Stallings wasn't happy with the production he was getting from his outfield in 1914 and began platooning at all three positions. Connolly, Larry Gilbert and Les Mann were the starting outfielders. But Ted Cather, acquired in mid-season from St. Louis, hit .297 in 50 games, and Herbie Moran, acquired from Cincinnati, hit .266 in 41 games, each of them platooning in all three outfield positions. Use of the five outfielders gave Stallings an added offensive punch. He juggled his lineup to get lefty-righty advantages over opposing pitching and knew which of his outfielders hit best against certain pitchers. While other managers had platooned from time to time, no one had done it with the consistency or success that Stallings did in 1914. He is credited with being the first master of platooning.

Stallings' short fuse was often lit when his pitchers became wild and put runners on base via walks. He died of heart disease nine years after he retired. Reportedly, when his health was deteriorating rapidly, a friend asked him how he developed heart trouble. "Oh, those bases on balls," said Stallings.

Year	Team	Record	Pct.	Standing
1897	Phil (N)	55–77	.417	Tenth
1898	Phil	19–27	.413	Eighth
1901	Det	74–61	.548	Third
1909	NY (A)	74–77	.490	Fifth
1910	NY	79–61	.564	Second
1913	Bos (N)	69–82	.457	Fifth
1914	Bos	94–59	.614	First
1915	Bos	83–69	.546	Second
1916	Bos	89–63	.586	Third
1917	Bos	72–81	.471	Sixth
1918	Bos	53–71	.427	Seventh
1919	Bos	57–82	.410	Sixth
1920	Bos	62–90	.408	Seventh
13 years		**880–900**	**.494**	

WORLD SERIES

Year	Team	Record	Pct.
1914	Bos	4–0	1.000

Edward Raymond Stanky

Born September 3, 1916, Philadelphia, Pennsylvania; died June 7, 1999, Mobile, Alabama; St. Louis Cardinals, December 10, 1951–May 28, 1955; Chicago White Sox, December 14, 1965–July 12, 1968; Texas Rangers, June 22, 1977

Eddie Stanky, known as "The Brat" during his playing days because of his scrappy, brash style, brought that same spirit to his approach to managing. As manager of the Chicago White Sox, he once refused to allow Vice President Hubert Humphrey into the Chicago clubhouse after a tough loss to the Minnesota Twins. He managed the St. Louis Cardinals for parts of four years and the Chicago White Sox for parts of three. Stanky had been retired for nine years when the Texas Rangers persuaded him to put on a uniform again and manage the Rangers. Stanky managed in one game, won it, and quit.

He was an infielder for 11 years with five National League teams. He broke in with the Chicago Cubs in 1943. Stanky was on the Brooklyn Dodgers in 1947, the year Jackie Robinson broke in and played in the World Series for the Dodgers. Brooklyn then traded Stanky to Boston, and he played in the World Series for the Braves in 1948. Three years later, he was in the World Series again, this time with the New York Giants, who got there by beating Brooklyn on Bobby Thomson's famous home run. He ended his career with the St. Louis Cardinals and became their manager in 1953.

Stanky was a full-contact type of player and a full-contact type of manager. He wanted his players to make contact with the opponent, slide hard, break up double plays and generally be in the other guy's face. Tom McCraw, who played first base for Stanky's White Sox, said Stanky taught White Sox players, in breaking up double plays, to always slide to the side of second base that the ball was hit to, putting the base runner in the path of the fielder coming over to make the play or who was tossing the ball for the force out. Either way, it was the best chance for the runner to take out the fielder — to make contact, according to Stanky. Another Stanky rule on the White Sox: pitchers were fined $50 if they didn't throw at a hitter when Stanky ordered it. Contact, once again.

Hank Sauer, a slugger for the Cubs when Stanky was managing the Cardinals, said he was hit by Cardinal pitches nine times in one year, most of the time with first base open (when an intentional walk would have served the same purpose). Sauer said the Cardinal pitchers were throwing at him on Stanky's orders.

In 1967, the White Sox were in first place much of the year, despite an anemic lineup in which Pete Ward led the offense with 18 home runs and 62 runs batted in and Don Buford and Ken Berry were the top hitters, both with .261 batting averages. But starting pitchers Gary Peters, Joel Horlen and Tommy John all had earned run averages under 2.50, and Hoyt Wilhem and Bobby Locker had 32 saves between them. Going into the last five games of the season, four teams still had a chance to win the pennant: the White Sox, Detroit, Boston and Minnesota. Chicago was given the best chance because they had two games with lowly Kansas City and three games with equally lowly Washington. The White Sox lost all five and Boston emerged on the final day as the American League champion. When Chicago started the 1968 season with 10 straight losses, making it 15 in a row, counting the disastrous end to the '67 season, the Stanky "contact" style had lost some of its luster. He was fired after 79 games and replaced by the man he had replaced, Al Lopez.

Dick Schofield, an infielder on Stanky's Cardinals, may have summed up Stanky's style best when he said, "He wanted you to play as if today's game was your first or your last."

Year	Team	Record	Pct.	Standing
1952	StL	88–76	.571	Third
1953	StL	83–71	.539	Third
1954	StL	72–82	.468	Fourth
1955	StL	17–19	.472	Fifth
1966	Chi (A)	83–79	.512	Fourth
1967	Chi	89–73	.549	Fourth
1968	Chi	34–45	.430	Ninth
1977	Tex	1–0	1.000	Second
8 years		**467–435**	**.518**	

Joseph Start

Born October 14, 1842, New York, New York; died March 27, 1927, Providence, Rhode Island; New York Mutuals, 1873

Joe Start was one of the leading hitters of early professional baseball. As a first base-man–outfielder for several teams in the National Association and then the National League, Start had 1,418 hits in a 16-year career, compiling a lifetime batting average of .299. In 1873, while playing for the New York Mutuals, Start was called on to manage the team for about a month, and he did pretty well. New York won 18 of 25 games with Start at the helm.

Year	Team	Record	Pct.	Standing
1873	NY	18–7	.720	Fourth

Charles Dillon Stengel

Born July 30, 1890, Kansas City, Missouri; died September, 29, 1975, Glendale, California; Brooklyn Dodgers, February 23, 1934–October 7, 1936; Boston Braves, October 25, 1937–January 27, 1944; New York Yankees, October 12, 1948–October 18, 160; New York Mets, October 2, 1961–August 30, 1965

Casey Stengel got four hits and a walk in his first big league game in 1912. That started a major league career — or, as player and then manager, two — in which he became one of the most colorful characters in baseball history. As manager of the New York Yankees from 1949 to 1960, his teams won 10 pennants in 12 years. No other manager has equaled that success record. Prior to taking over the Yankees, Stengel managed the Brooklyn Dodgers and Boston Braves, two bad teams that left him 166 games below .500. Despite the losing record, Yankee general manager George Weiss, an old friend, thought Stengel was smart and shrewd, despite his daffy antics on the field and his penchant for double-talk. Stengel came on board at the start of the 1949 season. The Yankees won five straight World Series championships. Cleveland interrupted the Yankee string in 1954. Then, in the next six years, the Yankees won five pennants and two World Series championships. The Yankees lost to the Pittsburgh Pirates in the 1960 World Series on Bill Mazeroski's home run in the bottom of the ninth inning of the seventh game. After the Series, Stengel was fired. He told the press his bosses thought he was too old. "I'll never make the mistake of being 70 again," he said. He wasn't out of work long. In 1961, the expansion New York Mets were looking for a manager who could help develop young players and draw crowds for the team's inaugural season, 1962. Stengel was a natural. He managed the Mets for four years, never winning more than 53 games in any one season.

As a player, he once caught a bird and put it under his hat while playing in the outfield for the Pittsburgh Pirates in Brooklyn. The Dodgers had recently traded Stengel to Pittsburgh. So in his first at-bat back in Brooklyn, he came to the plate, doffed his cap to the crowd — and the bird flew out. Once in the minor leagues, Stengel noticed a manhole in the outfield grass. When he took the field between innings, he quickly removed the cover before anyone noticed and crept down inside, staying close enough to the top to see the field. When a fly ball was hit in his direction, Stengel jumped out of the manhole and caught it. In 1925, he was president, manager and outfielder for Worcester in the Eastern League. At the end of a dismal season, Stengel the manager released Stengel the outfielder and Stengel the president released Stengel the manager. Then he quit as president.

This was the type of character that Weiss took a chance on when he brought Stengel to the proud tradition of the New York Yankees. Stengel wasn't worried. He told reporters, "I know I can make people laugh and some of you think I'm a damn fool. But I got the job because the people here think I can produce."

Stengel inherited veteran players like Joe DiMaggio, but he had a great eye for young talent. He made Yogi Berra his regular catcher and brought up Billy Martin from the Yankees Oakland farm club. He started an instructional school that was held before spring training each year, a forerunner to what is now the Instructional League. He developed a knack for platooning and juggling his lineup to make sure he had the right combinations in at the right situations. It was something he learned 30 years earlier when he played for John McGraw. The Yankees succeeded because Weiss got Stengel the players he needed and Stengel knew how to use them. Players such as Hector Lopez, Joe Collins and John Blanchard would have been everyday players on other teams. They filled roles on the Yankees, Lopez as a utility infielder and pinch hitter, Collins as the backup for first baseman Bill Skowron and Blanchard as a third string catcher and pinch hitter. Blanchard is in the record book for hitting four consecutive home runs — over a period of three games, because the first two he hit as a pinch hitter. Another indication of how Stengel moved his players around: infielder Gil McDougal led the American League in fielding percentage at three different positions — third base, shortstop and second base — in consecutive seasons. At one time Stengel had three outstanding catchers — Berra, Blanchard and Elston Howard — giving him the luxury of resting Berra and still having a catcher who could handle the pitchers and hit in the clutch. He also always had veterans who could come off the bench and help win a ball game, players such as Jackie Jensen and Enos Slaughter who were good role models for the younger players and who still knew how to hit. Stengel used 262 pinch hitters in 1954, a major league record; those pinch hitters hit .292. Ever the platooner, Stengel once pinch hit for Skowron, his slugging first baseman, in the first inning of a game. The Yankees had taken a 1–0 lead on Detroit, and had the bases loaded when the Tigers made a pitching change and brought in a right-hander to pitch to the right-handed hitting Skowron. Stengel countered by sending up left-handed batter Eddie Robinson who singled in two runs. Another trait of Stengel's Yankee teams is that they were always strong up the middle. They had Berra behind the plate, Mickey Mantle in center field and pitchers such as Allie Reynolds, Vic Raschi, Eddie Lopat and Whitey Ford. While the shortstop–second base combination varied, particularly in the early 1950s, the results were almost always the same. The Yankees led the American League in double plays in five of six years between 1952 and 1957, no matter whether Rizzuto, McDougald, Jerry Coleman, Billy Martin or Bobby Richardson was on the field. Stengel wrote about the importance of double plays in his autobiography, even on how to avoid them when your team is at bat (Never have two slow-footed right-handed hitters batting back-to-back in your lineup, he enjoined). "The double plays will murder you."

In Stengel's day, Yankee Stadium had a right-field wall that was just 296 feet from home plate. The Yankees took advantage of this by always having left-handed power hitters in the lineup and good left-handed pitchers on the staff. Stengel had a remarkable quality for getting the most out of a pitcher who was having a good year—and often, it was his only good year. Bob Grim was 20–6 in 1954 and never won more than 12 after that. Johnny Kucks was 18–9 in 1956 and never won more than eight after that. Tom Sturdivant won 16 games in 1956 and 1957 and never won more than nine after that. Luis Arroyo won 15 games in relief for the 1961 Yankees. His previous high was 11 wins, and that was as a starter for St. Louis in 1955. An example of the Stengel intuition, from the 1956 World Series: Don Larsen had been rocked by the Pirates in the second game, which the Yankees lost 13–8. Larsen was not a frontline starter for the Yankees and there was no reason to believe he would be any more effective later on in the Series. But Stengel started him in Game Five, and Larsen threw the only no-hitter in World Series history, and it was a perfect game. One of the reasons Stengel achieved success is that, for all of the fun he had with the fans and the press, he didn't develop close relationships with his players. The exceptions were Berra and Martin; yet Stengel traded Martin when he thought he had become a bad influence on the rest of the team.

The most famous example of Stengel's double talk occurred when he and Mantle were called to testify before a U.S. Senate subcommittee studying whether baseball should be included in anti-trust legislation. Here is a partial transcript from the *Congressional Record* of July 9, 1958:

> SENATOR LANGER: "I want to know whether you intend to keep on monopolizing the World's Championship in New York City."
>
> MR. STENGEL: "Well, I will tell you. I got a little concerned yesterday in the first three innings when I saw the three players I had gotten rid of, and said when I lost nine, what am I going to do—and when I had a couple of my players I thought so great that did not do so good up to the sixth inning, I was more confused but I finally had to go and call on a young man in Baltimore that we don't own and the Yankees don't own him and he is doing pretty good and I would actually have to tell you that I think we are more the Greta Garbo type now from success. We are being hated, I mean from the ownership on, we are being hated. Every sport that gets too great or one individual—but if we made 27 cents and it pays to have a winner at home, why would you have a good winner in your own park if you were an owner? That is the result of baseball. An owner gets most of the money at home and it is up to him and his staff to do better or they ought to be discharged."
>
> SENATOR KEFAUVER: "Mr. Mantle, do you have any observations...?"
>
> MR. MANTLE: "My views are just about the same as Casey's."

Year	Team	Record	Pct.	Standing
1934	Brklyn	71–81	.467	Sixth
1935	Brklyn	70–83	.458	Fifth
1936	Brklyn	67–87	.435	Seventh
1938	Bos (N)	77–75	.507	Fifth

Year	Team	Record	Pct.	Standing
1939	Bos	63–88	.417	Seventh
1940	Bos	65–87	.428	Seventh
1941	Bos	62–92	.403	Seventh
1942	Bos	59–89	.399	Seventh
1943	Bos	68–85	.444	Fifth
1949	NY (A)	97–57	.630	First
1950	NY	98–56	.636	First
1951	NY	98–56	.636	First
1952	NY	95–59	.617	First
1953	NY	99–52	.656	First
1954	NY	103–51	.669	Second
1955	NY	96–58	.623	First
1956	NY	97–57	.630	First
1957	NY	98–56	.636	First
1958	NY	92–62	.597	First
1959	NY	79–75	.513	Third
1960	NY	97–57	.630	First
1962	NY (N)	40–120	.250	Tenth
1963	NY	51–111	.315	Tenth
1964	NY	53–109	.327	Tenth
1965	NY	31–64	.326	Tenth
25 years		**1926–1867**	**.508**	

WORLD SERIES

Year	Team	Record	Pct.
1949	NY (A)	4–1	.800
1950	NY	4–0	1.000
1951	NY	4–2	.667
1952	NY	4–3	.571
1953	NY	4–2	.667
1955	NY	3–4	.429
1956	NY	4–3	.571
1957	NY	3–4	.429
1958	NY	4–3	.571
1960	NY	3–4	.429
10 years		**37–26**	**.587**

George Thomas Stovall

Born November 23, 1878, Independence, Missouri; died November 5, 1951, Burlington, Iowa; Cleveland Naps, 1911; St. Louis Browns, September 8, 1912–September 7, 1913; Kansas City Packers, 1914–1915

When George Stovall was named manager of the Cleveland Naps in 1911, Cleveland management had already made arrangements, without his knowledge, to bring Philadelphia A's first baseman Harry Davis in to manage the team in 1912. So Stovall went to the St. Louis Browns, where he managed for two years, and then finished his career by managing Kansas City in the Federal League for two years. His best year was his first, when he unknowingly was a lame duck.

Year	Team	Record	Pct.	Standing
1911	Cleve	74–62	.544	Third
1912	StL (A)	41–74	.357	Seventh

Year	Team	Record	Pct.	Standing
1913	StL	50–84	.373	Eighth
1914	KC (F)	67–84	.444	Sixth
1915	KC	81–72	.529	Fourth
5 years		**313–376**	**.454**	

Harry Duffield Stovey

Born Decmber 20, 1856, Philadelphia, Pennsylvania; died September 20, 1937, New Bedford, Pennsylvania; Worcester Ruby Legs, 1881; Philadelphia Athletics, 1885

Harry Stovey played just about every position in a 14-year professional career and had two stints at managing with two different teams. In 1881, he had the Worcester team in the National League and led them to an 8–18 record. Four years later, he got another chance, this time with Philadelphia in the American Association, and fared much better, finishing two games below .500 in 112 games.

Year	Team	Record	Pct.	Standing
1881	Wor	8–18	.308	Eighth
1885	Phil (AA)	55–57	.491	Fourth
2 years		**63–75**	**.456**	

Charles Evard "Gabby" Street

Born September 30, 1882, Huntsville, Alabama; died February 6, 1951, Joplin, Missouri; St. Louis Cardinals, October 30, 1929–July 24, 1933; St. Louis Browns, May 20, 1938–November 2, 1938

Gabby Street, who spent many years of his playing career as Walter Johnson's catcher at Washington, became the sixth manager in six years to start the season with the St. Louis Cardinals. The others were Branch Rickey, Rogers Hornsby, Bob O'Farrell, Bill McKechnie and Billy Southworth. McKechnie had won the pennant with the 1928 Cardinals but lost four straight to the New York Yankees in the World Series. So owner Sam Breadon ousted McKechnie in 1929 and replaced him with Southworth. In mid-season 1929, Breadon removed Southworth. Street, a coach, filled in for two games. The Cardinals won them both. McKechnie then managed the club the rest of the way. Street was given the managerial job in 1930 and won pennants in each of his first two years. But the Cardinals dropped to sixth in 1932 and were in fifth place after 91 games in 1933 when Breadon made the decision to fire Street. He was said to have been the man for the moment when he took over the Cardinals in 1930 but had lost control of the team by the time of his departure. Frankie Frisch took over that group of uncontrollables who came to be known as the Gas House Gang. Street's last managerial duty came with the St. Louis Browns in 1938.

Year	Team	Record	Pct.	Standing
1929	StL (N)	2–0	1.000	Fourth
1930	StL	92–62	.597	First
1931	StL	101–53	.656	First
1932	StL	72–82	.468	Sixth
1933	StL	46–45	.505	Fifth
1938	StL (A)	55–97	.362	Seventh
6 years		**368–339**	**.521**	

WORLD SERIES

Year	Team	Record	Pct.
1929	StL (N)	2–4	.333
1930	StL	4–3	.571
2 years		**6–7**	**.461**

John A. Stricker

Born February 15, 1860, Philadelphia, Pennsylvania; died November 19, 1937, Philadelphia; St. Louis Browns, 1892

Like so many players of his era, John "Cub" Stricker played many positions in his 11-year career in the National Association and the National League. In 1892, while still a player, he managed St. Louis for 23 games but was able to guide his team to victory in only six of them.

Year	Team	Record	Pct.	Standing
1892	StL	6–17	.261	Ninth

George Bevan Strickland

Born January 10, 1926, New Orleans, Louisiana; Cleveland Indians, April 2, 1964–July 3, 1964; August 20, 1966–October 3, 1966

George Strickland had been a shortstop for the Cleveland Indians and was a coach for them in 1966 when he replaced Birdie Tebbetts as manager to fill out the season. He never managed again.

Year	Team	Record	Pct.	Standing
1966	Cleve	15–24	.385	Fifth

Lawrence George "Moose" Stubing

Born March 21, 1938, Bronx, New York; California Angels, September 23, 1988–November 15, 1988

Moose Stubing managed the California Angels for eight games during the 1988 season. The Angels lost all eight of them, ending Stubing's major league managing career.

Year	Team	Record	Pct.	Standing
1988	Cal	0–8	.000	Fourth

Clyde Leroy Sukeforth

Born November 30, 1901, Washington, Maine; Brooklyn Dodgers, April 15, 1947–April 17, 1945

Clyde Sukeforth was a coach for the Brooklyn Dodgers when an unusual set of circumstances placed him in the position of managing the Dodgers for two games — and one of them stands out in baseball history. Dodger manager Leo Durocher was suspended for the 1947 baseball season by commissioner Happy Chandler for his alleged association with gamblers. Burt Shotton would be the next Dodger manager. But on Opening Day, Sukeforth was at the helm — and Jackie Robinson was at first base, becoming the first black man to play major league baseball. The Dodgers won, and won the next day, too, giving Sukeforth a perfect record as manager.

Year	Team	Record	Pct.	Standing
1947	Brklyn	2–0	1.000	First

Haywood Cooper Sullivan

Born December 15, 1930, Donalsonville, Georgia; Kansas City Athletics, May 15, 1965–November 28, 1965

Haywood Sullivan caught for the Boston Red Sox and Kansas City A's in a seven-year career and then worked for both teams when his playing days were over.

When Mel McGaha started the 1965 season as A's manager with a 5–21 record, he was dismissed and Sullivan took over. But Sullivan had the same problem McGaha had: a team that had the highest earned average in the American League and the second lowest total of home runs. The A's won 54 and lost 82 for Sullivan who later became general manager of the Red Sox.

Year	Team	Record	Pct.	Standing
1965	KC	54–82	.397	Tenth

Pat Sullivan

No biographical data available; Columbus Buckeyes, 1890

Information is scant about the baseball career of Pat Sullivan. He is listed as manager of the Columbus team in the American Association for three games in 1890, and his ball club won two of them.

Year	Team	Record	Pct.	Standing
1890	Col	2–1	.667	Second

Theodore Paul Sullivan

Born in 1852, County Clare, Ireland; died July 5, 1929, Washington, D.C.; St. Louis Browns, 1883; Kansas City Cowboys, 1884; Washington Nationals, 1888

Irishman Ted Sullivan managed three different teams in three different leagues in three different years in the early days of baseball. He had his greatest success with St. Louis in the American Association and didn't fare so well with Kansas City in the Union League and Washington in the National League.

Year	Team	Record	Pct.	Standing
1883	StL (AA)	53–27	.663	Second
1884	KC (U)	16–63	.211	Eleventh
1888	Wash (N)	36–57	.387	Eighth
3 Years		**105–147**	**.417**	

William Joseph Sullivan, Sr.

Born February 1, 1875; Oakland, Wisconsin; died January 28, 1965, Newberg, Oregon; Chicago White Sox, 1909

Billy Sullivan had Big Ed Walsh on the mound but not much firepower in his one year as manager of the Chicago White Sox. Walsh had a 1.41 earned run average but just a 15–11 record, evidence of the lack of offensive support that plagued all the pitchers.

Year	Team	Record	Pct.	Standing
1909	Chi (A)	78–74	.513	Fourth

Charles Sweasy

Born November 2, 1847, Newark, New Jersey; died March 30, 1908, Newark; St. Louis Reds, 1875

One year before the National League began operation, St. Louis fielded two teams in the National Association. Charlie Sweasy managed one of them, the Reds, for 19 games, but won only four of them.

Year	Team	Record	Pct.	Standing
1875	StL (Reds)	4–15	.211	Ninth

Robert Virgil Swift

Born March 6, 1915, Salina, Kansas; died October 17, 1966, Detroit, Michigan: Detroit Tigers, August 5, 1966–October 17, 1966

Bob Swift was a major league catcher for 14 years who played with the 1945 Detroit Tiger pennant winner. But he will always be remembered in baseball lore as the Tiger catcher in August of 1951 when Eddie Gaedel, a midget, came to bat for the St. Louis Browns in a publicity stunt by Browns owner Bill Veeck. Swift got down on his knees to catch as pitcher Bob Cain delivered four high pitches for a walk to Gaedel, who was then removed for a pinch runner. In 1966, Swift was the second of three Tiger managers, serving between Chuck Dressen and Frank Skaff. He posted a respectable record but took ill and stepped down.

Year	Team	Record	Pct.	Standing
1966	Det	32–25	.561	Third

Charles William Tanner

Born July 4, 1929, New Castle, Pennsylvania; Chicago White Sox, September 14, 1970–December 17, 1975; Oakland Athletics, December 18, 1975–November 5, 1976; Pittsburgh Pirates, November 5, 1976–October 7, 1985; Atlanta Braves, October 10, 1985–May 23, 1988

Chuck Tanner managed in the major leagues for 19 years. His 1979 Pittsburgh Pirate team won the World Series. Tanner was an innovative manager who motivated his players by keeping a positive attitude and discarding the Book from time to time. He took over an awful Chicago White Sox team in 1970 that lost 106 games. They had lost 93 of them when Tanner was brought in with 16 games left in the season. He told the players that he wanted to observe, so they kept the same lineup and the same pitching rotation for the remainder of the season. He did change pitchers when necessary during ball games. The club lost 13 of the 16 games, but Tanner learned a lot. He felt the team had a few standout players. But he determined the only way to build the club up was to trade some of the frontline players for promising youngsters. He and general manager Roland Hemond engineered some two-for-one deals in which Chicago let go of veteran outfielder Ken Berry and future Hall of Famer Luis Aparicio. They inserted young ballplayers like outfielder Pat Kelly and infielders Mike Andrews and Lee "BeBe" Richards. They fit into a lineup that already had slugging third baseman Bill Melton and outfielder Carlos May. Tanner went to spring training in 1971 determined to show his ball club they could be winners. Chicago won the Grapefruit League championship with Tanner making managerial moves in every game like the World Series championship was at stake. He wanted to instill the winning spirit. He made one other strategic move in 1971, converting veteran relief pitcher Wilbur Wood into a starter. Wood won 46 games in the next two years. The White Sox improved their record by 23 games over the previous year. In 1972, they added Dick Allen to the mix and became a pennant contender. Tanner had a penchant for zany strategy. In a game at Boston, he had his two sluggers, Allen and Melton, batting first and second. In the ninth inning, they hit back-to-back home runs to win the game. The next day, they were back in their normal spots in the order. "Lightning doesn't strike twice," said Tanner. He stayed as White Sox manager for five years.

After one unfulfilling year managing Oakland, Tanner was hired by the Pittsburgh Pirates. There he displayed the same kind of attitude and enthusiasm; this time he had the talent on the field to go with it. The Pirates finished second in 1977 and 1978. In 1979, with a theme of "We Are Family," the name of a popular song of the era, the Pirates won the National League pennant and the World Series in a seven-game thriller over the Baltimore Orioles.

At Pittsburgh, Tanner showed that his approach to the game hadn't changed since his days in Chicago. He stressed his positive attitude and told his players they couldn't get depressed over a loss, that the season was too long for that. Keep yourself mentally and physically fit and good things will happen, he said. Phil Garner, who later managed the Milwaukee Brewers, played for Tanner at Oakland and at Pittsburgh. He said Tanner's managerial style was to let hitters swing away in situations where most managers would bunt; to let runners run; and to go to the bullpen fast. Tanner ended his managerial career with a three-year stint with the Atlanta Braves.

Year	Team	Record	Pct.	Standing
1970	Chi (A)	3–13	.188	Sixth
1971	Chi	79–83	.488	Third
1972	Chi	87–67	.565	Second
1973	Chi	77–85	.475	Fifth
1974	Chi	80–80	.500	Fourth
1975	Chi	75–86	.466	Fifth
1976	Oak	87–74	.570	Second
1977	Pitt	96–66	.593	Second
1978	Pitt	88–73	.547	Second
1979	Pitt	98–64	.605	First
1980	Pitt	83–79	.512	Third
1981	Pitt	46–56	.451	Fourth
1982	Pitt	84–78	.519	Fourth
1983	Pitt	84–78	.519	Second
1984	Pitt	75–87	.463	Sixth
1985	Pitt	57–104	.354	Sixth
1986	Atl	72–89	.447	Sixth
1987	Atl	69–92	.429	Fifth
1988	Atl	12–27	.308	Sixth
19 Years		**1352–1381**	**.495**	

LEAGUE CHAMPIONSHIP SERIES

Year	Team	Record	Pct.
1979	Pitt	3–0	1.000

WORLD SERIES

Year	Team	Record	Pct.
1979	Pitt	4–3	.571

Elvin Walter Tappe

Born May 21, 1927, Quincy, Illinois; died July 12, 1999, Quincy, Illinois; Chicago Cubs (rotating coach), 1961–1962

Elvin Tappe was a reserve catcher and later a coach for the Chicago Cubs who came up with an idea to help the Cubs' minor league system. He thought coaches who specialized in various aspects of the game could rotate throughout the farm system and help young ballplayers. Owner Phil Wrigley liked the idea but decided to include the major league team in the coaching rotation. The result was that the Cubs had several "head coaches" instead of a manager for two years. Tappe was part of the rotation. The Cubs finished seventh the first year and ninth the next.

Year	Team	Record	Pct.	Standing
1961	Chi (N)	42–53	.442	Seventh
1962	Chi	4–16	.200	Ninth
2 Years		**46–69**	**.400**	

George J. Taylor

Born November 22, 1853, New York, New York; date of death unknown; Brooklyn Dodgers, 1884

George Taylor was a New York newspaperman who had a vision for a baseball team starting in Brooklyn. He got some friends to finance his idea, and he served one year as its manager and helped with the business of the team. The ball club was called the Brooklyn Dodgers and played six years in the American Association. The team, without Taylor, joined the National League in 1890.

Year	Team	Record	Pct.	Standing
1884	Brklyn	40–64	.385	Ninth

James Wren "Zack" Taylor

Born July 27, 1898, Yulee, Florida; died July 6, 1974, Orlando, Florida; St. Louis Browns, 1946; November 21, 1947–1951

Zack Taylor had a five-year run as manager of one of baseball's worst teams, the St. Louis Browns in the late 1940s and early 1950s. In 1951, he was at the helm of the Browns when two unusual circumstances occurred in the same week. In a game against the Philadelphia A's, Browns owner Bill Veeck arranged for fans in the stands to manage the team by holding up cards indicating what strategy the Browns should use. Someone in the dugout would hold up a sign with a question such as "Move Infield In?" after which

Zach Taylor

fans would hold up cards signaling "yes" or "no." The Browns won. A few days later, Taylor sent up 3'6" Eddie Gaedel to pinch hit for Frank Saucier in a game against the Detroit Tigers. The Browns lost 102 games that year, Taylor's last as a major league manager.

Year	Team	Record	Pct.	Standing
1946	StL (A)	13–17	.433	Seventh
1948	StL	59–94	.386	Sixth
1949	StL	53–101	.344	Seventh
1950	StL	58–96	.377	Seventh
1951	StL	52–102	.338	Eighth
5 Years		**235–410**	**.364**	

George Robert "Birdie" Tebbetts

Born November 10, 1912, Burlington, Virginia; died March 24, 1999, Orlando, Florida; Cincinnati Reds, September 29, 1953–August 14, 1958; Milwaukee Braves, September 2, 1961–October 5, 1962; Cleveland Indians, October 5, 1962–August 20, 1966

Birdie Tebbetts was a hard-nosed major league catcher who managed three major league teams and had a reputation for being a player's manager, someone who understood the pressures faced by ballplayers. He managed Frank Robinson in the slugger's rookie year. Robinson credits Tebbetts with setting goals that he knew the young Robinson could achieve. Robinson's confidence soared. Chuck Harmon, an outfielder, was Cincinnati's first black player. He lauds Tebbetts for helping smooth the way for him and giving him sound advice as to how to avoid trouble.

Tebbetts told his players, "All I ask of you is that you hustle 90 feet and give me 100 percent."

Tebbetts' greatest strength, probably developed from his 14 years as an American League catcher, was his handling of pitching staffs. His best team was the 1956 Reds, a club that featured the rookie Robinson and also had Ted Kluszewski, Wally Post and Gus Bell for home run punch, Ed Bailey behind the plate and a double play combination of Roy McMillan and Johnny Temple at shortstop and second base. The Reds tied the National League record with 221 home runs that year and finished third, two games behind Brooklyn. Tebbetts' team finished 28 games over .500 that year, with Brooks Lawrence winning 19 games and no other starter winning more than 13. (Tebbetts' 1957 Reds club set a record for most times going to the bullpen, 229.) He replaced Charlie Dressen in Milwaukee at the end of the 1961 season but was fired after finishing fifth with the Braves in 1962. Then it was on to Cleveland where he finished his managerial career in 1966. His personality had hardened over the years and, contrary to his days with Cincinnati, many Indian players didn't like him and didn't want to play for him.

Tebbetts never professed any great managerial strategy. He was a good handler of pitchers, and many of his former players said he was a good handler of men. He summed up his role as manager once by saying, "Whatever success you have as a manager belongs to the players. The only thing I bring with me is a great desire to win." Roy McMillan, his shortstop at Cincinnati, said Tebbetts' 1956 team would have won the National League pennant had it not been for one chancy acquisition by the Brooklyn Dodgers. Brooklyn picked up pitcher Sal Maglie from Cleveland in mid-season. Maglie, the former Giant ace, was believed to be on his way out. For Brooklyn, he went 12–2 to help them win the pennant, beating the Reds by two games. It was the closest Tebbetts ever got to a championship.

Year	Team	Record	Pct.	Standing
1954	Cin	74–80	.481	Fifth
1955	Cin	75–79	.487	Fifth
1956	Cin	91–63	.591	Third
1957	Cin	80–74	.519	Fourth
1958	Cin	52–61	.460	Seventh
1961	Mil	12–13	.480	Fourth
1962	Mil	86–76	.531	Fifth
1963	Cleve	79–83	.488	Fifth
1964	Cleve	79–83	.488	Sixth
1965	Cleve	87–75	.537	Fifth
1966	Cleve	66–57	.537	Fifth
11 Years		**781–744**	**.512**	

Oliver Wendell "Patsy" Tebeau

Born December 5, 1864, St. Louis, Missouri; died May 15, 1918, St. Louis; Cleveland Spiders, 1890–1898; St. Louis Cardinals, 1899–1900

Patsy Tebeau was a scrappy infielder who became manager of the Cleveland Spiders in 1890 and, while never winning a championship, had a run of three second-place finishes in a five-year span, largely due to Cy Young's pitching and Jesse Burkett's hitting. When Cleveland owner Frank Robison also bought the St. Louis Cardinals, Tebeau was shifted to St. Louis and managed there for two years. He was a man of sour disposition and was willing to fight to win. He once said, "A milk-and-water, goody-goody player can't wear a Cleveland uniform." His tactics worked in Cleveland. They didn't in St. Louis. Robison taunted Tebeau and Tebeau taunted his players. By August of his second year, Tebeau quit. Robison had acquired player John McGraw in the previous off-season. He tried to persuade McGraw to be the new manager but McGraw refused. Two years later, McGraw was managing the Giants. Tebeau's managerial career was over.

Year	Team	Record	Pct.	Standing
1890	Cleve (P)	18–17	.514	Seventh
1891	Cleve (N)	34–40	.459	Fifth
1892	Cleve	93–56	.624	Second

Year	Team	Record	Pct.	Standing
1893	Cleve	73–55	.570	Third
1894	Cleve	68–61	.527	Sixth
1895	Cleve	84–46	.646	Second
1896	Cleve	80–48	.625	Second
1897	Cleve	69–62	.527	Fifth
1898	Cleve	81–68	.544	Fifth
1899	StL (N)	84–67	.556	Fifth
1900	StL	48–55	.466	Fifth
11 Years		**732–575**	**.560**	

Fiore Gino Tenaci
(Gene Tenace)

Born October 10, 1946, Russeltown, Pennsylvania; Toronto Blue Jays, August 21, 1991–September 27, 1991

Gene Tenace was a catcher on the Oakland A's championship teams of the 1970s. In 1991, he was a Toronto Blue Jays coach who took over as manager for a little over a month when manager Cito Gaston had back surgery. Tenace had a successful run but never managed after that.

Year	Team	Record	Pct.	Standing
1991	Tor	19–14	.576	Second

Frederick Clay Tenney

Born June 9, 1859, Georgetown, Massachusetts; died July 3, 1952, Boston, Massachusetts; Boston Rustlers, 1905–1907, 1911

Fred Tenney had a great mentor in Frank Selee, who managed him when Tenney was a first baseman for Boston in the National League. Selee went on to manage the Chicago Cubs and had some great clubs. When Tenney got his chance to manage, he didn't have much talent to work with. The result was that Tenney has one of the worst managerial records, in terms of wins and losses, in baseball history. He served as player-manager for Boston, playing first base while he managed. After being fired as manager, he played two years with the Giants. When his days on the field were over with, he became a correspondent for *The New York Times*, giving the newspaper his expert opinion on happenings in baseball.

Year	Team	Record	Pct.	Standing
1905	Bos (N)	51–103	.331	Seventh
1906	Bos	49–102	.325	Eighth
1907	Bos	58–90	.392	Seventh
1911	Bos	44–107	.291	Eighth
4 Years		**202–402**	**.334**	

William Harold Terry

Born October 30, 1898, Atlanta, Georgia; died January 9, 1989, Jacksonville, Florida; New York Giants, June 3, 1932–February 6, 1942

Bill Terry was a great first baseman for John McGraw's New York Giants. His lifetime batting average of .341 is the highest of any National League left-handed batter. He is also the last National League player to hit over .400, hitting .401 in 1930.

When his playing career was over he succeeded John McGraw as manager of the Giants and won three pennants. Terry didn't win anything on the basis of his person- ality. He was brash, argumentative and demanding. Terry is remembered more for things he said as a manager than the things he did. At the start of the 1934 season, Terry was quoted as saying, "Is Brooklyn still in the league?" That comment infuriated the Dodgers but did not inspire them. They finished sixth while the Giants finished second behind the Cardinals. Terry bad-mouthed McGraw, claiming McGraw called all the pitches in a game — until the pitcher got in a jam. Then the pitcher and catcher were on their own, he said. When he retired, he said he wasn't worried about the future of baseball. "No business ever made more money with poorer management," he said. And when he was elected to the Hall of Fame in 1954, Terry said in his induction speech, "I don't know what kept me out, newspapermen, or that you just don't want me up here," apparently referring to baseball's hierarchy.

Terry's teams won 90 or more games five years in a row with lineups featuring him- self, Travis Jackson and Mel Ott and a pitching staff headed by Carl Hubbell.

A proud man who lived to be 90, Terry always signed autographs with his name fol- lowed by ".401," reminding everyone of his 1930 batting average.

Year	Team	Record	Pct.	Standing
1932	NY (N)	55–59	.482	Fifth
1933	NY	91–61	.599	First
1934	NY	93–60	.608	Second
1935	NY	91–62	.595	Third
1936	NY	92–62	.597	First
1937	NY	95–57	.625	First
1938	NY	83–67	.553	Third
1939	NY	77–74	.510	Fifth
1940	NY	72–80	.474	Sixth
1941	NY	74–79	.484	Fifth
10 Years		**823–661**	**.555**	

WORLD SERIES

Year	Team	Record	Pct.
1933	NY (N)	4–1	.800
1936	NY	2–4	.333
1937	NY	1–4	.200
3 Years		**7–9**	**.438**

Frederick L. Thomas

No biographical data available; Indianapolis Hoosiers, 1887

In an era when baseball managers sometimes didn't last more than a month, Fred Thomas fit the mold. He was gone after 29 games managing the American Association's Indianapolis entry in the National League.

Year	Team	Record	Pct.	Standing
1887	Ind	11–18	.379	Eighth

A.M. Thompson

Born in St. Paul, Minnesota; St. Paul White Caps, 1884

When officials tried to get the Union League off the ground, A.M. Thompson was called on to manage his hometown team in St. Paul. His Union League club lost six out of eight games, bringing his managerial career to a quick end.

Year	Team	Record	Pct.	Standing
1884	StP	2–6	.250	Ninth

John Thomas Tighe

Born August 9, 1913, Kearny, New Jersey; Detroit Tigers, October 4, 1956–June 10, 1958

Jack Tighe replaced Bucky Harris as manager of the underachieving Detroit Tigers, a team that had future Hall of Famer Al Kaline and future batting champion Harvey Kuenn in its everyday lineup and a pitching staff headed by future Hall of Famer Jim Bunning and 20-game winner Frank Lary. Tighe had the Tigers over .500 in 1957, but they finished fourth, 20 games behind the New York Yankees. In 1958, with the Tigers seven games under .500 after their first 49 games, Tighe was replaced by Bill Norman and never managed again.

Year	Team	Record	Pct.	Standing
1957	Det	78–76	.506	Fourth
1958	Det	21–28	.429	Fifth
2 Years		**99–104**	**.488**	

Joe Tinker

Joseph Bert Tinker

Born July 27, 1880, Muscotah, Kansas; died July 27, 1948, Orlando, Florida; Cincinnati Reds, 1913; Chicago Federals, 1914; Chicago Cubs, 1915–1916

Joe Tinker is the "Tinker" in "Baseball's Sad Lexicon," the famous Franklin P. Adams poem immortalizing "Tinker to Evers to Chance." He was the second baseman on the Chicago Cub dynasty that won four pennants in five years between 1906 and 1910. He also was the player-manager for Cincinnati, the Chicago Federals and then back with the Cubs.

Tinker is better remembered for his playing days than his managing. He is the only Cub player to steal home twice in the same game. The great athlete contracted diabetes after he retired and eventually had to have a leg amputated. He died in Orlando, Florida, on his 68th birthday.

Year	Team	Record	Pct.	Standing
1913	Cin	64–89	.418	Seventh
1914	Chi (F)	87–67	.565	Second
1915	Chi	86–66	.566	First
1916	Chi (N)	67–86	.438	Fifth
4 Years		**304–308**	**.497**	

Jeffrey Allen Torborg

Born November 26, 1941, Plainfield, New Jersey; Cleveland Indians, June 19, 1977–July 23, 1979; Chicago White Sox, November 3, 1988–October 11, 1991; New York Mets, October 11, 1991–May 19, 1993; Montreal Expos, May 31, 2001–February 2, 2002; Florida Marlins, February 12, 2002–present

Jeff Torborg was a reserve catcher through most of his major league career, from 1964 to 1973, but he was involved in some famous games. He caught Sandy Koufax's perfect game against the Chicago Cubs on September 9, 1965, Bill Singer's no-hitter on July 20, 1970, and Nolan Ryan's no-hitter on May 15, 1973. He also was behind the plate for the fifth of Don Drysdale's six consecutive shutouts in 1968.

He replaced Frank Robinson as manager of the Cleveland Indians in 1977 when the Indians finished fifth. They finished sixth in 1978 and were headed that way in 1979 when Torborg was fired. Ten years later he was hired as manager of the Chicago White Sox where he had his greatest success. Chicago finished second in two out of Torborg's three years there. After the 1992 season, he resigned to accept the managerial job with the New York Mets. But he didn't find the same success he did in Chicago. Torborg lasted a little over a year. He then moved to the broadcast booth, for eight years.

Torborg's style of managing was to push a run across any way he could rather than play for a big inning. The best teams he managed, the Chicago White Sox of 1989–1991, all led the American League in sacrifice bunts.

On May 31, 2001, he was hired to replace Felipe Alou as manager of the Montreal Expos. When the Expos owners sold the club to Major League Baseball and purchased the Florida Marlins, Torborg went with them.

Year	Team	Record	Pct.	Standing
1977	Cleve	45–59	.433	Fifth
1978	Cleve	69–90	.434	Sixth
1979	Cleve	43–52	.453	Sixth
1989	Chi (A)	69–92	.429	Seventh
1990	Chi	94–68	.580	Second
1991	Chi	87–75	.537	Second
1992	NY (N)	72–90	.444	Fifth
1993	NY	13–25	.342	Seventh
2001	Mon	47–62	.431	Fifth
9 Years		**539–613**	**.468**	

Joseph Paul Torre

Born July 18, 1940, Brooklyn, New York; New York Mets, May 31, 1977–October 4, 1981; Atlanta Braves, October 23, 1981–October 1, 1984; St. Louis Cardinals, August 1, 1990–October 23, 1995; New York Yankees, November 2, 1995–present

Of all of the managers in baseball history, only Casey Stengel experienced a bigger turn-around than Joe Torre. When he became manager of the New York Yankees in 1996, Torre had a career managing record that left him 109 games below .500. He made up that difference in his first four seasons as Yankee manager, winning the American League championship and the World Series in three of those years.

His success with the Yankees can be attributed to three factors: Owner George Steinbrenner, who had been quick to pull the plug on past managers, has stayed with Torre longer than any other of his managers; Steinbrenner has spent the money and made the deals to compete in the high stakes world of modern baseball; and finally, Torre has pushed the right buttons to get the best results.

Examples are numerous. The Yankees were willing to take chances with troubled players such as outfielder Darryl Strawberry and pitcher Dwight Gooden, both of whom had past drug problems but both of whom contributed to the Yankee success under Torre. At the same time, the Yankees acquired veter-

Joe Torre

ans such as catcher Joe Girardi, pitchers David Cone and David Wells (both of whom threw perfect games for New York) and outfielder Paul O'Neill. They also developed their own stars such as outfielder Bernie Williams, infielders Derek Jeter and Alfonso Soriano and relief ace Mariano Rivera. The result was an average of 100 wins in Torre's first four years.

Torre was a major league catcher for 18 years who retired with a career batting average of .297. In 1977, he was named player-manager of the New York Mets but retired as a player 18 days later. He had five losing seasons with the Mets and then was named manager of the Atlanta Braves, a team that also had a legacy of losing. Torre's Braves won the Eastern Division championship in 1982 but lost three straight games to the St. Louis Cardinals in the league championship series. After the 1984 season, he left the field to become a broadcaster but was lured back in 1990 to manage the Cardinals. He was over .500 most of the time with St. Louis but was fired 47 games into the 1995 season. Torre is the fourth man to have managed both the Mets and the Yankees. The others are Stengel, Dallas Green and Yogi Berra.

Torre has always preferred to play for one run rather than wait for the big inning to bail him out. He had made frequent use of his bullpen over the years — but for different reasons. With the Mets and Braves, his starting pitchers had trouble holding leads. With the Yankees, he had one of baseball's best stoppers in Rivera. Torre has also platooned more than he has used a set lineup. With his early teams, he looked for the right combination of players. With the Yankees, it was more a matter of making use of all the talent. His 1998 Yankee team won 114 games in the regular season, second most in baseball history — Frank Chance's 1906 Cub team won 116, as did Lou Piniella's Seattle club in 2001.

Torre may have been speaking for all managers when, as manager of the Mets, he said, "When we lose, I can't sleep at night. When we win, I can't sleep at night. But when we win, I wake up feeling better."

Year	Team	Record	Pct.	Standing
1977	NY (N)	49–68	.419	Sixth
1978	NY	66–96	.407	Sixth
1979	NY	63–99	.389	Sixth
1980	NY	67–95	.414	Fifth
1981	NY	17–34	.333	Fifth
1981	NY	24–28	.462	Fourth
1982	Atl	89–73	.549	First
1983	Atl	88–74	.543	Second
1984	Atl	80–82	.494	Second
1990	StL	24–34	.410	Sixth
1991	StL	84–78	.510	Second
1992	StL	83–79	.510	Third
1993	StL	87–75	.530	Third
1994	StL	53–61	.460	Fourth
1995	StL	20–27	.420	Sixth
1996	NY (A)	92–70	.560	First
1997	NY	96–66	.590	Second
1998	NY	114–48	.700	First
1999	NY	77–49	.600	First
2000	NY	87–74	.540	First
2001	NY	95–65	.594	First
19 Years		**1455–1375**	**.514**	

League Championship Series

Year	Team	Record	Pct.
1982	Atl	0–3	.000
1996	NY (A)	4–2	.667
1997	NY	4–1	.800
1998	NY	4–2	.667
1999	NY	4–2	.667
2000	NY	4–2	.667
2001	NY		
6 Years		**24–12**	**.667**

World Series

Year	Team	Record	Pct.
1996	NY (A)	4–2	.667
1998	NY	4–0	1.000
1999	NY	4–0	1.000
2000	NY	4–1	.800
4 Years		**16–3**	**.843**

Richard Joseph Tracewski

Born February 3, 1935, Eynon, Pennsylvania; Detroit Tigers, June 9–12, 1979

Detroit Tiger coach Dick Tracewski filled in as manager in 1979 after Les Moss was fired and before Sparky Anderson came on board. Tracewski's Tigers won two out of the three games he managed.

Year	Team	Record	Pct.	Standing
1979	Det	2–1	.667	Fifth

Harold Joseph "Pie" Traynor

Born November 11, 1899, Framingham, Massachusetts; died March 16, 1972, Pittsburgh, Pennsylvania; Pittsburgh Pirates, March 27, 1934–1939

Pie Traynor was a great third baseman for the Pittsburgh Pirates in his playing days and then managed them for six years. He hit over .300 10 times in his career, finishing with a lifetime batting average of .320. He drove in more than 100 runs seven times, including five years in a row. He scored more than 100 runs twice. He led the National League in putouts seven times and assists three times.

Traynor managed the Pirates from 1934 to 1939. He was in the dugout in May of 1935 when an aging Babe Ruth hit three home runs against the Pirates, including the only one to ever clear the roof at Forbes Field. Five days later, Ruth retired. Traynor was also in the dugout in September of 1938 when Gabby Hartnett hit the famous home run into the darkness of Wrigley Field that catapulted the Cubs past the Pirates into first place and an eventual pennant. It was a heart-breaking finish for Traynor and the Pirates. After a sixth-place finish in 1939, Traynor bowed out as manager but remained in the organization as a scout and coach for many years.

Year	Team	Record	Pct.	Standing
1934	Pitt	47–52	.475	Fifth
1935	Pitt	86–67	.562	Fourth
1936	Pitt	84–70	.545	Fourth
1937	Pitt	86–68	.558	Third
1938	Pitt	86–64	.573	Second
1939	Pitt	68–85	.444	Sixth
6 Years		**457–406**	**.530**	

Thomas Trebelhorn

Born January 27, 1948; Milwaukee Brewers, September 25, 1986–October 9, 1991; Chicago Cubs, October 13, 1993–October 17, 1994

Tom Trebelhorn managed the Milwaukee Brewers for five full seasons and part of a sixth and had only one losing season with them but could not get them any higher than third place. At the end of the 1991 season, he was replaced by Phil Garner. In 1994, he managed the Chicago Cubs in the strike-shortened season. Before the season began, Trebelhorn was reminded that the Cubs had not won a World Series since 1908. "Anybody can have a bad century," he said. The Cubs posted a 49–64 record that year and Trebelhorn was fired and replaced by Jim Riggleman.

Year	Team	Record	Pct.	Standing
1986	Mil	6–3	.667	Sixth
1987	Mil	91–71	.562	Third
1988	Mil	87–75	.537	Third
1989	Mil	81–81	.500	Fourth
1990	Mil	74–88	.457	Sixth
1991	Mil	83–79	.512	Third
1994	Chi (N)	49–64	.434	Second
7 Years		**471–461**	**.505**	

Samuel W. Trott

Born in 1858, Washington D.C.; died June 5, 1925, Cantonsville, Maryland; Washington Statesmen, 1891

Sam Trott had a brief stay as a baseball manager. In 1891, he started the season as manager of the Washington ball club in the American Association but was gone after the team lost eight of its first 12 games.

Year	Team	Record	Pct.	Standing
1891	Wash	4–8	.333	Eighth

Robert Edwards "Ted" Turner

Born November 19, 1938, Cincinnati, Ohio; Atlanta Braves, May 11, 1977

Ted Turner

Ted Turner will be remembered for many things. He founded the Cable News Network (CNN), created the first "super station" (WTBS in Atlanta), assembled one of baseball's most successful modern franchises (the Atlanta Braves) and managed the Braves for one game. The Braves dominated the National League in the 1990s, but 20 years earlier, they struggled for several years. In 1977, an impatient Turner relieved manager Dave Bristol of his duties for two games. Coach Vern Benson managed in one of the games. Turner inserted himself as manager of the next game, which the Braves lost. Bristol was then reinstated as manager.

Year	Team	Record	Pct.	Standing
1977	Atl	0–1	.000	Sixth

Robert Alexander Unglaub

Born July 31, 1881, Baltimore, Maryland; died November 29, 1916, Baltimore; Boston Red Sox, 1907

Bob Unglaub, a first baseman, was called on to be the third of four managers for the Boston Red Sox in 1907, losing 20 of 28 games. The Red Sox finished seventh. Unglaub returned to first base and played three more seasons. He never managed again in the major leagues.

Year	Team	Record	Pct.	Standing
1907	Bos (A)	8–20	.286	Seventh

Robert John Valentine

Born May 13, 1950, Stamford, Connecticut; Texas Rangers, May 17, 1985–July 9, 1992; New York Mets, August 26, 1996–present

Bobby Valentine was an 11-year major league infielder who managed the Texas Rangers for eight years and in 2001, began his sixth year as manager of the New York Mets. He has the most wins of any Ranger manager, led the Mets to the National League playoffs in 1999 and to the World Series in 2000.

Valentine was an aggressive ballplayer who played every position but pitcher in his career. After retiring as a player, he coached for Cincinnati and the Mets and had several minor league managing jobs. He has a reputation for driving his players as hard as he drove himself when he played. His aggressive style has had mixed results. At Texas, the Rangers showed a 25-game improvement from 1985 to 1986. At New York in 1997, his Mets team finished 87–75 — a marked improvement over their 1996 season in which they were 20 games below .500. But he also alienated some players by making them work harder and by his "rah-rah" style. Pitcher Pete Harnisch was treated for depression and blamed Valentine for much of his problem. When catcher Todd Hundley was in a prolonged slump, Valentine surmised he wasn't getting enough sleep. The New York press picked up on the story and referred to Hundley and Valentine as "Sleepy" and "Dopey." In 1999, Valentine was ejected from a game for arguing a call and showed up in the dugout later in the game wearing a disguise of glasses and a false mustache. He was ousted again.

His 1998 Mets team was in the playoff hunt until the last day of the season. His 1999 club made the playoffs but was eliminated by the San Diego Padres in the League Championship Series. But in 2000, the Mets made it to the playoffs as the wild card entry, won the playoffs and played the Yankees in the first "subway World Series" since 1956. The Mets lost in five games.

Valentine is married to the daughter of Ralph Branca, the former Dodger pitcher who gave up the home run to Bobby Thomson of the Giants in the 1951 National League playoffs. During his playing career, Valentine wore uniform number 13, the same number Branca wore in his career.

Year	Team	Record	Pct.	Standing
1985	Tex	53–76	.411	Seventh
1986	Tex	87–75	.537	Second
1987	Tex	75–87	.463	Sixth
1988	Tex	70–91	.435	Sixth
1989	Tex	83–79	.512	Fourth
1990	Tex	83–79	.512	Third
1991	Tex	85–77	.525	Third
1992	Tex	45–41	.523	Fourth
1996	NY (N)	12–19	.387	Fourth
1997	NY	88–74	.543	Third
1998	NY	88–74	.543	Second
1999	NY	97–66	.595	Second
2000	NY	94–68	.580	Second
13 Years		**960–906**	**.514**	

DIVISIONAL PLAYOFFS

Year	Team	Record	Pct.
1999	NY	2–4	.333
2000	NY	4–1	.800
2 Years		**6–5**	**.545**

WORLD SERIES

Year	Team	Record	Pct.
2000	NY	1–4	.200

George Edward Martin Van Haltren

Born March 30, 1866, St. Louis, Missouri; died September 29, 1945, Oakland California; Baltimore Orioles, 1891–1892

George Van Haltren managed Baltimore teams in two different leagues for short spurts in 1891 and 1892, just prior to the glory years of the franchise under manager Ned Hanlon.

Year	Team	Record	Pct.	Standing
1891	Bal (AA)	4–2	.667	Third
1892	Bal (N)	1–14	.067	Twelfth
2 Years		**5–16**	**.238**	

James Barton "Mickey" Vernon

Born April 22, 1918, Marcus Hook, Pennsylvania; Washington Senators, November 19, 1960–May 22, 1963

When the original Washington Senators pulled up stakes and moved to Minnesota to become the Twins, the American League established an expansion franchise in Washington. In an effort to keep fans interested, Mickey Vernon, one of the old Senators' greatest players, was hired as manager. Vernon was still a fan favorite, but he didn't have any players who matched his abilities when he was a player. Vernon's Senators lost 100 and 101 games in his first two years. They were headed in that direction again when he was fired after 30 games of the 1963 season.

Year	Team	Record	Pct.	Standing
1961	Wash	61–100	.379	Ninth
1962	Wash	60–101	.373	Tenth
1963	Wash	14–26	.350	Tenth
3 Years		**135–227**	**.373**	

William Charles Virdon

Born July 9, 1931, Hazel Park, Michigan; Pittsburgh Pirates, November 23, 1971–September 6, 1973; New York Yankees, January 3, 1974–August 2, 1975; Houston Astros, August 19, 1975–August 10, 1982; Montreal Expos, October 13, 1982–August 27, 1984

Bill Virdon was a National League outfielder for 12 years and was Rookie of the Year in 1955 with the St. Louis Cardinals. He played 10 years with the Pittsburgh Pirates and retired in 1968. In 1972, he was hired to replace Danny Murtaugh as manager of the Pirates and guided them to a first place finish. They lost the League Championship Series, three games to two, to the Cincinnati Reds. When the Pirates slipped in 1973, Virdon was fired late in the season and was replaced by Murtaugh. The Yankees hired him in 1974 after American League president Joe Cronin ruled the Yankees couldn't hire their first choice, Dick Williams, because he was still under contract to Oakland. Virdon directed the Yankees to a second place finish. In 1975, though, he faced the same fate as he had in Pittsburgh. The Yankees were struggling. Billy Martin was between jobs. Yankee owner George Steinbrenner fired Virdon and hired Martin. At the same time, the Houston Astros were looking to make a managerial change. Virdon took over in Houston and stayed eight years, helping the Astros to their first post-season play in 1980 when they lost the league championship series to the Philadelphia Phillies in five games. He concluded his managerial career with a stint in Montreal.

No Virdon team ever made it to the World Series but no manager ever came closer. His 1972 Pirate team lost to Cincinnati in the League Championship Series when the winning run scored on a wild pitch in the ninth inning. In 1980, four of the five games of the LCS with the Philadelphia Phillies went extra innings. In 1981, in division playoffs after a split season, the Astros won the first two games and then lost three in a row to the Dodgers.

Virdon was a quiet man who showed patience with pitchers and had a tendency to let his hitters swing away. Most of his teams were near the bottom of the league in sacrifice bunts attempted. When he retired after the 1984 season, Virdon was within five games of having 1,000 wins as a major league manager.

Year	Team	Record	Pct.	Standing
1972	Pitt	96–59	.619	First
1973	Pitt	67–69	.493	Third
1974	NY (A)	89–73	.549	Second
1975	NY	53–51	.510	Third
1975	Hous	17–17	.500	Sixth
1976	Hous	80–82	.494	Third
1977	Hous	81–81	.500	Third
1978	Hous	74–88	.457	Fifth
1979	Hous	89–73	.549	Second
1980	Hous	93–70	.571	First
1981	Hous	28–29	.491	Third
1981	Hous	33–20	.623	First
1982	Hous	49–62	.441	Fifth
1983	Mon	82–80	.506	Third
1984	Mon	64–67	.489	Fifth
13 Years		**995–921**	**.519**	

DIVISIONAL PLAYOFF

Year	Team	Record	Pct.
1981	Hous	2–3	.400

LEAGUE CHAMPIONSHIP SERIES

Year	Team	Record	Pct.
1972	Pitt	2–3	.400
1980	Hous	2–3	.400
2 Years		**4–6**	**.400**

Oscar Joseph Vitt

Born January 4, 1890, San Francisco, California; died January 31, 1963, Oakland, California; Cleveland Indians, October 20, 1937–November 12, 1940

To look at statistics alone, the observer would think that Ossie Vitt had one of the most successful careers of any manager of the Cleveland Indians. In three years, his teams averaged 87 wins and had two third place finishes and one second place finish during the time of one of the Yankee dynasties. In 1937, Vitt, who had been a successful minor league manager for 12 years, led the Newark Bears to 109 victories. The Bears are perhaps the most famous of minor league teams. All but one of its players eventually made it to the major leagues. Vitt was then hired to manage the Indians. And while he enjoyed success with the Indians in terms of wins and losses, many of his players hated him and plotted against him. In 1939, a delegation of 12 players went to owner Alva Bradley to complain about how Vitt mismanaged the team, criticized players publicly and ought to be replaced. Bradley wanted to take the comments under advisement and decide what to do. He told the players to keep their complaints quiet. But a Cleveland newspaper reporter already knew about the turmoil and published a story about it. Bradley, put on the spot, felt compelled to back his manager. Vitt not only survived the 1939 season, but had the Indians in the 1940 pennant race until the final day when Detroit rookie Floyd Giebell beat Bob Feller to win the pennant for the Tigers. Vitt did not return for the 1941 season.

Year	Team	Record	Pct.	Standing
1938	Cleve	86–66	.566	Third
1939	Cleve	87–67	.565	Third
1940	Cleve	89–65	.578	Second
3 Years		**262–198**	**.570**	

Christian Frederick Wilhelm Von der Ahe

Born November 7, 1851, Hille, Germany; died June 7, 1913, St. Louis, Missouri; St. Louis Browns, 1892, 1895, 1896, 1897

Chris Von der Ahe was a German-born brewer and saloon keeper in St. Louis who bought the St. Louis baseball team — then called the Browns and later the Cardinals — as a pastime giving people something to do while they drank his beer. He named himself as manager on four different occasions, though he hardly ever took the field. Von der Ahe had a good time with the ball club, but it suffered some of its leanest years under his direction.

Year	Team	Record	Pct.	Standing
1892	StL (N)	56–94	.373	Eleventh
1895	StL	2–12	.143	Eleventh
1896	StL	0–2	.000	Eleventh
1897	StL	1–2	.333	Twelfth
4 Years		**59–110**	**.349**	

John Vukovich

Born July 31, 1947, Sacramento, California; Chicago Cubs, June 13–14, 1986; Philadelphia Phillies, September 23, 1988–October 3, 1988

John Vukovich has been a longtime major league coach whose name is frequently mentioned when managerial vacancies occur. But his only two shots have been interim positions, two games with the Cubs in 1986 and nine games with the Phillies two years later.

Year	Team	Record	Pct.	Standing
1986	Chi (N)	1–1	.500	Fifth
1988	Phil	5–4	.556	Sixth
2 Years		**6–5**	**.545**	

Charles F. "Heinie" Wagner

Born September 23, 1881, New York, New York; died March 20, 1943, New Rochelle, New York; Boston Red Sox, 1930

The Boston Red Sox of the 1920s and early 1930s had trouble getting out of the American League cellar. An example is 1930 when Heinie Wagner had his only season as a major league manager.

Year	Team	Record	Pct.	Standing
1930	Bos (A)	52–102	.338	Eighth

John Peter "Honus" Wagner

Born February 24, 1874, Carnegie, Pennsylvania; died December 6, 1955, Carnegie; Pittsburgh Pirates, 1917

Honus Wagner was one of baseball's greatest players. He hit over .300 for 17 consecutive seasons and won eight batting titles in a 12-year period. He had 3,430 hits. Only five players have done better than that. Wagner was a loyal Pirate who was a coach on the ball club for 19 years. He was called on to manage only once. Nixie Callahan started the 1917 season as manager. The Pirates lost 40 of their first 60 games. Wagner filled in while Pirate management figured out their next move. The Pirates lost four out five with Wagner managing. They hired Hugo Bezdek to take his place. Bezdek managed for a couple of seasons and later went on to become Penn State University's first great football coach.   Wagner never managed again.

Year	Team	Record	Pct.	Standing
1917	Pitt	1–4	.200	Eighth

Harry William Walker

Born October 22, 1918, Pascagoula, Mississippi; St. Louis Cardinals, May 28, 1955–October 12, 1955; Pittsburgh Pirates, October 19, 1964–July 18, 1967; Houston Astros, June 18, 1968–August 26, 1972

Harry "The Hat" Walker was a major league outfielder for 11 years who played in three World Series with the St. Louis Cardinals. His father and his brother, both nicknamed Dixie, were also major league ballplayers. He got his first chance to manage when St. Louis fired Eddie Stanky in 1955. Walker set the all-time record for use of relief pitchers that year, using 274, breaking Eddie Stanky's record of 262 set the year before. But Walker did it in only 118 games. The Cardinals were in fifth when Walker took over but finished seventh. Walker was not rehired. In fact, he didn't manage again for 10 years. In 1965, he took over for Danny Murtaugh as manager of the Pittsburgh Pirates and guided them to two straight years of winning 90 games or more, finishing third both years. Walker had a different style than Murtaugh and did not get along as well with his players. That didn't matter when they were winning 90 games, but when they split the first 84 games of the next season and were in sixth place at the All-Star break, it did matter. Walker was fired and Murtaugh returned. Walker then managed the Houston Astros for five years. He took over for Grady Hatton early in 1968 with the Astros 15 games below .500. They were 49–52 for Walker, a big improvement, and the next year, they climbed to .500 at 81–81. They never did any better than that, though, in Walker's five years there. He retired, having managed more than 1,200 games. His good years at Pittsburgh afforded him a lifetime winning percentage.

Year	Team	Record	Pct.	Standing
1955	StL	51–67	.432	Seventh
1965	Pitt	90–72	.556	Third
1965	Pitt	92–70	.568	Third
1967	Pitt	42–42	.500	Sixth
1968	Hous	49–52	.485	Tenth
1969	Hous	81–81	.500	Fifth
1970	Hous	79–83	.488	Fourth
1971	Hous	79–83	.488	Fourth
1972	Hous	67–54	.554	Third
9 Years		**630–604**	**.511**	

Roderick John "Bobby" Wallace

Born November 4, 1873, Pittsburgh, Pennsylvania; died November 3, 1960, Torrance, California; St. Louis Browns, January 14, 1911–June 1, 1912; Cincinnati Reds, September 13, 1937–October 15, 1937

Bobby Wallace was the first American League shortstop elected to the Hall of Fame. Playing for the St. Louis Browns, he led the American League in assists three times and once had 27 assists in a game — a record that may someday be tied but will never be broken in a nine-inning contest. He was among the first shortstops to develop a style of picking up ground balls and throwing to first base in one fluid motion, instead of picking up the ball, coming to standing position, and then throwing.

He managed the Browns for a little over a year, with only an eighth place finish to show for it, and umpired with veteran American League umpire Billy Evans for about a year, but decided he'd rather play than ump. Twenty-five years after his first managerial experience with the Browns, Cincinnati hired him to manage the Reds, filling in for the remainder of a disappointing season. The Reds had high hopes for the 1938 season but were 51–78 under Chuck Dressen. Wallace had been a longtime scout for the Reds. He was given the reins for the remainder of the year with the understanding that a new manager would be onboard the following year. The Reds failed to hustle for their lame duck manager and lost 15 of their last 20 games, including 14 in a row to end the season. The next year, Bill McKechnie took over and brought home champions in 1939 and 1940.

Forty years after Wallace retired as a player, he was elected to the Hall of Fame in 1953.

Year	Team	Record	Pct.	Standing
1911	StL (A)	45–107	.296	Eighth
1912	StL	12–27	.308	Eighth
1937	Cin	5–20	.200	Eighth
3 Years		**62–154**	**.287**	

Edward Augustine Walsh

Born May 14, 1881, Plains, Pennsylvania; died May 20, 1959, Pompano Beach, Florida; Chicago White Sox, 1924

Ed Walsh was one of the greatest pitchers in major league baseball for more than a decade in the early part of the 20th century. Blessed with a great arm, Walsh won 195 games for the Chicago White Sox in a 14-year career in which he struck out nearly three times as many batters as he walked and finished with a lifetime earned run average of 1.82.

Walsh retired as a player in 1917, two years before the Black Sox scandal tainted his former team. When eight White Sox players were banished by Commissioner Kenesaw Mountain Landis, team owner Charles Comiskey needed some big names to help draw people into the ballpark. In 1924, he hired Johnny Evers, the famed old Cub second baseman of Tinker-to-Evers-to-Chance fame, to manage the ball club. With three games left in the season and the White Sox mired in sixth place, Comiskey replaced Evers with Walsh, another old Chicago favorite. The White Sox lost two out of three under his direction. Walsh never managed again but did try his hand at umpiring. That turned out to be another short career for the Hall of Fame pitcher.

Year	Team	Record	Pct.	Standing
1924	Chi (A)	1–2	.333	Sixth

Michael John Walsh

Born August 6, 1852, Baltimore, Maryland; died March 17, 1924, Springfield, Missouri; Louisville Eclipse, 1884

Mike Walsh took over for Joe Gerhardt as manager of the American Association's Louisville Eclipse in 1884. Gerhardt had gotten the team off to a 39–18 start, good for third place. Under Walsh, they played almost as well and retained third place at the end of the season, Walsh's only season as a manager.

Year	Team	Record	Pct.	Standing
1884	Lou	29–22	.569	Third

William Henry "Bucky" Walters

Born April 19, 1909, Philadelphia, Pennsylvania; died April 20, 1991, Abington, Pennsylvania; Cincinnati Reds, August 6, 1948–September 26, 1949

Bucky Walters won 198 games in a 19-year career as a major league pitcher, including 10 years with the Cincinnati Reds. In 1939 and 1940, he averaged almost 25 wins a year for the two Red pennant winners. In 1948, he was named to replace Johnny Neun as Reds manager.

The Reds were in the process of trying to regroup after some sub-par years. In the next two years, they traded away Frankie Baumholtz and Hank Sauer, two outfielders who later had several good years with the Chicago Cubs. Meanwhile the Reds continued to flounder. After a seventh-place finish in 1949, Walters was fired and never managed again.

In 1950, he tried to return to the mound, appearing in one game with the Boston Braves. He pitched four innings, allowed two runs on five hits and did not get the decision.

Year	Team	Record	Pct.	Standing
1948	Cin	20–33	.377	Seventh
1949	Cin	61–90	.404	Seventh
2 Years		**81–123**	**.397**	

John Waltz

No biographical data available; Baltimore Orioles, 1892

John Waltz was the second of three managers for Baltimore in 1892, filling in for only two games. He was succeeded by Ned Hanlon, who was to have baseball's first early dynasty on a team that groomed future stars like John McGraw and Hughie Jennings. Waltz, in his brief tenure, didn't win a game.

Year	Team	Record	Pct.	Standing
1892	Bal	0–2	.000	12th

John Montgomery Ward

Born March 3, 1860, Bellefante, Pennsylvania; died March 4, 1925, Augusta, Georgia; New York Gothans/Giants, 1884, 1893–1894; Brooklyn Wonders, 1890; Brooklyn Bridegrooms, 1891–1892

John "Monte" Ward was an outstanding pitcher until he hurt his right arm, his pitching arm, while sliding into a base. While his arm was healing, he taught himself to throw left-handed and played center field for a year. He never regained strength enough in his right arm to pitch again. Ward was moved to shortstop, where he had a Hall of Fame career.

He was the first leader of the Brotherhood of Professional Base Ball Players, and through it he helped start the ill-fated Players League. He was also part owner of the Boston Braves for a year. Though his pitching career was cut short, he achieved many milestones, including winning 47 games for Providence one year and throwing a perfect game. He is believed to be the first pitcher to issue an intentional walk. As a hitter, he had more than 2,100 hits and was an excellent base runner.

He managed two different Brooklyn teams and the National League's New York club twice, compiling a .562 winning percentage. As a manager, he never had a championship team, but had two second-place finishes and one third-place finish in his six years.

Year	Team	Record	Pct.	Standing
1884	NY	6–8	.429	Fourth
1890	Brklyn (P)	76–56	.576	Second
1891	Brklyn (N)	61–76	.445	Sixth
1892	Brklyn	95–59	.617	Second
1893	NY	68–64	.515	Fifth
1894	NY	88–44	.667	Second
6 Years		**394–307**	**.562**	

George Ware

No biographical data available; Providence Grays, 1878

George Ware was one of baseball's pioneer managers, handling the Providence team for part of the 1878 season, the third year of the National League. Providence finished third under his direction, which was the only time he managed.

Year	Team	Record	Pct.	Standing
1878	Prov	33–27	.550	Third

John Wathan

Born October 4, 1949, Cedar Rapids, Iowa; Kansas City Royals, August 27, 1987–May 22, 1991; California Angels, May 22, 1992–August 28, 1992

John Wathan was a 10-year catcher for the Kansas City Royals from 1976 to 1985 who was hired to manage the Royals in 1987. He experienced success in his first few seasons, bringing the club home in second place in 1989. But after a sixth-place finish in 1990 and a dismal start in 1991, Wathan was fired. In 1992, he was the second of three managers the California Angels used that year and has not managed since then.

Year	Team	Record	Pct.	Standing
1987	KC	21–15	.580	Second
1988	KC	84–77	.520	Third
1989	KC	92–70	.560	Second
1990	KC	75–86	.460	Sixth
1991	KC	15–22	.400	Sixth
1992	Cal	39–50	.430	Fifth
6 Years		**326–320**	**.506**	

Harvey L. Watkins

No biographical data available; New York Metropolitans, 1895

Harvey Watkins was one of three managers for the New York ball club in 1895. George Davis and Jack Doyle preceded him and had records of 17–17 and 31–31. Watkins was able to improve on their performances, as New York won one more game than it lost under Watkins' reign — which turned out to be his only reign.

Year	Team	Record	Pct.	Standing
1895	NY	18–17	.514	Ninth

William Henry Watkins

Born May 5, 1859, Brantford, Ontario, Canada; died June 9, 1937, Port Huron, Michigan; Indianapolis Hoosiers, 1884; Detroit Wolverines, 1885–1888; Kansas City Cowboys, 1888–1889; St. Louis Browns, 1893; Pittsburgh Pirates, 1898–1899

Bill Watkins was a successful 19th-century manager who was in high demand after his Detroit ball club won the National League championship in 1887. From then on, he was hired by other clubs with expectations of similar success. It didn't happen. At Kansas City, his teams finished eighth and seventh; at St. Louis, the Cardinals finished tenth under his direction; and at Pittsburgh, he finished eighth and then was fired about a month into his second season. In Watkins' day, field managers were also managers of many other operations. In fact, at Pittsburgh, his title was president-manager. He was plagued by owners' second-guessing him and making player changes without consulting him. He retired in 1899 after a managerial career of nine years with five different teams.

Year	Team	Record	Pct.	Standing
1884	Ind	4–19	.174	Twelfth
1885	Det	28–28	.451	Sixth
1886	Det	87–36	.707	Second
1887	Det	79–45	.637	First
1888	Det	49–45	.521	Third
1888	KC	3–11	.214	Eighth

1889	KC	55–82	.401	Seventh
1893	StL	57–75	.432	Tenth
1898	Pitt	72–76	.486	Eighth
1899	Pitt	8–16	.333	Tenth
9 Years		**437–433**	**.502**	

Earl Sidney Weaver

Born August 14, 1930, St. Louis, Missouri; Baltimore Orioles, July 11, 1968–November 11, 1982; June 13, 1985–October 6, 1986

Earl Weaver said he believed in good pitching, good defense and in three-run homers. In his 17 years as manager of the Baltimore Orioles, he won 100 or more games five times. Only Joe McCarthy topped that. Weaver's teams won 90 or more games 11 times. He is another example of an unexceptional ballplayer who became a great manager. Weaver was an astute judge of talent and had the knack for inserting the right players for the right situations. "They're not all great players," he once said, "but they can all do something." He believed in going for the big inning—playing for the three-run homer. "If you play for one run, that's all you'll get," he said. Weaver's teams therefore bunted very little, as the manager believed that was giving an out away—and you have only 27 before the game is over. Weaver didn't believe in the hit-and-run, either, and didn't have a sign for it.

For all the philosophy about run producing, Weaver knew the key to winning was good pitching, and the Orioles always seemed to have good pitching. Hall of Fame right-han-

Earl Weaver

der Jim Palmer once said the only thing Weaver knew about pitching was that he couldn't hit it. But the pitching coaches he hired, George Bamberger and Ray Miller, were considered the best in the game. Five times during his 17 years as manager, the Orioles had a Cy Young Award winner. His 1971 club had four 20-game winners: Mike Cuellar, Pat Dobson, Jim Palmer and Dave McNally. The Orioles also always had depth in their bullpen, with people like Moe Drabowsky, Stu Miller, Eddie Watt and Dick Hall.

Weaver was a student of the game and a strategist who took pride in juggling lineups to fit specific situations. He got Elrod Hendricks as one of his catchers to work with Mike Cuellar, a Cuban, because Hendricks could communicate with him. It turned Cuellar's career around. Weaver platooned two average ballplayers, John Lowenstein and Gary Roenicke in left field, and together they became a run-producing force. Weaver loved platooning and sometimes platooned more than two players at a position. Another Weaver innovation was his use of defensive specialists. He used a number of players over the years who were great fielders but not great hitters. Believing he should have his best defensive team on the field early in the game (most managers rely on late-inning defensive substitutions), Weaver put defensive specialists in his starting lineup. Mark Belanger made a living that way at shortstop and there were others. But Weaver would pinch-hit for these players in key situations — when he needed the three-run homer, for example. And then he would put in another good defensive player for the pinch hitter.

Baltimore's team statistics confirm their manager's strategy. Under Weaver, the Orioles had the lowest earned average and the best fielding percentage eight times. They also led the American League in complete games six times and were always at the bottom of the league in bunts attempted.

Weaver believed in knowing how to get the most out of his players. With Brooks Robinson and Frank Robinson, both of whom were established stars and future Hall of Famers, Weaver left them alone. With Cuellar, the pitcher whom Weaver brought along slowly, he said, "I gave him more chances than I gave my first wife."

Weaver had a fiery temper and was ejected from 91 games in his career, three times from both games of a doubleheader. He was suspended four times. He once caused the Orioles to forfeit a game because he didn't like the way the tarp was rolled up in foul territory in Toronto. Weaver complained about it before the game and refused to have his players take the field. Umpire Marty Springstead waited 15 minutes and then declared the game a forfeit.

Under Weaver, the Orioles won six Eastern Division titles, four American League pennants and one World Series championship. He was elected to the Hall of Fame in 1996.

Year	Team	Record	Pct.	Standing
1968	Bal	48–34	.585	Second
1969	Bal	109–53	.673	First
1970	Bal	108–54	.667	First
1971	Bal	101–57	.639	First
1972	Bal	80–74	.519	Third
1973	Bal	97–65	.599	First
1974	Bal	91–71	.562	First
1975	Bal	90–69	.566	Second
1976	Bal	88–74	.573	Second
1977	Bal	97–64	.602	Second
1978	Bal	90–71	.559	Fourth
1979	Bal	102–57	.642	First
1980	Bal	100–62	.617	Second
1981	Bal	31–23	.574	Second
1981	Bal	28–23	.549	Fourth
1982	Bal	94–68	.580	Second
1985	Bal	53–52	.505	Fourth
1986	Bal	73–89	.451	Seventh
17 Years		**1480–1060**	**.583**	

LEAGUE CHAMPIONSHIP SERIES

Year	Team	Record	Pct.
1969	Bal	3–0	1.000
1970	Bal	3–0	1.000
1971	Bal	3–0	1.000

Year	Team	Record	Pct.
1973	Bal	2–3	.400
1974	Bal	1–3	.250
1979	Bal	3–1	.750
6 Years		**15–7**	**.682**

WORLD SERIES

Year	Team	Record	Pct.
1969	Bal	1–4	.200
1970	Bal	4–1	.800
1971	Bal	3–4	.429
1979	Bal	3–4	.429
4 Years		**11–13**	**.458**

Wesley Noreen Westrum

Born November 8, 1922, Clearbrook, Minnesota; died, May 28, 2002; New York Mets, November 18, 1965–September 19, 1967; San Francisco Giants, June 27, 1974–November 20, 1975

Wes Westrum was Leo Durocher's catcher with the great New York Giant teams of the early 1950s. He was the manager who succeeded Casey Stengel for the New York Mets but had about the same degree of success as Stengel had. He took over a tenth-place team in 1965, and that's where the Mets finished. In 1966, they moved up to ninth. But in 1967, they were in tenth place again when Westrum was replaced by Gil Hodges. Westrum managed the San Francisco Giants for parts of two years and brought them home in third place in 1975.

Year	Team	Record	Pct.	Standing
1965	NY (N)	19–48	.284	Tenth
1966	NY	66–95	.410	Ninth
1967	NY	57–94	.377	Tenth
1974	SF	38–48	.442	Fifth
1975	SF	80–81	.497	Third
5 Years		**260–366**	**.415**	

Harry Eugene Wheeler

Born March 3, 1858, Versailles, Indiana; died October 9, 1960, Cincinnati, Ohio; Kansas City Unions, 1884

Harry Wheeler had a five-year playing career in which he played several positions. He managed briefly, for about a week in 1884. His Kansas City team in the Union Association played four games during that time but could not come up with a win.

Year	Team	Record	Pct.	Standing
1884	KC	0–4	.000	Eighth

James Laurie "Deacon" White

Born December 7, 1847, Caton, New York; died July 7, 1939, Aurora, Illinois; Cleveland Forest Citys, 1872; Cincinnati Reds, 1879

Deacon White managed Cincinnati for 16 games in 1879, splitting them. Five years later, his brother, Will White, also managed the Cincinnati ball club for part of one season.

Year	Team	Record	Pct.	Standing
1872	Cleve	0–2	.000	Seventh
1879	Cin	9–9	.500	Fifth
2 years		**9–11**	**.450**	

Joyner Clifford "Jo-Jo" White

Born June 1, 1909, Red Oak, Georgia; died October 9, 1986, Tacoma, Washington; Cleveland Indians, August 3, 1960

Jo-Jo White, a Cleveland Indians coach, served as interim manager of the Indians for one game in 1960, bridging the gap between the departure of Joe Gordon and the arrival of Jimmy Dykes. Gordon and Dykes, who had been managing the Detroit Tigers, were involved in the only deal in major league history in which managers were traded for each other. White won his only game as manager.

Year	Team	Record	Pct.	Standing
1960	Cleve	1–0	1.000	Fourth

William Henry White

Born October 11, 1854, Caton, New York; died August 31, 1911, Port Carling, Ontario, Canada; Cincinnati Red Stockings, 1884

Will "Hoop-la" White managed the Cincinnati ball club for one year and didn't do too badly, 43–25, but it wasn't good enough for him to make it to the end of the season. He left with his team in fourth place.

Year	Team	Record	Pct.	Standing
1884	Cin (AA)	43–25	.632	Fourth

William Warren White

No biographical data available; Baltimore Lord Baltimores, 1874

William Warren White, who went by his middle name, played six seasons in the National Association and had one disastrous stretch as manager of the Baltimore ball club. White's team was able to win only nine out of 47 games, ending his career as a manager.

Year	Team	Record	Pct.	Standing
1874	Balt	9–38	.191	Eighth

Delbert Quentin Wilber

Born February 24, 1919, Lincoln Park, Michigan; Texas Rangers, September 7, 1973

Del Wilber filled in as manager of the Texas Rangers after Whitey Herzog's departure and before Billy Martin arrived to take over. Texas lost 105 games that year, but Wilber won the only game he managed.

Year	Team	Record	Pct.	Standing
1973	Tex	1–0	1.000	Sixth

Irvin Key "Kaiser" Wilhelm

Born January 26, 1874, Wooster, Ohio; died May 21, 1936, Rochester, New York; Philadelphia Phillies, March 7, 1921–1922

Kaiser Wilhelm took over for Bill Donovan as manager of the Philadelphia Phillies in 1921 as the Phillies limped home in seventh place. In 1922, the Phillies had what sportswriters referred to as the "2 O'Clock Infield," so named because the fielders were brilliant in fielding practice before the game—about 2 o'clock—but not so good when the game started. The Phillies finished seventh in 1922, finishing Wilhelm's short managerial career. He was in the dugout the day his Phillies came back from a 25–6 deficit only to lose to the Cubs 26–23—still the most runs ever scored in a major league game.

Year	Team	Record	Pct.	Standing
1921	Phil (N)	20–32	.385	Eighth
1922	Phil	57–96	.373	Seventh
2 Years		**77–128**	**.376**	

Richard Hirshfield Williams

Born May 7, 1928, St. Louis, Missouri; Boston Red Sox, September 28, 1966–September 23, 1969; Oakland Athletics, October 2, 1970–October 21, 1973; California Angels, July 1, 1974–July 23, 1976; Montreal Expos, October 5, 1976–September 8, 1981; San Diego Padres, November 18, 1981–February 24, 1986; Seattle Mariners, May 8, 1986–June 6, 1988

Dick Williams was a tough, no-nonsense manager who three times took underachieving teams and led them to championships. In 1966, the Boston Red Sox finished ninth. In 1967, Williams' first year, the Red Sox won the pennant and lost to the St. Louis Cardinals in a seven-game World Series. Oakland had never won a pennant when Williams arrived in 1971. They won the championship in his first year and in the next two years as well. The Montreal Expos lost 107 games in 1976. Williams arrived in 1977. Two years later they won 95 and followed that up with a 90-win season, narrowly missing the championship in those two years. The San Diego Padres had experienced just one winning season in 14 years when Williams arrived to manage them in 1982. He guided them to two .500 seasons (81–81) and then won the National League championship in 1984. Williams also managed the California Angels and Seattle Mariners during his career.

Williams believed it wasn't enough for players to know what it means to win. Rather, he said, "they must know what it takes to win." Williams had powerhouse teams in Boston with sluggers like George Scott and Carl Yastrzemski and at Oakland with Reggie Jackson. In San Diego, he had slugger Steve Garvey and the best pure hitter in the National League in Tony Gwynn. Yet teams managed by Williams led the league in sacrifice bunts eight times.

He was fortunate to have good hitters on most of his teams, and he had a knack for recognizing young talent and allowing it to develop. But Williams believed that pitching and defense were essential elements to winning.

Williams, because of his gruffness and his strong disciplinarian tendencies, was sometimes accused of not communicating with his players. But he said his critics were missing the point. A team loses because it doesn't execute, not because it doesn't communicate, said Williams.

He joined Bill McKechnie and Billy Martin as the only managers to win championships with three different teams.

Year	Team	Record	Pct.	Standing
1967	Bos	92–70	.568	First
1968	Bos	86–76	.531	Fourth
1969	Bos	82–71	.536	Third
1971	Oak	101–60	.627	First
1972	Oak	93–62	.600	First
1973	Oak	94–68	.580	First
1974	Cal	36–48	.429	Sixth
1975	Cal	72–89	.447	Sixth
1976	Cal	39–57	.406	Fourth
1977	Mon	75–87	.463	Fifth
1978	Mon	76–86	.469	Fourth
1979	Mon	95–65	.594	Second
1980	Mon	90–72	.556	Second
1981	Mon	30–25	.545	Third
1981	Mon	14–12	.538	Second
1982	SD	81–81	.500	Fourth
1983	SD	81–81	.500	Fourth
1984	SD	92–70	.568	First
1985	SD	83–79	.512	Third
1986	Sea	58–75	.436	Sixth
1987	Sea	78–84	.481	Fourth
1988	Sea	23–33	.411	Sixth
21 Years		**1571–1451**	**.520**	

LEAGUE CHAMPIONSHIP SERIES

Year	Team	Record	Pct.
1971	Oak	0–3	.000
1972	Oak	3–2	.600
1973	Oak	3–2	.600
1984	SD	3–2	.600
4 Years		**9–9**	**.500**

WORLD SERIES

Year	Team	Record	Pct.
1967	Bos	3–4	.429
1972	Oak	4–3	.571
1973	Oak	4–3	.571
1984	SD	1–4	.200
4 Years		**12–14**	**.462**

James Andrew Williams

Born January 3, 1848, Columbus, Ohio; died October 24, 1918, North Hempstead, New York; St. Louis Browns, 1884; Cleveland Blues, 1887–1888

Jimmy Williams managed two teams in the American Association, achieving some success with the St. Louis franchise and then falling on hard times with Cleveland for two years.

Year	Team	Record	Pct.	Standing
1884	StL (AA)	67–40	.626	Fourth
1887	Cleve	39–92	.298	Eighth
1888	Cleve	19–41	.317	Seventh
3 Years		**125–173**	**.419**	

James Francis "Jimy" Williams

Born October 4, 1943, Santa Maria, California; Toronto Blue Jays, October 25, 1985–May 15, 1989; Boston Red Sox, November 20, 1996–August 16, 2001; Houston Astros, November 1, 2001–present

Jimy Williams has been one of the most successful modern-day managers. In 1999, he was the American League manager of the year with the Boston Red Sox, who were the wildcard entry in the post-season playoffs for the second year in a row but who did not make it to the World Series either year. Williams, whose playing career consisted of 14 games as a reserve infielder with the St. Louis Cardinals in 1966 and 1967, won 86, 96 and 87 games in his first three years as manager of the Toronto Blue Jays and had second-, third- and fourth-place finishes to show for it. But when the Blue Jays got off to an awful start in 1989, Williams departed, only to watch as Toronto rebounded and won its division race. Eight years later, Williams got another chance to manage and averaged 88 wins in a five-year stint with the Red Sox. But he and general manager Dan Duquette didn't get along and Williams was fired on August 16, 2001, with his Red Sox 65–53, in second place in the American League East. Pitching coach Joe Kerrigan replaced him. He was, ironically, quickly hired by the Astros, who'd fired Larry Dierker for having led strong teams to the playoffs but not to the Series.

Year	Team	Record	Pct.	Standing
1986	Tor	86–76	.530	Fourth
1987	Tor	96–66	.590	Second
1988	Tor	87–75	.530	Third
1989	Tor	12–24	.333	Fifth
1997	Bos	78–84	.480	Fourth
1998	Bos	92–70	.560	Second
1999	Bos	94–68	.580	Second
2000	Bos	85–77	.525	Second
2001	Bos	65–53	.550	
9 Years		**630–540**	**.540**	

DIVISIONAL PLAYOFFS

Year	Team	Record	Pct.
1998	Bos	1–3	.250
1999	Bos	3–2	.600
2 Years		**4–5**	**.444**

LEAGUE CHAMPIONSHIP SERIES

Year	Team	Record	Pct.
1999	Bos	1–4	.200

Theodore Samuel Williams

Born August 30, 1918, San Diego, California; died July 5, 2002; Washington Senators/Texas Rangers, February 21, 1969–October 4, 1972

Ted Williams was one of the greatest hitters in base-ball history. He is the last man to hit over .400 for a season —.406 in 1941— and had a lifetime batting average of .344. He played his entire career with the Boston Red Sox. When Williams was hired to manage the Washington Senators, he took a team that had finished tenth in 1968 and brought them home in fourth place in 1969, winning 21 more games than they did the previous year. The magic didn't last, however, and Williams was gone after three successive losing seasons, including the team's first year in Texas, in which they lost 100 games. Williams demanded much from his players, and his expectations of them may have been affected by his own tremendous abilities.

Ted Williams

Year	Team	Record	Pct.	Standing
1969	Wash	86–76	.531	Fourth
1970	Wash	70–92	.432	Sixth
1971	Wash	63–96	.396	Fifth
1972	Tex	54–100	.351	Sixth
4 Years		**273–364**	**.429**	

Maurice Morning Wills

Born October 2, 1932, Washington D.C.; Seattle Mariners, August 4, 1980–May 6, 1981

Maury Wills was an outstanding shortstop for the Los Angeles Dodgers and was the premier base stealer of his era. In 1962, he stole 104 bases, setting the all-time single-season record and becoming the first man to steal more than 100 bases. The record has since been surpassed by Lou Brock, Vince Coleman and Rickey Henderson. Wills was hired to manage the Seattle Mariners in 1980, lasting parts of two dismal seasons.

Year	Team	Record	Pct.	Standing
1980	Sea	20–38	.345	Seventh
1981	Sea	6–18	.250	Seventh
2 Years		**26–56**	**.317**	

James Wilson

Born July 23, 1900, Philadelphia, Pennsylvania; died May 31, 1947, Bradenton, Florida; Philadelphia Phillies, November 15, 1933–September 30, 1938; Chicago Cubs, November 17, 1940–May 1, 1944

Jimmie Wilson has the dubious distinction of having the worst managerial record of anyone managing 1,000 games or more, finishing with a winning percentage of .401. He also has the worst win-loss differential — 242 more losses than wins. In Philadelphia, he was victimized by an owner, Gerry Nugent, who got rid of many of the Phillies' best players for cash. In Wilson's first year, 1934, his best player was Chuck Klein, winner of the Triple Crown in 1933. Nugent sold Klein to the Cubs for $65,000. Wilson worked to convert an infielder with a great arm, Bucky Walters, into a pitcher. Walters went 9–9 in his first full season as a pitcher — and then was sold to the Boston Red Sox. Slugger

Dolph Camilli went to the Dodgers. Wilson resigned shortly before the end of the 1938 season, saying, "Even Connie Mack can't win without any players."

In 1941, the Cubs hired him to replace Gabby Hartnett. The Cubs had won three pennants in the 1930s. Under Wilson, they finished sixth twice, fifth once and were in eighth place in 1944 when he was fired. Charlie Grimm replaced him and was at the helm when the Cubs won their last pennant in 1945.

Year	Team	Record	Pct.	Standing
1934	Phil (N)	56–93	.376	Seventh
1935	Phil	64–89	.418	Seventh
1936	Phil	54–100	.351	Eighth
1937	Phil	61–92	.399	Seventh
1938	Phil	45–103	.304	Eighth
1941	Chi (N)	70–84	.455	Sixth
1942	Chi	68–86	.442	Sixth
1943	Chi	74–79	.484	Fifth
1944	Chi	1–9	.100	Eighth
9 Years		**493–735**	**.401**	

Robert Paul Wine

Born September 17, 1938, New York, New York; Atlanta Braves, August 26, 1985–October 10, 1985

Bobby Wine was a major league infielder for 12 years who had one brief chance at managing. He finished out the 1985 season for the Atlanta Braves but did not return at the helm in 1986.

Year	Team	Record	Pct.	Standing
1985	Atl	16–25	.390	Fifth

Ivey Brown Wingo

Born July 8, 1890, Gainesville, Georgia; died March 1, 1941, Norcross, Georgia; Cincinnati Reds, 1916

Ivey Wingo was the interim manager for the Cincinnati Reds, filling in after Buck Herzog was fired and before Christy Mathewson took over the club. Under Wingo, the Reds split two games.

Year	Team	Record	Pct.	Standing
1916	Cin	1–1	.500	Eighth

Bobby Brooks Winkles

Born March 11, 1932, Swifton, Arkansas; California Angels, October 11, 1972–June 26, 1974; Oakland Athletics, June 10, 1977–May 23, 1978

Bobby Winkles was a highly successful college baseball coach at Arizona State University who was hired by Gene Autry and the California Angels in 1973. He was the first manager in major league history to go straight from coaching college ball to the big leagues. He brought with him a college playbook he had written, and a set of rules that included short haircuts and the wearing of coats and ties on road trips. The players respected Winkles' enthusiasm but some called him "Joe College" and "Dr. Strange Play."

The Angels finished with a modest 79–83 record, good for fourth, in his first season. There was friction between Winkles and veteran outfielder Frank Robinson, whom the Angels acquired in 1973. Robinson had been a Most Valuable Player in both leagues, had won the Triple Crown with Baltimore in 1966. Destined for the Hall of Fame, he was a legend and had his eye on someday being a manager. Many of the Angels players sought his advice and counsel. Winkles thought Robinson was undermining him. The tension grew and, after the Angels got off to a slow start in 1974, general manager Harry Dalton thought a change was needed. To Dalton, the former Baltimore general manager who had acquired Robinson for the Orioles in 1966, the next move was obvious: He fired Winkles. Nolan Ryan, who pitched for the Angels during those years, said Winkles was a good baseball man but he tried to impose college standards on grown men who were making a living playing ball. Ryan said it's possible to demand "rah-rah" spirit of kids for the length of a college season, but not on adults who have to play 162 games. In 1977, Charlie Finley hired Winkles to manage the Oakland A's, but within a year and a half, Winkles was out of that job too. In 1975, two years after his run-ins with Winkles, Robinson was hired as manager of the Cleveland Indians.

Year	Team	Record	Pct.	Standing
1973	Cal	79–83	.488	Fourth
1974	Cal	32–46	.410	Sixth
1977	Oak	37–71	.343	Seventh
1978	Oak	24–15	.615	Sixth
4 Years		**172–215**	**.444**	

William Van Winkle Wolf

Born May 12, 1862, Louisville, Kentucky; died May 16, 1903, Louisville; Louisville Colonels, 1889

When the Louisville ball club of the American Association went looking for a manager in 1889, it didn't have to look far. Louisville native William Wolf, whose nickname was "Chicken," led the team for one year, a miserable one in which Louisville lost 51 of its 66 games. After the season, Wolf went home and never managed again.

Year	Team	Record	Pct.	Standing
1889	Lou	15–51	.227	Eighth

Harry Sterling Wolverton

Born December 6, 1873, Mount Vernon, Ohio; died February 4, 1937, Oakland, California; New York Yankees, November 21, 1911–January 8, 1913

Harry Wolverton was hired to replace Hal Chase as manager of the New York Yankees after New York finished sixth in 1911. Wolverton was a flamboyant man who had achieved great success as a minor league manager. He arrived in New York wearing a sombrero, smoking a cigar and promising a first-place finish for the Yankees in 1912. It was an exciting year. On May 15, Detroit star Ty Cobb went into the stands and attacked a heckler, precipitating a near riot at Hilltop Park, predecessor to Yankee Stadium. On July 25, Yankee outfielder Bert Daniels hit for the cycle. On August 15, Guy Zinn stole second, third and home in one inning and stole home in another inning. But when the season was over, the Yankees had won only 50 games. They lost 102. Their .329 percentage remains the lowest in Yankee history. Wolverton and his sombrero were gone after that one disastrous year.

Year	Team	Record	Pct.	Standing
1912	NY (A)	50–102	.392	Eighth

George A. Wood

Born November 9, 1858, Boston, Massachusetts; died April 4, 1924, Harrisburg, Pennsylvania; Philadelphia Athletics, 1891

George Wood managed the Philadelphia team in the American Association and had a pretty good year, 54–46, in 1891. But the American Association was on its way out and so was Wood. He never managed again.

Year	Team	Record	Pct.	Standing
1891	Phil (AA)	54–46	.540	Fourth

James Leon Wood

Born December 1, 1844, Brooklyn, New York; died November 30, 1886; Chicago White Stockings, 1871; 1874–1875; Troy Haymakers, 1872; Brooklyn Eckfords, 1872; Philadelphia Philadelphias, 1873

Jimmy Wood was one of the best second basemen of his era, combining the ability to hit with outstanding fielding. He managed Chicago in 1871 and achieved some success, but the Great Chicago Fire caused economic distress throughout the city and left the White Stockings without the funds to field a team. Wood managed the Troy, New York, ball club and again achieved success but then lost 12 of 15 with the Brooklyn Eckfords the same year. In 1873, he moved on to manage Philadelphia Philadelphias and had his team in second place most of the season.

In 1874, Chicago was back in business and Wood was back managing Chicago. But his career was cut short by a strange accident. In the off-season, he had developed an abscess on his leg. He tried to cut it out with a knife and suffered a severe gash which eventually became infected. He could no longer play but tried to continue managing. By the time he sought proper medical attention, the leg was so infected it had to be amputated. His career was over at the end of the season, and 11 years later, Wood was dead at the age of 42.

Year	Team	Record	Pct.	Standing
1871	Chi	19–9	.679	Second
1872	Troy	15–10	.600	Fifth
1872	Brklyn Eck	3–15	.167	Ninth
1873	Phil Phil	28–15	.651	Second
1874	Chi	10–13	.435	Fifth
1875	Chi	30–37	.468	Sixth
5 years		**105–99**	**.514**	

Alfred Hector Wright

Born March 30, 1842, Cedar Grove, New Jersey; died April 20, 1905; Philadelphia Athletics, 1876

Al Wright had the distinction of managing in the first year of the National League, but he didn't fare too well. His Philadelphia team lost 45 of 59 games, ending Wright's managerial career.

Year	Team	Record	Pct.	Standing
1876	Phil	14–45	.237	Seventh

George Wright

Born January 28, 1847, New York, New York; died August 31, 1937, Boston, Massachusetts; Providence Grays, 1879

George Wright was a shortstop on the first professional baseball team, his brother Harry's Cincinnati Red Stockings in 1869. He once hit 49 home runs in 56 games for the Red Stockings, who would play 130 games without a loss in 1869 and 1870. In 1879, he managed the Providence Grays in the National League, winning the championship. He and Harry were elected to the Hall of Fame for their many contributions to the early years of baseball. Later, George Wright developed a similar love for tennis and helped promote that sport as well. He remains the only man in history to win a championship in his one and only year as manager.

Year	Team	Record	Pct.	Standing
1879	Prov (N)	59–25	.702	First

William Henry "Harry" Wright

Born January 10, 1835, Sheffield, England; died October 3, 1895, Atlantic City, New Jersey; Boston Red Stockings, 1871–1881; Providence Grays, 1882–1883; Philadelphia Quakers/Phillies, 1884–1893

Harry Wright enjoyed his greatest success as the organizer and field manager of the Cincinnati Red Stockings, the greatest team of the 19th century and one that played before the National Association was formed. The Red Stockings won 56 straight games in 1869 and continued the streak in 1870 with 74 more wins before losing to the Brooklyn Atlantics in extra innings, stopping the amazing streak at 130. When the National League was formed, Wright managed for 18 years and won 1,042 games. Wright outfitted his teams in the first baseball uniform of sorts — knickers, a style which has lasted for more than a century, with modifications. Wright was the first to patent a scorecard and the first to take a team on a foreign tour.

Harry Wright

Early reports of Wright's managing indicate that he was a patient man, a fine teacher and someone who never criticized players after a defeat (he believed they were not then in the proper frame of mind to respond to it). Wright's style was to talk to his team when things had gone well, pointing out to them how they could do even better in the future.

Year	Team	Record	Pct.	Standing
1871	Bos	20–10	.667	Third
1872	Bos	39–8	.830	First
1873	Bos	43–16	.729	First
1874	Bos	52–18	.743	First
1875	Bos	71–8	.899	First
1876	Bos (N)	39–31	.557	Fourth
1877	Bos	42–18	.700	First
1878	Bos	41–19	.683	First
1879	Bos	54–30	.643	Second
1880	Bos	40–44	.476	Sixth
1881	Bos	38–45	.458	Sixth
1882	Prov	52–32	.619	Second
1883	Prov	58–40	.592	Third
1884	Phil (N)	39–73	.348	Sixth
1885	Phil	56–54	.509	Third
1886	Phil	71–43	.623	Fourth
1887	Phil	75–48	.610	Second
1888	Phil	69–61	.531	Third
1889	Phil	63–64	.496	Fourth
1890	Phil	78–54	.591	Third
1891	Phil	68–69	.496	Fourth
1892	Phil	87–66	.569	Fourth
1893	Phil	72–57	.558	Fourth
23 Years		**1225–885**	**.581**	

Rudolph Preston York

Born August 17, 1913, Ragland, Alabama; died February 2, 1970, Rome, Georgia; Boston Red Sox, July 2, 1959

Rudy York, an American League slugger for 13 years in the 1930s and '40s, was a Boston Red Sox coach when he was called on to fill in for one game in 1959 after Pinky Higgins was fired and before Billy Jurges was hired as his replacement. The Red Sox lost York's one and only game as manager.

Year	Team	Record	Pct.	Standing
1959	Bos	0–1	.000	Eighth

Thomas Jefferson York

Born July 13, 1851, Brooklyn, New York; died February 17, 1936, New York, New York; Providence Grays, 1878, 1881

Tom York was a journeyman outfielder with six teams in the National Association, National League and American Association, spending most of that time with Providence in the National League. He finished his career with a lifetime batting average of .274. In two of those seasons he was called on to manage Providence and did well both times, finishing with a winning percentage above .600 for 93 games.

Year	Team	Record	Pct.	Standing
1878	Prov	33–27	.580	Third
1881	Prov	23–10	.697	Second
2 years		**56–37**	**.602**	

Edward Frederick Joseph Yost

Born October 13, 1926, Brooklyn, New York; Washington Senators, May 22, 1963

Eddie Yost was an American League third baseman for 18 years, all but two of the years with woeful Washington Senator ball clubs. As a player, he was best known for his ability to get on by drawing walks. He drew more than 100 bases on balls eight times in his career and led the American League six times.

In 1963 Yost was a coach with the Senators when he filled in for one game between the managerial tenures of Mickey Vernon and Gil Hodges. The Senators lost the game.

Year	Team	Record	Pct.	Standing
1963	Wash	0–1	.000	Eighth

Denton True "Cy" Young

Born March 29, 1867, Gilmore, Ohio; died November 4, 1955, Peoli, Ohio; Boston Red Sox, March 6, 1907–April 1907

Cy Young was one of the greatest pitchers of all time. In 22 seasons, he won 511 games and lost 313, both unequaled marks. In 1907, he was asked to take over for Jimmy McAleer as manager of the Boston Red Sox, following a last-place finish in 1906. Young lasted only seven games before he was restated as player only. The Red Sox had four managers that season and moved up to seventh place, winning 59 games and losing 90. Young pitched the team to 22 of the 59, lost 15 and had an earned run average of 1.99.

Cy Young

Year	Team	Record	Pct.	Standing
1907	Bos (A)	3–4	.429	Seventh

Nicholas Emanuel Young

Born September 12, 1840, Fort Johnson, New York; died October 31, 1916, Washington D.C.; Washington Olympics, 1871, 1872; Washingtons, 1873

Nick Young was one of the most prominent names in the early days of professional baseball. He played, managed, umpired and helped form the National Association of Professional Baseball Players in 1871, the game's first major league. He was league secretary for all five years that it lasted. When the National League was formed in 1876, Young was elected its first secretary. He continued to serve in that capacity, and in 1884 was also elected league president. By that time he was also treasurer. During his long association with baseball, Young also ran an umpires school. He helped manage Washington ball clubs during three seasons but his teams lost twice as many as they won.

Year	Team	Record	Pct.	Standing
1871	Wash Olymp	15–15	.500	Fifth
1872	Wash	2–7	.222	Tenth
1873	Wash	8–31	.205	Seventh
3 years		**25–53**		

Charles Louis "Chief" Zimmer

Born November 23, 1860, Marietta, Ohio; died August 22, 1949, Cleveland, Ohio; Philadelphia Phillies, 1903

In the early 1900s, the Philadelphia Phillies were struggling. They had been hit hard by the raiding, particularly, by the Philadelphia A's of the newly formed American League. Barney Dreyfus, owner of the Pittsburgh Pirates, wanted the Phillies to succeed because the rivalry was good for his business and good for the National League. He loaned money to the ball club and also arranged for his veteran catcher, Chief Zimmer, to be the manager. Zimmer, a catcher with 19 years of experience, seemed well prepared for his first — and, it turned out, only — turn as manager. But it was a horrible year. Philadelphia won only 49 games and finished seventh. And in one of their games, more than 500 fans were injured when a section of the left field stands collapsed. A fire had broken out across the street from the ballpark. Fans flocked to the outfield seats not to watch the game but to get a better view of the fire. The added weight caused the stands to fall. Zimmer lasted one year and then became an umpire.

Year	Team	Record	Pct.	Standing
1903	Phil (N)	49–86	.363	Seventh

Donald William Zimmer

Born January 17, 1931, Cincinnati, Ohio; San Diego Padres, April 27, 1972–October 1, 1973; Boston Red Sox, July 19, 1976–October 1, 1980; Texas Rangers, November 12, 1980–July 28, 1982; Chicago Cubs, November 20, 1987–May 21, 1991; New York Yankees, March 10–18, 1999

Don Zimmer managed five major league teams in a baseball career of more than 50 years. He came close to leading two teams to the World Series, one in each league, but didn't quite make it. His Boston Red Sox lost a one-game divisional playoff to the New York Yankees in 1978, a game best remembered for Bucky Dent's home run that broke the game open. In 1989, Zimmer's Chicago Cubs clawed their way into the league championship series but lost to the San Francisco Giants, three games to one. That series is best remembered because the two first basemen, Will Clark of the Giants and Mark Grace of the Cubs, each hit well over .500.

Zimmer was known for his often unorthodox signal-calling. Often, he relied on instinct rather than percentages in choosing to bring a right-hander in to pitch to a left-handed batter or to have a batter swing away when a bunt was clearly in order.

He played hunches with certain players, too. In 1978, he continued to use Butch Hobson at third base even though Hobson had a sore throwing arm and made so many errors,

43, that his final fielding percentage was under .900, something that hadn't happened since the early 1900s. The Red Sox won 99 games that year, but let a 14.5 game lead slip away. The free fall hurt Zimmer's popular support in Boston.

His Cubs players remember him as a general leading his troops. "Every season was a war and every game was a battle," said Rick Wrona, who was a backup catcher on the 1989 Eastern Division champions. Wrona said Zimmer didn't want any fraternization between his players and the opposition. So when the Cubs did their wind sprints, instead of running across the back of the outfield during the opponents' batting practice, they would run from third base down the foul line and back. Gary Scott, a rookie third baseman in the early 1990s, said he got a base hit in a spring training exhibition game against the Oakland A's. When he reached first base, Mark McGwire, the A's first baseman spoke to him. Scott said he looked over in the Cub dugout and saw Zimmer glaring at him so he didn't say a word to McGwire.

In 1991, the Cubs were 18–19 and in fourth place when Cub management told Zimmer his contract would be re-evaluated at the end of the year. Zimmer said, "I've been in baseball 50 years. Evaluate me now." He was fired.

Zimmer's leadership qualities and knowledge of the game are still respected in both leagues, though it appears his managing days are past. He has served for several years as bench coach of the New York Yankees, for whom he was pressed into service as interim manager in March of 1999. Manager Joe Torre had been sidelined for cancer treatments; Zimmer filled in for 36 games.

Zimmer said one of the toughest parts of his job was cutting players. "Monkeying around with people's lives is never fun," he said during spring training of 1989. "On the other hand, 24 players are monkeying around with my life."

Year	Team	Record	Pct.	Standing
1972	SD	54–88	.380	Sixth
1973	SD	60–102	.370	Sixth
1976	Bos	42–34	.550	Third
1977	Bos	97–64	.600	Second
1978	Bos	99–64	.600	Second
1979	Bos	91–69	.560	Third
1980	Bos	82–73	.520	Fourth
1981	Tex	33–22	.600	Second
1981	Tex	24–26	.480	Third
1982	Tex	38–58	.390	Sixth
1988	Chi (N)	77–85	.470	Fourth
1989	Chi	93–69	.570	First
1990	Chi	77–85	.470	Fourth
1991	Chi	18–19	.480	Fourth
1999	NY (A)	21–15	.583	First
14 Years		**906–873**	**.509**	

LEAGUE CHAMPIONSHIP SERIES

Year	Team	Record	Pct.
1989	Chi	1–3	.250

Appendix A

Most and Fewest
Games Managed

The following chart helps indicate the difficulty of managing in the major leagues. Of the 588 managers since 1876, only 98, or 17 percent, have lasted for 1,000 games or more — the equivalent of about seven seasons. Only 64 of the 98 had winning records overall. Here is a list of managers who have appeared in at least 1,000 games. In a few cases, wins and losses do not equal total number of games because of games that ended in a tie.

NAME*	GAMES	RECORD	PCT.
Connie Mack	7,878	3776–4025	.484
John McGraw	4,879	2840–1984	.589
Bucky Harris	4,410	2159–2219	.493
George "Sparky" Anderson	4,028	2194–1834	.545
Gene Mauch	3,942	1902–2037	.483
Casey Stengel	3,812	1926–1827	.508
Leo Durocher	3,740	2010–1710	.540
Walter Alston	3,653	2040–1613	.558
Bill McKechnie	3,650	1898–1724	.524
Joe McCarthy	3,489	2126–1335	.614
Ralph Houk	3,156	1619–1531	.514
Bobby Cox	**3,051**	**1754–1345**	**.559**
Tom Lasorda	3,038	1599–1439	.520
Dick Williams	3,023	1571–1451	.520
Jimmy Dykes	2,960	1407–1538	.478
Clark Griffith	2,916	1491–1367	.522
Joe Torre	**2,835**	**1455–1375**	**.514**
Fred Clarke	2,822	1602–1179	.576
Wilbert Robinson	2,813	1397–1395	.500
Chuck Tanner	2,738	1352–1381	.495
Miller Huggins	2,569	1413–1134	.555
Bill Rigney	2,561	1239–1321	.484

***Boldface** type indicates managers who are still active.

Name*	Games	Record	Pct.
Earl Weaver	2,541	1480–1060	.583
Al Lopez	2,459	1422–1026	.581
Frank Chance	2,429	1597–932	.593
Lou Boudreau	2,404	1162–1224	.487
John McNamara	2,393	1160–1233	.484
Tom Kelly	2,384	1140–1244	.478
Charlie Grimm	2,370	1287–1069	.546
Whitey Herzog	2,336	1281–1055	.548
Lou Piniella	**2,292**	**1226–1066**	**.535**
Billy Martin	2,276	1258–1018	.553
Adrian "Cap" Anson	2,254	1297–957	.575
Frankie Frisch	2,245	1137–1078	.513
Frank Selee	2,202	1299–872	.598
Jim Fregosi	2,123	1028–1095	.484
Jim Leyland	2,100	1069–1031	.509
Danny Murtaugh	2,068	1115–950	.540
Charles Dressen	2,039	1037–993	.511
Bobby Valentine	**2,028**	**1042–986**	**.514**
Davey Johnson	2,026	1148–878	.567
Red Schoendienst	1,999	1041–955	.522
Alvin Dark	1,949	994–954	.510
Harry Wright	1,917	1042–848	.551
Bill Virdon	1,917	995–921	.519
Steve O'Neill	1,876	1039–819	.559
Paul Richards	1,836	923–901	.506
Billy Southworth	1,815	1064–729	.593
Art Howe	**1,781**	**889–892**	**.499**
Don Zimmer	1,743	885–858	.507
Fred Hutchinson	1,666	830–827	.501
Mike Hargrove	**1,632**	**858–777**	**.525**
Frank Chance	1,597	932–640	.593
Patrick "Patsy" Donovan	1,595	683–878	.438
Buck Rodgers	1,559	784–774	.503
Phil Garner	1,559	730–829	.468
Birdie Tebbetts	1,528	781–744	.512
Lee Fohl	1,518	713–792	.474
Jack McKeon	1,504	770–733	.512
Bill Terry	1,496	823–661	.555
Rogers Hornsby	1,494	680–798	.460
Roger Craig	1,475	738–737	.500
Bill Barnie	1,475	646–829	.438
Burt Shotton	1,468	697–763	.477
Dave Bristol	1,422	658–764	.464
Gil Hodges	1,415	660–754	.467
Felipe Alou	1,408	691–717	.491
Dusty Baker	**1,394**	**745–649**	**.534**
Fred Haney	1,393	629–757	.454
Charles Comiskey	1,382	824–533	.607
Gus Schmelz	1,355	623–703	.470
Pat Moran	1,342	748–586	.561
Patsy Tebeau	1,337	732–575	.560
Cito Gaston	1,320	683–637	.517
Fielder Jones	1,298	685–582	.541
Mayo Smith	1,278	662–611	.520
Branch Rickey	1277	597–664	.473

NAME	GAMES	RECORD	PCT.
Luke Sewell	1260	606–644	.485
Jimmie Wilson	1,237	493–735	.401
Harry Walker	1,235	630–604	.511
Hugh Duffy	1,221	535–671	.444
Pat Corrales	1,211	572–634	.474
Jimy Williams	1,170	630–540	.540
Danny Ozark	1,160	618–542	.533
Jeff Torborg	1,152	539–613	.468
Bill Killefer	1,149	523–623	.456
Tris Speaker	1,138	616–520	.542
Herman Franks	1,128	605–521	.537
Hank Bauer	1,128	594–534	.527
Pinky Higgins	1,087	543–541	.502
Jim Riggleman	1,085	486–598	.448
Jim Mutrie	1,077	658–419	.611
Darrell Johnson	1,063	472–590	.444
Jack Hendricks	1,055	520–528	.496
Al Buckenberger	1,049	493–540	.477
Owen "Donie" Bush	1,045	497–539	.480
William Carrigan	1,004	489–500	.494
Mel Ott	1,004	464–530	.467

Managers with One-Game Careers

Often, men who are named as interim managers stay on for several games or are called on several times to serve as a fill-in manager. Some go on to become full-time skippers. But ten times in baseball history, interim managers have been in charge for only one game. Here is how they fared.

Name	Team	Year	Record
Roy Johnson	Chicago (N)	1944	0–1
William Burwell	Pittsburgh	1947	1–0
Rudy York	Boston (A)	1959	0–1
Jo-Jo White	Cleveland	1960	1–0
Andrew Cohen	Philadelphia	1960	1–0
Del Wilber	Texas	1973	1–0
Vernon Benson	Atlanta	1977	1–0
Ted Turner	Atlanta	1977	0–1
Marty Martinez	Seattle	1986	0–1
Bob Schaefer	Kansas	1991	1–0

Wins and Winning Percentage

Best Winning Percentage

1.	Joe McCarthy	.614
2.	Jim Mutrie	.611
3.	Charles Comiskey	.607
4.	Frank Selee	.598
5.	Frank Chance	.593
6.	Billy Southworth	.593
7.	John McGraw	.589
8.	Earl Weaver	.583
9.	Sparky Anderson	.581
10.	Al Lopez	.581

Most Wins

1.	Connie Mack	3,731
2.	John McGraw	2,763
3.	Sparky Anderson	2,194
4.	Bucky Harris	2,157
5.	Joe McCarthy	2,125
6.	Walter Alston	2,040
7.	Leo Durocher	2,008
8.	Casey Stengel	1,905
9.	Gene Mauch	1,902
10.	Bill McKechnie	1,896

Chronological Roster
of Managers

HOUSTON ASTROS
Houston Colt .45s (1962–1964),
Houston Astros (1965–present)

Harry Craft   1962–1964
Chalmer Lumen "Lum"
  Harris   1964–1965
Grady Hatton   1966–1968
Harry Walker   1968–1972
Francis "Salty" Parker   1972
Leo Durocher   1972–1973
Preston Gomez   1973–1975
Bill Virdon   1975–1982
Bob Lillis   1982–1985
Hal Lanier   1986–1988
Art Howe   1989–1993
Terry Collins   1994–1996
Larry Dierker   1997–2001
Jimy Williams   2002–

ATLANTA BRAVES
Boston Beaneaters (1883–1906),
Boston Doves (1907–1908), Boston
Pilgrims (1909–1911), Boston
Braves (1911–1935), Boston Bees
(1936–1940), Boston Braves
(1941–1952), Milwaukee Braves
(1953–1965), Atlanta Braves
(1966–present)

Frank Selee   1890–1901
Albert Buckenberger   1902–
  1904
Fred Tenney   1905–1907
Joe Kelley   1908
Frank "Mike" Bower-
  man   1909
Harry Smith   1909
Fred Lake   1910
Fred Tenney   1911
John Kling   1912
George Stallings   1913–1920
Fred Mitchell   1921–1923
Dave Bancroft   1924–1927
John Slattery   1928
Rogers Hornsby   1928
Emil Fuchs   1929
Bill McKechnie   1930–1937
Casey Stengel   1938–1943
Bob Coleman   1944–1945
Del Bissonette   1945
Billy Southworth   1946–
  1951
Tommy Holmes   1951–
  1952
Charlie Grimm   1952–1956
Fred Haney   1956–1959
Chuck Dressen   1960–1961

George "Birdie" Tebbetts
  1961–1962
Bobby Bragan   1963–1966
Billy Hitchcock   1966–1967
Ken Silvestri   1967
Chalmer "Lum" Harris
  1968–1972
Eddie Mathews   1972–1974
Clyde King   1974–1975
Connie Ryan   1975
Dave Bristol   1976–1977
Ted Turner   1977
Dave Bristol   1977
Bobby Cox   1978–1981
Joe Torre   1982–1984
Eddie Haas   1985
Bobby Wine   1985
Chuck Tanner   1986–1988
Russ Nixon   1988–1990
Bobby Cox   1990–present

ST. LOUIS CARDINALS
Patsy Donovan   1901–1903
Charles "Kid" Nichols
  1904– 1905
Jimmy Burke   1905
Matt Robison   1905

John McCloskey 1906–1908

Roger Bresnahan 1909–1912

Miller Huggins 1913–1917

John Hendricks 1918

Branch Rickey 1919–1925

Rogers Hornsby 1925–1926

Bob O'Farrell 1927

Bill McKechnie 1928

Billy Southworth 1929

Charles "Gabby" Street 1929

Bill McKechnie 1929

Charles "Gabby" Street 1930–1933

Frankie Frisch 1933–1938

Mike Gonzales 1938

Francis "Ray" Blades 1939– 1940

Mike Gonzales 1940

Billy Southworth 1940–1945

Eddie Dyer 1946–1950

Marty Marion 1951

Eddie Stanky 1952–1955

Harry Walker 1955

Fred Hutchinson 1956–1958

Stan Hack 1959

Solly Hemus 1959–1961

Johnny Keane 1961–1964

Albert "Red" Schoendienst 1965–1976

Vern Rapp 1977–1978

Jack Krol 1978

Ken Boyer 1978–1980

Jack Krol 1980

Dorrel "Whitey" Herzog 1980

Albert "Red" Schoendienst 1980

Dorrel "Whitey" Herzog 1981–1990

Joe Torre 1991–1995

Mike Jorgensen 1995

Tony LaRussa 1996–present

CHICAGO CUBS

White Stockings (1876–1894), Colts (1887–1906), Orphans (1898), Cubs (1902–Present)

Cap Anson 1892–1897

Tom Burns 1898–1899

Tom Loftus 1900–1901

Frank Selee 1902–1905

Frank Chance 1905–1912

John Evers 1913

Henry O'Day 1914

Roger Bresnahan 1915

Joe Tinker 1916

Fred Mitchell 1917–1920

Johnny Evers 1921

Bill Killefer 1921–1925

Walter "Rabbit" Maranville 1925

George Gibson 1925

Joe McCarthy 1926–1930

Rogers Hornsby 1930–1932

Charlie Grimm 1932–1938

Charles "Gabby" Hartnett 1938–1940

Jimmy Wilson 1941–1944

Roy Johnson 1944

Charlie Grimm 1944–1949

Frankie Frisch 1949–1951

Phil Cavarretta 1951–1953

Stan Hack 1954–1956

Bob Scheffing 1957–1959

Charlie Grimm 1960

Lou Boudreau 1960

Avitus "Vedie" Himsl 1961

Harry Craft 1961

Elvin Tappe 1961

Lou Klein 1961

Elvin Tappe 1961–1962

Lou Klein 1962

Charlie Metro 1962

Bob Kennedy 1963–1965

Lou Klein 1965

Leo Durocher 1966–1972

Carroll "Whitey" Lockman 1972–1974

Jim Marshall 1974–1976

Herman Franks 1977–1979

Joe Amalfitano 1979

Preston Gomez 1980

Joe Amalfitano 1980–1981

Lee Elia 1982–1983

Charlie Fox 1983

Jim Frey 1984–1986

John Vukovich 1986

Gene Michael 1986–1987

Frank Lucchesi 1987

Don Zimmer 1988–1991

Joe Altobelli 1991

Jim Essian 1991

Jim Lefebvre 1992–1993

Tom Trebelhorn 1994

Jim Riggleman 1995–1999

Don Baylor 2000–2002

Bruce Kimm 2002–present

ARIZONA DIAMOND-BACKS

1998–present

Buck Showalter 1998–2000

Bob Brenley 2001–present

LOS ANGELES DODGERS

Brooklyn Superbas (1899–1910), Brooklyn Dodgers (1911–1957), Los Angeles Dodgers (1957–present)

Ned Hanlon 1899–1905

Patsy Donovan 1906–1908

Harry Lumley 1909

Bill Dahlen 1910–1913

Wilbert Robinson 1914–1931

Max Carey 1932–1933

Casey Stengel 1934–1936

Burleigh Grimes 1937–1938

Leo Durocher 1939–1946

Clyde Sukeforth 1947

Burt Shotton 1947

Leo Durocher 1948

Burt Shotton 1948–1950

Chuck Dressen 1951–1953

Walter Alston 1954–1976

Tom Lasorda 1976–1997

Bill Russell 1997–1998

Glenn Hoffman 1998

Davey Johnson 1999–2000

Jim Tracy 2001–present

MONTREAL EXPOS

Gene Mauch 1969–1975

Karl Kuehl 1976

Charlie Fox 1976

Dick Williams 1977–1981

Jim Fanning 1981–1982

Bill Virdon 1983–1984

Jim Fanning 1984

Robert "Buck" Rodgers
1985–1991
Tom Runnells   1991–1992
Felipe Alou   1992–2001
Jeff Torborg   2001
Frank Robinson 2002–present

SAN FRANCISCO GIANTS

New York Giants (1901–1957), San Francisco Giants (1958–present)

George Davis   1900–1901
Horace S. Fogel   1902
George Smith   1902
John McGraw   1902–1932
Bill Terry   1932–1941
Mel Ott   1942–1948
Leo Durocher   1948–1955
Bill Rigney   1956–1960
Tom Sheehan   1960
Alvin Dark   1961–1964
Herman Franks   1965–1968
Clyde King   1969–1970
Charlie Fox   1970–1974
Wes Westrum   1974–1975
Bill Rigney   1976
Joe Altobelli   1977–1979
Dave Bristol   1979–1980
Frank Robinson   1981–1984
Danny Ozark   1984
Jim Davenport   1985
Roger Craig   1985–1992
Dusty Baker   1993–present

FLORIDA MARLINS

Rene Lachemann   1993–1996
John Boles   1996
Jim Leyland   1997–1998
John Boles   1999–2001
Tony Perez   2001
Jeff Torborg   2002–present

NEW YORK METS

Casey Stengel   1962–1965
Wes Westrum   1965–1967
Francis "Salty" Parker   1967
Gil Hodges   1968–1971
Lawrence "Yogi" Berra
1972–1975
Roy McMillan   1975

Joe Frazier   1976–1977
Joe Torre   1977–1981
George Bamberger
1982–1983
Frank Howard   1983
Davey Johnson   1984–1990
Bud Harrelson   1990–1991
Mike Cubbage   1991
Jeff Torborg   1992–1993
Dallas Green   1993–1996
Bobby Valentine   1996–present

SAN DIEGO PADRES

Preston Gomez   1969–1972
Don Zimmer   1972–1973
John McNamara   1974–1977
Bob Skinner   1977
Alvin Dark   1977
Roger Craig   1978–1979
Gerry Coleman   1980
Frank Howard   1981
Dick Williams   1982–1985
Steve Boros   1986
Larry Bowa   1987–1988
Jack McKeon   1988–1990
Jim Riggleman   1991–1994
Bruce Bochy   1995–present

PHILADELPHIA PHILLIES

Quakers/Phillies (1883–1889), Phillies (1890–1942), Bluejays (1943–1944), Phillies (1945–present)

Bob Ferguson   1883
Blondie Purcell   1883
Harry Wright   1884–1893
Arthur Irwin   1894–1895
Billy Nash   1896
George Stallings   1897–1898
William Shettsline   1898–1902
Charles "Chief" Zimmer   1903
Hugh Duffy   1904–1906
Billy Murray   1907–1909
Charles "Red" Dooin   1910–1914
Pat Moran   1915–1918
Jack Coombs   1919

Clifford "Gavvy" Cravath
1919–1920
Bill Donovan   1922
Irvin "Kaiser" Wilhelm
1921–1922
Art Fletcher   1923–1926
John "Stuffy" McInnis
1927
Burt Shotton   1928–1933
Jimmie Wilson   1934–1938
John "Honus" Lobert   1938
James "Doc" Prothro
1939–1941
John "Honus" Lobert   1942
Stanley "Bucky" Harris
1943
Freddie Fitzsimmons   1943–1945
Ben Chapman   1945–1948
Allen "Dusty" Cooke   1948
Eddie Sawyer   1948–1952
Steve O'Neill   1952–1954
Terry Moore   1954
Mayo Smith   1955–1958
Eddie Sawyer   1958–1960
Andy Cohen   1960
Gene Mauch   1960–1968
George Myatt   1968
Bob Skinner   1968–1969
George Myatt   1969
Frank Lucchesi   1970–1972
Paul Owens   1972
Danny Ozark   1973–1979
Dallas Green   1979–1981
Pat Corrales   1982–1983
Paul Owens   1983–1984
John Felske   1985–1987
Lee Elia   1987–1988
John Vukovich   1988
Nick Leyva   1989–1991
Jim Fregosi   1991–1996
Terry Francona   1997–2000
Larry Bowa   2001–present

PITTSBURGH PIRATES

Alleghenys (1887–1889), Innocents (1890), Pirates (1891–present)

Fred Clarke   1900–1915
James "Nixey" Callahan
1916–1917
Honus Wagner   1917
Hugo Bezdek   1917–1919

George "Moon" Gibson 1920–1922
Bill McKechnie 1922–1926
Owen "Donie" Bush 1927–1929
Jewel Ens 1929–1931
George "Moon" Gibson 1932–1934
Harold "Pie" Traynor 1934–1939
Frankie Frisch 1940–1946
Virgil "Spud" Davis 1946
Billy Herman 1947
Bill Burwell 1947
Billy Meyer 1948–1952
Fred Haney 1953–1955
Bobby Bragan 1956–1957
Danny Murtaugh 1957–1964
Harry Walker 1965–1967
Danny Murtaugh 1967
Larry Shepard 1968–1969
Alex Grammas 1969
Danny Murtaugh 1970–1971
Bill Virdon 1972–1973
Danny Murtaugh 1973–1976
Chuck Tanner 1977–1985
Jim Leyland 1986–1996
Gene Lamont 1997–2000
Lloyd McClendon 2001–present

CINCINNATI REDS
Reds/Red Stockings (1876–1880; 189–1943); Redlegs (1944–1945); Reds (1946–present)

Charlie Gould 1876
Lip Pike 1877
Cal McVey 1878–1879
Deacon White 1879
John Clapp 1880
Pop Snyder 1882–1884
Will White 1884
Dan O'Leary 1884
O.P. Caylor 1885–1886
Gus Schmelz 1887–1889
Tom Loftus 1890–1901
John "Bid" McPhee 1901–1902
Frank Bancroft 1902
Joe Kelley 1902–1905
Ned Hanlon 1906–1907
John Ganzel 1908
Clark Griffith 1909–1911
Henry O'Day 1912
Joe Tinker 1913
Charles "Buck" Herzog 1914–1916
Ivy Wingo 1916
Christy Mathewson 1916–1918
Henry "Heinie" Groh 1918
Pat Moran 1919–1923
Jack Hendricks 1924–1929
Dan Howley 1930–1932
Owen "Donie" Bush 1933
Bob O'Farrell 1934
Burt Shotton 1934
Chuck Dressen 1934–1937
Bobby Wallace 1937
Bill McKechnie 1938–1946
John Neun 1947–1948

William "Bucky" Walters 1948–1949
Luke Sewell 1950–1952
Earl Brucker Sr. 1952
Rogers Hornsby 1952–1953
Colonel Mills 1953
George "Birdie" Tebbetts 1954–1958
Jimmy Dykes 1958
Mayo Smith 1959
Fred Hutchinson 1959–1964
Dick Sisler 1964–1965
Don Heffner 1966
Dave Bristol 1966–1969
George "Sparky" Anderson 1970–1978
John McNamara 1979–1982
Russ Nixon 1982–1983
Vern Rapp 1984
Pete Rose 1984–1989
Tommy Helms 1989
Lou Piniella 1990–1992
Tony Perez 1993
Davey Johnson 1993–1995
Ray Knight 1996–1997
Jack McKeon 1997–2000
Bob Boone 2001–present

COLORADO ROCKIES
Don Baylor 1993–1998
Jim Leyland 1999
Buddy Bell 2000–2002
Clint Hurdle 2002–present

AMERICAN LEAGUE

ANAHEIM ANGELS
Los Angeles Angels (1961–1964), California Angels (1965–1995), Anaheim Angels (1996–present)

Bill Rigney 1961–1969
Harold "Lefty" Phillips 1969–1971
Del Rice 1972
Bobby Winkles 1973–1974
Dick Williams 1974–1976

Norm Sherry 1976–1977
Dave Garcia 1977–1978
Jim Fregosi 1978–1981
Gene Mauch 1981–1982
John McNamara 1983–1984
Gene Mauch 1985–1987
Octavio "Cookie" Rojas 1988
Lawrence "Moose" Stubing 1988
Doug Rader 1989–1991
Buck Rodgers 1991–1994

Marcel Lachemann 1994–1996
John McNamara 1996
Joe Maddon 1997
Terry Collins 1997–1999
Joe Maddon 1999
Mike Scioscia 2000–present

OAKLAND ATHLETICS
Philadelphia Athletics (1901–1954), Kansas City Athletics

(1955–1967), Oakland Athletics (1968–present)

Connie Mack   1901–1950
Jimmy Dykes   1951–1953
Eddie Joost   1954
Lou Boudreau   1955–1957
Harry Craft   1957–1959
Bob Elliott   1960
Joe Gordon   1961
Hank Bauer   1961–1962
Eddie Lopat   1963–1964
Mel McGaha   1964–1965
Haywood Sullivan   1965
Alvin Dark   1966–1967
Luke Appling   1967
Bob Kennedy   1968
Hank Bauer   1969
John McNamara   1969–1970
Dick Williams   1971–1973
Alvin Dark   1974–1975
Chuck Tanner   1976
Jack McKeon   1977
Bobby Winkles   1977–1978
Jack McKeon   1978
Jim Marshall   1979
Billy Martin   1980–1982
Steve Boros   1983–1984
Jackie Moore   1984–1986
Jeff Newman   1986
Tony LaRussa   1986–1995
Art Howe   1996–present

TORONTO BLUE JAYS
Roy Hartsfield   1977–1979
Bobby Mattick   1980–1981
Bobby Cox   1982–1985
Jimy Williams   1986–1989
Cito Gaston   1989–1997
Mel Queen   1997
Tim Johnson   1998
Jim Fregosi   1999–2000
Buck Martinez   2001–2002
Carlos Tosca   2002–present

MILWAUKEE BREWERS
Seattle Pilots (1969), Milwaukee Brewers (1970–present)

Joe Schultz   1969
Dave Bristol   1970–1972
Roy McMillan   1972
Del Crandall   1972–1975

Harvey Kuenn   1975
Alex Grammas   1976–1977
George Bamberger   1978–1980
Robert "Buck" Rodgers   1980
George Bamberger   1980
Robert "Buck" Rodgers   1980–1982
Harvey Kuenn   1982–1983
Rene Lachemann   1984
George Bamberger   1985–1986
Tom Trebelhorn   1986–1990
Phil Garner   1991–1999
Davey Lopes   2000–2002
Jerry Royster   2002–present

BALTIMORE ORIOLES
(Original)
John McGraw   1901–1902
Wilbert Robinson   1902

BALTIMORE ORIOLES
St. Louis Browns (1902–1954), Baltimore Orioles (1954–present)

Jimmy McAleer   1902–1909
Jack O'Connor   1910
Bobby Wallace   1911–1912
George Stovall   1912–1913
Jimmy Austin   1913
Wesley "Branch" Rickey   1913–1915
Fielder Jones   1916–1918
Jimmy Austin   1918
Jimmy Burke   1918–1920
Leo Fohl   1921–1923
Jimmy Austin   1923
George Sisler   1924–1926
Dan Howley   1927–1929
Bill Killefer   1930–1933
Allen Sothoron   1933
Rogers Hornsby   1933–1937
Jim Bottomley   1937
Charles "Gabby" Street   1938
Fred Haney   1939–1941
James "Luke" Sewell   1941–1946
James "Zack" Taylor   1946

Harold "Muddy" Ruel   1947
James "Zack" Taylor   1948–1951
Rogers Hornsby   1952
Marty Marion   1952–1953
Jimmy Dykes   1954
Paul Richards   1954–1961
Chalmer "Lum" Harris   1961
Billy Hitchcock   1962–1963
Hank Bauer   1964–1968
Earl Weaver   1968–1982
Joe Altobelli   1983–1985
Earl Weaver   1985–1986
Cal Ripken Sr.   1987–1988
Frank Robinson   1988–1991
Johnny Oates   1991–1994
Phil Regan   1995
Davey Johnson   1996–1997
Ray Miller   1998–1999
Mike Hargrove   2000–present

CLEVELAND INDIANS
Cleveland Blues (1901), Cleveland Bronchos (1902–1904), Cleveland Naps (1905–1914), Cleveland Indians (1915–present)

Jimmy McAleer   1901
Bill Armour   1902–1904
Napoleon Lajoie   1905–1909
Jim McGuire   1909–1911
George Stovall   1911
Harry "Jasper" Davis   1912
Joe Birmingham   1912–1915
Lee Fohl   1915–1919
Tris Speaker   1919–1926
Jack McCallister   1927
Roger Peckinpaugh   1928–1933
Walter Johnson   1933–1935
Steve O'Neill   1935–1937
Oscar Vitt   1938–1940
Roger Peckinpaugh   1941
Lou Boudreau   1942–1950
Al Lopez   1951–1956
Kerby Farrell   1957
Bobby Bragan   1958

Joe Gordon   1958–1960
Joyner "Jo–Jo" White   1960
Jimmy Dykes   1960–1961
Mel Harder   1961
Fred McGaha   1962
George "Birdie" Tebbetts
1963–1966
George Strickland   1966
Joe Adcock   1967
Alvin Dark   1968–1971
John Lipon   1971
Ken Aspromonte   1972–1974
Frank Robinson   1975–1977
Jeff Torborg   1977–1979
Dave Garcia   1979–1982
Mike Ferraro   1983
Pat Corrales   1983–1987
Howard "Doc" Edwards
1987–1989
John Hart   1989
John McNamara   1990–1991
Mike Hargrove   1991–1999
Charlie Manuel   2000–2002
Joel Skinner   2002–present

TAMPA BAY DEVIL RAYS

Larry Rothschild   1998–2001
Hal McRae   2001–present

SEATTLE MARINERS

Darrell Johnson   1977–1980
Maury Wills   1980–1981
Rene Lachemann   1981–1983
Del Crandall   1983–1984
Chuck Cottier   1984– 1986
Marty Martinez   1986
Dick Williams   1986– 1988
Jim Snyder   1988
Jim Lefebvre   1989–1991
Bill Plummer   1992
Lou Piniella   1993–present

TEXAS RANGERS

Washington Senators (1961–1971), Texas Rangers (1972–present)

Mickey Vernon   1961–1963
Gil Hodges   1963–1967
Jim Lemon   1968

Ted Williams   1969–1972
Dorrel "Whitey" Herzog
1973
Del Wilbur   1973
Billy Martin   1973–1975
Frank Lucchesi   1975–1977
Eddie Stanky   1977
Connie Ryan   1977
Billy Hunter   1977–1978
Pat Corrales   1979–1980
Don Zimmer   1981–1982
Darrell Johnson   1982
Doug Rader   1983–1985
Bobby Valentine   1985–1992
Toby Harrah   1992
Kevin Kennedy   1993–1994
Johnny Oates   1995–2001
Jerry Narron   2001–present

BOSTON RED SOX

Boston Somersets (1901–1904), Boston Puritans (1904–1906), Boston Red Sox (1907–present)

Jimmy Collins   1901–1906
Charles "Chick" Stahl   1906
Denton "Cy" Young   1907
George Huff   1907
Bob Unglaub   1907
Jim "Deacon" McGuire
1907–1908
Fred Lake   1908–1909
Patsy Donovan   1910–1911
Garland "Jake" Stahl   1912–1913
William Carrigan   1913–1916
Jack Barry   1917
Ed Barrow   1918–1920
Hugh Duffy   1921–1922
Frank Chance   1923
Lee Fohl   1924–1926
William Carrigan   1927–1929
Charles "Heinie" Wagner
1930
John "Shano" Collins
1931–1932
Marty McManus   1932–1933
Stanley "Bucky" Harris
1934
Joe Cronin   1935–1947
Joe McCarthy   1948–1950

Steve O'Neill   1950–1951
Lou Boudreau   1952–1954
Michael "Pinky" Higgins
1955–1959
Rudy York   1959
Billy Jurges   1959–1960
Michael "Pinky" Higgins
1960–1962
Johnny Pesky   1963–1964
Billy Herman   1964–1966
James "Pete" Runnels   1966
Dick Williams   1967–1969
Eddie Popowski   1969
Eddie Kasko   1970–1973
Darrell Johnson   1974–1976
Don Zimmer   1976–1980
Ralph Houk   1981–1984
John McNamara   1985–1988
Joe Morgan   1988–1991
Butch Hobson   1992–1994
Kevin Kennedy   1995–1996
Jimy Williams   1997–2001
Bill Kerrigan   2001–2002
Grady Little   2002–present

KANSAS CITY ROYALS

Joe Gordon   1969
Charlie Metro   1970
Bob Lemon   1970–1972
Jack McKeon   1973–1975
Dorrell "Whitey" Herzog
1975–1979
Jim Frey   1980–1981
Dick Howser   1981–1986
Mike Ferraro   1986
Billy Gardner   1987
John Wathan   1987–1991
Hal McRae   1991–1994
Bob Boone   1995–1997
Tony Muser   1997–2002
John Mizerock   2002
(Interim)
Tony Peña   2002–present

WASHINGTON SENATORS

Washington Senators (1901–1960) / Minnesota Twins (1961–present)

James Manning   1901
Tom Loftus   1902–1903
Malachi Kittredge   1904
Pat Donovan   1904

Garland "Jake" Stahl   1905–1906
Joe Cantillon   1907–1909
Jim McAleer   1910–1911
Clark Griffith   1912–1920
George McBride   1921
Jesse Milan   1922
Owen "Donie" Bush   1923
Stanley "Bucky" Harris   1924–1928
Walter Johnson   1929–1932
Joe Cronin   1933–1934
Stanley "Bucky" Harris   1935–1942
Ossie Bluege   1943–1947
Joe Kuhel   1948–1949
Stanley "Bucky" Harris   1950–1954
Chuck Dressen   1955–1957
Harry "Cookie" Lavagetto   1957–1961
Sam Mele   1961–1967
Cal Ermer   1967–1968
Billy Martin   1969
Bill Rigney   1970–1972
Frank Quillici   1972–1975
Gene Mauch   1976–1980
John Goryl   1980–1981
Billy Gardner   1981–1985
Ray Miller   1985–1986
Tom Kelly   1986–present

DETROIT TIGERS
George Stallings   1901
Frank Dwyer   1902
Ed Barrow   1903–1904
Bobby Lowe   1904
Bill Armour   1905–1906
Hugh Jennings   1907–1920
Ty Cobb   1921–1926
George Moriarty   1927–1928
Stanley "Bucky" Harris   1929–1932
Del Baker   1933
Mickey Cochrane   1934–1938
Del Baker   1938–1942
Steve O'Neill   1943–1948
Robert "Red" Rolfe   1949–1952
Fred Hutchinson   1952–1954
Stanley "Bucky" Harris   1955–1956

Jack Tighe   1957–1958
Henry "Bill" Norman   1959
Jimmy Dykes   1959–1960
Billy Hitchcock   1960
Joe Gordon   1960
Bob Scheffing   1961–1963
Chuck Dressen   1963–1966
Frank Skaff   1966
Bob Swift   1966
Mayo Smith   1967–1970
Billy Martin   1971–1973
Joe Schultz   1973
Ralph Houk   1974–1978
Les Moss   1979
Dick Tracewski   1979
George "Sparky" Anderson   1979–1995
Buddy Bell   1996–1998
Larry Parrish   1998–1999
Phil Garner   2000–2002
Louis Pujols   present

CHICAGO WHITE SOX
Clark Griffith   1901–1902
Jim Callahan   1903–1904
Fielder Jones   1904–1908
Billy Sullivan   1909
Hugh Duffy   1910–1911
Jim Callahan   1912–1914
Clarence "Pants" Rowland   1915–1918
William "Kid" Gleason   1919–1923
John Evers   1924
Eddie Collins   1925–1926
Ray Schalk   1927–1928
Russell "Lena" Blackbourne   1928–1929
Owen "Donie" Bush   1930–1931
Lew Fonseca   1932–1934
Jimmy Dykes   1934–1946
Ted Lyons   1946–1948
Jack Onslow   1949–1950
John "Red" Corriden   1950
Paul Richards   1951–1954
Marty Marion   1954–1956
Al Lopez   1957–1965
Eddie Stanky   1966–1968
John "Les" Moss   1968
Al Lopez   1968–1969
Don Gutteridge   1969–1970
Marion "Bill" Adair   1970
Chuck Tanner   1970–1975

Paul Richards   1976
Bob Lemon   1977–1978
Larry Doby   1978
Don Kessinger   1979
Tony LaRussa   1979–1986
Doug Rader   1986
Jim Fregosi   1986–1988
Jeff Torborg   1989–1991
Gene Lamont   1992–1995
Terry Bevington   1996–1997
Jerry Manuel   1998–present

NEW YORK YANKEES
Highlanders   (1903–1912), Yankees (1913–present)

Clark Griffith   1903–1908
Norman "Kid" Elberfeld   1908
George Stallings   1909–1910
Hal Chase   1910–1911
Harry Wolverton   1912
Frank Chance   1913–1914
Roger Peckinpaugh   1914
Bill Donovan   1915–1917
Miller Huggins   1918–1929
Art Fletcher   1929
Bob Shawkey   1930
Joe McCarthy   1931–1946
Bill Dickey   1946
Johnny Neun   1946
Stanley "Bucky" Harris   1947–1948
Charles "Casey" Stengel   1949–1960
Ralph Houk   1961–1963
Lawrence "Yogi" Berra   1964
Johnny Keane   1965–1966
Ralph Houk   1966–1973
Bill Virdon   1974–1975
Billy Martin   1975–1978
Dick Howser   1978
Bob Lemon   1978–1979
Billy Martin   1979
Dick Howser   1980
Gene Michael   1981
Bob Lemon   1981–1982
Clyde King   1982
Billy Martin   1983
Lawrence "Yogi" Berra   1984–1985
Billy Martin   1985
Lou Piniella   1986–1987
Billy Martin   1988

Lou Piniella   1988
Dallas Green   1989
Russell "Bucky" Dent
   1989–1990

Stump Merrill
   1990–1991
Buck Showalter
   1992–1995

Don Zimmer   1999
   (Interim)
Joe Torre   1996–present

Bibliography

Alexander, Charles C. *John McGraw*. New York: Viking Penguin, 1988.
_____. *Ty Cobb*. New York: Oxford University Press, 1984.
Allen, Lee. *The Cincinnati Reds*. New York: G.P. Putnam's Sons, 1948.
Alston, Walter, and Si Burick. *Alston and the Dodgers*. Garden City, New York: Doubleday, 1966.
Anderson, Dave. *Pennant Races: Baseball at Its Best*. New York: Doubleday, 1994.
Asinof, Eliot. *Eight Men Out*. New York: Holt, Rinehart and Winston, 1963.
Aylesworth, Thomas, and Benton Minks. *The Encyclopedia of Baseball Managers*. New York: Crown, 1990.
Baumgartner, Stan, and Frederick Lieb. *The Philadelphia Phillies*. New York. G.P. Putnam's Sons, 1953.
Dark, Alvin, and John Underwood. *When in Doubt, Fire the Manager*. New York: E.P. Dutton, 1980.
Dickson, Paul. *Baseball's Greatest Quotations*. New York: Harper-Collins, 1991.
Gallagher, Mark. *Day by Day in New York Yankees History*. New York: Leisure Press, 1983.
Graham, Frank. *The Brooklyn Dodgers*. New York: G.P. Putnam's Sons, 1945.
Herzog, Dorrel, and Kevin Horrigan. *White Rat: A Life in Baseball*. New York: Harper & Row, 1987.
Ivor-Campbell, Frederick, Robert L. Tiemann, and Mark Rucker. *Baseball's First Stars*. Cleveland: The Society for American Baseball Research, 1996.
James, Bill. *The Bill James Guide to Baseball Managers from 1870 to Today*. New York: Scribner, 1997.
Johnson, Davey, and Peter Golenbock. *Bats*. New York: G.P. Putnam's Sons, 1986.
Lewis, Franklin. *The Cleveland Indians*. New York: G.P. Putnam's Sons, 1949.
Lieb, Frederick G. *The St. Louis Cardinals: The Story of a Great Baseball Club*. New York: G. P. Putnam's Sons, 1947.
McKeon, Jack, and Tom Friend. *Jack of All Trades*. Chicago: Contemporary Books, 1988.
Mosedale, John. *The Greatest of All: The 1927 New York Yankees*. New York: Dial Press, 1974.
Myers, Doug. *Essential Cubs*. Chicago: Contemporary Books, 1999.
Newhan, Ross. *The California Angels: The Complete History*. New York: Simon & Schuster, 1982.
Peary, Danny. *We Played the Game*. New York: Hyperion, 1994.
Phillips, John. *The Tigers vs. the Cubs: The 4-F World Series of 1945*. Perry, Ga.: Capital Publishing, 1997.
Piniella, Lou, and Maury Allen. *Sweet Lou: Lou Piniella*. New York: G.P. Putnam's Sons, 1986.
Pluto, Terry. *The Curse of Rocky Colavito*. New York: Simon & Schuster, 1994.
Pope, Edwin. *Baseball's Greatest Managers*. New York: Doubleday, 1960.
Rathgeber, Bob. *Cincinnati Reds Scrapbook*. Virginia Beach, Va.: JCP Corp., 1982.
Reidenbaugh, Lowell. *Cooperstown: Where the Legends Live*. New York: Crescent Books, 1997.
Richter, Ed. *View from the Dugout*. Philadelphia: Chilton Books, 1963.
Robinson, Frank, and Berry Stainback. *Extra Innings*. New York: McGraw-Hill, 1988.
Sahadi, Lou. *The Pirates: We Are Family*. New York: Times Books, 1980.
Schoor, Gene. *Seaver*. Chicago: Contemporary Books, 1986.

Smith, Ron. *The Sporting News Chronicle of Baseball*. New York: BDD Books, 1993.

Vanderberg, Bob. *Sox: From Lane and Fain to Zisk and Fisk*. Chicago: Chicago Review Press, 1984.

Werber, Bill, and C. Paul Rogers III. *Memories of a Ballplayer*. Cleveland: The Society of American Baseball Research, 2001.

Williams Dick, and Bill Plaschke. *No More Mr. Nice Guy*. New York: Harcourt Brace Jovanovich, 1990.

Index